MICMAC DICTIONARY

Albert D. DeBlois

Mercury Series
Canadian Ethnology Service
Paper 131

Published by
Canadian Museum of Civilization

© Canadian Museum of Civilization 1996

CANADIAN CATALOGUING IN PUBLICATION DATA

DeBlois, Albert D.
Micmac dictionary
(Mercury series, ISSN 0316-1854)
(Paper / Canadian Ethnology Service,
ISSN 0316-1862; no. 131)
Includes an abstract in French.
ISBN 0-660-15966-X

1. Micmac language — Dictionaries.
2. English language — Dictionaries — Micmac.
I. Canadian Museum of Civilization.
II. Canadian Ethnology Service.
III. Title.
IV. Series.
V. Series: Paper (Canadian Ethnology Service);
no. 131.

PM1793.D42   1996   497.3   C96-980386-9

PRINTED IN CANADA

Published by
Canadian Museum of Civilization
100 Laurier Street
P.O. Box 3100, Station B
Hull, Quebec
J8X 4H2

Senior production officer: Deborah Brownrigg
Cover design: Roger Langlois Design

Front cover: Micmac quillwork chair seat, ca.
1850–1860. This chair seat made from porcupine
quills and birchbark was beautifully crafted in
traditional Micmac designs and colours. The quills
were dyed naturally with plant roots and berries and
applied unflattened on birchbark backing. Canadian
Museum of Civilization, III-F-267

OBJECT OF THE MERCURY SERIES

The Mercury Series is designed to permit the rapid dissemination of information pertaining to the disciplines in which the Canadian Museum of Civilization is active. Considered an important reference by the scientific community, the Mercury Series comprises over three hundred specialized publications on Canada's history and prehistory.

Because of its specialized audience, the series consists largely of monographs published in the language of the author.

In the interest of making information available quickly, normal production procedures have been abbreviated. As a result, grammatical and typographical errors may occur. Your indulgence is requested.

Titles in the Mercury Series can be obtained by writing to:

> Mail Order Services
> Canadian Museum of Civilization
> 100 Laurier Street
> P.O. Box 3100, Station B
> Hull, Quebec
> J8X 4H2

or by calling: 1-800-555-5621

BUT DE LA COLLECTION

La collection Mercure vise à diffuser rapidement le résultat de travaux dans les disciplines qui relèvent des sphères d'activités du Musée canadien des civilisations. Considérée comme un apport important dans la communauté scientifique, la collection Mercure présente plus de trois cents publications spécialisées portant sur l'héritage canadien préhistorique et historique.

Comme la collection s'adresse à un public spécialisé, celle-ci est constituée essentiellement de monographies publiées dans la langue des auteurs.

Pour assurer la prompte distribution des exemplaires imprimés, les étapes de l'édition ont été abrégées. En conséquence, certaines coquilles ou fautes de grammaire peuvent subsister : c'est pourquoi nous réclamons votre indulgence.

Vous pouvez vous procurer la liste des titres parus dans la collection Mercure en écrivant au :

> Service des commandes postales
> Musée canadien des civilisations
> 100, rue Laurier
> C.P. 3100, succursale B
> Hull (Québec)
> J8X 4H2

ou en appelant au : 1 800 555-5621

Abstract

The *Micmac Dictionary* is derived from texts and anecdotes collected over the past thirty-five years from speakers of Micmac in Nova Scotia, New Brunswick, Prince Edward Island and Quebec. The Micmac – English section consists of some 7,850 Micmac entries with their English equivalents. The comprehensive English – Micmac keyword index should render the dictionary more accessible to native speakers of Micmac as well as to students of the language.

Résumé

Ce dictionnaire micmac provient de textes et d'anecdotes recueillis au cours des trente-cinq dernières années auprès d'interlocuteurs de langue micmaque de Nouvelle-Écosse, du Nouveau-Brunswick, de l'Île-du-Prince-Édouard et du Québec. La section micmac-anglais comporte près de 7850 entrées en micmac accompagnées de leurs équivalents anglais. Constitué de mots clés, l'index anglais est exhaustif. Il se prête à une consultation facile, aussi bien pour les Autochtones qui parlent cette langue que pour toutes les personnes désireuses de l'apprendre.

Celles et ceux qui désirent recevoir en français de plus amples renseignements sur cette publication sont priés de s'adresser au :

Service canadien d'ethnologie
Musée canadien des civilisations
100, rue Laurier
C.P. 3100, succursale B
Hull (Québec) J8X 4H2

TABLE OF CONTENTS

ACKNOWLEDGEMENTS vii

INTRODUCTION ix

    SCOPE ix

    DIALECT VARIATION ix

    ORTHOGRAPHY ix

    ORDER OF ENTRIES xiii

    FORM OF ENTRIES xiii

ABBREVIATIONS xv

POSSESSED NOUNS

MICMAC - ENGLISH 1

ENGLISH - MICMAC 101

ACKNOWLEDEMENTS

We would like to acknowledge the cooperation and hospitality provided by the following people in the course of our research on the Micmac language: Chief Louis Peters (Bear River), Mrs. Teresa Thomas (Indianbrook), Chief Ben Christmas (Membertou), Grand Chief Gabriel Sylliboy (Eskasoni), Mrs. Mildred Milliet (Big Cove), Mr. Joseph Augustine (Red Bank), Mr. Emanuel Metallic (Restigouche), Mrs. Mary Caplin (Restigouche), Mrs. Irene Labobe Halley (PEI), Mrs. Murdina Marshall (Eskasoni), Mr. William Prosper (Eskasoni), and Mr. Bernie Francis (Membertou). Ms. Janet Vicaire (Restigouche) contributed to an earlier lexicon, printed under the auspices of the Department of Indian Affairs. Liliane Bourbeau, my wife, partipated actively in the preparation of the succeeding **Micmac Lexicon** (DeBlois, Albert D., and Alphonse Metallic, 1984. Ottawa: National Museum of Man, Mercury Series, No 91, pp. xviii 392.) and offered many helpful suggestions.

We are especially grateful to Allan Ford, Université de Montreal, who most generously made available computer time, terminal and personnel that made it possible to include an English - Micmac index of the Lexicon of much greater scope than originally envisioned. Work on the Lexicon was, in part, supported by an F.C.A.C. research grant to him (N%84EQ0362). Field work was supported by the Canadian Museeum of Civilization, then known as the National Museum of Canada.

We would like to thank Gilles Pineault (Université de Montreal, Department de Linguistique) for his invaluable aid in preparing the required computer programme for the Lexicon, and supervising its output.

We wish also to thank Edward Laine (History Division, Canadian Museum of Civilization) for his suggestions regarding the formatting of the dictionary and, while circumstances did not allow for its application here, to acknowledge the elaborate methodology he has developed for using a computer to automate the generation of separate Micmac-English and English-Micmac data sets from a Micmac-English data base.

Finally, we wish to thank Michael Allsopp for his expertise and skill in formatting the Dictionary as it now stands, and for his meticulous attention to details in ensuring its successful completion

INTRODUCTION

...y is a corrected, revised and expanded version of the ... (Micmac - English, English - Micmac) dictionary, its ...ccurately as possible, one or more English equivalents ...d that teachers, students, writers, and any others who ...Micmac language will find the dictionary useful.   It ...o interpreters and translators.

SCO... ...on of a lexical entry has largely been a matter of circu... ...t on the kind of source material available and, to a lesse... ...of the individuals involved in the compilation of the dic... ...material for the dictionary does encompass a variety ... ...citations from such widely dispersed localities as Big ... New Brunswick, Bear River, Indianbrook (Shubenac... ...and PEI, in addition to the tape recordings collected a...

DIALECT V... ...ary items obtained in other communities have much th... ...s in Restigouche.   In many instances, however, eithe... ..., or both, have been found to differ noticeably from ... ...this has been observed, the alternate forms or meaning... ...ave been included in the dictionary.

Again, it ha... ...nsiderable differences in the speech of older and younge... ...e is evidence for positing a three-level dialect distincti... ...speaker: elderly vs. middle aged vs. young. One might... ...nger the speaker, the greater the possibility that the wo... ...dergone assimilation (compare <ankaptm ~ ankattm ... ...the longer and less assimilated forms are still widely u... ...as ben taken to select these forms, where obtained, fo...

ORTHOGRAPHY.   The orthography used to transcribe the Micmac entries in this dictionary is, in several ways, different from that found in the **Micmac Lexicon** which, itself, was a considerable modification of the traditional thirteen (13) letter alphabet used by elders literate in the Micmac language, and the subsequent changes introduced by Father Pacifique in his **Leçons Grammaticales**. Adjustments have been made for greater clarity and should cause no undue problems. Though there is still no universally agreed upon orthography and orthographic conventions for writing Micmac, there has been a considerable rapproachment between those used throughout the Atlantic provinces in recent years. For the most part, they are compatible, and easily convertible from the one to the other. The orthographies employed are based upon the distinctive sounds of Micmac which consist of eight obstruents / p, t, k, k^w, q, q^w, č, s /, three sonorants / l, m, n /, and two semi-vowels / w, y /. The vowels are / a, e, i, o, u /, which occur in both short and long varieties, and schwa / ə /.

The changes from the **Micmac Lexicon** are as follows: (1) **k** replaces **g**, (2) **q** replaces **ĝ**, (3) a colon after the vowel replaces the grave accent above to mark vowel length, (4) an additional symbol **y** is introduced, (5) an apostrophe replaces **ê** as the symbol for a mid to high back unrounded vowel ("schwa"), (6) the apostrophe is also used to mark intervocalic open juncture, which takes the form of an aspiration or an hiatus, (7) there are no vowel sequences.

Obstruents are voiceless in clusters but voiced between vowels. By convention, the vowel schwa, though always present and pronounced, is only written between an obstruent (**p, t, j, k, q, s**) and a sonorant (**l, m, n**) when internal open juncture (realized phonetically by a perceptible lengthening of the sonorant and voicing of an immediately following obstruent) occurs. In such cases, the schwa signals the upcoming open juncture, as well as marking the occurence of the schwa vowel. It should be noted that in the *phonetic transcriptions*, which are enclosed within brackets, the apostrophe here represents preglottalization of the succeeding obstruent.

Thus, we write <**plamu** [pəlamu] 'salmon'>, <**tmi:kn** [təmiːgən] 'axe'>, <**Kluskap** [kəluskap] 'Glooscap'>, <**smt′k** [səm'tək] 'at once'>, <**temtm** [tem'təm] 'I bite it off'>, <**kwitn** [k^{w}idən, k^{w}idn̩] 'canoe'>, <**a:kwesn** [aːg^{w}ezən] 'hat'>, <**mesn′k** [mezənək] 'I catch hold of it'>, <**etekl** [edegəl] 'they stand there'>, <**ejikla:tu** [ejigəlaːdu] 'I take it away'>, *but* <**pejit′ms′k** [pejidəm·zək], 'he cut it in two accidentally'>, <**k′lpisun** [kəl·bizun] 'anchor'>, <**k′nki:kuk** [kən·giːguk] 'your (sg) parents'>.

Elsewhere, as well, the written sequence schwa plus sonorant signals the occurence of open juncture before a following single obstruent. When there is a following geminate obstruent, however, there is no juncture. Thus, we write <**n′njan** [nən·jan] 'my child'>, **'nkaqan** [ən·gaɣan] 'measurement'>, <**m'ntu** [mən·du] 'devil'>, *but* <**l'nppok** [lən'pok] '(spring) water'>

The occurence of open juncture following a sonorant that is not preceded by schwa is signalled by gemination of the sonorant or, in order to avoid alternate spellings of a lexical item, the introduction of a hyphen: <**malltew** [mal·deǫ] 'blood'>, <**wennju:su:n** [ɥen·juːzuːn] 'apple'>, <**kunntew** [kun·deo] 'rock'>, <**palltaqan** [pal·daɣan] 'gunwhale'>, and <**puwi:kn-ji:j** [puɥiːɡənjiːč] 'Puerto Rican'>, <**ejikl-te:m** [ejigəl·deːm] 'I knock it away'>. Between vowels, as noted above, the apostrophe marks intervocalic open juncture, which here takes the form of an aspiration or an hiatus: <**t'mte:'e:n** [təm·deːheːn] 'chop it off!'>, <ke'itu [ke-idu] (compare the dialect variant <kejitu) 'I know (it)'>.

The first consonant of a word initial cluster consisting of any combination of nasals (m, n) or liquid (l) is syllabic and is followed by open juncture: <**llutaqan** [l̩'ludaɣan] 'fence'>, <**nnu** [n̩·nu] 'person'>, <**nmi** [n̩·mi] 'granny!'>, <**lmu:j** [l̩'muːč] 'dog'>. If a word initial cluster consists of a liquid (l) plus obstruent, the liquid is also syllabic and is followed by open juncture: <**lpa:tuj** [l̩'baːduč] 'boy'>, <**lketu** [l̩'gedu] 'mushroom'>, <**lsipuktuk** [l̩'zibu'ktuk] 'Big Cove'>.

On the other hand, if the word initial cluster consists of a nasal (m, n) followed by an obstruent, the nasal is voiceless and semi-syllabic, and there is no open juncture: <**mpo:qon** [m̥'poːɣon] 'bed'>, <**mkikn** [m̥'kigən] 'hook'>, <**mqwan** [m̥'xwan] 'spoon'>, <**mtl'n** [m̥'tələn] 'ten'>, <**npuwinu** [n̥'puɥinu] 'hearse'>, <**ntlu:tew** [n̥'təluːdeǫ] 'smoke'>, <**nsisqon** [n̥'si'sxon] 'my nose'>, <**ntuksuwinu** [n̥'tu'ksuɥinu] 'provider'>, <**nkutuko:pj** [n̥'kudugoːpč] 'recluse'>.

When there is no open juncture wthin the word, the consonants and vowels are said to be in close transition: <**temte:m** [tem'teːm] 'I chop it off'>, <**winpasit** [ɥin'pasit] 'he hustles'>, <**puktew** [pu'kteǫ] 'fire'>, <**kitpu** [ki'tpu] 'eagle'>, <**maltejjuwey** [mal'te'ččuɥei] 'hammer'>, <**wiyus** [ɥiius] 'meat'>.

The first consonant of word initial obstruent clusters is sometimes pronounced with a slight, preceding, non-distinctive vocalic: <**kti** [ᵊ'kti] 'your (sg) dog'>, <**psew** [ᵊ'pseǫ] 'gunpowder'>, <**skwew** [ᵊ'skʷeǫ] 'female fowl'>, <**tku** [ᵊ'tku] 'wave'>.

In hopes of rendering the dictionary more pertinent, an additional symbol (the "bullet") has been introduced in the Micmac - English section to mark off meaningful units of compound or complex forms that have undergone modification in the process. If an open juncture has resulted from the modification, a hyphen is used in place of the bullet. In either case, the unmodified form, which is listed elsewhere in the dictionary, is then provided within parentheses: <ali·sqotm *ti* (soqtm) 'I chew it about'>, <nikani·ksma:tu *ti* (kesma:tu) 'I push it ahead'>, <wel-p′sk *ii* (eps′k) 'it heats up properly'>, <nutkul-pa:sit *ai* (epa:sit) 'he kneels down'>

The modified list of symbols used to transcribe Micmac forms is as follows:

Symbols	Examples
a	atkitemit, tami, m'ta
a:	a:pi, wa:w, ala:
e	epit, nepat, je mu
e:	e:pit, ne:pat. nike:
i	ika:q, wituwit, nipi
i:	i:k, wi:k, nmi:
j	ji:nm, keji:k, nujjaq, kikjiw, nmu:j
k	kopit, teke:k, m'ntuwa:ki
l	lusknikn, piley, witapal
m	meski:k, tmi:kn, temte:m
n	nepk, mena:tu, kunntew, wen
o	oqwa:t, soqtm, ketloqo
o:	o:platu, ko:pikn
p	patliya:s, nusapun, tepkik, put'p
q	qopisun, apt'sqe:k, na:qi, soqqwat
s	sipu, wastew, pusit, wapus
t	tiya:m, amatpat, matuwes, mijjit
u	utan, kelusit, kulkwis, sisku
u:	u:n, kelu:sit, nemitu:n, nuku:
w	wow, kewte:m, kawiksaw, kwitn, nkwis, sikkw, moqwa
y	wayopskw, eykik, tewiyey
′	p′tewey, nt′p, temtm′n, m′ntu, tmte:′e:n
-	ejikl-te:m, awan-kijjet, aji-winjit, weli-kisk'k

ORDER OF ENTRIES. Dependent nouns (noun stems that may only occur in possessed form) are listed separately at the beginning of the dictionary. They are usually entered using the first person singular prefix (**n-, nt-** 'my'): <**nkij** *an* [my] 'mother'>, <**ntus** *an* [my] 'daughter'>. Occasionally, the third person prefix (**w-**) is more suitable: <**wilqi** [his] 'penis' [animal]>.

Otherwise, both here and in the main section that follows, the arrangement is alphapetical, *with no distinction being made between long and short vowels.*

FORM OF ENTRIES. Micmac nouns are either *animate* (*an*) or *inanimate* (*in*) in grammatical gender. With the exception of homonyms of different genders, however, *only* animate nouns are marked as such in the dictionary.

The form of the majority of noun plurals is predictable from that of the singular: animate nouns form their plurals in **-k**, inanimate noun in **-(')l**: <**wow** *an* 'pot'>, <**wowk** (pl) *an* 'pots'>; <**jujij** *an* 'serpent'>, <**jujijk** (pl) *an* 'serpents'>; <**wa:w** 'egg'>, <**wa:w'l** (pl) 'eggs'>; <**wisse:j** 'nest'>, <**wisse:jl** 'nests'>.

There are exceptions, however. In such cases, the unpredictable plural forms are provided in parentheses: <**muwin (muwinaq)** *an* 'bear'>, <**ji:nm (ji:nmuk)** *an* 'man'>, <**ksu:skw (ksu:skuk)** *an* 'hemlock'>, <**lpa:tu (lpa:tu:k)** *an* 'young man'>, <**e:pit (e:pijik)** *an* 'woman'>, <**wisnaw (wisnaq)** *an* 'perch'>; <**kunntew (kunntal)** 'rock'>, <**nitu (nitu:l)** '(my) whisker'>, <**tulkowey (tulkowe:l)** 'cannon'>. A special case is the now almost universal replacement of the inanimate plural marker **-(')l** by **-n** when the singular form ends in **n**. Example: <**kwitn (kwitnn)**, rather then the infrequently heard **(kwitn'l)** 'canoe'>.

Micmac verb forms are always entered as whole, fully inflected (sentence) words. English verbs, on the other hand, whether they appear as glosses or as main entries in the index, are given in their *infinitive* forms only. Thus, while the Micmac expressions <**nepk**> and <**nemi:k**> may be literally translated as 'he is dead' and 'I see her', respectively, they are glossed in the dictionary simply as <'dead'> and <'see'>.

Micmac verbs are categorized as being either *intransitive* or *transitive*. They are listed in the dictionary in the independent order form for *third person singular actor* if intransitive, and for *first person singular actor with third person singular object* if transitive.

The intransitive verb may be inflected for *animate* actor (*ai*), or *inanimate actor* (*ii*), or both. Where both forms occur, and are not homonyms, they are given separate entries. Examples, with full translations provided here and throughout the rest of the introduction, are as follows: <**nepat** *ai* 'he / she is sleeping'>, <**pekisink** *ai* 'he / she arrives'>, <**meskilk** *ai* 'he / she / it is big'>, <**epsit** *ai* 'he / she / it is hot'>, *but* <**pekisk** *ii* 'it arrives'>, <**meski:k** *ii* 'it is big'>, <**eptek** *ii* 'it is hot'>, <**kikpesaq** *ii* 'it is raining'>, and <**musike:k** *ai, ii* 'it is empty'>.

Intransitive verbs that occur only in the plural are given in the form for third person 'dual' actor or, where appropriate, in that for third person 'plural' actor: <**aknutmajik** (pl) *ai* 'they negotiate'>, <**kittoqopultijik** (pl) *ai* 'they sit around in a circle'>.

Intransitive verbs whose stems end in -**m** drop the -**m** in inflections with a third person actor. In order to exhibit the full form of the stem, the inflection with a first person singular actor is provided in parentheses: <**alaqami:k (alaqami:m)** *ai* 'he/she snowshoes' ('I snowshoe')>, <**na:kwekewa:q (na:kwekewa:m)** *ai* 'he/she is paid by the day' ('I am paid by the day')>

Intransitive verbs may have a *participle* use: the verb behaves syntactically like a noun. Many entries that have been listed as nouns seem clearly to have an underlying verbal base, and many entries that have been recorded as intransitive verbs are also used nominally. Where this situation has been noted, the entry is marked for both uses: <**nutnawet** *ai (an)* 'he assists at mass' ('alter boy'), <**tepkise:k** *ai (an)* 'he/she's a loner', <**nuji wsuwa:teket** *ai (an)* 'he's the one who hauls in' ('policeman'). <**e:pit** *an* 'woman' (the one who sits'?). Compare <**epit** *ai* 'he/she sits'>.

A transitive verb may be inflected for an *animate object* (*ta*) or for an *inanimate object* (*ti*). They are given separate listings in the dictionary: <**kesalk** *ta* 'I like him or her'>, <**kesatm** *ti* 'I like it'>; <**nemi:k** *ta* 'I see him or her'>, <**nemitu** *ti* 'I see it'>; <**wettelaq** *ta* 'I purchase him, her or it from there'>, <**wettel'm** *ti* 'I purchase it from there'>; <**paqa:l'k** *ta* 'I bite him, her or it'>, <**paqa:tu** *ti* 'I bite it'>; <**anko:tm** *ti* 'I take care of or preserve it'>, <**ankweyaq** *ta* 'I take care of or preserve him, her or it'>. If transitive verbs have a participle use, this has not been noted.

xiv

Forms that are neither nouns or verbs are referred to as *particles*. Particles have no inflection and, like the inanimate nouns, are left unmarked: **<miyamuj** 'for sure!'>, **<me: pa** 'anyhow'>, **<awisiw** 'seldom'>, **<tam pas′k tami** 'anywhere'>

ABBREVIATIONS

ai	animate intransitive verb
an	inanimate intransitive
BC	Big Cove, New Brunswick
CB	Cape Breton, Nova Scotia
do	direct object
EG	Éel Ground. New Brunswick
ESK	Esksasoni (Cape Breton), Nova Scoia
Fr	French
ii	inanimate verb
in	inanimate noun
loc	local form of noun
MARIA	Maria, Quebéc
MEM	Membertou (Cape Breton), Quebec
PEI	Prince Edward Island
pl	plural
RB	Red Bank, Nova Scotia
SH	Indianbrook (Shubenacadie), Nova Scotia
ta	transitive animate verb
ti	trsnsitive inanimate verb
voc	vocative form of noun

POSSESSED NOUNS

na:qi (my) flesh

nijan *an* (my) child

nijapo:ti (my) purse [SH]

nijimij (my) buttocks; (my) anus

nijinj (nijinjik) *an* (my) meat (of a nut or seed); (my) fish roe

nijink (pl) *an* (my) children [BR]

nijinuwan (my) cheek

nijjus *an* (my) stepchild

nijkikm (my) wart

ni:k (my) house; (my) dwelling

nikma:j *an* (my) spouse

nikmaj *an* (my) neighbour; (my) housemate [SH]

nikmaq *an* (my) immediate family; (my) relative; (my) chum [SH]

ni:kmatut (voc) *an* (my) people

nili (my) navel; (my) belly button

niliksi (my) gut

nilisqi *an* (my) wing

nilmus *an* (my) sister-in-law (male speaker) [BC, PEI]; (my) brother-in-law (female speaker) [BC, PEI]

nilnu (my) tongue [BR]

nilqi (my) penis [SH]

nilu *an* (my) game [ESK]

ni:naji:j (dim) *an* (my) little one [SH]

ninnu (my) tongue

ninoqwey (my) rump

ninu (my) food; (my) provisions; (my) larder; (my) game [BR]

ni:p (my) penis

nipit (my) tooth

nipitokom (my) gum

niskamij *an* (my) grandfather [SH]; (my) stepfather [BC]

niskamiji:skw *an* (my) grandmother; (my) stepmother [BC]

nitap (nitapaq) *an* (my) male friend

nitape:skw (nitape:skwaq) *an* (my) female friend

nitku *an* (my) eyelash

nitn (my) nostril

nitu (my) whisker

njijaqamij *an* (my) spirit; (my) soul; (my) shadow

njijaqamiju:wey (my) shadow

njijaqamiju:wiyey (my) shadow [SH]

njiknam *an* (my) younger brother

njikun *an* (my) knee

njikwi:ji:j *an* (my) mother-in-law [SH]

njikwi:jij *an* (my) mother-in-law [SH]

njilj *an* (my) father-in-law

nji:n'mum *an* (my) man; (my) husband

nji:n'mumt'p *an* (my) ex-husband

nji:taqan (my) neck

njoqj'te:kn (my) palate

njoqolqote:kn'm (my) palate

njukwi:ji:j *an* (my) mother-in-law

nkajikn (my) foreleg

nkamlamun (my) heart

nkamlamuti(m) (my) breath [SH]

nkat (my) foot

nkata:law (nkata:laq) *an* (my) calf (of the leg) [SH]

nkekkuni *an* (my) godparent [NB]

nkekkusk *an* (my) godparent; (my) godmother [BC]

nkekunit *an* (my) godparent [CB]

nke:kwatpan (my) pate (top of the head)

nkij *an* (my) mother

nkijewijik (pl) *an* (my) parents (mother dominant)

nkiju:wem *an* (my) mother (term of endearment)

nkisikum *an* (my) dear old man (term of affection, wife to husband)

nkisikuwi:skum *an* (my) dear old woman (term of affection for a wife)

nk'jinuwan (my) cheek [BR]

nk'jinuwan (my) cheek [SH]

nklamuksis *an* (my) uncle (also, a term of respect for an older man) [SH]

nklitam (my) birthmark

nklnikn *an* (my) godchild [CB, BC]

nknnikn *an* (my) godchild

nkoji:j *an* (my) nephew or niece; (my) stepdaughter; (my) granddaughter [BR]

nk'site:taqan (my) valuable [BR, SH]

nk'tlams'tmaqan (my) belief [BC]

nkujinuwan (my) cheek [SH]

nkwe:ji:j *an* (my) younger sister

nkwis *an* (my) son

nkwitji:j (dim) *an* (my) little son

n'liksi (my) gut

n'lis *an* (my) aunt; (my) grandmother [BR]; (my) aunt (mother's sister) [BC]

n'luk *an* (my) gland; (my) swelling

nluskunikn'm *an* (my) elbow

n'magtam *an* (my) brother-in-law (male speaker) [BC]; (my) sister-in-law (female speaker) [BC]

n'makkatem (my) dress [BC]

nmakkupe:l'm *an* (my) partner (the godparent of my child) [SH]

n'malltem (my) blood

nmaposm (my) pocket (Fr *ma) poche*)

nmaqaqjikeweym (my) big toe

n'maqjikewe: m (my) toe

n'maqtam *an* (my) brother or sister-in-law

n'matletm (my) blouse [PEI]

nma:tletm (my) gown

nmi (voc) (my) old woman (term of affection and respect)

n'mi:jan *an* (my) feces

n'mijkamij *an* (my) grandfather

n'mis *an* (my) older sister

n'mi:sikwan *an* (my) eyebrow

nm'lakejm *an* (my) mammary [SH]

nm'litam (my) birthmark [BC]

n'msekun *an* (my) eyelash [SH]

n'mtesan *an* (my) last-born

n'muksn *an* (my) shoe

n'muksnapi (my) shoelace

n'munntek (my) sack

n'munnti (my) scrotum

n'musti (my) belly; (my) pouch; (my) abdomen

n'naqapem *an* (my) chum; (my) partner; (my) housekeeper; (my) servant; (my) adoptee [BC]

n'nijan *an* (my) child [SH]

nnijkikm (my) wart

n'nikamij'skw *an* (my) mother-in-law [SH]

n'niskamij *an* (my) grandfather [NB, EG]

n'niskamiji:skw *an* (my) grandmother; (my) mother-in-law [SH]

n'njan *an* (my) child

n'nki:kw (n'nki:kuk) *an* (my) parent

nn'snaqan'm *an* (my) foster (adopted) child [SH]

n'nuji (my) head [SH]

no:kuma:j(i:j) *an* (my) distant cousin (elder to youth)

no:kumaw (no:kumaq) *an* (my) cousin; (my) relative [SH]

no:kwin (my) backbone; (my) spinal cord

nowikn (my) backbone [SH]

npaqam (my) back

npaqamiptn (my) back of the hand

npijo:qati(m) (my) quiver

npikaqan (my) rib

npi:nem (my) opinion [SH]

npitn (my) hand

np'kikw (my) eye [BR, BC, SH]

nplaqan (my) lap; (my) groin

np'lkoqom *an* (my) steady (girl or boyfriend); (my) fiancee

np'n *an* (my) lung

npoqomatim (my) weapon [CB]

npo:qon (my) bed

np'siktiyem (my) anal track; (my) anus

np'skun (my) chest; (my) breast [BR, SH]

np'ssan (my) sleeve; (my) forearm; (my) forelimb [SH]

np'ssanikat (my) foreleg [SH]

np'tn my) hand

np'tnokom (my) arm [SH]

npukukw (my) eye

npukukwe:l (my) glasses

npukumaqan (my) weapon [BC]

npu:kw (my) eye

npu:kwe:l (pl) (my) glasses; (my) specs

npuskun (my) chest; (my) breast

npuskuney (my) brassiere; (my) chest protector (in baseball)

nqon *an* (my) eel

nqosi *an* (my)f ingernail; (my) hoof

nqotaqan (my) throat

nsaqatp (my) skull [BR]

nsaqtaqan *an* (my) testicle

nsaski (my) crotch

nsi *an* (my) hoof [SH]

nsi (my) lip

nsis *an* (my) older brother

nsiskw (my) face

nsisqon (my) nose

nsit *an* (my) fetlock [SH]

nsitun (my) voice; (my) voice box; (my) windpipe

nsitunapi:l (pl) (my) vocal cords

ns'kun (my) hip; (my) rump

ns'kuti (my) urine

nsm *an* (my) niece
nsmji:j *an* (my) niece
nsmu *an* (my) (animal) horn
ns'tuwaqan (my) ear
nsukun (my) hip; (my) rump [SH]; (my) tailbone
nsukuni (my) tail
nsukuti (my) urine
nsukwis *an* (my) aunt
nsukwis *an* (my) sister-in-law (woman speaking) [PEI]; (my) brother-in-law (man speaking) [PEI]
nsukwisewijik (pl) *an* (my) aunt and uncle (aunt dominant)
ntalasutmaqan'm (my) religion [PEI]
ntalikam (my) belonging; (my) possession
ntalikem (my) possession [SH]
ntalsutaqan (my) possession
ntalsuwikn (my) indigestion; (my) liver [NB]
ntalsuwikn (my) ulcer [BC]; (my) digestive tract
nta:pim *an* (my) net
ntaposm (my) pocket
ntaptu:n (my) cane; (my) crutch
ntaqam *an* (my) snowshoe
nta:qan (my) paddle
ntaqan (my) paddle; (my) oar [SH]
nta:sutmaqan'm (my) religion
ntatqa:lam *an* (my) calf (of the leg)
nte:j *an* (my) puppy [BR]
ntelkw (my) inner fat (around the kidneys)
nte:pitem *an* (my) wife
nte:pitemt'p *an* (my) ex-wife
nte:pite:sm *an* (my) girlfriend; (my) fiancee
ntettuwoqon'm (my) bill; (my) debt
nti *an* (my) dog
ntijin (my) thumb
ntijinikat (my) big toe [BR]
ntinin (my) flesh
ntisikn (my) stocking
nt'ksite:taqan (my) treasure; (my) valuable
n'tku *an* (my) eyelash
ntlamilu (my) stomach; (my) innards
ntlaw (ntlaq) *an* (my) shoulder blade
ntlmaqan (my) shoulder
ntlmaqanatkw (my) shoulder blade
nt'lpa:tum *an* (my) boyfriend [SH]
nt'lpa:tu:sm *an* (my) boyfriend [PEI]
ntlu:suk *an* (my) son-in-law
ntlu:suwe:skum *an* (my) daughter-in-law

ntluwikn (my) finger
ntluwiknikat (my) toe [BR]
ntnuwan *an* (my) vein; (my) tendon [SH]
nto:jm (my) toe
ntoqon (my) dress
ntoqwan (my) dress [BR]; (my) quilt [BC]
nt'p (my) brain
nt'pi (my) root (a fine root used for stitching quill basket covers)
nt'p'ssan (my) sleeve [PEI]
nt'pun (my) place; (my) seat
nt'sikn (my) stocking [PEI]
ntukwape:kn (my) jaw
ntukwejan (my) forehead
ntul (my) means of transportation (boat, car, etc.)
ntun (my) mouth
ntupun (my) bed; (my) seat [PEI]
ntus *an* (my) daughter
ntuskun'm (my) liver
ntu:taqan (my) paddle; (my) oar
ntutem *an* (my) gentleman friend [BC]
ntutji:j (dim) *an* (my) little daughter
ntuttem *an* (my) totem; (my) gentleman friend [SH]; (my) fellow clansman
ntuttemi:skw *an* (my) lady friend [SH]
ntuttemi:skwe:j *an* (my) young lady friend [SH]
ntuttemji:j *an* (my) young gentleman friend [SH]
ntuwaqan (my) knife
ntuwe:m *an* (my) domestic animal (e.g. a horse, cat, etc.); (my) pet
ntuwowm *an* (my) pot
nuja:kaj (my) vein [BR]
nuja:lam *an* (my) nasal mucus
nuji:j *an* (my) grandchild
nujininuwan (my) cheek [BC]
nujipo:ti (my) purse [BC]
nujj *an* (my) father
nujjiji:j *an* (my) daddy [SH]
nujjiwejik (pl) *an* (my) parents (father dominant)
nujkikm (my) wart [BR, SH]
nujkim (my) sore; (my) scab [SH]
nukumij *an* (my) grandmother; (my) mother-in-law [SH]; (my) aunt [BR]
nullsu *an* (my) testicle
nuluks, nuluks'ji:j *an* (my) nephew [BR]
nulukun (my) thigh
nulukw *an* (my) abscess; (my) tonsil [SH]

numapposm (my) pocket [PEI]
numis *an* (my) older sister [PEI]
nunnji (my) head
nusapun (my) head hair
nusaqatp (my) skull [SH]
nutapaqan (my) team (of horses) [SH]
nuta:pi *an* (my) net [ESK]
nutapsun (my) clothing; (my) belonging
nu:ta:qan (my) paddle [BC]
nutepaqan (my) sleigh; (my) car; (my) team (of horses)
nutmaqan *an* (my) pipe
nutmawey (my) tobacco
nutmi:kn (my) axe
nutumo:taqan'm (my) property
nwikew'm (my) fat (outer layer)
nwisawe:m (my) appendix [SH]
nwisawo:m (my) appendix
wilqi (his) penis (animal)
w'nisqi (his) wing [BR]
wpmepikaj (his) hip [SH]

- MICMAC - ENGLISH -

A

a'ej "uh!" (hesitation form; noun and verb substitute) [SH]

a'ij "uh!" (hesitation form; noun and verb substitute) [PEI]

a'itetapu coincidentally

a:jela:sit *ai* get in the way; become a hindrance

a:jela:s'k *ii* get in the way; become a hindrance

a:jelisink *ai* lie in the way

a:jelpit *ai* {epit} sit in the way

a:jel-pukuwik *ii* stand in the way

a:jel-pukuwit *ai* stand in the way

a:jeltek *ii* sit in the way

a:jijkopilaqan bandage

a:jijkopilk *ta* bandage

a:jijkopil'm *ti* bandage

aji-kate:ket *ai* go for eels [NB]

aji-klu:lk *ii* {kelu:lk} better

aji-klu:sit *ai* {kelu:sit} better

aji-pikweln'k *ta* have much more of [BR]

aji-pikweln'm *ti* have much more of [BR]

ajipjulk *ta* encourage

ajipjutu *ti* encourage

aji-pukwenn'k *ta* have much more of

aji-pukwenn'm *ti* have much more of

aji-winjik *ii* worse

aji-winjit *ai* worse

ajiyet *ai* o'clock; advance (in time)

ajiyoqjimin *an* blackberry [SH]

ajje:mat *ai* play ball

akase:wa:l'k *ta* hire; lease

akase:wa:tu *ti* hire; lease

akase:wit *ai* enlist; hire on

aklasiyew *an* Englishman; white man [BR]

aklasiyewimk *ta* speak English to [BR]

aklasiyewi:sit *ai* speak English [BR]

akmetuk (loc) alongside

aknimk *ta* tell on; report on; relate what happens; confess

ak'ntiyewimk Sunday [BC]

aknutm *ti* tell on; report on; relate what happens; confess

aknutmajik (pl) *ai* talk over; agree on; negotiate

aknutmaq *ta (do)* tell (something) to

aknutmaqan news; report

a:k'tiyepis *an* sea porpoise

a:kusn hat

a:kwesn hat [BR]

ala that

ala: that [BR]

ala:l'k *ta* carry (with oneself); carry around

alalsumk *ta* own all of [BC]

ala:lukwek *ii* float around; float about

ala:lukwet *ai* float around; float about

alame:s mass (Fr *à la messe*)

alamk *ta* look around for

alanku:sit *ai (an)* a peddler

alankuwalk *ta* peddle about

alankuwat *ai* peddle about

alankuwetu *ti* peddle about

alapilaqan knapsack

alapilawemkewey stretcher; briefcase

alapit *ai* look around

alaptm *ti* look around for

ala:q (ala:m) *ai* swim about

alaqami:k (alaqami:m) *ai* {aqami:k} snowshoe about

alaqteket *ai* sail around (about)

alasenmat *ai* walk around with a light

ala:sit *ai* go about; spread around (as a sickness)

ala:s'k *ii* go about; spread around (as a sickness)

alasukwet *ai* wade around in the water

alasumteket *ai* wade around in the snow

alasutmaqan prayer [BR]

alasutmat *ai* pray [BR]

alasutmo:kuwom church [BR]

ala: te:l over that way [SH]

ala tet over there

ala: tet way over there [SH]

alatija:sit *ai* scurry about

ala:tu *ti* carry (with oneself); carry around

alawey pea

alaw'lalk *ta* carry around on the back

alaw'latm *ti* carry around on the back

alaw'let *ai* carry around on the back

alikew (alikal) clothing; clothes

alikja:t *ai* show one's buttocks

alikje:yaq *ta* show one's buttocks to (in an argument) [SH]

alikjo:kwet *ai* bend and show one's buttocks

alipqamit *ai* skate about [ESK]
ali:puluwet *ai* ride a horse
aliskalk *ta* feel around for
aliskatm *ti* feel around for
ali·sqopk *ta* {soqp'k} chew
ali·sqotm *ti* {soqtm} chew
aliyo:qsat *ai* coast about [ESK]
al-ja:t *ai* stagger; stumble about
alje:maqan *an* ball [BR]
alje:mat *ai* play ball [BR] [BC]
al-k'ltaqan'k *ta* {keltaqank} take (a dog) for a walk on a leash
al-komit *ai* paddle about (while eeling) [PEI]
al-kopijik (pl) *ai* sit all about
Allpo:s *an* Alphonse (Fr *Alphonse*)
alma *an* German (Fr *Allemand*) [SH]
almanntiyew *an* overseas Frenchman; German
alm'stapuwek *ii* shriveled up
alm'stapuwet *ai* shriveled up
alm'sta:q *ii* soggy
alm'sta:t *ai* soggy
al-nanntunawet *ai* {nanntunawet} feel one's way around (as a blind man) [SH]
alo:stasit *ai* hint; insinuate
al-p'k *ta* {soqp'k} chew on
alqo:qwek *ii* float about [BR]
alqo:wek *ii* float about
alqo:wet *ai* float about
alsink *ai* fly or glide around
als'k *ii* fly or glide around
alsumk *ta* own [SH]; control [BC]; boss
alsumukwat *ai (an)* an escapee
alsusit *ai (an)* boss [SH]
alsusuti authority [PEI]
alsutaqan personal property; something owned [SH]
alsutm *ti* own [SH]; control [BC]; boss
alt some
al-tawet *ai* {etawet} go about begging
al-tm *ti* {soqtm} chew on
al-tuqwa:t *ai* make the sound of footsteps
aluk cloud [BR]
alukiyaq *ii* turn cloudy
alukkwalk *ta* follow around
alukkwatm *ti* follow around
a:lulk *ta* guide (by boat)

alu:l'k *ta* row about
alu:saq *ii* skinny; lean
alu:sat *ai* skinny; lean
alusol (pl) measles (Fr *la rougeole*)
alusolewit *ai* have the measles
a:lutasit *ai (an)* a guide (by boat)
aluwa:l'k *ta* reject
aluwamk *ta* reject (because of the appearance)
aluwaptm *ti* reject (because of the appearance)
aluwasa:sit *ai* appear in moving silhouette
aluwa:tu *ti* reject
amalamk *ta* take a quick look at; glance at
amalamkuk where there are many varieties of sand [SH]
amalamkw *an* fine sand [SH]
amalaptm *ti* take a quick look at; glance at
amaliknoqji:j *an* mud turtle [SH]
amaliksawet *ai* carve; whittle [SH]
amaliks'k *ta* carve
amaliksm *ti* carve
amalisknuwet *ai* crochet
amaljikwej *an* raccoon [SH]
amalkat *ai* dance
amal-lukwalk *ta* {elukwalk} decorate
amal-lukwatm *ti* {elukwatm} decorate
amaloqsawet *ai* whittle [PEI]; carve
amalpaqamej *an* chipmunk; ground-squirrel [CB]
amalsawet *ai* whittle
amaltaqa:l'k *ta* put a design on; decorate; garland
amaltaqa:taqan design; decoration
amaltaqa:tu *ti* put a design on; decorate; garland
amaltaqawi:kas'k *ii* embroidered; a mixed design
amaltaqi:sawet *ai* embroider
amaltaqi:s'k *ta* embroider
amaltaqi:sm *ti* embroider
amaqan'm *ti* rub; annoint [SH]
amasapit *ai* far-sighted
amaseji:jk *ii* a little ways distant
amasek *ii* far
amase:ke:k *ai* stingy [SH]
amaskipnn'k *ta* torture

amassit *ai* silly; foolish; irresponsible

amassuwajit *ai* act the fool

amatpa:t *ai* retarded

amatpat *ai* giddy [ESK]

amatpesmat *ai* act foolishly; act unbalanced

a:meken'm *ti* rub; annoint

a:mekn'k *ta* rub; annoint

a:meknusit *ai* rub (something) on oneself

ami: (voc) *an* elderly person (term of respect and affection) [SH]

ami-klu:lk *ii* {kelu:lk} sort of good; so-so

ami-klu:sit *ai* {kelu:sit} sort of good; so-so

ami·ns'tuwe:k *ai* {nestuwe:k} partly sane

ami-p'sit *ai* {epsit} slightly warm

ami-p'tek *ii* {eptek} warm (of the weather) [BR]

amipulk *ta* rub on; rub in

amipusit *ai* rub self against

amiputu *ti* rub on; rub in

ami-siskuwapuwaq *ii* slightly muddy in color

ami·staqanat *ai* {kepistaqanat} slightly deaf; hard of hearing [SH]

ami·tke:k *ii* {teke:k} somewhat cold (weather)

ami·tkik *ii* {tekik} coolish

ami·tkit *ai* {tekit} coolish

amjaqam *ti* spread on

amjaqamat *ai* spread on

amjaq-amuksit *ai* spread (in mixed colors)

amjaq-amu:q *ii* spread (in mixed colors)

amjaqq *ta* spread on

amjaqto:sit *ai* dab or sprinkle self (with powder or perfume)

amjilakwej *an* pinfish [CB]

amjimoqpit *ai* stuck

amjimoqtek *ii* stuck

amjimoqtesink *ai* caught; stuck

amjimoqtesk *ii* caught; stuck

amjimoqwa:l'k *ta* get stuck inside

amjimoqwa:tu *ti* get stuck inside

amjoqtelikn pear [SH]

am-k'pistaqanat *ai* {kepistaqanat} hard of hearing

amkwes first; at one time

amkwes elukutimk Monday; the first work day

amkwesewa:j *an* the first one; the oldest one (person)

amkwesewa:juwit *ai* the first person

amkwesewey *an, in* the first one

am'lmaw (am'lmaq) *an* mackerel

am'lmekw *an* mackeral [BR]

am-p'tek *ii* {eptek} warm (of the weather)

amqoqjaji:j *an* toad [SH]

amqwanji:j *an* spoon

amsala:sit *ai* go wrong; break down

amsala:s'k *ii* go wrong; break down

amsalimk *ta* insult; give the run around to

amskwes first [BR]

ams'tk *ta* overhear [SH]

ams'tm *ti* overhear [SH]

ams'tmat *ai* hear vaguely about

amsute:kan *an* doll [SH]

amu *an* bee

amuj yes (in contradicting a negative statement); necessarily so (an interjection)

amujpa has to be; of necessity (an interjection)

amu:k *ii* appear; look so [SH]

amuksit *ai* appear; look so [SH]

a:muni·tke:k *ii* {teke:k} extremely cold [PEI]

amuwesusi bee hive

amuwow (amuwaq) *an* bee [BR]; wasp

anakwe:j *an* flounder

anapik pack basket [SH]

anapi:kan lean-to

anapikan lean-to [BR]; brush camp [BR]

anapiw partly; in part; aside

anapiw pemkopit *ai* sit on one side

anastawto:kwek *ii* unsteady [CB]

anastawto:kwet *ai* unsteady [CB]

anawtik *ii* cheap; inexpensive

anawtit *ai* cheap; inexpensive

aniyamukwet *ai* get one's just desserts (for cruelty committed)

aniyapsu:tlk *ta* punish; make do penance

aniyapsuwinu *an* missionary; penitent; one who sacrifices; saint [SH]

aniyapsuwinuwi:skw (aniyapsuwinuwi:skwaq) *an* nun

ankamk *ta* look at; view

ankamsuti(yey) mirror; looking glass [SH]

ankaptm *ti* look at; view

anko:tm *ti* take care of; look after; preserve

anko:way fur [ESK]

ankuna:l'k *ta* encase; enclose with

ankuna:tu *ti* encase; enclose with
ankutey just like; just the same as
ankuwa:l'k *ta* give an additional amount to;
supplement
ankuwa:taqan supplement
ankuwa:tu *ti* give an additional amount to;
supplement
ankuwowey fur
ankweyaq *ta* take care of; look after; bring
up; raise; preserve
an-nanntunawet *ai* {nanntunawet} feel one's
way around (as a blind man)
anntaknikwej *an* monkey [SH]
anntakuwej *an* black man
anntakuwejkwej *an* black woman
anntakuwejuwe:kati New Carlisle
anntakuwe:skw (anntakuwe:skwaq) *an*
black woman
anntanqanawejit (anntanqanawejijik) *an*
monkey [SH]
anntanqanawejuwa:l'k *ta* make a monkey of
[SH]
anqaney ancient [BR]
anqoni:kn covering; sheet [SH]
anqono:simkewey bedding [SH]
anqono:sun blanket; shawl [SH]
ansale:wit (ansale:wijik) *an* angel
ansma just; exactly
ansmajiw right on! [ESK]
an'stawe:k *ai, ii* delicate; uneven
an'stawite:l'mk *ta* unsure of (about)
an'stawite:tm *ti* unsure of (about)
an'stawpit *ai* unsafe
an'stawtek *ii* unsafe
ansuwe:k *ii* unfortunate; too bad
ansuwi-te:l'mk *ta* {tel-te:l(')mk} feel bad
about; distrust [PEI]
ansuwi-te:tm *ti* {tel-te:tm} feel bad about;
distrust [PEI]
antawe:s *an* Russian (red-headed) woodpecker [SH]
Antle *an* Andrew (Fr *André*)
apaja:sit *ai* come back; return
apaji·kwsuwa:l'k *ta* {kwesuwa:l'k} take back
apaji·kwsuwa:tu *ti* {kwesuwa:tu} take back
apaji·tqwa:majik (pl) *ai* {toqwa:majik} reunite
apajiyaq *ii* return; regain conciousness

apajukkwalk *ta* follow back
apajukkwatm *ti* follow back
apalqaqamej *an* chipmunk; ground-squirrel
apankimk *ta* pay for
apankitaq *ta* pay for something
apankitatimk pay day
apankitm *ti* pay for
apankituwowey contribution; payment
apank'talinik pay day [PEI]
apank'tuwowey pay check [PEI]
a:papi *an* rope, fishing line; coupled pipe [CB]
a:papi:j *an* thread; spool or thread
apaqtu:jk a little way off shore
apaqtuk off shore
apaqtukewa:j *an* European
apatalk *ai* back from eating [ESK]
apatankiyet *ai* fall backwards [PEI]
apatapekiyejit (apatapekiyejijik) *an* turkey
apatl'ka:t *ai* walk or stride back
apatpa:q *ii* reversing tide [SH]
apatte:k *ta* chase back; win back
apattek *ii* luck [SH]
apatte:m *ti* chase back; win back
apatte:mat *ai* win back
apattesink *ai* spring back
apattesk *ii* spring back
apatto:sit *ai* do (something) in reverse order
(e.g. skip rope backwards, paddle in reverse)
apatu *ti* save; preserve
a:petna:s'k *ii* gusty (of the wind)
a:pi *an* fishnet
api *an* bow [BR]
a:pij scarf [ESK]
apikji:j *an* mouse
apikjilu *an* skunk
apikjilute:k *ta* hit with a skunk (in cribbage)
apiksiktaq *ta* forgive; pardon; overlook (an
offense)
a:pimit *ai* have a net
apipunsit *ai* spend or pass the winter
apiskaq *ta* fetc.h [NB]
apiskm fetc.h [NB]
apistanewj (apistanewjik) *an* marten
apitapuwek *ii* shrivel
apitapuwet *ai* shrivel
apita:q *ii* bloated; risen (as dough)
apita:t *ai* bloated; risen (as dough)

apita:taqan soda
apiya:jijkewatp fiddlehead [SH]
a:piya:q (a:piya:m) *ai* have a net [SH]
a:piyet *ai* fish with a net
apj again [BR]
apja:'it *ai* never return
apja:sit *ai* never return
apje:jijit *ai* tiny
apje:ji:jk *ii* tiny
apje:jit *ai* small
apje:jk *ii* small
apj-elmit *ai* laugh at length
apjelmultimkewey grain of rice [BR]
apji constantly
apji:jkmuj *an* black duck
apjiku:niyet *ai* bleed (to death)
apjimk *ta* outtalk
apjimt'k (apjimtm) *ai* cry at length
apjitoq (apjitu) *ai* out of breath (as a result of having a tantrum)
apj kt'k again another [SH]
apjoqji:jit *ai* small and round
apjoqji:jk *ii* small and round
apjun handle [SH]
apjuna:tu *ti* put a handle on [SH]
apknuwalk *ta* pacify [BR]
apkwa:'ik *ii* loose; untied [PEI]
apkwa:'it *ai* loose; untied [PEI]
apkwa:l'k *ta* untie; undo
apkwa:sit *ai* become untied
apkwa:s'k *ii* become untied
apkwa:tu *ti* untie; undo
apli:kmuj *an* rabbit [SH]; hare?
apo:qajej *an* woodpecker [BC]
apo:qatej *an* woodpecker [SH]
apoqnej *an* woodpecker [RB]
apoqonmaq *ta* help; assist
apoqonmatimk assistance; help
app again
app iktik again another
app n'miskaq *ta* {nemiskaq} go fetc.h
app n'miskm *ti* {nemiskm} go fetc.h
app'sqi:kn key [BR]
apsa:l'k *ta* make smaller
apsalkikwat *ai* have tiny eyes [PEI]
apsalqikwa:ji:jit *ai* have tiny eyes

apsalqikwat *ai* have small eyes
apsalqo:tnat *ai* have a small mouth [SH]
apsalqutnat *ai* have a small mouth
apsaqqutnat *ai* have a small mouth
apsatpat *ai* have a small head
apsa:tu *ti* make smaller
apsikjat *ai* have small buttocks
apsiptnat *ai* {npitn} have small hands or paws
apsi:s'k *ta* alter (clothing)
apsisknuwet *ai* fine-weave; knit
apsi:sm *ti* alter (clothing)
apsisqonat *ai* {nsisqon} have a small or narrow nose
apskwitk *ii* form an eddy
apso:qiptnat *ai* have small arms
apso:qonikatat *ai* have small legs
apso:qonmat *ai* have a small penis
aps'sitat *ai* have a small foot
aps'sk *ta* cut into narrow strips
aps'sm *ti* cut into narrow strips
aps'sqate:ket *ai* make kindling
aps'te:m *ii* cut small
apsute:kan *an* doll
aptapjiyet *ai* gripped with fright
aptaqanet *ai* starve
aptaqatk (aptaqatm) *ai* stay permanently
aptekwat *ai* have freckles
apt-elmit *ai* laugh at length
aptelmultimkewey grain of rice
aptlama:l'k *ta* smother; block off the air from
aptlama:tu *ti* smother; block off the air from
aptlamik *ii* suffocate
aptlamit *ai* suffocate
aptlamsink *ai* lose one's breath (in a gale); breathless
aptluwajik (pl) *ai* locked together; clenched (two dogs fighting or copulating)
aptluwat *ai* hold one's breath
aptoqwet *ai* learn (by holding on to something) to walk; balance
apt'sqa:m *ti* lock up, in or out
apt'sqa:q *ta* lock up, in or out
apt'sqate:k *ta* lock up, in or out (quickly)
apt'sqate:m *ti* lock up, in or out (quickly)
apt'sqi:kn key
apt'tesink *ai* stuck inside

apt'tesk *ii* stuck inside
aptu:n cane
apu:jenk *ta* warm up (by body heat)
apu:jen'm *ti* warm up (by body heat)
apukji:j *an* mouse [BR]
apukjik soon; after while
apukjilu *an* skunk [PEI] [BR]
apukunajit *ai* February [ESK]
apu:s'k *ta* warm up (by the fire); liquefy
apu:sm *ti* warm up (by the fire); liquefy
aputansk'pit *ai* tipped over [PEI]
aputansk'tek *ii* tipped over [PEI]
aputaska:l'k *ta* turn upside down
aputaska:tu *ti* turn upside down
aputaskikwalk *ta* pry loose; turn over (with a
  tool)
aputaskikwatm *ti* pry loose; turn over (with a
  tool)
aputaskiyaq *ti* fall backwards
aputaskiyet *ta* fall backwards
aputask'tesink *ai* fall backwards
apuwa:l'k *ta* thaw out
apuwaqaj hindquarter; round of meat [SH];
  hammer (of a flint lock gun) [CB]
apuwa:tu *ti* thaw out
aqalasiyew *an* Englishman (Fr *anglais*);
  white man
aqalasiyewimk *ta* speak English to
aqalasiyewi:sit *ai* speak English
aqam *an* snowshoe [SH]
aqami:k (aqami:m) *ai* snowshoe [SH]
aqamoq *an* ash tree [SH]; white ash [RB]
aqamoqe:kati ash grove [SH]
aqata'ik *ii* half
a:qatapit *ai* half shot (from drinking)
a:qatatpa:t *ai* half-witted
aqati half [BR]
aqatiyepis *an* sea porpoise [SH]
aqawikalk *ta* hide; conceal
aqawikatm *ti* hide; conceal
aqjikatek *ii* shady
aq'ntiye:wit *ai* observe Sunday
aq'ntiye:wumk Sunday
aq'ntiye:wuti week
aqq and; then
aqtamkiyaq *ii* half-full

aqtamkiyet *ai* half-full
aqtatpa:q *ii* midnight
aqupit *ai* hidden
aqutek *ii* hidden
aquwoqomqek (loc) at (on) the turn
aquwoqomwa:sit *ai* make a turn; veer off
aquwoqomwa:s'k *ii* make a turn; veer off
asamaja:l'k *ta* do fancily or elegantly
asamaja:tu *ti* do fancily or elegantly
asamaje:k *ai, ii* fancy; elegant
a:se:k (loc) beyond; on the other side
a:sey the other side of a partition or obstacle;
  room [SH]
asiketk (asiketm) *ai* instigate; stir up trouble
a:siku:s May [CB]
asimk *ta* instigate; goad; incite
a:sisapekit *ai* climb over; crawl over
a:sisa:sit *ai* go over
a:siseket *ai* throw over
a:sispit *ai* over; beyond; across
a:sistek *ii* over; beyond; across
asita:teket *ai* get revenge; do back to; pay
  back; retaliate [PEI]
asite-klulk *ta* {kelulk} reply or talk back to [SH]
asite:l'mk *ta* have intercourse with; permit;
  allow [NB]
asitemk *ta* reply to in kind
a:s'kaq *ta* meet
aska:sit *ai* walk with a limp
askatesink *ai* limp
askayaq *ta* annoy; disturb; harm; aggravate
  [BC]
a:s'km *ti* meet
as'kom six (in counting)
as'komapekit *ai* crawl across [BR]
as'komasikwet *ai* wade across [BR]
as'koma:sit *ai* go across [BR]
as'komi:kwe:k (as'komi:kwe:m) *ai* swim
  across [BR]
as'komi:pit *ai* run across [BR]
as'commkaqan ferry; bridge [BR]
as'kom'nkaqan bridge [SH]
as'komoqtek *ii* lie across [BR]
as'komoqtesk *ii* fall across [BR]
as'kom-te:sijik (pl) *ai* six
as'kom-te:sinska:q sixty (in counting) [BR]

as'kom-te:siska:q sixty (in counting); sixty times
as'kom-te:sitpa:q *ii* six nights
as'kom-te:s'kl (pl) *ii* six
as'kom-te:soqsijik (pl) *ai* six (of something cylindrical in shape)
as'kom-te:sunkik (pl) *ta* have six of
asko:tm *ti* annoy; disturb; harm; aggravate [BC]
asoqoma:q (asoqoma:m) *ai* swim across
asoqoma:sit *ai* cross over
asoqoma:s'k *ii* cross over
asoqomasukwet *ai* wade across
asoqomi·ksma:l'k *ta* {kesma:l'k} push across
asoqomi·ksma:tu *ti* {kesma:tu} push across
asoqommtaqan ferry; bridge
asoqomoqtesink *ai* fall across
asoqomoqtesk *ii* fall across
asoqomute:ket *ai* ferry across
asoqonnkaqan railroad bridge [SH]
assma just; exactly
assumk *ta* own
assusit *ai (an)* boss
assusuti authority
assutaqan ownership
assutm *ti* own
a:sukwesukwijik (pl) *ai* meet or come together (by boat)
a:su:n blanket
a:su:nkewk *ta* clothe
asu:set *ai* pace back and forth
asu:teskaq *ta* walk back and forth to; kick back and forth
asu:teskm *ti* walk back and forth to; kick back and forth
a:sutmaqan prayer
a:sutmat *ai* pray
a:sutmessewatm *ti* pray for (Fr *messe*)
a:sutmessewk *ta* pray for (Fr *messe*)
a:sutmo:kuwom church
a:t that
atakali *an* frog [SH]
atapaqalk *ta* wind up [PEI]
atapaqam *ti* wind (up)
atapaqq *ta* wind (up)
a:taqali *an* bullfrog
atel a while ago

atelk *ai, ii* in addition to [SH]
atiyewit *ai* say goodbye
atiyu goodbye (Fr *adieu*, Basque *adiu*)
atkikwa:t *ai* wrinkled (of the head and neck)
atkikwati wrinkle
atkitemit *ai* weep
atkitemu:l'k *ta* make cry
atkitemuwaqan weeping [BC]
atknawet *ai* deal
atkne:k *ta* deal for [PEI]
atknewk *ta* deal(cards)
atk'temit *ai* weep [CB]
atlasmit *ai* rest
atlasmu:l'k *ta* rest; give a rest to
atlasmu:teket *ai* take a break; take a short rest
atla:wekn cloth
atlawekn cloth
atla:y *an* shirt (Basque pidgin *atouray*; Basque *atorra*)
a:tnamkewey item or event pertaining to the game of checkers
a:tnaqan *an* checker
a:tnaqaney checker board
a:tnaqanwi:kasit *ai* checkered
a:tnaqanwi:kas'k *ii* checkered
a:tnat *ai* play checkers
a:toq right on! [ESK]
atoqwa:su *an* trout
atoqwa:suwe:ket *ai* fish for trout
atpi:sewk *ta* go change the diaper (of an infant)
attikna:sit *ai* labor; work to one's limit
attikna:s'k *ii* labor; work to its limit
a:tukwaqan story; tale
a:tukwaqanek (loc) Eel Ground [RB]
a:tukwet *ai* tell a story
a:tukwewinu *an* storyteller
a:tukwewk *ta* tell a story to
atupikej Brook Village, N.S.
atu:tuwej *an* squirrel
atu:tuwejuwi:sit *ai* imitate a squirrel
atuwa:sa:kw *an* animal floating on its back [BR]
atuwa:sikwe:k swim on the back [BR]
atuwa:skwa:q (atuwa:skwa:m) *ai* swim on the back

atuwa:skwesink *ai*   lie on one's back
atuwa:skwetesink *ai*   fall backwards
atuwomk   sand
atuwomkemin *an*   strawberry [BR] [RB]
awaluktesk *ii*   form into clouds [BR]
awana:qiyet *ai*   uncertain; unaware
awane:jit *ai*   do or perform awkwardly
awane:k *ai*   awkward
awaneyaq *ta*   operate or handle poorly
awani·tplu:teket *ai*   {teplu:teket} have poor
     judgement
awani·wsket *ai*   {wesket} an unskilled
     fisherman
awan-kijjet *ai*   {ekijjet} read poorly
awan-lukwet *ai*   {elukwet} a poor worker
awan-mila:sit *ai*   a poor player
awano:tm *ti*   operate or handle poorly
awan-ta:sit *ai*   {tel-ta:sit} forget
awan-ta:suwalk *ta*   forget about
awan-ta:suwatm *ti*   forget about
awaqan   trail [SH]
awa:qi:kn   crooked knife
awije:jit *ai*   scarce; rare
awije:jk *ii*   scarce; rare
awisiw   seldom
awisku:k (awisku:kaq) *an*   spy [SH]
awiyalusink *ai*   encircled with a halo (as the
     sun or moon)
awiyo:qopilaqan   quill box [SH]
awjo:l'k *ta*   transport [BC]
awjo:tu *ti*   transport [BC]
aw na   instead
awo:wejit (awowejijik) *an*   spider [BR]
awo:wejituwo:pi   spider web [BR]
awti   road; trail
awti:j   path; trail
awtiket *ai*   make or clear a road or path
awtit *ai*   charged for; on salary
ayij   "uh!" (hesitation form; noun and verb
     substitute) [PEI]

E

e: yes

e:'e yes

ejala:l'k *ta* in no position to help; unable to help

ejaqaluwej *an* yellow perch [RB]

ejaqannjeteskmat *ai* trip; stub one's toe; wear out one's shoe on one side

ejaqje'ite:k *ta* knock down to the knees

ejaqje'iteskaq *ta* knock down with the feet

ejaqjepit *ai* stoop

ejela:sit *ai* helpless [SH]

ejela:tu *ti* in no position to help; unable to help

ejiklajija:sit *ai* go away quickly; fly away [CB]

ejiklako:jink *ai* bent (head part) away

ejikla:l'k *ta* take away

ejiklamukwiyet *ai* face away

ejikla:sit *ai* go away; depart

ejikla:tu *ti* take away

ejikleket *ai* throw away

ejikli·ksma:l'k *ta* {kesma:l'k} push away

ejikli·ksma:tu *ti* {kesma:tu} push away

ejikli:kwe:k (ejikli:kwe:m) *ai* swim away [SH]

ejikliwsit *ai* move away; change one's place of residence; move across (the river)

ejikl-ko:jink *ai* bent (head part) away [BR]

ejikl-sink *ai* flown away [CB]

ejikl-te:k *ta* drive away; knock away

ejikl-te:m *ti* drive away; knock away

ejiklu:jink *ai* bent (at the waist) away [SH]

ejiljet *ai* read; count [BR]

e:jint (e:jintaq) *an* Indian agent

ejkwe:mat *ai* sob

ejkwit *ai* hiccough [BC]; sneeze

ejkw'jk squash; pumpkin [SH]

ejoqjemk *ta* outargue; interrupt (in conversation)

e:k corner [SH]

ekel occasionally; once in a while

ekijjet *ai* read; count [BR]

ekimk *ta* recite; read; count (off)

ekinuwa:l'k *ta* tell [SH]; inform [SH]

ekipjik soon [BR]

ekitm *ti* recite; read; count (off)

Ekiyan *an* Stephen [BC]

ekiyaq *ii* downtide [RB]

ekkatpat *ai* hard-headed [BC]; thick-headed

ek'ntiye:wimk Sunday [CB]

eksitpu:kw *ii* morning

eksitpu:kwatal'mkewey {etlatalk} breakfast food

eksitpu:kwewulkw early morning train, boat, etc.

eksitpu:kwiyet *ai* rise early in the morning

eksitpu:kwowey breakfast; item or event pertaining to the morning

eksitpu:nuk tomorrow morning

eksupukuwa:l'k *ta* lie to; tell a whopper to

eksuwet *ai* tell a lie

eksuwo:qon lie

ekulamsn *an* gale [BR]; tornado; hurricane

ekuma:tu *ti* anchor

ekumik *ii* anchored

ekumit *ai* anchored

ekwija:l'k *ta* put in the water

ekwija:tu *ti* put in the water

ekwijink *ai* sit (set) in the water; float

ekwitamemk fishing [CB]; ice fishing

ekwitamet *ai* fish [SH] [BC]; jig fish

ekwitk *ii* sit (set) in the water; float

ela:kipulk *ta* saw

ela:kittu *ti* saw; grind or scrape

ela:l'k *ta* take or bring toward; pursue

elalqek *ii* tunnel; a long hole

ela:lukwet *ai* drift toward [BC] (waltes term)

ela:m *ti* serve

ela:mat *ai* serve self [ESK]; help self [ESK]

ela:miket *ai* ladle; dish out [SH]

elamkiyaq *ii* granular

elamkiyet *ai* granular

elamko:l'k *ta* pile

elamko:tasit *ai* piled; stacked

elamko:tas'k *ii* piled; stacked

elamko:tu *ti* pile

ela:muwet *ai* ladle; dish out

elanku:sit *ai (an)* a peddler [BC]

elanqate:m *ti* beat (ash) into strips

elanqayejit (elanqayejijik) *an* tripe

elapalk *ta* bless

elapaqte:k *ta* splash water on

elapaqte:m *ti* splash water on

elapaqtesmk *ta* line; mark (with a line)

elapaqtesteket *ai* cast (a fishing line)

elapaqto:sit *ai* splash oneself

elapatu *ti* bless
elapit *ai* look toward
elapska:tasit *ai* embossed (of bead work)
elapsk'pit *ai* short and round
elapsk'tek *ii* short and round
elapte:k (elapte:m) *ai* walk with a cane or crutch
elaptoq (elaptu) *ai* make tracks toward
ela:q (ela:m) *ai* swim toward
ela:q *ta* serve
elaq[1] *ta* resemble
elaq[2] *ta* tell [SH]
elaqalk *ta* throw toward; let go
elaqalsewk *ta* play for (in cards and board games)
elaqalsewsit *ai* play for self; run for office
elaqpa:l'k *ta* bind; lace; entwine
elaqpa:teket *ai* bind; lace
elaqpa:tu *ti* bind; lace; entwine
elaqpilk *ta* shield or conceal (with a cloth)
elaqpil'm *ti* shield or conceal (with a cloth)
elaqpit *ai* spread out [SH]
elaqpo:l'k *ta* lace up
elaqpo:tu *ti* lace up
elaqsensit *ai* make the bed; spread out the blanket
elaqsink *ai* fly toward
elaqs'k *ii* fly toward
elaqtaq[1] *ta* insinuate about
elaqtaq[2] *ta (do)* throw at [ESK]
elaqteket *ai* sail toward
elaqtu *ti* throw toward; let go; release
elaska:l'k *ta* point
elaska:tu *ti* point
elasknk *ta* hand over
elaskn'm *ti* hand over
elask'te:m *ti* split up (as kindling) [SH]
elaskukwet *ai* play cards
elasukwet *ai* wade toward (in the water)
elasumteket *ai* wade toward (through the snow)
elat *ai* bear a family resemblance
elateja:sit *ai* go over to quickly; rush over toward
elatejimk *ta* drag over
elatejitu *ti* drag over
elatpo:jink *ai* lean one's head toward

elatqek *ii* bushy; dense (as a thicket)
ela:tu *ti* take or bring toward; pursue
elaw'let *ai* lug or carry toward (on the back)
elekepilawet *ai* close the drapes (on windows)
eleket *ai* throw; drop; sow; throw in (for office)
elekete:ket *ai* cultivate; hoe; harrow
eleketoq (eleketu) *ai* raffle (off)
eleke:wi:skw *an* queen; queen card
eleke:wit (eleke:wijik) *an* king; king card (Basque *errege*)
eleke:wiya:timk Ephiphany
eleko:l'k *ta* lay out; spread out
eleko:tu *ti* lay out; spread out
elenqwe:set *ai* go forth on foot; stroll toward
eletqek *ii* grove; orchard
eletqo:l'k *ta* coil
eletqo:tu *ti* coil
eli:k *ta* make; build
eli-kimskuwalk *ta* sneak up on [BR]
eli-kimskuwatm *ti* sneak up on
eli-kimskuwet *ai* sneak up [BR]
eli·kjepilawet *ai* {kejipilm} make the bottom part (of a basket) [SH]
eli·kjipil'm *ti* {kejipilm} weave the bottom (of a basket) [SH]
elikpetamit *ai* strip ash [SH]
elikpete:ket *ai* pound ash (to make basket splints)
elikp'ta:q *ti* smoke toward
eli·ksma:l'k *ta* {kesma:l'k} push toward
eli·ksma:tu *ti* {kesma:tu} push toward
e:liku *ti* serve food [BC]
eliku:niyet *ai* bleed toward
elikuwa:laq *ii* drip
elikuwa:lat *ai* drip
elikuwaq *ii* have a grain (as of wood)
elikuwet *ai* lean toward
elikwalk *ta* pry toward
elikwatm *ti* pry toward
eli:kwe:k (eli:kwe:m) *ai* swim toward [BR]
eli-nisku:niyet *ai* bleed down toward [BR]
eli:pit *ai* rush toward
elipqama:l'k *ta* roll [NB]
elipqama:tu *ti* roll [NB]
elipqamit *ai* ice skate
elipqamu:l'k *ta* roll

elipqamulk *ta* slide
elipqamu:tu *ti* roll
elipqamutu *ti* slide
elipqiyaq *ii* layered
elipqiyet *ai* layered
eli:pukwet *ai* stagger toward
elipulk *ta* rake toward; stroke toward
eliputu *ti* rake toward; stroke toward; shove toward
eli:sawet *ai* sew
eli:sawewk *ta* sew for
eli:sewet *ai* sew [SH]
eli:s'k *ta* sew
eliska:sit *ai* offer one's hand [BC]
elisknuwalk *ta* braid; knit
elisknuwatm *ti* braid; knit
elisknuwet *ai* knit; weave; spin [BR]; braid
eli:sm *ti* sew
elisma:sit *ai* lie down [BR]
elisqanpeka:tu *ti* weave a handle on [SH]
eli:sqaqanek *ii* point toward [BR]
elistaq *ta* disobey
elist'k (elistm) *ai* disobey [PEI]
elistm *ti* disobey
elisukwit *ai* paddle toward
elitaq *ta* make something for [BR]
elita:sit *ai* dependent on
elita:suwalk *ta* depend on
elita:suwatm *ti* depend on
elitk *ii* flow toward
elitu *ti* make
eli:tuwat *ai* wear or have a moustache
eliyaq *ii* go
eliyet *ai* go
eljaqam *ti* spread; smear
eljaqq *ta* spread; smear
elk also; too
e:l'k[1] *ai* swim forth [BC]
e:l'k[2] *ta* serve [BC]
elkaq *ta* cause (a body part) to get sore (from sleeping on it)
elkesawet *ai* plow
elkesm *ti* plow (the land)
elkete:ket *ai* cultivate; hoe; harrow
elkimk *ta* send forth; send over; send there
el-kimskwet *ai* sneak up to
elkitm *ti* send forth; send over; send there

elkm *ti* cause (a body part) to get sore (from sleeping on it)
elko:jink *ai* faced toward
elkomiktaq *ta* call out to (for assistance)
elkusuwet *ai* climb (up)
el-kuta:l'k *ta* pour into
el-kuta:tat *ai* pour oneself a drink
el-kuta:tu *ti* pour into
elkwi:tm *ti* swim toward [BR]
e:l'm *ti* serve [BC]
elma:l'k *ta* take or bring back home [BR]
elmalqei hole [BR]
elmalqe:ji:j small hole
elmalqey hole [BR]
elmapekit *ai* crawl home [BR]
elmaqteket *ai* sail home [CB]
elma:tu *ti* take or bring back home [BR]
elmikimk *ta* send home [BR]
elmi-nikani·pqa:sit *ai* {paqa:sit} go ahead down in the water [BR]
elmi-pisaqqaniyet *ai* {pisaqqan} bubble along [SH]
elmi-walqwasiyet *ai* {walqwe:k} set (as the sun) [CB]; descend (into the hollow) [CB]
elmiwktaqamu:k Nova Scotia mainland [BR]
elmiyaq *ii* go home; depart for home [BR]
elmiyet *ai* go home; depart for home [BR]; depart [BR]
elm'joqtek *ii* set (as a table); piled up along
el'm'kitm *ti* send [SH]
el'm'kiyaq *ii* recede (tide) [SH]
elm'kiyaq *ii* recede (of the tide) [BR]
elm'l'kat *ai* go home on foot
elmoqwe:set *ai* scoot home [CB]
elm'piskwa(:)t *ai* {piskwa(:)t} enter a dwelling [BR]
elmu:jink *ai* bend away from [SH]
elnaqsit *ai* bed down (as an animal) [BC]
eln'k *ta* hand over
eln'kalk *ta* carry or pack on the shoulder
eln'katm *ti* carry or pack on the shoulder
eln'ket *ai* carry or pack on the shoulder
eln'm *ti* hand over
eln'ma:l'k *ta* insert; stick into
eln'ma:tu *ti* insert; stick into
eln'mik *ii* stuck into

eln'mit stuck into
elnmte:k *ta* drive or hammer in [BR]
elnmte:m *ti* drive or hammer in
elnmtesm(')k *ta* hurl in (as a spear [BR]
elo:l'k *ta* bring (in bulk); place (in bulk)
elo:pisit *ai* suspended (as on a rope or string
elo:pitek *ii* suspended (as on a rope or string
eloqeket *ai* throw lengthwise [BR]
eloqo(n)maqa:taqan cigarette [BR]
eloqo(n)maqa:tu *ti* wrap up lengthwise [BR];
    roll a cigarette [BR]
eloqomkiyatm *ti* fit a handle on an axe
eloqomqwalk *ta* trim to fit
eloqomqwatm *ti* trim to fit
eloqosink *ai* laid out lengthwise
eloqosk *ii* laid out lengthwise
eloqpit *ai* long and cylindrical
eloqs'k *ta* carve
eloqsm *ti* carve
eloqtek *ii* long and cylindrical
eloqtesmk *ta* chop or push down toward
eloqtestu *ti* chop or push down toward
eloqtnema:t *ai* have bad breath
eloqwa:l'k *ta* lay down lengthwise
eloqwalk *ta* trim to fit [BR]
eloqwatm *ti* trim to fit [BR]
eloqwatu *ti* lay down lengthwise
elo:tu *ti* bring (in bulk); place (in bulk)
elp too; also
el-paniksink *ai* drifted up against
el-paniks'k *ii* drifted up against
elpaq'nte:m *ti* splash [BR]
elpilk *ta* send across by rope or cable
elpil'm *ti* send across by rope or cable
elpiso:tulk *ta* wrap; bundle up (with a scarf)
el-pukuwik *ii* upright; vertical
el-pukuwit *ai* upright; vertical
el-pukuwo:tasit *ai* stacked upright
el-pukuwo:tas'k *ii* stacked upright
el-puwalk *ta* want there
el-puwatm *ti* want there
elqamkuk over the hill; on the other side [SH]
elqamkwejat *ai* brace oneself (to keep one's
    balance or to slow down)
elqanapit *ai* beneath the surface [BR]
elqawet *ai* hang out laundry [BC]
elqo:suwet *ai* climb (up) [EG]

elqowet *ai* hang out laundry
elsaqapit *ai* flat and rigid
elsaqas'k *ii* flat and rigid
elsaqa:tu *ti* set a trap [BR]
elsaqtek *ii* layered; divided [SH]
elsipuktuk Big Cove [NB]
elsita:sit *ai (an)* instep
elsma:l'k *ta* lay down
elsma:sit *ai* lie down
elsma:tu *ti* lay down
elsumukwat *ai* flee toward
elsusit *ai* cut self [BR]
elsu:tmaq *ta (do)* blame on
elsutmaq *ta (do)* defer to [BC]
elt too; also
eltaqa:l'k *ta* string up (as a clothesline) [BC];
    string toward
eltaqa:m *ti* shoot toward
eltaqanewet *ai* spin (thread)
eltaqa:teket *ai* string a line [RB]; set a net [RB]
eltaqa:tu *ti* string up (as a clothesline) [BC];
    string toward
eltaqayaq *ii* reach or stretc.h toward (as a
    cable or rope)
eltaqayet *ai* reach or stretc.h toward (as a
    cable or rope)
eltaqpit *ai* long and flexible
eltaqsawet *ai* cut sheens (for basket making)
eltaqtek *ii* long and flexible
eltaqte:ket *ai* weave
el-teja:l'k *ta* drive to (in a vehicle)
el-teja:tu *ti* drive to (in a vehicle)
eltek *ii* lead to
elteskaq *ta* chase toward
eltnuwalk *ta* knit [SH]
eltnuwatm *ti* knit [SH]
eltnuwet *ai* knit; purr (as a cat) [SH]
el'tqek *ii* coiled
el'tqet *ai* coiled
el-tu *ti* make; build
el-tuknapskek *ii* round and hollow
el-tuknapsk'sit *ai* round and hollow
el-tukne:k *ai* hollow
el-tukwi:k (el-tukwi:m) *ai* run toward
elu:jink *ai* bend toward
elukkwalk *ta* follow toward
elukkwatm *ti* follow toward

elu:knawet *ai* knead dough [PEI]

eluktu *ti* carry toward on one's back or shoulder

eluktulk *ta* carry toward on one's back or shoulder

elu:kwalk *ta* point toward

elu:kwalk *ta* point toward

elukwalk *ta* repair; fix; gut (as a fish)

elu:kwatm *ti* point toward

elu:kwatm *ti* point toward

elukwatm *ti* repair; fix

elu:kwek *ii* point toward

elukwe:k *ta* work; make work

elukwek *ii* work

elu:kwet *ai* point toward

elukwet *ai* work

elukwetu *ti* use for work

elukwewk *ta* work for

elu:kwit *ai* gag; choke on (food)

elulk *ta* hire; ask (someone) to do something; seek assistance from

elusknawet *ai* knead dough

eluskwatamit *ai* spit

elutaq *ta* impersonate; imitate

eluwe:wa:l'k *ta* fool; trick

eluwe:wit *ai* quick-tempered; short-tempered

eluwe:wiyaq *ii* crazy

eluwe:wiyet *ai* crazy

eluwi:tmasit *ai* take an oath; swear off; make a pledge

eluwi:tmasuti oath

emeko:teket *ai (an)* treat (people) badly; tyrant

emeko:tm *ti* mistreat

emekwatalk *ai* eat improperly

emekwe:k *ai* act improperly

emekweyaq *ta* mistreat

emisqapit *ai* nude; naked

emisqa:sit *ai* strip self nude

emisqatesink *ai* strip (while dancing); stripped (of clothing)

emisqe:k *ai, ii* naked; bare

emisqo:t'lk *ta* strip (a person)

emittukwalk *ta* visit

emittukwatm *ti* visit

emittukwet *ai* visit

em'lsiktmat *ai* see or hear an apparition or ghost; spooked

emqata:q *ta* loan to

emqatuwi:k *ta* loan to

emqatuwi:ketu *ti* loan

emqwanji:j *an* spoon [BR]

emteskatalk *ai* {etlatalk} eat fussily; a fussy eater

emteskit *ai* vain; snobbish; envious [BC]

emteski-te:l'mk *ta* {tel-te:l'mk} act superior to; place oneself above

emteski-te:tm *ti* {tel-te:tm} act superior to; place oneself above

emtoqwalk *ta* worship

emtoqwatm *ti* worship

enaqan *an* spruce bough (used as floor covering in wikwam) [SH]

enaqet *ai* spread spruce boughs [SH]

enaqsit *ai* hurry off [CB]; hurry up [CB]

e:n'k *ta* lose

enkalk *ta* scale; measure out; weigh

enkaqan measurement

enkatm *ti* scale; measure out; weigh

enkejit (enkejijik) *an* caterpillar

enkemkewey measuring instrument

enket *ai* scale or measure (pertaining to wood)

e:n'm *ti* lose

enma:l'k *ta* take or bring home

enmalqey hole

enmapej *an* carrot [ESK]

enmapet (enmapejik) *an* carrot

enmaqqey hole

enmateja:l'k *ta* convey or drive home (in a vehicle)

enmateja:sit *ai* hurry that way; hurry home

enmateja:tu *ti* convey or drive home (in a vehicle)

enma:tu *ti* take or bring home

enmaw'lalk *ta* carry home

enmaw'latm *ti* carry home

enmejepit *ai* face the other direction

enmejetek *ii* face the other direction

enmikimk *ta* send home

enmikitm *ti* send home

enmikiyaq *ii* recede (tide)

enmikjepit *ai* reserved

enmikjesink *ai* lie facing in the opposite direction

enmikjetek *ii* reserved

enmikjo:kwet *ai* stoop facing backwards

enmiktaqamu:k Nova Scotian mainland

enmipkowe:k along the edge of a cliff

enmisa:kwatp'tesink *ai* run with one's hair bobbing up and down

enmisink *ai* lie facing away

enmisk *ii* lie facing away

enmit *ai* laugh [NB]

enmitk *ii* flow away

enmiyaq *ii* go home; depart

enmiyet *ai* go home; depart

enm'kate:pit *ai* trot or scoot along home; beat it home

enm'kitm *ti* send

enm'lamit *ai* gasp

enm'l'ka:t *ai* walk away

enm'nqwe:set *ai* go home in a huff

enmoqowet *ai* carry (pertaining to the voice)

enmoqtesink *ai* stagger along; stagger home

enm'piskwa:t *ai* {piskwa:t} enter a dwelling

enm'teskaq *ta* chase home

enmu:jink *ai* bend back facing in the opposite direction

enmukkwalk *ta* follow along; follow home

enmukkwatm *ti* follow along; follow home

enn'ma:l'k *ta* stick in

enn'ma:tu *ti* stick in

ennmte:k *ta* drive or hammer in

ennmte:m *ti* drive or hammer in

ennmtesm'k *ta* hurl in

ennmtestu *ti* hurl in

enqa:l'k *ta* stop

enqalk[1] *ta* leave behind

enqalk[2] *ta* strain

enqanapit *ai* beneath the surface

enqanatek *ii* beneath the surface

enqan'm *ti* strain

enqapit *ai* stopped

enqa:sit *ai* stop

enqa:s'k *ai* stop

enqatek *ii* stopped

enqatm *ti* leave behind

enqa:tu *ti* stop

ensanoqonik *ii* dangerous

ensanoqonit *ai* dangerous

entu *ti* lose

epa:l'k *ta* seat

epa:sit *ai* sit down

epasma:sit *ai* lie down [CB]

epa:suwalk *ta* sit on; sit next to

epa:suwatm *ti* sit on; sit next to

epatku-pukuwik *ii* lean against

epatku-pukuwit *ai* lean against

epatkwi·ksma:l'k *ta* {kesma:l'k} push or shove against

epatkwi·ksma:tu *ti* {kesma:tu} push or shove against

epatuwepit *ai* set against

epatuwetek *ii* set against

epekwitk *ii* calm water; Prince Edward Island

epetoqsit *ai* moan

epipnatm *ti* knead

epipnet *ai* bake bread

epistamit *ai* sop up (with bread); eat the main course (fish, pork) [BC]

e:pit (e:pijik) *an* woman

epit *ai* seated; placed; located at

e:pite:ji:j *an* young girl

e:pite:s *an* an unmarried woman; a young woman

e:pite:siw-qamiksit *ai* act like a girl

e:pite:siwwet *ai* enter into womanhood (post menstrual)

e:pitewe:ket *ai* hunt or seek for a woman

e:pitewe:sm *an* woman-chaser [PEI]

e:pitewit *ai* become a woman

e:pitew-qamiksit *ai* act like a woman; act effeminately

e:pitewsm (e:pitewsmuk) *an* woman-chaser

e:pitji:jiwwet *ai* enter into womanhood (ready for marriage)

epitm *ti* sit on; brood; hatch

epkenikn manure; fertilizer

epkenk *ta* fertilize

epken'm *ti* fertilize

e:pluwi·psaq *ii* {pesaq} heavy snowfall [ESK]

epme:tkwaj *an* temple; side of the head [SH]

epme:tkwete:k *ta* slap along the side of head [SH]

epoqek *ii* light and warm (of a breeze)

eppa:q *ii* warm liquid
eppaqsijik (pl) *ai* warm (of a liquid)
eppetek *ii* lukewarm water
epqwalk *ta* shelter
epqwas'k temporary shelter
epqwatm *ti* shelter
epsaqtejk *an* stove
epsawek *ii* radiate; give off heat
epsawet *ai* radiate; give off heat
epsimkewey fever
epsit *ai* hot
eps'k *ta* heat; warm up
epskuninet *ai* have dry tuberculosis
epsm *ti* heat; warm up
eptaqan *an* dish; record
eptaqano:kuwom china cabinet; cupboard
eptek *ii* hot (eptek is also used for the weather)
eptekwat *ai* have freckles; freckled
eptekwati freckle
eptoqalk *ta* leave in care of somebody; leave for safekeeping; temporarily abandon
eptoqatm *ti* leave in care of somebody; leave for safekeeping; temporarily abandon
epuktaqanat *ai* have heartburn
epune:k below; downstairs
e:s (e:sik) *an* clam; ace card
esa:m *ti* banish; fire; refuse; turn down
esamqwatm *ti* drink [BR]
esamuqo:tlk *ta* give a drink to; water
esamuqwat *ai* drink
esapoqo:tlk *ta* give a drink to [SH]; water
esapoqwat *ai* drink [SH]
esapoqwatm *ti* drink [SH]
esa:q *ta* banish; fire; refuse; turn down
ese:k *ta* banish; fire; refuse; turn down
e:se:ket *ai* hunt for clams
eseta:sit *ai* move back
esetekja:l'k *ta* bring backwards
esetekjapekit *ai* crawl backwards
esetekja:tu *ti* bring backwards
esetekjeket *ai* shove backwards
esetekji·ksma:l'k *ta* {kesma:l'k} push back
esetekji·ksma:tu *ti* {kesma:tu} push back
esetekji·pija:sit *ai* go in backwards
esetekji·psa:l'k *ta* {pesa:l'k} skin inside out [SH]

esetekji·psa:tu *ti* {pesa:tu} skin inside out [SH]
eseti·ksma:l'k *ta* {kesma:l'k} push back [SH]
eseti·ksma:tu *ti* kesmatu} push back [SH]
eseti·pija:sit *ai* enter backwards
eseti·psa:l'k *ta* {pesa:l'k} turn inside out
esinapito:tu *ti* squeeze together (ash strands in basketry) [ESK]
esinnteskaq *ta* pack or tamp down
esinnteskm *ti* pack or tamp down
esinoqjo:tu *ti* press down (basket splints) [BC]
esipulk *ta* sharpen; file; grind
esiputu *ti* sharpen; file; grind
esiyamkek[1] *ii* rilely [BR]
esiyamkek[2] Campbellton
eske:k *ai, ii* raw [BC]
eskik *ii* green (of foliage); uncured
eskikloqon green twig [SH]
eskipe:k *ta* expect
eskipetu *ti* expect
eskit *ai* green (of foliage); uncured
eskmalk *ta* wait for
eskmaqtmat *ai* pregnant; expecting (a baby)
eskmat *ai* wait
eskmatm *ti* wait for
eskm'na:q before (takes a negative verb)
eskmoqon slime; semen
esknuwapatij Burnt Church [RB]
eskoqsit *ai* left untouched by fire
eskoqtek *ii* left untouched by fire
esk'pk *ta* eat raw
esk'tamit *ai* eat raw food
esk'tm *ti* eat raw
esk'tm'kewey cucumber
eskutesm'k *ta* break
eskwaqanik (eskwaqanikaq) *an* fish-hawk
eskwit *ai* sneeze
eskwitesm(')k *ta* break [BR]
eskwiyaq *ii* leftover; remainder
eskwiyet *ai* leftover; remainder
esm(')k *ta* feed [BR]
esne:k *ai, ii* low; flat
espe:k *ai* important; high up (in rank); High Mass [SH]
espek *ii* leak
espet *ai* leak
espi:sit *ai* use high-sounding language

es'pkwa:l'k *ta* bring up a child [SH]

es'pkw'tl'k *ta* raise a child [SH]

esp'pit *ai* sit (or set) up high

esp'pukuwik *ii* stand up high; hold a high position

esp'pukuwit *ai* stand up high; hold a high position

esp'tek *ii* sit (or set) up high

espulqek *ii* deep

essasit *ai* dyed

essawiya:l'k *ta* dye

essawiyalk *ta* dye [SH]

essawiyaqan dye

essawiyatm *ti* dye [SH]

essawiya:tu *ti* dye

essawiyet[1] *ai* fade

essawiyet[2] *ai* dye [SH]

essit *ai* ripe

ess'k *ta* dye

ess'm *ti* dye

ess'ntaqo:tu *ti* thin down (of splints) [SH]

eta emphatic particle

etamk *ta* ask of; request from

e:tamkw (e:tamkwaq) *an* bank beaver [RB]

e:taqaq *ta* stand next in line to (of succession); stand behind [SH]

e:ta:s every [SH]

etawaqtmaq *ta* beg for

etawaqtmat *ai* ask for a favor

etawet *ai* beg a favor; hope

etek *ii* seated; placed; located at; set, located or situated there

etekji·ksma:l'k *ta* {kesma:l'k} push back

etekji·ksma:tu *ti* {kesma:tu} push back

etepne:k *ta* catch up with

etepne:m *ti* catch up with

etl(i) where; progressive aspect (grammar)

etlanqatesk *ii* shimmer (heat)

etlapensit *ai* scratch oneself

etlaqqisewet *ai* blab away

etlatalk *ai* eat

etl-elmit *ai* laugh [SH]

etl-enmit *ai* laugh

etlewistu *ai* talk

etli:k *ta* create; make

etlikmiyet *ai* steam and boil

etlikp'ta:q *ii* smoke; steam

etlikp'ta:t *ai* smoke; steam

etliktuknit *ai* stay or pass the night

etliku:niyet *ai* bleed; hemmorage

etlintoq (etlintu) *ai* sing

etlipiyasit *ai* dry; cured (of wood)

etlipiyask *ta* dry; cure (wood)

etlipiyasm *ti* dry; cure (wood)

etlipiyatek *ii* dry; cured (of wood)

etlipulk *ta* rub; stroke; pet

etliputu *ti* rub; stroke; pet

etlitat *ai* suckle from the breast

etli-te:l'mk *ta* {tel-te:l'mk} assume; believe; think

etli-te:tm *ti* {tel-te:tm} assume; believe; think

etlitu *ti* create; make

etlo:piyet *ai* swing

etloqs'k *ta* cook

etloqsm *ti* cook

etloqtek *ii* cooked

etl-seknk *ta* construct or build with brick or cement blocks

etl-sekn'm *ti* construct or build with brick or cement blocks

etl-te:k[1] *ta* have intercourse with

etl-te:k[2] *ta* beat; strum; play

etl-te:m *ti* beat; strum; play

etl-te:mat *ai* copulate

etl-temit *ai* {atkitemit} cry

etl-tesink *ai* beat or move rythmically; shake; dance; where one got injured

etl-tesk *ii* beat or move rythmically; shake; dance; where one got injured

e:tmapit *ai* sit (set) in the forefront

e:tma-pukuwit *ai* stand in the forefront

e:tmatek *ii* sit (set) in the forefront

etnesink *ai* nest (as a bird) [SH]

etoqtalk *ta* bake; cook [SH]

etoqtasit *ai* roast [BR]

etoqtatm *ti* bake; cook [SH]

etoqtet *ai* cook [SH]; bake

ettamit *ai* eat poorly

ettek *ii* ripe

ettoqalk[1] *ta* shore up; support [BR]

ettoqalk[2] *ta* leave for safekeeping [BR]

ettoqatm leave for safekeeping [BR]

etuk perhaps; should?

etuk jel maybe so; probably
etu:kutewe:k (pl) *an* scapular
etu:kwesmit *ai* rest one's head on
etulkomit *ai* hold or carry something under the arm
Etuwe:l *an* Edward (Fr *Edouard*)
ewayatpat *ai* silly; foolish [SH]
ewayatpete:k *ta* knock senseless or silly [SH]
ewe:ka:l'k *ta* loosen
ewe:ka:tu *ti* loosen
ewe:ke:k *ai, ii* roomy; uncrowded
eweke:k *ta* make use of
eweketu *ti* make use of
ewe:kiska:l'k *ta* exercise; break in
ewe:kiskalsit *ai* exercise; loosen up
ewe:kiska:tu *ti* exercise; break in
ewi:kat *ai* make a camp or dwelling; build a house
ewi:kewk *ta* build a house for
ewi:kikek *ii* write
ewi:kikemkewey writing pad; pencil
ewi:kiket *ai* write
ewi:k'k *ta* write; mark down
ewi:km *ti* write; mark down
ewi:kmaq *ta* write to
ewipk *ii* calm (of water)
ewisit *ai* pick berries [CB]
ewissukwalk *ta* cook [SH]
ewissukwateket *ai* cook [SH]
ewissukwatm *ti* cook [SH]
ewi:t'k *ta* mention; name
ewi:tm *ti* mention; name
ewjo:l'k *ta* haul back and forth; transport
ewjo:tat *ai (an)* a delivery man
ewjo:tu *ti* haul back and forth; transport
e:w'k *ta* use; make use of
ew'lamsit *ai* catch one's breath
ew'lamsn *an* gale; tornado; hurricane
ew'le:jit *ai* poor; poor condition
ew'le:jiwanu *an* poor person [SH]
ew'le:jiwaqan hard times
ew'le:jiwinu *an* poor person
ew'le:jk *ii* poor; poor condition
ew'let *ai* tell lies [PEI]
e:w'm *ti* use; make use of

ew'nasa:sit *ai* act foolish; act up; hustle about [BR]
ew'nasi·mknasit *ai* {meknasit} pick up hurriedly [BR]
ew'nasi·mk'nk *ta* {meknk} pick up improperly
ew'nasi·mkn'm *ti* {mekn'm} pick up improperly
ew'nasisink *ai* lie awkwardly
ew'nasiyaq *ii* confused; mixed up (crazy)
ew'nasiyet *ai* confused; mixed up (crazy)
ew'naskwatpa:l'k *ta* make dizzy; make someone's head turn
ew'naskwatpetesink *ai* dizzy from a blow on the head
ew'naskwetesink *ai* nod [BR]
ew'naskwiyet *ai* dizzy
ew'ne:k *ii* blue
ew'niyaq *ii* get foggy [SH]; turn blue
ewqwam garment
ewsa:l'k *ta* shake; rough up
ewsami-apje:jk *ii* too small [CB]
ewsa:tu *ti* feint; bluff; pretend to do
ewsimk *ta* bluff; kid
ewsi·npat *ai* {nepat} feign sleep; pretend to sleep [BR]
ewsitutk (ewsitutm) *ai* show off
ewskwapek *ii* twitch
ewskwapet *ai* twitch
ewskwit *ai* sneeze
ewt'pa:sit *ai* sit down on top of; sit down atop
ewt'paskaq *ta* sit on
ewt'paskm *ti* sit on; hold back (of money)
ewt'pa:suwalk *ta* sit on top of; sit atop
ewt'pa:suwatm *ti* sit on top of; sit atop
eyk (ey'm) *ai, ii* be there; reside [BC]
eyt *ai* be there; reside [BR]

I

ijipanji:j *an* kitten beaver [SH]

ika:l'k *ta* release; place; put

ikalk *ta* protect; defend; fight for; take the side of; favor

ikalsit *ai* defend self

ikanawtiket (ikanawtikejik) *ai (an)* {awtikwet} blaze a trail; a trail blazer; head swamper

ikani-te:tm *ti* {tel-te:tm} read entrails [SH]; predict [SH]

ikanitqa:sit *ai* run up ahead [SH]

ikan-pukuwit *ai (an)* stand at the head [SH]; a leader [SH]

ikanus *an* leader [SH]

ika:q *ii* arrive

ika:t *ai* arrive

ika:taqalk *ta* plant; sow

ika:taqan cultivated land or field; garden

ika:taqatm *ti* plant; sow

ika:taqewk *ta* sow or plant for

ika:taquk *ai* plant; put in a garden; sow

ika:taqulk *ta* plant; sow

ika:taqutm *ti* plant; sow

ikatm *ti* protect; defend; fight for; take the side of; favor

ikatne:siwinu *an* a horse racer

ikatne:we:sm (ikatne:we:smuk) *an* a racer

ikatne:wet *ai* race; win (a race)

ika:tu *ti* release; place; put

ikekkwet *ai* in heat (said of a dog); lose one's mind; fall sick

ikewkwet *ai* act up [PEI]

ikn'maq *ta (do)* give to; allow; permit

ikn'muwetu *ti* give away

ikte:k (ikte:m) *ai* yawn [SH]

iktewsit *ai* yawn [PEI]

iktik *an, in* another (one)

iktiki-sapo:nuk the day after tomorrow

iktiki-w'la:ku {wela:kw} the day before yesterday

ikto:sit *ai* yawn

ilaji:kewk *ta* prepare for; prepare lodging for

ilaji:kewsit *ai* get ready; get prepared

ilajit *ai* prepare (for); get ready (for); pack

ilajuktaq *ta* prepare for; get ready for

ilajuktm *ti* prepare for; get ready for

ila:l'k *ta* adjust; set; fix

ilamk *ta* sight; look over; examine

ilanqa:l'k *ta* fold right; fold properly

ilanqa:tu *ti* fold right; fold properly

ilapewnusit *ai* put on make up

ilapsk'smu:kwet *ai* stretc.h out for a rest

ilapt'k *ta* examine; look over

ilaptm *ti* sight; look over; examine

ila:sit *ai* get well; recover

ilaska:l'k *ta* re-align

ilaska:tu *ti* re-align

ilaskukwaqan card playing [SH]

ilaskuwaqan card playing [BC]

ilaskuwet *ai* play cards [BC]

ilaskw (ilaskuk) *an* playing card [SH]

ila:tu *ti* adjust; set; fix

ileko:tm *ti* spread [PEI]

ilisma:sit *ai* change position (while lying prone)

ilisqa:l'k *ta* limber; massage; put back in place (as a joint)

ilisqa:tu *ti* limber; massage; put back in place (as a joint)

ilkwenk *ta* guide or steer (by the head or bow)

ilkwen'm *ti* guide or steer (by the head or bow)

ilkwi:t'k *ta* steer

ilkwi:tm *ti* steer

illjo:qonk *ta* balance; steady

illjo:qon'm *ti* balance; steady

illjo:qwa:l'k *ta* put right side up; put straight; settle

illjo:qwa:tu *ti* put right side up; put straight; settle

iloqamk *ta* check over [BC]

iloqomoqwa:l'k *ta* wrap(as a gift)

iloqomoqwa:taqan cigarette [SH]; gift package; wrapping paper

iloqomoqwa:tu *ti* wrap(as a gift)

iloqwa:l'k *ta* place or put in a proper position lengthwise; straighten out

iloqwa:tu *ti* place or put in a proper position lengthwise; straighten out

ilpilk *ta* dress properly; tie up properly

ilpil'm *ti* dress properly; tie up properly

ilpilsit *ai* get properly dressed; tie self up

il-pukuwa:sit *ai* stand into position

ilsaqam *ti* partition off

ilsaqa:tu *ti* cock (a gun); set (a trap)

ilsumk *ta* judge; sentence
ilsutaqan trial
ilsuteket *ai* give orders; plan
ilsutm *ti* judge; sentence
ilta:l'k *ta* shut; close down; damper
iltaqa:l'k *ta* close [BC]; straighten out
iltaqalk *ta* hitch up (a horse) [SH]
iltaqane:walk *ta* prepare; organize; set up
iltaqane:watm *ti* prepare; organize; set up
iltaqank *ta* guide or direct (a horse) by the reins
iltaqa:tu *ti* close [BC]; straighten out
iltaqayet *ai* recover from illness
iltaqo:l'k *ta* straighten (out) (as pipe or a net)
iltaqotm *ti* hitch up (a wagon) [SH]
iltaqo:tu *ti* straighten (out) (as pipe or a net)
ilta:tu *ti* shut; close down; damper
ilteket *ai* shut firmly
iltijiyeket *ai* slam shut
inaqan right (side)
inaqanek on the right
inaqaneke:l toward the right
inaqanmit *ai* right-handed
innklan England [CB]
i:pusit *ai* embark frequently; embark regularly
ise:k *ai* have a good time
isey half [BR]
istu-napuwi:k'k *ta* draw or trace unevenly or crookedly
istu-napuwi:km *ti* draw or trace unevenly or crookedly
istu:pit *ai* crooked
istu:s'k *ta* cut unevenly or crookedly
istu:sm *ti* cut unevenly or crookedly
istu:tek *ii* crooked
istuwa:l'k *ta* do or make crooked
istuwa:tu *ti* do or make crooked
istuwe:k *ai, ii* different; strange; crooked [BC]
istuwik *ii* crooked; uneven; bent; dishonest
istuwikata:t *ai* {nkat} have a clubfoot; clubfooted
istuwikit *ai* crooked; uneven; bent; dishonest
i:ta:s every
i:wesuwaskw sweet flag (a medicinal herb) [RB]

iwtoqoto:sit *ai* skip around [SH]; spin around [BC]
iyap (iyapaq) *an* bull (moose, caribou, etc.) [SH]
iyapjiw forever

J

jajik-amuksit *ai* look healthy
jajike:k *ai* healthy [BR]
jajikiw along the edge [SH]
jajikoqpit *ai* lie alongside
jajikoqtek *ii* lie alongside
jajikpit *ai* alongside [SH]
jajiktek *ii* alongside [SH]
jajiktuk (loc) along the shore [SH]
jakej *an* crab [BR] [SH]; lobster
jakeju:p'k *ta* clean out; bum dry; eat the faeces of
jakejuwe:ket *ai* trap lobsters
jakj'ke:j *an* salt water perch [RB]
jakkwet *ai* talk loud [PEI]
jakwek *ii* sound loud; talk loud
jakwet *ai* sound loud; talk loud
jaman hair bun [BC]
jammpo:qiyet *ai* sommersalt
japikwetaq *ta* wink at
japikwetuwet *ai* wink
jaqala:l'k *ta* do quickly
jaqala:sit *ai* go or move suddenly
jaqala:tu *ti* do quickly
jaqali-piyas'k *ta* {etlipiyas'k} quick-dry (clothing)
jaqali-piyasm *ti* quick-dry (clothing)
jaqalipnet *ai* fall suddenly ill
jaqal'k *ai, ii* quick
jaqal-te:k *ta* finish off quickly (as in boxing or cards); make a quick killing; make money quickly
jaqal-te:m *ti* finish off quickly (as in boxing or cards); make a quick killing; make money quickly
jaqje'ite:k *ta* knock down
jaqje'ite:m *ti* knock down
jaqjete:k *ta* knock down
jaqjete:m *ti* knock down
jaqpije'ite:m *ti* slap [SH]
ja:wa:tat *ai* chew tobacco
ja:wey chewing tobacco
jejuwejk bell
jejuwejk'ji:j small bell; sleigh bell
jejuwejkwatp steeple
je:k[1] *an* jack (in cards)
je:k[2] stories [BC]
je:kit *an* jacket [SH]

jel mu not even [BR]
je mu not even; not as much
jena:sit *ai* slow down; calm down (of the wind)
jena:s'k *ii* slow down; calm down (of the wind)
jenpit *ai* quiet
jentek *ii* quiet
jenu *an* giant; wind giant
je pe:kwamuksin long time no see!
jesmuwit *ai* calve; give birth to a calf; carry a calf [SH]
je tliya even so
jijikulqek *ii* narrow (of a canoe) [BR]
jijikwatej *an* sand piper; snipe [RB]
jijikwe:jit *ai* narrow
jijikwe:jk *ii* narrow
jijiwa:qiyaq *ii* rusty
jijiwa:qiyet *ai* rusty
jijjawiknej *an* raisin
jijjema:q *ii* smell bad; stink
jijjema:t *ai* smell bad; stink
jijje:taq *ii* distorted (of sound)
jijkluwewj (jijkluwewjik) *an* sheep
jijkluwewjiwapi wool; yarn
jijkluwewjiwapiyey woolen material
jijuwaqa meanwhile [SH]; sometimes
jijuwejk bell
jijuwejkwatp steeple
jikajiyet *ai* restless
jikalukk (jikalukum) *ai* paddle or pole alone or singlehanded
ji:ka:taw (ji:ka:taq) *an* dressed wood [SH]
jikatej *an* snipe [RB]
ji:kate:k *ta* hew; dress; trim; shape (to fit)
ji:kate:ket *ai* dress; trim (wood)
ji:kate:m *ti* hew; dress; trim; shape (to fit)
jikaw *an* bass
jikawepit *ai* inactive; dull; boring
jikawetek *ii* inactive; dull; boring
jikijo:n (jikijo:naq) *an* rooster [SH]
jikistaqanat *ai* {jiks'taq} eavesdrop
ji:kitlo:q *an* teakettle
jik'ji:j(i:j) *an* periwinkle [RB]; sea snail [RB]
jikk'putaqan rake
jikk'puteket *ai* rake

ji:kmaqan slapstick (a piece of rolled up birch bark used in drumming)
jikmaqan drum [SH]
jikmit *ai* growl
jikmuktaq *ta* growl at
jikmuktm *ti* growl at
jikmuwatk type of tree (used in medicine) [PEI]
jikni:ket *ai* root (as a pig)
jikp'k *ta* eat all of; consume
jiks'taq *ta* listen to
jiks'tm *ti* listen to
jiks'tmakwet *ai* approach and listen [SH]
jiktaqam *ti* smooth out [SH]
jiktaqawet *ai* smooth sheens (for basketry)
jiktek *ii* calm (water) [PEI]; quiet
jik'tli:kej *an* kingfisher [ESK]; chickadee [BC]
jik'tlo:q (jik'tlo:qq) *an* kettle
jiktm *ti* eat all of; consume
jiku:k *ii* calm water
jikwapa:n tide [BR]
jikwapan incoming tide [SH]
jila:kipulk *ta* mark (with a saw)
jila:kittu *ti* mark (with a saw)
jilapa:l'k *ta* mark; scrape; scratch
jilapaqte:k *ta* mark (with a line or string)
jilapaqte:m *ti* mark (with a line or string)
jilapa:teket *ai* mark
jilapa:tu *ti* mark; scrape; scratch
jilapsk'te:m *ti* scrape off a protuberance
jilaptoq (jilaptu) *ai* make footprints
jilaqami:k (jilaqami:m) *ai* make tracks with snowshoes
ji:law (ji:laq) *an* bass [RB]
jile:k *ai* injured; hurt
jiloqs'k *ta* blaze (with a knife)
jiloqsm *ti* blaze (with a knife)
jiloqte:k *ta* blaze (with an axe)
jiloqte:m *ti* blaze (with an axe)
jil pas'k just only
jilpit *ai* marked; spotted
jilsawet *ai* mark or scar (with a knife)
jils'k *ta* knick (with a knife)
jilsm *ti* knick (with a knife)
jilta:sik *ii* marked; scarred
jilta:sit *ai* marked; scarred
jilte:k *ta* mark or scar (with an axe)

jiltek *ii* marked; spotted
jilte:m *ti* mark or scar (with an axe)
ji:maqan oar
ji:matm *ti* paddle; row
ji:met *ai* row; paddle
jimpeknawet *ai* wring out; milk (a cow)
jimpekn'k *ta* wring out
jimpekn'm *ti* wring out
jinewalk *ta* mess up
jinewatm *ti* mess up
jinewit *ai* messed up
jink'ja:l'k *ta* squeeze; press
jink'ja:tu *ti* squeeze; press
ji:nm (ji:nmuk) *an* man
ji:nmji:j *an* young man
ji:nmji:ju:wet *ai* enter into manhood (post puberty)
ji:nmu-qamiksit *ai* act like a man
ji:nmuwe:sm (ji:nmuwe:smuk) *an* man chaser
ji:nmuwit *ai* become a man; enter into manhood (i e become ready for marriage)
jinqamisteket *ai* rinse out
jipalk *ta* fear; afraid of
jipaluwejit *ai (an)* a recluse
jipaluwet *ai (an)* a recluse
jipaqa:l'k *ta* frighten
jipasit *ai* scared; frightened
jipatm *ti* fear; afraid of
jipjawej *an* robin [SH]
jipji:j *an* bird
jipji:ju:kisutnat *ai* have a voice like a bird
jipkaq *ta* make tense; frighten
jiptuk perhaps; maybe; unless
jiptuke:l perhaps [CB]
jipu:ji:j brook
jipuktuk Halifax, N.S.
jipuktukwewa:j *an* Haligonian
jitlo:mukwaqan cradle; crib
jitnaqa:m *ti* smooth out
jitnaqe:kney clothing iron
jitnaqi:kney clothing iron [BC]
jiyakewj (jiyakewjik) *an* mink
jiyoqjimusi-a:qamikt maple grove [SH]
jiyoqsimusi rock maple tree [SH]
jiyoqsimusi apu maple syrup [SH]
jki:n je:k you bet! (an exclamation)

joqsimusi rock maple tree
joqsimusi apu maple syrup
jujij *an* crawling creature; lizard; serpent
juji:ji:j *an* insect; bug
jujiju:nat *ai* have the hand of an insect [BC]
jujijuwikan blackhead [BC]
jupijka:m *an* horned serpent

K

kajj-amu:k *ii* an unpleasant (ugly) color
kajj-amuksit *ai* an unpleasant (ugly) color
kajuwewj *an* cat
kajuwewji:j *an* kitten
kakaju:man teaberry [BR]
ka:kaka babytalk (said by a baby who is tired or in need of a change) [SH]
kakknawa:ki Kahnawake
kakwejink *ai* half frozen [SH]
ka:kwetk *ii* half frozen [SH]
kakwetk *ii* half frozen [SH]
ka:l one quarter (of time, etc.) (Fr *quart*)
kale:m Lent (Fr *carême*)
kale:mewimk Lent [SH]
kale:mewumk Lent
kalipu *an* sleigh; pung [BC]; caribou [RB]
kaliyulk sleigh (Fr *carriole*)
kalkiyey quarter (coin)
kalkunawey hardtack; biscuit [BC]
kalla'ink (loc) Carlyle
kalqwasiyet *ai* sunset
kaltiyey quarter (coin) [SH]
kalun gallon
kamlamit *ai* breathe
kamso:k (loc) Canso [SH]
kanata Canada
kanatiyes *an* Canadian
kanatiye:si:s *an* young Canadian man
kanatiyesuwi:skw *an* Canadian woman
kanatiyesuwi:skwe:j *an* young Canadian woman
kaniye:wit *ai* win; earn (Fr *gagner*)
kanntakknuwejit *an* monkey [PEI]
kanntakwey *an* black man [PEI]
kannti *an* candy [BC]
kapaqtesk gooseberry [RB]
kapiten *an* captain (Fr *capitaine*)
kapjakwej *an* robin
kap'ji: night Hallowe'en (Fr *gabegie*)
Kapliye:l *an* Gabriel (Fr *Gabriel*)
kaqaju:man teaberry [SH]
ka:qakuju:man teaberry
kaqalamit *ai* {kamlamit} stop breathing
kaqa:l'k *ta* finish; terminate; end; take all of
kaqa-lukwet *ai* {elukwet} finish working
kaqama:sit *ai* stand up
kaqama:s'k *ii* stand up

kaqamik *ii* stand
kaqamit *ai* stand
kaqamklek *ii* burned out (as a stove)
kaqamklet *ai* burned out (as a stove)
kaqamutaq *ta* stand against
kaqamutm *ti* stand against
ka:qan door
kaqani entranceway; door [BR]
ka:qanipsi entranceway poles (for a wikwam) [SH]
ka:qanipsun (skin) door flap
kaqa-nu:kwa:l'k *ta* finish burning up
kaqa-nu:kwa:tu *ti* finish burning up
kaqa-pija:l'k *ta* hang up
kaqa-pija:tu *ti* hang up
kaqa-pijink *ai* hang
kaqa-pitk *ii* hang
ka:qaquj *an* crow
kaqaqw dried or smoked moosemeat [SH]
kaqa:teket *ai* finish; end
kaqa:tu *ti* finish; terminate; end; take all of
kaqawa:sit *ai* go by quickly
kaqawa:s'k *ii* go by quickly
kaqi-alsutm *ti* own all of [BC]
kaqi·kjiji:k *ta* keji:k} know all about
kaqi·kjijitu *ti* {kejitu} know all about
kaqi-kwesmat *ai* finished bearing or producing children
kaqi net finished [BC]; over with [BC]
kaqi-petkwe:k *ai* stiff all over [BC]
kaqi:siskekipuna:q *ii* so many years old
kaqi:siskekipuna:t *ai* so many years old
kaqi:sk often
kaqiyaq *ii* finished; ended; dead [BR]
kaqiyet *ai* finished; ended; dead [BR]
kaqjek *ii* brittle; dried up
kaqjet *ai* brittle; dried up
kaq-kisa:l'k *ta* finish doing
kaq-kisa:tu *ti* finish doing
kaqm'te:mat *ai* copulate in a standing position
kaqoqsit *ai* burned out
kaqoqtek *ii* burned out
kaqo:tm *ti* finish with; use up
kaqpesaw (kaqpesaq) *an* smelt
kaqqamew moose fat
kaqqaq *ta* wear out (an article of clothing)
kaqqm *ti* wear out (an article of clothing)

kaqqmat *ai* wear out (one's clothing)
kaqsit *ai* burned up or out
kaqs'k *ta* burn
kaqsm *ti* burn
kaqtaqayaq *ii* reach the end
kaqtaqayet *ai* reach the end
kaqte:k *ta* finish striking
kaqtek *ii* burned up or out
kaqteskmat *ai* wear out (one's footwear)
kaqtukwaw (kaqtukwaq) *an* thunder
kaqtukwawik *ii* thunder
kaqtukwewe:sn *an* the Thunderer (a mythical spirit); thunder stick; gun [CB]
ka:s train
kasa:l'k *ta* wipe or rub off
kasapuwek *ii* wash away; wash off
kasapuwet *ai* wash away; wash off
kasa:tu *ti* wipe or rub off
kasawo:q iron
ka:s'k *ta* wipe
kaskimtlnagan {mtl'n} hundred [BR]
kaskimtlnaqani-puna:t one hundred years old [BR]
kask'ptnnaqan hundred
kask'ptnnaqani-puna:t *ai* one hundred years old
ka:sm *ti* wipe
kaspalaw *an* gaspereau [RB]
kastiyo:mi molasses
kast'pl *an* constable; policeman
kastuk *an* hemlock
kastulastuk *an* cedar bough (left in infant's crib until turns black; cure for fever)
ka:t (ka:taq) *an* eel
kataqam upper (rear) section of wikwam [SH]
kata:skw'l (pl) seaweed [PEI]
katawe:ket *ai* net for eels [BC]
katew (kataq) *an* eel [BR]
katewaqanntaqan brisket [SH]
ka:tewe:ket *ai* hunt for eels [SH]
Katli:n *an* Catherine (Fr *Cathérine*)
ka:tomi eelskin
ka:to:min *an* gooseberry; a kind of berry [BR]
katu for instance; what about?; but
kawak'pa:sit *ai* turn around (while seated)
kawaqtejk a kind of berry (pea-sized and green); currant; gooseberry

kawaqtejkumusi gooseberry bush
kawaska:l'k *ta* overturn
kawaska:sit *ai* turn over; (religious) convert [PEI]
kawaska:tu *ti* overturn
kawaskeka:l'k *ta* turn over
kawaskeka:tu *ti* turn over
kawaskeket *ai* turn something over
kawaskisma:sit *ai* turn self over
kawask'smtesink *ai* turn over (while prone)
kawask'tniyaq *ii* change direction (of the wind)
kawaskulapa:sit *ai* turn one's head around
kawaskuwi:tm *ti* {ewi:tm} say backwards
kawatkw (kawatkuk) *an* spruce
kawey quill work
kawi *an* porcupine quill
kawiksaw (kawiksaq) *an* thorn; thistle; burdock
kawikso:musi thorn wood genus [SH]
kawiye:ket *ai* do quill work
kawiyey quill work
kawiyo:qolaqan quill box [SH]
ke: come on! [CB]; please [BC]
ke'ipaqte:m *ti* drive in (as a nail)
ke'iteket *ai* intelligent; knowledgeable
ke'itine:k *ai* clever; mature
ke'itmk *ii* known
ke'itu *ti* know about; have knowledge of
ke: jel come on then! (an exclamation)
keji:k *ta* know about; have knowledge of
keji:kas'k *ii* the corner
kejikaw recently [SH]
kejikiyaq *ii* the corner
kejikow recently; a short while ago
kejimoqpit *ai* in the way
kejimoqtek *ii* in the way
kejipilk *ta* secure; tie up (with a rope) [SH]
kejipil'm *ti* secure; tie up (with a rope) [SH]
kejitapaqte:m *ti* drive in (as a nail)
kejiteket *ai* intelligent; knowledgeable
kejitme:k *ai* clever [BC]; precocious
kejitmk *ii* known
kejitu *ti* know about; have knowledge of
kejkapa:l'k *ta* scratch (with fingernails)
kejkapa:tu *ti* scratch (with fingernails)

kekapit *ai* nearsighted [SH]
ke:kapskwesk Pabineau [RB]
keket almost; soon
kekina:maq *ta* teach
kekina:matimkewey learning
kekina:matnewey learning [SH]
kekina:muwet *ai* teach
kekitlmaqanat *ai* have big shoulders [PEI]
kekkunasit *ai* kept for safekeeping
kekkunas'k *ii* kept for safekeeping
kekkunawet *ai* godparent
kekkunk *ta* have; hold; possess
kekkun'm *ti* have; hold; possess
kekna:l'k *ta* decorate
kekna:sit *ai* dress up (in finery)
kekna:tu *ti* decorate
keknesit *ai* dressed
kekno:tlk *ta* dress; trim (as a Christmas tree)
kek'ntiye:wimk Sunday [SH]
keknu:kijjet *ai* {ekijjet} read properly or correctly
keknukwalk *ta* mark
keknukwatiket *ai* blaze (a trail); leave a direction marker
keknukwatm *ti* mark
keknu:lukwet *ai* {elukwet} work correctly
keknu:qamiksit *ai* behave
keknu:telaq *ta* {pekwatelaq} buy the proper or right one
keknu:tel'm *ti* {pekwatel'm} buy the proper or right one
keknu:tmaq *ta* teach to; show how (to do)
keknu:tmasit *ai* learn
keknuwa:l'k *ta* set right; prove; do correctly or properly
keknuwa:taq *ta (do)* inform; notify
keknuwa:teket *ai* do what is proper or correct
keknuwa:tu *ti* set right; prove; do correctly or properly
keknuwe:k *ai, ii* special; a certain thing, one; act respectfully; live correctly
keknuwimk *ta* speak truthfully to
ke:koqpit *ai* lie atop
ke:koqtek *ii* lie atop
ke:ko:tu *ti* place atop
kekpewisk dew

ke:kuluskwa:l'k *ta* put one's arms around the neck of
ke:kupit *ai* sit or set atop
ke:kupn hilltop
ke:ku-pukuwit *ai* stand atop
ke:kutek *ii* sit or set atop
ke:kutesink *ai* land atop
ke:kwa:l'k *ta* put or set on top
ke:kwa:sit *ai* get atop
kekwa:sit *ai* move slowly
kekwa:s'k *ii* move slowly
ke:kwatpan pate
ke:kwa:tu *ti* put or set on top
ke:kwe:k (loc) up above
kekwe:k *ai, ii* slow
ke:kwey upstairs
ke:kwi:pit *ai* run atop
kekwi:pit *ai* run slowly
ke:kwi-pukuwit *ai* stand atop [SH]
ke:kwisink *ai* lie atop
ke:kwisma:l'k *ta* {elsmal'k} lay on top
ke:kwisma:tu *ti* {elsma:tu} lay on top
ke:l (ke:laq) *an* heart (in cards) (Fr *coeur*) [SH]
kelapaqam *ti* screw on; fasten
kelapaqq *ta* screw on; fasten
kelapaqte:k *ta* pound on; stitch on
kelapaqte:m *ti* pound on; stitch on
keleyaq *ta* keep watch over; hold in safekeeping
keliket *ai* protect; guard; watch over; cling to
kelikwet *an* burdock; thistle
kelkaq *ta* hold down with one's body; hold (the family) together as a unit (pl); restrain [PEI]
kelkm *ti* hold down with one's body; hold (the family) together as a unit (pl); restrain [PEI]
kelkunk *ta* have; hold; possess [BR]
kelkwiske:k *ii* sprained; fractured
kelkwisketesk *ii* sprained
kelkwisketesm'k *ta* fracture
kelkwisketestu *ti* fracture
keln'k *ta* hold [NB]
kelo:tm *ti* keep watch over; hold in safekeeping
kelpilk *ta* tie up
kelpil'm *ti* tie up

kelpisit *ai* tied up [PEI]
keltaqamiktuk frozen ground [ESK]
keltaqank *ta* hold; restrain (by leash or rope)
keltaqan'm *ti* hold; restrain (by leash or rope)
keltaqpilk *ta* tie
keltaqpil'm *ti* tie
kelte:k¹ *ta* support (from falling) [PEI]
kelte:k² *ta* put a claim, deposit, retainer or a down payment on
kelte:m *ti* put a claim, deposit, retainer or a down payment on
kelt'k *ii* frozen [ESK]
kelu:lk *ii* good; nice
kelulk *ta* speak to
keluluwemk marriage agreement [BC]
keluluwet *ai* request permission (of parents) to marry daughter; propose [PEI]; mediate a marriage agreement
kelumk *ta* request; ask for
kelu:si:ji:jit *ai* little and fancy
kelusimkewey telephone [SH]
kelu:sit *ai* good; nice
kelusit *ai* speak; talk
kelutm *ti* request; ask for
kemutmk *ta* steal from
kemutnalk *ta* steal
kemutna:timk Hallowe'en [SH]
kemutnatm *ti* steal
kemutnek *ii* steal; cheat
kemutnet *ai* steal; cheat
ke:n thank you [SH]
kenkunk *ta* have; hold; possess
kenkun'm *ti* have; hold; possess
kenn'k *ta* hold
kenn'm *ti* hold
kepa:tat *ai* have a hoarse voice or throat
kepe:k *ai, ii* blocked or plugged (of the ear or nose)
kepijoqwa:l'k *ta* block; plug
kepijoqwa:tu *ti* block; plug
kepi:sit *ai* have a husky voice
kepistaqanat *ai* {ns'tuwaqan} deaf
kepitnetoqsit *ai* speak hoarsely; sound hoare
kepitni:sit *ai* speak with a nasal twang [BC]
kepiyet *ai* hoarse
kepjoqiket *ai* lock up
kepjoqikn plug; cork

kepjoqi:s'k *ta* seam
kepjoqi:sm *ti* seam
kepjoqpit *ai* blocked; shut; plugged [SH]
kepjoqte:k *ta* plug up
kepjoqtek *ii* blocked; shut; plugged [SH]
kepjoqte:m *ti* plug up
kepmite:l'mk *ta* honor; pay homage to; respect
kepmite:tm *ti* honor; pay homage to; respect
keppewisk *ii* morning dew
kepsaqa:l'k *ta* shut; close
kepsaqa:tu *ti* shut; close
kepsaqtejk *an* stove [SH]
kepska:l'k *ta* put to sleep
kepskit *ai* doze off
kepskiyet *ai* drift off to sleep
kepsoqk *ta* lock in
kepsoqom *ti* lock in
kepsoqpit *ai* closed; shut
kepsoqtek *ii* closed; shut
kepta:l'k *ta* put or take off; unload; remove; lift off
keptaqalk *ta* throw off
keptaqtu *ti* throw off
kepta:sit *ai* get off; get out of
kepta:s'k *ii* get off; get out of
kepta:tu *ti* put or take off; unload; remove; lift off
keptin *an* captain [CB]
kep't'k *ii* frozen water
kep't'kewiku:s November
ke:s while
kesa:l'k *ta* hurt
kesalk *ta* like; love
kesaluwejit (kesaluwejijik) *an* burdock
kesaluwet *ai* love
kesaqek *ii* steep
kesaqet *ai* steep
kesaqtiyat *ai* have diarrhea
kesasek *ii* lit up
kesaset *ai* lit up
kesasit *ai* bright
kesatek *ii* bright
kesatenmat *ai* sun-blinded
kesatm *ti* like; love
kesi-ankamk *ta* stare at

kesi-ankaptm *ti* stare at
kesik *ii* winter
kesikaq *ii* slippery; fast (as a sled, etc.)
kesikat *ai* slippery; fast (as a sled, etc.)
kesikawa:sik *ii* move fast
kesikawa:sit *ai* move fast
kesikawatpi:pit *ai* run fast with head bobbing [BR]
kesikawewo:kwet *ai* speak loudly
kesikawi:pit *ai* run fast
kesikawitk *ii* a swift current
kesikawitnet *ai* snort
kesikawiyaq *ii* go fast [SH]
kesikawiyaqewey automobile [SH]
kesikawiyet *ai* go fast [SH]
kesikawlamit *ai* {kamlamit} breathe hard or heavily
kesikawlusit *ai* make a loud crack; twang [CB]
kesikawta:q *ii* make a loud noise
kesikawtesiket *ai* make a loud noise or report
kesikawtewesikek *ii* make a loud rapport (as a cannon or gun)
kesikawtewesiket *ai* make a loud rapport (as a cannon or gun)
kesikawtoqsit *ai* make a loud noise (with the voice)
kesikawwek *ii* talk loudly
kesikawwet *ai* talk loudly
kesikewey *an* in something associated with winter
kesikewiku:s December
kesi·ksinukwat *ai* {kesinukwat} very sick
kesima:q *ii* have a strong unpleasant odor
kesi-maqapskek *ii* large and round
kesi-maqapsk'sit *ai* large and round
kesima:t *ai* have a strong unpleasant odor
kesi-m'lkiknat *ai* {melkiknat} very strong
kesimt'k (kesimtm) *ai* cry hard; wail
kesinukuwik *ii* hurt; ache
kesinukuwit *ai* hurt; ache
kesinukwat *ai* sick [BR]
kesipa:l'k *ta* scratch
kesipa:tu *ti* scratch
kesi-pawalk *ta* covet [BR]
kesi-pewalk *ta* covet [SH]
kesi-pitoqsit *ai* very tall

kesipiyaq *ii* itchy
kesipiyemkewey itchyness
kesipiyet *ai* itchy
kesipk *ta* hurt (by biting hard)
kesipkuwek *ii* scratchy; itchy (of a garment)
kesipkuwet *ai* scratchy; itchy (of a garment)
kesipoqwat *ai* scrape [SH]
kesippeket *ai* break (a rope, string or chain) in two
kesi·psa:l'k *ta* {pesa:l'k} skin
kesi·psaqalk *ta* {pesaqalk} skin (e.g. a fish) [BR]
kesipte:k *ta* scratch hard; scratch with an instrument
kesipte:m *ti* scratch hard; scratch with an instrument
kesipto:sit *ai* scratch oneself (as an animal)
kesipukwa:l'k *ta* lie to [BR]
kesi-puwalk *ta* covet
kesi-puwatm *ti* covet
kesispa:l'k *ta* wash
kesispalsit *ai* take a bath
kesispapal'k *ta* prewash; hose down
kesispapalsit *ai* take a sponge bath; take a shower [BR]
kesispapalsit *ai* take a sponge bath; take a shower [BR]
kesispapatu *ti* prewash; hose down
kesispa:tekemkewey washing machine
kesispa:teket *ai* wash (floors, etc.)
kesispa:tu *ti* wash
kesistaqanewet *ai* wash (clothes)
kesi-s'wikna:t *ai* {sewikna:t} very weak (from being sick)
kesite:k *ta* hurt badly
kesi-te:lmk *ta* {tel-te:l'm(')k} think highly of; fond of; proud of; value; prize; admire
kesitesink *ai* get hurt badly (from a fall)
kesite:taqan treasure [PEI]
kesi-te:tm *ti* tel-te:tm} think highly of; fond of; proud of; value; prize; admire
kesite:wet *ai* attractive
kesitewipnet *ai* groan [SH]
kesi·twaqji:jit *ai* {tewaqji:jit} very short
kesi-wesmat *ai* {wesmuwit} have nice shaped antlers or horns [BR]

kesi-w'lismat *ai* have nice shaped antlers or horns [BR]

ke:s'k just a minute!; hold on!

keska:l'k[1] *ta* make disappear

keska:l'k[2] *ta* widen

keskamukwa:l'k *ta* make or cause to vanish or disappear; dissolve; erase

keskamukwa:sit *ai* dissolved; vanished

keskamukwa:s'k *ii* dissolved; vanished

keskamukwa:tu *ti* make or cause to vanish or disappear; dissolve; erase

keskamukwiyaq *ii* fade (away); fade out of sight

keskamukwiyet *ai* fade (away); fade out of sight

keskapekiyaq *ii* fade out of sight; Maria (Québec); widen (of a river)

keska:sit *ai* disappear; become invisible

keska:s'k *ii* disappear; become invisible

keska:t *ai* lost

keskatesink *ai* disappear in a flash; vanish

keskatesk *ii* disappear in a flash; vanish

keska:tu[1] *ti* make disappear

keska:tu[2] *ti* widen

keske:k *ai, ii* wide

keskel'mk *ta* reluctant to part with

keskeltm *ti* reluctant to part with

keskeltmat *ai* stingy [BC]

keskija:l'k *ta* put over

keskijaqsink *ai* fly over

keskija:sit *ai* go or pass over

keskija:tu *ti* put over

keskissink *ai* flown over

keskiss'k *ii* blown over; flown over

keskitlmaqanat *ai* have large upper arms

keskitlmaqasit *ai* broad-beamed; broad-hipped

keskiyaqasit *ai* broad-shouldered

keskma:l'k *ta* take or bring by the shortest route; make disappear

keskm-ap'lkikwa:l'k *ta* make someone see things that are not there; put magic on

keskm-ap'lkikwa:t *ai* see things that are not there; see a mirage; hallucinate

keskm-ap'lkikwa:teket *ai* do magic tricks

keskm-ap'lkikwa:tu *ti* make someone see things that are not there; put magic on

keskma:sit *ai* take a shortcut

keskma:taqan sleight of hand

keskma:teket *ai* perform magic

keskma:tu *ti* take or bring by the shortest route; make disappear

keskm'naq before

keskmsit *ai* possess magic; a magician; get lucky

kesk'mtek *ii* a shortcut

keskmu:k *ii* blurred

keskmuksit *ai* blurred

keskoqomaqasit *ai* broad-beamed [SH]

keskukk *ii* heavy

keskulk *ai* heavy

keskulq'q *ii* wide and deep (e.g., a canoe, chair)

keskunasit *ai* carry a heavy load

keskustaq *ta* overhear

keskustm *ti* overhear

keskute:k *ta* catch or get on time

keskute:m *ti* catch or get on time

keskuteskaq *ta* catch by surprise; catch on time

keskuteskm *ti* catch by surprise; catch on time

keskuteskmat *ai* on time (for)

ke:skw while [SH]

ke:skwaq echo [SH]

keskwaq echo [SH]

keslek *ii* stink [SH]

keslet *ai* stink [SH]

kesma:l'k *ta* push

kesmapewit *ai* look strange or weird

kesmaqalk *ta* shove

kesmaqtu *ti* shove

kesma:tu *ti* push

kesmeket *ai* shove

kesmikit *ai* well-built; well-proportioned; streamlined

kesmi:sit *ai* speak in an odd or unusual way; speak with an accent

kesmoqja:l'k *ta* push (on, in or by a vehicle); give a boost

kesmoqja:tu *ti* push (on, in or by a vehicle); give a boost

kesmoqjeket *ai* give a boost
kesmpisit *ai* well-dressed; fancily dressed
kesmteskaq *ta* bump into; shove (with foot)
kesmteskm *ti* bump into; shove (with foot)
ke:s mu before (takes a negative verb form)
kesnqo:we:k *ai* frivolous; trifling
kesnukw-amuksit *ai* look sick
kesnukwat *ai* sick
kesnukwi-ankamkusit *ai* look sick
kesnukwitoqsit *ai* sound sickly
kespaqami:k *ii* the end of the world
kespiyaq *ii* the end [SH]; get dull
kespiyatoqsit *ai* the end of the story (the sound)
kesp'k *ii* dull; blunt
kesplk *ta* dull; blunt
kesp'plk *ta* blunt
kesp'tek Saturday
kesp'tu *ti* dull; blunt
kespukuwa:l'k *ta* lie to [BC]
kespukwitk Annapolis Valley [SH]
kespukwitkewaq (pl) *an* (Annapolis) valley people [BR]
kespukwitnewa:j *an* (Annapolis) valley person [BR]
kespu:taq *ta* defeat (in a game)
kespu:tuwet *ai (an)* the winner
kestaqanewet *ai* do the laundry
kestetapu coincidentally [BC]
kestuna:l'k *ta* choke; throttle
kestunepilaqan gallows
kestunepilk *ta* hang; garrot
ketalqa:l'k *ta* take out of
ketalqa:tu *ti* take out of
ketalqikwalk *ta* pry out
ketalqikwatm *ti* pry out
keta:maq *ta* reply to; agree with [BC]
ke:tamskw (ke:tamskuk) *an* extra large (bank) beaver [BR]
keta:muwemk (formal) agreement [BC]
ke:tane:k *ai* make self noticed [PEI]
ketank *ta* strive to obtain; hate; spite; hunt for
ketanqikalk *ta* stalk [CB]
ketanteket *ai* hunt; spiteful; strive; hate; vindictive

ketantu *ti* strive to obtain; hate; spite; hunt for
ketanuwet *ai* spiteful
ketapa:q *ii* sink
ketapa:sit *ai* submerge
ketapa:t *ai* sink
ketapekiyatm *ti* sing [CB]
ketapekiyet *ai* sing
ketapet (ketapejik) *an* ox [SH]
ketapet *ai* dive
ketapetesink *ai* dive
ketapja:l'k *ta* take with one's bare hands
ketapja:sit *ai* do something barehanded
ketapja:tu *ti* take with one's bare hands
ketapsknk *ta* take barehanded
ketapskn'm *ti* take barehanded
ketaqama:sit *ai* eat lunch [BC]
ketaqa:sit *ai* rush; hurry
ketaqqa:l'k *ta* lift out of [BC]
ketaqqa:tu *ti* lift out of [BC]
ketemenejik (pl) *ai* die from a disease; perish
ketemetesultijik (pl) *ai* die in an accident
ke:tipnet *ai* harvest roots or tubers (e.g. potatoes, carrots, turnips)
ke:tipnewinu *an* potato picker or harvester
ke:tiyap (ke:tiyapaq) *an* full-grown bull (moose, etc.) [SH]
ketkaqamiksit *ai* ill-mannered
ketkatalk *ai* eat ill-manneredly; eat what no one else would eat
ketke:k *ai* indecent
ketki-te:l'mk *ta* {tel-te:l'm(')k} abhor; shrink from [BC]
ketki-te:tm *ti* {tel-te:tm} abhor; shrink from [BC]
ketkiyet *ai* drunk; an inadequate lover
ketkujetesink *ai* fall prone
ketkujetesk *ii* fall prone
ketkukjesink *ai* lie prone (on the belly)
ketkunit *ai* sleep over; sleep there
ketkwijetesink *ai* fall face first
ketkwijetesk *ii* fall face first
ketkwi:k (ketkwi:m) *ai* run
ketlams'taq *ta* believe in
ketlams'tm *ti* believe in
ketl etuk certainly; absolutely; for sure
ketlewey believe it! (an exclamation)

ketloq for certain! [SH]
ketma:q *ta* clean out (of food)
ketme:k *ta* clean out (of food)
ketmenet (ketmenejik) *ai (an)* deceased
ketmete:k *ta* wipe out; finish off
ketmete:m *ti* wipe out; finish off
ketmete:mat *ai* wiped out; finished off
ketmoqsit *ai* burned completely out
ketmoqtek *ii* burned completely out
kettiyalk *ta* abort
ketu:k (ketu:m) *ai* start to holler or sing
ketuk *ai* start to holler or sing [BR]
ketuksit *ai* sleepy
ketuksiyet *ai* get sleepy
ketuktnukqwanet *ai* want an alcoholic drink
ketu:lmiyet *ai* {elmiyet} want or intend to go
  home
ketu:maq *ta* make music for; play for
ketu:muwet *ai* make music; play a musical
  instrument
ketu:pkisink *ai* {pekisink} expected to arrive
ketutamit *ai* crave (food, sex)
ketuwapemk *ta* need; want to use
ketuwapetm *ti* need; want to use
ketuwapsit *ai* struggle; help oneself
ketuwapsmu:tlk *ta* rescue [PEI]
ketuwi·pkisink *ai* {pekisink} expected to arrive
  [BR]
ketu-w'njanit *ai* expect a baby
kewaqsink *ai* blown down (by a heavy wind)
kewaqs'k *ii* blown down (by a heavy wind)
kewa:salk *ta* topple [BR]
kewa:satm *ti* topple [BR]
kewe:salk *ta* topple [SH]
kewe:satm *ti* topple [SH]
kewisina:l'k *ta* make hungry [CB]
kewisinji:jit *ai* somewhat hungry
kewisink *ai* hungry
kewiyaq *ii* fall over; topple
kewiyet *ai* fall over; topple
kewjik *ii* cold
kewjiptnewjit *ai* {np'tn} have cold hands
kewjisqonat *ai* {nsisqon} have a cold nose
  [ESK]
kewjit *ai* cold
kewjiya:qiyet *ai* chilly; have the chills
kewk'k *ta* force down with one's weight

kewkm *ti* force down with one's weight
kewkunk *ta* have; hold; possess
kews'k *ta* topple; fell (by cutting)
kews'm *ti* topple; fell (by cutting)
kewtaqsikit *ai* have cold feet
kewte:k *ta* knock down
kewte:m *ti* knock down
kijimuk outside [BR]
kijipan(ji:j) *an* kitten beaver [RB]
kijka:ji:jk a little bit
kijka:tata:n right on! (an interjection)
kiju: (voc) *an* mother!
kiju:mi (voc) *an* grandmother! [PEI]
ki:k *ai, ii* sharp
ki:kaj still; yet [BR]; in spite of
ki:kaja:l'k *ta* force; rape
ki:kaja:sit *ai* argue; go for spite;
  argumentative; confrontational
ki:kaja:tu *ti* force; rape
ki:kaje:k *ai* act for spite [PEI]; tease [BC]
ki:kajeyaq *ta* aggravate; tease; do for spite
ki:kaji-e:w'mk *ta* use forcefully
ki:kajimk *ta* dare [BR]; goad [SH]; exaggerate
  to
ki:kaji·nmikimk *ta* {enmikimk} force to go
  home
ki:kajo:tm *ti* aggravate; tease; do for spite
ki:kamko:n *an* canoe pole [BC]
ki:kassit *ai* tease
ki:kass'mk *ta* force feed
ki:kassuwinu *an* a teaser
ki:kasuwaskw muskrat root
ki:kat-akanutaq *ta* exaggerate about
ki:kat-akanutm *ti* exaggerate about
ki:ke:k in the corner [SH]
kikjakutijik (pl) *ai* close relatives or relations
kikjapit *ai* nearsighted
kikjisqonat *ai* {nsisqon} pug nosed
kikjiw near; close by
kikjiw eloqpit *ai* lie near [SH]
kiklikjnk *ta* tickle
kikliksik *ii* ticklish
kikliksit *ai* ticklish
kikli:kwej *an* hen [BR]; rooster [BR]; chicken
  [PEI]
kikli:wej *an* hen [SH]
kikpesa:ji:jk *ii* shower; rain slightly

kikpesan rain
kikpesanamukwiyaq *ii* look like rain
kikpesanawe:k *ii* misty [BR]
kikpesanewiyaq *ii* turn to rain [SH]
kikpesaq *ii* rain
kikpewisk *ii* morning dew [PEI]
kikto:qo-pukuwa:sit *ai* turn about [NB]
kikto:qoto:sit *ai* skip rope
ki:kwaju *an* wolverine
ki:kwesu *an* muskrat
ki:kwesuwaskw muskrat root (good for cold,
   mix with gin after boiling in water; chew on it)
ki:l you (sg)
kilewewey *an, in* yours (pl)
ki:lewey *an, in* yours (sg)
kilikwejit (kilikwejijik) *an* ant [SH]
kilow you (pl)
kilowewey *an, in* yours (pl)
kimamk *ta* peek at; spy on
kimapit *ai* peek
kimaptm *ti* peek at; spy on
kime:k *ai* sneaky [SH]
kim-elmit *ai* laugh secretly [BR]; smile to
   oneself
kim-elmuktasit *ai* laugh to oneself [SH]
kim-enmit *ai* laugh secretly [SH]
kime:s *an* beetle
kimewistoq (kimewistu) *ai* whisper
kimewo:kwet *ai* talk softly; talk secretively
kimiyet *ai* sneak around
kimskwet *ai* tiptoe
kimtelaq *ta* ambush
kimtemit *ai* {atkitemit} cry inside; cry silently
kimteskaq *ta* sneak up on
kimteskawit *ai* walk on tiptoes [PEI]
kimteskm *ti* sneak up on
kimutna:l'k *ta* kidnap; steal [SH]
kimutnalk *ta* kidnap; steal
kimu:tuk carefully; stealthfully; sort of
kina:masuti education
kina:matimk learning
kina:matnewey education; learning [SH]
kina:muwet *ai* teach
kinap *an* a legendary person of great strength
ki:naqan cradleboard
kinateja:sit *ai* strut around
kina:teket *ai* perform extraordinary feats

kinawaklapa:sit *ai* face about [CB]
kinawska:l'k *ta* overturn [BR]
kinawskipa:sit *ai* turn around (while seating
   down)
kinawski-pukuwa:sit *ai* turn around (while
   standing up) [BR]
kinawskismtesink *ai* turn over (while prone)
   [BR]
kinawskituniyaq *ii* change direction (of the
   wind) [BR]
kinawsklapa:sit *ai* turn one's head about [BR]
kinawsk'pa:sit *ai* turn around (while seated)
   [BR]
kinawskwi-wi:tm *ti* {ewi:tm} translate [BR]
kinijkej *an* peaked cap [SH]
kinikwejij *an* thistle [BC]; stinging nettle
kinipewa:j *an* branch (used to hold a tea kettle
   over a fire to boil water)
kiniskayipulk *ta* sharpen
kiniskayiputu *ti* sharpen
kini:skwakum the point of a tree [SH]
kiniskwejewey peaked cap [BC]
kiniskwe:k *ai, ii* pointed; have a sharp point
kiniskwik *ii* sharply pointed
kiniskwikit *ai* sharply pointed
kini:swikuwom the point of a wikwam [SH]
kin-lu:kwalk *ta* {elu:kwalk} praise [BC]
kin-pukuwit *ai* stand like a ginap; stand tall
kinta:q *ii* noisy [EG]
kin-tewoqsink *ai* snore
kintoqsit *ai* a loud mouth [EG]
kinu we; us (inclusive)
kinujink *ai* vain; conceited
kinuwa:l'k *ta* revive [SH]; duplicate [SH]
kinuwalk *ta* brag about
kinuwatm *ti* brag about
kinuwa:tu *ti* revive [SH]; duplicate [SH]
kinuwet *ai* brag; boastful
kinuwewey *an* in ours (inclusive)
kipoqamk *ta* catch a glimpse of; look at
   furtively; glance at
kipoqaptm *ti* catch a glimpse of; look at
   furtively; glance at
kipoqtelaq *ta* crease (with a bullet or arrow)
kipoqtel'm *ti* crease (with a bullet or arrow)
kiptoqapsk'sit *ai* round (globular) [CB]
ki:s completed action; already

kisa:l'k *ta* fix; repair
kisapsknk *ta* catch; reach; get hold of; attain
kisapskn'm *ti* catch; reach; get hold of; attain
kisatalk *ai* finished eating [BR]
kisa:tasit *ai* fixed; prepared
kisa:tas'k *ii* fixed; prepared
kisa:tu *ti* fix; repair
kise:k *ai* have fun; have a good time; enjoyable; fun to be with
kisi:k *ta* finish making
kisiku *an* old man
kisiku:l'ka:t *ai* walk like an old person
kisiku:lkw old canoe or boat [BR]
kisiku:mskw *an* old beaver
kisiku:qamiksit *ai* act like an old person
kisiku:skw (kesiku:skwaq) *an* old woman
kisiku:skwe:j *an* spinster
kisiku:sm (kisiku:smuk) *an* old animal
kisiku:waq *ii* get old
kisikuwa:sit *ai* act like an old person [BR]
kisiku:wet *ai* get old
kisikuwey *an* in something old
kisikuwi:skw (kisikuwi:skwaq) *an* old woman
kisikuwiyet *ai* get old [BR]
kisikuwo:p *an* old man [SH]
kisikwek *ii* full grown; mature
kisikwekewiku:s August-September
kisikwenikn *an* adopted child
kisikwenk *ta* grow; raise; rear
kisikwen'm *ti* grow; raise; rear
kisikwet *ai* full grown; mature
kisintoq (kisintu) *ai* finish singing
kisipiyasit *ai* dried out
kisipiyatek *ii* dried out
kisi:s'k *ta* sew
kisi:sm *ti* sew
kisitaqan home made item
kisite:l'mk *ta* {tel-te:l'mk} invent
kisite:tm *ti* {tel-te:tm} invent
kisitu *ti* finish making
kisiyaqan home made item
ki:s'k *ta* finished cooking
kiskaja:l'k *ta* get ready; prepare; get revenge on

kiskaja:tu *ti* get ready; prepare; get revenge on
kiskaje:k *ai* ready or available immediately
kiskajiyet *ai* measure up; able
kiskatpit *ai* ready; prepared
kiskat-pukuwit *ai* stand at the ready (said of the sun when it is on the verge of rising) [BR]
kiskatte:k *ta* fix up; impregnate [SH]
kiskattek *ii* ready; prepared
kiskiyaq *ii* get dark [SH]
kiskuk today
kislassit *ai* ripe
kislastek *ii* ripe
ki:sm *ti* finished cooking
kisna or
kisoqek atop a hill
kiso:qon lots of fun! (an interjection)
kisoqsit *ai* already cooked; finished being cooked
kisoqtek *ii* already cooked; finished being cooked
kispa:q *ii* floodtide [BR]
kispasasit *ai* cured (of lumber); dried out (of lumber)
kispasas'k *ii* cured (of lumber); dried out (of lumber)
kispasawemkewey dryer
kispasit *ai* dry
kispask *ta* dry
kispasm *ti* dry
kispatek *ii* dry
kispisun *an* belt
kispnapewit *ai* look tired
kispnek *ii* tired
kispnet *ai* tired
kispnetoqsit *ai* sound tired
kispniyet *ai* feel tired
kispnulk *ta* make tired
ki:s sa:q long ago; once upon a time
kisteju *an* slave
kiste:k[1] *ta* finish beating
kiste:k[2] *ta* impregnate
kistelaq *ta* impregnate
kiste:m *ti* finish beating
kisu:k'k (kisu:km) *ai* warmly dressed
kisu:l you are created! (expression of surprise) [BR]

kisu:lk you are created! (expression of surprise)

kisupa:q *ii* lukewarm (of a liquid)

kisupaqsijik (pl) *an* lukewarm (of a liquid)

kisu:piso:tlk *ta* dress warmly

kisu:snik nnu:k Indians are created! (expression of surprise)

kisuwe:k warm (of a house) [ESK]

ki:taqan grindstone

kitaqasit *ai* sore (of a person)

kitaqek *ii* sore (of a body part)

kitaqet *ai* sore (of a body part)

kitk both

kitmaqan *an* count stick (in waltes game) [CB]

kitn'mat *ai* have a hard time

kitn'meyaq *ta* give a hard time to

kitn'mo:tm *ti* give a hard time to

kitpu *an* eagle

kitto:qakatultijik (pl) *ai* follow one another in a circle

kitto:qa:l'k *ta* turn or swing around

kitto:qa:sit *ai* turn around; go around

kitto:qa:s'k *ii* turn around; go around

kitto:qaska:l'k *ta* turn around to point in a different direction

kitto:qaska:tu *ti* turn around to point in a different direction

kitto:qateskatultijik (pl) *ai* chase each other around (in a circle)

kitto:qa:tu *ti* turn or swing around

kitto:qi·ksma:l'k *ta* {kesma:l'k} push around

kittoqi·ksma:tu *ti* {kesma:tu} push around

kitto:qiyaq *ii* spin

kitto:qiyet *ai* spin

kitto:qopeka:l'k *ta* swing around (in a circle)

kitto:qopeka:tu swing around (in a circle)

kitto:qopilk *ta* wrap around

kitto:qopil'm *ti* wrap around

kitto:qopiya:tijik (pl) *ai* sit around in a circle

kitto:qopultijik (pl) *ai* sit around in a circle

kittoqoqsit *ai* round (cylindrical, tubular) [CB]

kittukwakik *ii* round (circular) [CB]

kittukwakit *ai* round (circular) [CB]

ki:waje:k *ai* pleasing

kiwaje:k *ai* dull; listless

kiwajeyaq *ta* long or yearn for

ki:wajiyaq *ii* honest; a fact; true; so

ki:wajiyet *ai* honest; a fact; true; so

kiwajo:tm *ti* long or yearn for

kiwanska:sit *ai* turn back [SH]

kiwask *ii* heat lightning

kiwaska:sit *ai* turn over [BC]

kiwaski-wi:tm *ti* {ewi:tm} translate [CB]; name backwards

kiwatteskaq *ta* sadden (by one's departure)

ki:wesuwaskw sweet flag (a medicinal plant or herb) [RB]

kiwikatm *ti* stock a pantry with provisions [BR]

kiwiksit *ai* grub up [BR]; beg [CB]; provision

kiwiyo:qiyaq *ii (in)* wheel; tire [SH]

kiwkw *ii* earthquake

kiw'nik *an* otter

kiwto:qa:l'k *ta* swing or spin around [SH]; wave around [SH]

kiwto:qa:tu *ti* swing or spin around [SH]; wave around [SH]

kiwto:qi·ksma:l'k *ta* {kesma:l'k} push in a circle [SH]

kiwto:qi·ksma:tu *ti* {kesma:tu} push in a circle [SH]

kiwto:qoto:sit *ai* skip rope [SH]; spin around [BC]

kiwto:qwa:sit *ai* circle around

kiyaspi-kisk'k the last day

kiyaspiyaq *ii* the end; the last

kiyaspiyet *ai* make a habit of

kji-ansale:wit (ansale:wijik) *an* Archangel

kji-apluwew *an* rat [SH]; rascal

kjikan city

kjikanji:j village; town

kjikapa:n tide

kjikapan incoming tide

kji-kaqaquj *an* raven

kji-kawa:suwinu *an* a fast runner

kjiku:s *an* December; great (Christmas) month [CB] [BC]

kji-m'ntu *an* Satan

kjimskiku sweetgrass [BC]; poison ivy [BR]

kji-niskam *an* Great Spirit

kji-pa:tliya:s *an* bishop

kji-pa:tliya:s ewkwam the Bishop's garment! (exclamation of surprise)

kjipulkowey epilepsy

kji-sape:wit *an (an)* patron saint; blessed

kji-saqamaw *an* Grand Chief [CB]
kjitloqomuwaqan rocking chair; cradle
kjitmey *an* in real one
kkijinu female honorific (used in addressing an old woman or a chief's wife) [SH]
klakw (klakwaq) *an* sculpin [SH]
klamen so; therefore; thus
klap (klapaq) *an* club (in cards) [SH]
klapis finally
klaptan *an* blacksmith
klatpetaw (klatpetaq) *an* hornpow (a kind of fish)
klep (klepaq) *an* club (in cards)
klitam birthmark
klitaw (klitaq) *an* red raspberry [SH] [BC] [RB]; strawberry
kl'muwej[1] *an* boil; carbuncle
kl'muwej[2] *an* mosquito [BR]
kl'muwejimin *an* blackberry [BC]
kl'muweji-wapskw coal
klo:kowey closet; clothes hangar [CB]
kloqiyej *an* whipperwill; swamp robin
kloq'ntiyej *an* seagull
kloqowej *an* star
k'lpisun anchor; sinker
k'lsu *an* testicle
klu *an* condor
klujje:wey cross [BC] (Fr *crucifix?*)
klujjewtaqto:sit *ai* skip the cross (in jump rope) [SH]
klujjewta:sit *an* crucifix [SH]
klujjewto:sit *ai* make the sign of the cross [BC]
klujjewto:t weltamultimk Good Friday
kluk (klukk) *an* gland; swelling; abcess; lump
kluluwet *ai (an)* a matchmaker
klumk wheat
kluskap *an* Glooscap (a culture hero)
kluskapewit *ai* fib; tell lies; tell tall tales
kmeniye:wit *ai* receive holy communion
kme:s *an* beetle [SH]
kmetuk on the side
k'mtn *an* mountain [SH]
kmu:j (kmu:jik) *an* tree [BR]; lumber tree
kmu:j *in* stick; piece of lumber (sg only)
kmu:je:kaqan lumbering
kmu:je:ket *ai* cut lumber
kmu:jemin *an* red raspberry

kmu:ji:j small stick [BR]
kmu:ji:kan frame house or building
kmutnalk *ta* steal
kmutnatm *ti* steal
kmutnes *an* thief
kmutnet *ai* steal
kmutte:k *ta* beat with a stick
kmutte:m *ti* beat with a stick
kmuwej *an* boil [BR]
kmuweju:sit *ai* have boils [EG]
kna:ji:j *an* nit
kna:taqan decoration; decorative object
knek *ii* far
knek wetakutijik (pl) *ai* distant relatives or relations
kni:sikn braid [BC]; hair bun
kniskunej *an* swordfish
kniskwastu *an* fir, pine or spruce needle
kniskwatkiyej *an* grosbeak
kniskwikn Frenchman (slang)
knukwaqan marker
knukwatikn *an* letter (of the alphabet); mark; blaze (on a tree)
ko:kemin *an* thornbush berry [SH]
kokomin *an* thornberry [BR]
ko:kumin *an* thornbush berry
ko:kuminaqsi *an* thornbush
ko:layl coal oil; kerosene
komkotamu *an* sturgeon [RB]
komkwej *an* sucker (fish)
komkwejuwi:kaqan character used to write Micmac
komkwejuwi:kiket *ai* {ewi:kiket} write with Micmac characters
ko:pikn *an* dip net (for salmon) [SH]
kopit (kopitaq) *an* beaver
kopite:skw (kopite:skwaq) *an* female beaver
kopitewe:ket *ai* hunt or trap beaver
kopkej *an* sawwhet [SH]
ko:pukwet[1] *ai* drenched (by heavy seas) [BC]
ko:pukwet[2] *ai* guilty (by association) [BC]
koqkwej *an* sawwhet [RB]
koqoli:kwej *an* hen; chicken; pullet
koqowey n't what is this (that) [BR]
koqqaja:teket *ai* do correctly [SH]
koqqaji-w'naqto:sit *ai* {wenaqto:sit} skip correctly [BR]

koqqwa:l'k *ta* grab
koqqwa:tu *ti* grab
koqwattek *ii* straight; right [SH]
ko:qwejij *an* spider
ko:qwejijiwa:pi spider web
koqwey what?
koqwey ta what for?
koqwey net what is this?; what is that?
koqwey wjit what for?; why not?
k'petaq summit
k'pnno:l *an* government (Fr *gouverneur*)
k'p'tay up; above; overhead; the summit
kp'te:sn south
ksaltimkewey {kesalk} love; loving
k'satalk *ai* finished eating
ksin {kesik} past winter
ksinuk forthcoming winter
ksipo:qwan {kesipa:l'k} scratching place [SH]
ksispa:taqan {kesispa:tu} soap [SH]
ksispa:tekemkewey {kesispa:tu} dryer; object pertaining to the washing of clothes
ksite:taqan {kesite:tm} something or someone cherished or valued; something or someone precious
ks'keltaqan {keskeltm} something or someone held dear
ksno:qon *an* frivolous person [RB]
ksno:qonewey triviality (pejorative) [RB]
ksnqoweyey useless object; worthless object
ksnuko:kuwom {kesnukwat} hospital
ksnukowaqan {kesnukwat} sickness
ks'pukuwa:taqan {kespukuwa:tu} lie [PEI]
ksu:skw (ksu:skuk) *an* hemlock [SH]
ksuskwate:kn tent flap [SH]
kta:n ocean
ktantaqan {ketantu} hatred
ktantekewinu *an* {ketantu} hunter; person who hates
ktapekiyaqan {ketapekiyet} song
ktik *an* in other; another
ktiki nipn last summer
ktiki sapo:nuk the day after tomorrow
ktiki w'la:kwe:k {wela:kw} the night before last
ktipun last winter
kt'k *an, in* (an) other [SH]
kt'kiyewinuj *an* {ketkiyet} drunkard

kt'kiyewuti {ketkiyet} drunkenness
kt'k w'la:kw {wela:kw} the night before last [BR]
kujjinu honorific used in addressing an old man; our (inclusive) father
kujm outside
kujmuk outside; outdoors
ku:ku:kwes *an* owl [RB]; screech owl
ku:ku:wes *an* owl
kukwa:sit *ai* stoop to drink (human or animal)
kukwej *an* giant [BR]
kukwejultimk tag (game)
kukwejuwit *ai* "it" (in tag game)
kukwes *an* giant [SH]; a legendary, greedy wildman
ku:la:ji:j tub [SH]
kulaman so [BC]; therefore [BC]; thus [BC]
kulapuwalk *ta* parboil
kule:k *ai* try [BR]
kulje:wey cross [SH]
kuljewta:sit (kuljewta:sijik) *an* crucifix
kuljewto:sit *ai* cross oneself
kuljiyewey cross [SH]
kulkwikmk earwax [SH]
kulkwi:s *an* pig
kulkwis *an* coasting sled; tobaggan [BR]
kulkwi:su:mi pork fat; lard [SH]
kulkwisuwatp short sled with wide runners [SH]
kulkwi:suwey pork
kulkwi:suwimi pork fat; lard [BR]
kullpatkij *an* maggot
kullpisun anchor [CB]; sinker
kumaqan whip
kume:s *an* beetle [PEI]
kunnte:j stone
kunntew (kunntal) rock; stone
kunntewapskek *ii* rocky
kupniye:wit receive communion
kups'ji:j *an* cup [SH]
kuta:l'k *ta* pour
kutana:sit *ai* go down (the mission); go to town
kutank (loc) down the mission
kutapikwalk *ta* desalinate; desalt (by soaking in several changes of water)
kutapikwatm *ti* desalinate; desalt (by soaking in several changes of water)
kutapuwalk *ta* sink [BC]
kutapuwatm[1] *ti* parboil

kutapuwatm[2] *ti*   sink [BC]
kuta:tat *ai*   pour
kutatesmk *ta*   spill
kutatestat *ai*   spill
kutatestu *ti*   spill
kuta:tu *ti*   pour
kuteket *ai*   spill
kutputi   chair
kuwaskuwi:tm *ti*   translate [BC]
kuwasun   a dead (sagging) tree [BR]
kuwikn   marrow bone
kuwow (kuwaq) *an*   pine
kwaptm'n   horizon
kwa:taqan   pillow [SH]
kwe: qreetings! (obsolete [Iroquois?])
kweja:l'k *ta*   test [BR]; try out [BR]
kweja:l'sit *ai*   try [BR]
kwejaqama:l'k *ta*   boil [BR]
kwejaqama:tu *ti*   boil [BR]
kwejaqamiyaq *ii*   boil [BR]
kwejaqamiyet *ai*   boil [BR]
kweja:tu *ti*   test [BR]; try out [BR]
kweji·ks'kuteskaq *ta*   {keskuteskaq} try to catch
kweji·ks'kuteskm *ti*   keskuteskm} try to catch
kweji·msnk *ta*   {mesnk} try to grasp
kweji·msn'm *ti*   {mesn'm} try to grasp
kweji-n'mi:k *ta*   {nemi:k} try to see
kweji-n'mi:k *ta*   {nemi:k} try to see
kweji-n'mitu *ti*   {nemitu} try to see
kweji-pawnatqa:t *ai*   try to get out of a thicket
kweji·psemk *ta*   {pesemk} sniff
kweji·psetu *ti*   {pesetu} sniff
kwe:kwiyamkek   Port Hood, N.S.; water embankment [CB]
kweltamit *ai*   feast
kweltanat *ai*   feast [SH]
kwe:maq *ta*   hail; greet
kwesiket *ai*   foretell [SH]; tell fortunes [SH]
kwestaw'let *ai*   gifted [BR]
kwetaluktuwet *ai (an)*   a (ceremonial) greeter [BC]
kwetamat *ai*   smoke [BR]
kwetapa:l'k *ta*   sink [BC]
kwetapa:q *ii*   sink [BR]
kwetapa:sit *ai*   submerge [BR]
kwetapa:tu *ti*   sink [BC]
kwetapet (kwetapejik) *an*   ox [CB]

kwetapet *ai*   dive [BR]
kwetej *an*   Iroquois Indian
kwetmat *ai*   smoke [BR]
kwetnasa:l'k *ta*   try on
kwetnasa:tu *ti*   try on
kwetp'k *ta*   taste [BR]; try the taste of [BR]
kwettm *ti*   taste [BR]; try the taste of [BR]
kwilaq *ta*   look for; search for
kwil'm *ti*   look for; search for
kwiluwasit *ai*   search about
kwimu *an*   loon [CB]
kwinu *an*   loon [SH]
kwi:s (voc)   son!; boy! (term of affection)
kwi:sit *ai*   jump (used in reference to a fish only)
kwitamaqan   fishing [CB]; fishery [BC]
kwitamet *ai*   cast (as in fishing)
kwitji:j (voc)   sonny!
kwitn   canoe
kwitna:q (kwitna:m) *ai*   go by canoe
kwitnu:j   small canoe

la:jijjaqan *an* glove [NB]

la:kittaqan file; rasp

lakka:p cellar (Fr *la cave*)

lakko:l cord of wood (Fr *la corde*)

lakko:la:laq *ii* equal or equivalent to a cord (of wood)

laklem cream (Fr *la crème*)

laklem amu:k *ii* cream colored

laklem amuksit *ai* cream colored

laklus pitcher (Fr *la cruche*) [SH]

la:maqan *an* dipper; ladle

lame:k *ai, ii* underneath; below; inside

lame:kewey slip (undergarment)

lamikuwom {wikuwom} interior (of a dwelling)

lamikuwome:j *an* {wiguwom} slipper [ESK]

lamipjan palm (of the hand)

lamipkikwam {np'kikw} eyeball [BR]

lamipkikwan eyeball [SH]

lamiptn {np'tn} palm (of the hand)

lamkmu:k underground

lampo:q bottom of the river or lake

lamqamu:k (loc) underground

lamqwan *an* undershirt [SH]

lamukuwom interior of a dwelling [SH]

lamukuwomk (loc) inside the house [SH]

lamulkuk (loc) below deck [CB]

lamutta:lt mustard (Fr *le moutarde*)

lapaltnewey holy water (Fr *le baptême*)

lapasaqan gauge (for baskets)

lapatikn holy water sprinkler (Fr *le baptême*)

lapawji:jitewey tin

lapa:y *an* tub (Fr *la baille*)

lape:lis yard (of measurement) (Fr *la verge*)

lape:w *an* rooster [SH]

lapew male animal

lape:wi:skw *an* female animal [SH]

lapikot *an* smallpox; smallpox vaccination (Fr *la picote*)

lapikotewit *ai* have smallpox

lapilas *an* flax seed (Fr *la filasse*)

lapli:sikn silk

laplusan jail (Fr *la prison*)

lapol *an* bowl (Fr *le bol*)

la:puktaqan snare (rabbit)

la:puktaqanikalk *ta* snare

la:puktaqaniket *ai* set (rabbit) snares

lapukwan three-master sailing ship (Fr *la boucane*)

laputi spy glass

laputi:l pair of binoculars

lapuwe:l *an* frying pan (Fr *la poêle*)

laqala:ns barn (Fr *la grange*)

la:qan deep wound or gash

laqpa:taqan shoelace [SH]

laqpilaqan drape; wooden hoop support around inside of wikwam [SH]

laqpisuti apron

laqpo:taqan binding; lacing

lasinamey chimney (Fr *la cheminée*) [SH]

lasiyantejk lantern [SH]

lasiyet *an* plate (Fr *l'assiette*)

lasiyetji:j *an* saucer [SH]

laskukutimk card playing

laskukwaqan game of cards

laskukwet *ai* play cards

laskuwaw (laskuwaq) *an* snowshoe

laskw (laskuk) *an* playing card

lasqo:plaw (lasqo:plaq) *an* board

las'tikjapekit *ai* crawl backwards [SH]

lasup soup (Fr *la soupe*)

lasupe:ji:j savory

lasuwi:p *an* Jew [SH] (Fr *le Juif*)

la:taqsun *an* bucket; pail

la:taqsuna:laq *ii* equivalent to a pail

la:taqsuna:lat *ai* equivalent to a pail

la:ti tithe [BC]

lati:m tithe (Fr *la dîme*)

latto:law *an* bull; stud horse (Fr *le taureau*)

lawtis should; ought to [SH]

lekepilaqan window shade; blind; curtain [SH]

lekka:p cellar (Fr *les caves*)

leklans barn (Fr *les granges*)

lenpok spring water

lentuk *an* deer

leppiye (no plural) foot; feet (in measurement) (Fr *les pieds*)

lesqe:kn clothes trunk; coffin

lessow *an* bucket (Fr *les seaux*) [BR]

lesuwi:p (lesuwi:paq) *an* Jew (Fr *les Juifs*)

likpenikn basket

likpeta:w *an* (white) ash (tree)

likpete:knapi ash strip (for weaving baskets)

lipqamu:k layered; stratified; underground

lisknuwapi braid or strand (Maria)
lisknuwaqan sheen (for weaving baskets) [SH]; weaving; knitting
listukujewa:tuwat *ai* speak or imitate the Restigouche dialect
lke:kn hoe
lkeso:qon plow
lketu *an* mushroom [SH]
lketuweket *ai* gather mushrooms [SH]
lkowaqana:l'k *ta* {lukwaqana:l'k} bother; trouble
lkowaqana:tu *ti* bother; trouble
lkusuwaqan {elkusuwet} ladder
lkwetuk *an* female mammal [SH]
lkwetukji:j *an* heifer
llim too much
llipqama:taqan (toy) top [NB]
llutaqan fence
llutaqanatkw fence post
lluwikn'k seven (in counting)
lluwikn'k te:sinska:q seventy (in counting)
lluwiman choke-cherry [RB]
lmu:j (lmu:jik) *an* dog [BR]
lmu:ju:paq *ii* neap tide [SH]
lnapskw Indian rock [SH]
lnaqanatkw handle; axe handle [BR]
lnaqantkw handle; axe handle [SH]
lnim because [CB]; too much
l'npok spring (water) [SH]
lnu *an* Indian [BR]; person
lnu:kwat *ai* dance Indian style [BC]
lnu:tesink *ai* dance Indian style
lnutesink *ai* dance Indian style [SH]
lnuwe:kati Indian village (reserve) [BR]
lnuweyey pertaining to Indians [BR]
lnuwipi Indian paddle [SH]
lnuwi:skw *an* Indian woman [BR]
lnu-wi:tm *ti* {ewi:tm} say in Micmac (in Indian) [BR]
lokowit *ai* lucky
lo:ks (lo:ksik) *an* log
Lola *an* Lawrence (Fr *Laurent*)
lo:q well; so; so that
lo:q etuk so probably [SH]
loqomoqa:taqan {iloqomaqa:tu} wrapper; cigarette [SH]
loqte:kn trap
loqte:knikalk *ta* trap; set a trap for

loqte:kniket *ai* trap; set traps
loqtnema:t *ai* have bad breath
loqwistaqan (basket) hoop [BR]
lpa really! (an emphatic particle); even so
lpa jikaw all gone! (an emphatic particle)
lpa mu not even (takes negative verb form)
lpa:tu *an* young man (16–18 years of age) [SH]
lpa:tuj *an* boy
lpa:tu:ji:j *an* small boy
lpa:tujuwit *ai* become or be a boy
lpa:tu:s *an* young man
lpa:'uj *an* boy
lpa:'ujuwit *ai* become or be a boy
lpa wijey all the same; same here (an emphatic paricle)
lsipuktuk (loc) Big Cove
l'sqi:kn coffin; casket; trunk [BC]
l'tqa:mun *an* arrowhead; harpoon [BR]
lukowaqan {elukwet} work
lukowaqana:teket *ai* bothersome
lukowaqane:kmuti tool kit; tool box
lukowaqanit *ai* bothersome; troublesome
lukowinu *an* {elukwet} worker [SH]
luks *an* a mythical being
luks'ji:j *an* youngster; kid
lukwaqana:l'k *ta* bother; trouble
lukwaqana:tu *ti* bother; trouble
lu:kwejk compass; pointer [SH]
lukwe:k between [SH]
lukwetuk *an* female mammal
lukwewaqana:teket *ai* {elukwet} make or cause trouble
lukwewinu *an* {elukwet} worker [BR]
lukwistaqan (basket) hoop [SH]
lupapl rhubarb [BC]
lu:se:kn furnace poker
lusknikn dough; biscuit; bannock
luskwatikn spit; saliva
lusniknekaluj *an* cubit (of measurement) [ESK]
lu:sukwewa:sit *ai* act like a son-in-law
lu:sukwewa:timk bride-price activity
lu:suweskwewa:sit *ai* perform the duties of a prospective daughter-in-law
lu:suweskwewit *ai* act like a daughter-in-law
lu:ta:qan paddle
lutmaqan gossip; rumour; hearsay
lutmaqaniket *ai* spread rumours

lutqamun *an* harpoon [SH]
luwi:tmasuti {eluwitmasit} oath [BR]; pledge

M

ma a future negative particle
ma: a future negative particle
majaqtat *ai* copulate
maja:sit *ai* leave; move
maja:sitewiku:sk September [SH]
majiyaqa:l'k *ta* scold
majjoqtelikn *an* arrow
majo:qiyaq *ii* wobble
majo:qiyet *ai* wobble
majukkwalk *ta* keep in time with; follow; tag along with [PEI]
majukkwatm *ti* keep in time with; follow; tag along with [PEI]
majulkalk *ta* keep in time with; follow [SH]
majulkwatm *ti* keep in time with; follow [SH]
maju:pa:q *ii* high tide [RB]
makasan store (Fr *magasin*)
makasana:sit *ai* go shopping
ma:kn *an* moccasin
makot dress
makota:q (makota:m) *ai* wear a dress
makun slush (on the river)
malapit see poorly
mala:sit *ai (an)* a slowpoke
malatalk *ai* eat little
male:k *ai* lazy
Ma:li Virgin Mary
Mali *an* Mary; Marie [BC] (Fr *Marie*)
Mali:j(i:j) *an* Mary (dim)
mali:japa:qawey golden-thread (root)
malikatat *ai* walk poorly
malike:w *an* keg; barrel
malike:wa:t *ai* equal or equivalent to a barrel
malikewe:j Mollygowatch [CB]
malikeyaq *ta* play with; amuse
malikimk *ta* mock [BC]; tease [BC]
maliki-te:l'mk *ta* {tel-te:l'mk} mock; consider incapable
maliki-te:tm *ti* {tel-te:tm} mock; consider incapable
malikitm *ti* make fun of; laugh at [BC]
malikmk *ta* mock; tease
maliko:tm *ti* play with; amuse
malikwat *ai* mentally lazy
malikwek *ii* grow slowly
malikwet *ai* grow slowly
Mali Lo:s *an* Mary Rose (Fr *Marie-Rose*)

malimqwanj hazlenut [BR]
malipqwanj hazlenut
malipqwanjmusi hazelnut bush or tree
mali:sit *ai* speak poorly; a Malecite Indian
maliye:wit *ai* marry
maliye:wuti marriage
malja:t *ai* slow; backward
maljat *ai* physically weak
maljewe:j *an* youngster
maljewe:juwit *ai* young
malkaq *ta* put off schedule
malkupaqteskaq *ta* hold or pin down by covering
malkupaqteskm *ti* hold or pin down by covering
mallpale:wi:skw (mallpale:wi:skwaq) *an* woman doctor
mallpale:wit (mallpale:wijik) *an* doctor
mallpale:witewapewit *ai* look like a doctor
malltew blood
malltewa:l'k *ta* get blood on
malltewa:tu *ti* get blood on
malltewik *ii* bloody
malltewit *ai* bloody
malltewiyaq *ii* bleed
malltewiyejit *an* beet [SH]
malltewiyet *ai* bleed
malltews'k *ta* cut (so as to cause blood to flow)
malltewsm *ti* cut (so as to cause blood to flow)
malltewte:k *ta* hit (so as to cause blood to flow)
malltewte:m *ti* hit (so as to cause blood to flow)
malltewtesink *ai* bleed (as the result of a fall)
malltewtesk *ii* bleed (as the result of a fall)
malltewtesmk *ta* get or make bloody
malltewtestu *ti* get or make bloody
malqomk *ta* eat
malqotm *ti* eat
malqwi:kn pole or weighty object used to secure or hold down wikwam covering [SH]
mals flint [SH]
malsan *an* merchant (Fr *marchand*)
malsanewey merchandize
malsano:kuwom general store [SH]
malsa:sik *ii* flinted (as a gun) [SH]
malsnawey soft maple
maltejjuwey hammer [SH]
maltejjuweyatkw hammer handle [SH]
maltejuwey hammer [BC] [CB] (Fr *marteau*)
malukunat *ai* have a weak back [BR]

mam (voc) mother! [SH]
mamam food; drink; bottle (baby talk) [SH]
ma:muni·ksalk *ta* {kesalk} like very much
ma:muni·psaq *ii* {pesaq} snow heavily
ma:munlaq *ii* rain heavily; pour
manapsk'te:m *ti* chip off a protuberance
manasu:lkw warship [SH]
mapos pocket (Fr *ma poche*)
mappos pocket (Fr *ma poche*)
maqa:l'k *ta* enlarge
maqalqasit *ai* have a large hole
maqalqikwat *ai* have large eyes
maqamikew (maqamikal) land; ground
maqamikewa:sit *ai* go by land
maqana:l'k *ta* confuse; baffle; outwit
maqanat *ai* confused; baffled; out-witted
maqanimk *ta* outtalk; put down
maqapskek *ii* large and round
maqapsk'sit *ai* large and round
maqapsk'tiyat *ai* have a big and round belly
maqapskusuwat *ai* have large testicles
maqa:q *ii* wide and round (cylindrical); big (in girth)
maqata:q lend to
maqatewey temporary thing; loan
maqatkwik *ii* big waves; heavy seas
maqatpat *ai* have a big head
maqa:tu *ti* enlarge
maqatuwi:ket *ai (an)* a lender
ma:qi carcass; flesh [SH]
maqijjikwat *ai* have a big bowel movement; have a large stool
maqikjat *ai* have big buttocks
maqipskunat *ai* {npuskun} have a large breast or chest
maqiptnat *ai* {npitn} have large hands
maqi:sit *ai* speak with a deep or husky voice
maqiske:k *ai, ii* wide
maqisqonat *ai* {nsisqon} have a large nose
maqistaqanat *ai* {ns'tuwaqan} have large or long ears (Big Cove term for a Micmac from Restigouche)
maqitnat *ai* {nitn} have wide nostrils
maqiwilnuwit *ai* {nilnu} have a large tongue
maqiwtulit *ai* {ntul} have a large boat [BR]
maqo:qiptnat *ai* {npitn} have large arms
maqo:qonikata:t *ai* {nkat} have large legs

maqoqsit *ai* wide and round (cylindrical); big (in girth)
maqsitat *ai* have large feet
maqtawa:qewey penny [NB]
maqtawe:k *ai, ii* black
maqtawikneksit *ai* dark complected
maqtawi:tuwat *ai* {wituwit} black-bearded
maqtawoqsit *ai* darkened; tanned
maqtawoqtek *ii* darkened; tanned
maqtew-amu:k *ii* blackish; darkish
maqtew-amuksit *ai* blackish; darkish
maqtewe:k *ai, ii* black [BR]
maqtewikjat *ai* black-bottomed
maqtewiman *an* blackberry; potato (alternate form) [SH]
maqtewipqaji:jit (maqtewipqaji:jijik) *an* spade (in cards) [SH]
maqtunat *ai* {ntun} have a big mouth
maskelket *ai* separated (in marriage)
maskel'mk *ta* hate
maskeltm *ti* hate
masko:l'k *ta* store; put away (in bulk)
masko:tu *ti* store; put away (in bulk)
maskute:k *ta* put away quickly
maskute:m *ti* put away quickly
maskwa:l'k *ta* put away [PEI]
maskwa:tu *ti* put away [PEI]
maskwe:s *an* young birch tree
maskwe:siman cherry
maskwe:simanaqse:kati birch grove [SH]
maskwe:simanaqsi *an* cherry tree
maskwe:simusi *an* birch genus
maskwi *an* white birch bark
masqo:tasit *ai* saved up; accumulated
masqupit *ai* hidden internally
masqute:k *ta* hide; put away quickly
masqutek *ii (in)* hidden internally; uterus
masqute:m *ti* hide; put away quickly
masqwa:l'k *ta* put away; store; save
masqwa:tasit *ai* jailed; put away (in a mental institution)
masqwa:tu *ti* put away; store; save
massaqiyet *ai* sexually aroused or stimulated
massaqte:ket *ai* instigate; arouse; stimulate
masu:mi perfume
ma:susi fiddlehead [RB]
mataluwat *ai* wag the tail

matama:sit go towards the road or path

matawa:sit *ai* reach the end of the path [BC]; complete the job [BC]

Matiyu *an* Matthew (Fr *Mathieu*)

matkete:ket *ai* cultivate; hoe [SH]

matkwa:sit *ai* bow down

matkwetaq *ta* bow to

matkwetm *ti* bow to

Matle:n *an* Madelein (Fr *Madeleine*)

matlet blouse

matlot (matlotaq) *an* sailor (Fr *matelot*) [SH]

matnakket *ai* fight; struggle

matnakkewaqan fighting; battle

matnakkewinu warrior

matnk *ta* fight or struggle against

matn'm *ti* fight or struggle against

mat'ntijik (pl) *ai* fight

mat'ntimk war; battle

matnukteskewey head cheese

mato:qiyaq *ii* sway

mato:qiyet *ai* sway

mattaqa:taq *ta (do)* telephone [BC]

mattaqa:tmkewey telephone [SH]

mattaqa:tu *ti* pull on to make a sound (as a bell); telephone [BR]

mattaqte:k *ta* pluck (as a string)

mattaqte:ket *ai* send a wire or a telegram [SH]

mattaqte:m *ti* pluck (as a string)

mattejjuwey hammer

matte:k *ta* beat; spank; thrash; vanquish

mattelaq *ta* shoot at

mattelikn *an* arrow [BR]

mattelm *ti* shoot at

matte:m *ti* beat; spank; thrash; vanquish

mattesink *ai* shake

mattesk *ii* shake

matu:lukwet *ai (an)* {elukwet} do odd jobs; a handyman

matu:mimajit *ai* live simply

matu:n'mat *ai* frugal

matu:p'k *ta* {soqp'k} eat the scraps; eat the leftovers of

matu:te:maq *ta* trim (someone's) hair

matu:tm *ti* {soqtm} eat the scraps; eat the leftovers of

matuwapetesink *ai* glance

matuwa:sit *ai* wander off unintentionally

matuwatalk *ai* eat poorly; have a snack

matuwe:k[1] *ai* a part-time worker

matuwe:k[2] *ai* simple; unsophisticated

matuwes *an* porcupine

matuwesewey porcupine meat

maw also

maw-aknutmajik (pl) *ai* talk together

maw-amk'pijik (pl) *an* piled together

maw amk'tekl (pl) *ii* piled together

mawa:tajik (pl) *ai* share; chip in together

mawe:kik (pl) *ai* live together; gathered together

mawi-apoqonatultijik (pl) *ai* congregate to help each other [BC]

mawiaqa:teket *ai (an)* an organizer [BC]

mawi-klu:lk *ii* {kelu:lk} pretty good

mawiknat *ai* omnipotent

mawi·ktlams'tasultijik (pl) *ai* {ketlams'taq} share the same belief [BC]

mawi-mijijultijik (pl) *ai* {mijisit} gathered together (to eat) [SH]

mawisetesink *ai* fall in a heap

mawisetesk *ii* fall in a heap

mawiseteskaq *ta* crumple

mawiseteskm *ti* crumple

mawita:jik (pl) *ai* gather together; hold a meeting

mawi-winjik *ii* pretty bad [SH]

mawi-w'lta:sit *ai* {wel-ta:sit} very happy or pleased

mawi-w'lta:suwaqan {wel-ta:sit} joyful time or occasion

mawiya:tijik (pl) *ai* gather; swarm (as bees)

mawiyejik (pl) *ai* gather together; congregate

mawiyo:mi formal meeting or gathering

mawkamik *ii* corpulent; very fat

mawkamit *ai* corpulent; very fat

maw·kijjet *ai* {ekijjet} count; add up

maw·kiljet *ai* {ekiljet} figure; calculate [SH]

maw·kimk *ta* {ekimk} include in the count; call together (pl)

maw·kitm *ti* include in the count; call together (pl)

maw-klulk *ii* {kelu:lk} pretty good

maw-klu:sit *ai* {kelu:sit} pretty good

mawksa:l'k *ta* build a fire within

mawksa:teket *ai* make or build a fire (in a stove or furnace)

mawksa:tu *ti* build a fire within

mawkutamit *ai* chew and swallow
maw-lukwalk *ta* {elukwalk} include in the repairs
maw-lukwatm *ti* {elukwatm} include in the repairs
maw-mekisiw'ltimk pusu: puna:newimk *a* gathering for purposes of eating a meal in common and to extend New Year's greetings
maw-nutmamk {nutmat} conference; assembly
mawo:l'k *ta* gather up
mawo:tasit *ai (an)* a collector; a gatherer
mawo:tu *ti* gather up
maw-piley very new
mawpisit *ai* bundled
mawpit *ai* bunched together
mawpitek *ii* bundled; tied or bundled together
mawtejjuwey drumstick
mawte:k *ta* collect; save
mawtek *ii* bunched together
mawte:m *ti* collect; save
maw-winjik *ii* pretty bad
maw-winjit *ai* pretty bad
me: still; yet; anyway
me: ap some more [SH]
me: aq more than
me: ijka some more
me:j even still
mejik-amuksit *ai* look dirty
mejik-apewit *ai* have a dirty face
mejike:k *ai, ii* dirty
mejikiptnat *ai* {npitn} have dirty hands [PEI]
mejikkumet *ai* wear dirty clothes
mejiku:lkw dirty sink [BR]
mejikulkw dirty canoe [BR]
mejitnewt one more time
mejjikwat *ai* defecate
mejjilsit *ai* defecate on oneself
me:jka some more
mejka: some more!
mejkiyet *ai* undergo rigor mortis; get stiff
me:ka:sik *ii* flow rapidly [SH]
me:ka:sit *ai* greedy; get worse
me:ka:s'k *ii* greedy; get worse
me:ka:teket *ai* show off; overdo; do more than expected; do much
meka:teket *ai* do much
me:ke:k *ai* stuck up; haughty; inconsiderate
meken'k *ta* have much of

meken'm *ti* have much of
mekepk *ta* eat plenty of; eat in abundance
mekete:k *ta* gather; collect; pick plenty of; win plenty of
mekete:m *ti* gather; collect; pick plenty of; win plenty of
meketm *ti* eat plenty of; eat in abundance
me:ki·ksitesink *ai* {kesitesink} badly injured [SH]
me: kisikuwit *ai* older
me:ki-te:l'manej kkijnaq Mother's Day
me:ki-te:l'manej kujjinaq Father's Day
me:ki-te:l'mk *ta* {tel-te:l'mk} respect [PEI]
me:ki-te:l'mk *ta* think highly of; respect [PEI]
me:ki-telsit *ai* have a high opinion of oneself
me:ki-te:tasit *ai* highly praised; honored
me:ki-te:tas'k *ii* highly praised; honored
me:ki-te:tm *ti* think highly of; respect [PEI]
me:kitutk *ai* put on airs [PEI]
me:ki·wju:s'k *ii* {weju:s'k} gale force wind [SH]
me:ki-w'la:teket *ai* {wela:teket} do wondrous things [SH]
mekloqiyaq *ii* turn red (as of the sky) [SH]
meknk *ta* gather; collect; pick up; choose
mekn'm *ti* gather; collect; pick up; choose
me:ko:pj (me:ko:pjik) vain person; stuck up person; snob
me: koqwey anything else?
meko:tik *ii* expensive
meko:tit *ai* expensive
mektaq *ta* disbelieve; doubt
mektm *ti* disbelieve; doubt
mekunik *ii* icy; slushy
me:kusit *ai* ask a high price
mekwa'ik in the center; in the middle
mekwa:l'k *ta* make red
mekw-amu:k *ii* reddish
mekw-amuksit *ai* reddish
mekwapskek *ii* round and red
mekwapsk'sit *ai* round and red
mekwasa:l'k *ta* stick on; glue on
mekwasa:tu *ti* stick on; glue on
mekwasitalk *ta* pull strings (to get a job or to get in an organization)
mekwaspit *ai* attached (as an integral part)
mekwastek *ii* attached (as an integral part)
mekwa:taqan rouge

mekwa:tat *ai* put on rouge
mekwatesink *ai* flash red
mekwatesk *ii* flash red; northern lights [SH]
mekwa:tu *ti* make red
mekwe:jit (mekwe:jijik) *an* beet
mekwe:k *ai, ii* red
mekwe:saqa:sit *ai* turn red; blush
mekwe:saqsit *ai* red-faced
mekwik *ii* swollen
mekwit *ai* swollen
mekwulkw red canoe [SH]
melkajit *ai* withstand the cold [BC]
melka:l'k *ta* harden
melkapek *ii* tough (to eat) [SH]
melkapekisk *ii* tough and stringy
melkapjit *ai* have a strong grip
melkaqanatpat *ai* bald-headed
melka:sit *ai* hardened; solidified
melka:s'k *ii* hardened; solidified
melka:tu *ti* harden
melke:k *ai, ii* hard; solid
melki-ji:n'm *an* strong man; solid man
melkikit *ai* solidly built
melkikiyaq *ii* rigid [BC]
melkikiyet *ai* rigid [BC]
melkiknaq *ii* strong
melkiknat *ai* strong
melki:taqanat *ai* {nji:taqan} have a strong neck
melkita:t *ai* brave
melkiyaqasit *ai* muscular; tough
melk'jat *ai* constipated; have a hard stool
melk'tqasit *ai* strong and stringy [BC]
melk'tqek *ii* strong and stringy [BC]
melkunasit *ai* hang on tight [BC]
melkwiskat *ai* stiff with fright (from a nightmare)
meluwij especially! [ESK]
meluwijoqo na honestly! seriously!
memkatpat *ai* bald [SH]
memke:k *ai, ii* bare; cleared
memkoqte:ket *ai* make a clearing
memkoqte:m *ti* clear out; make bare
memk'te:maq *ta (do)* cut someone's hair short or thin [BR]
memkwan temple (of the head) [SH]
me: muljiwe:juwit *ai* younger
menaje:jit *ai* fragile; delicate; brittle
menaje:jk *ii* fragile; delicate; brittle

menakwisink *ai* wobbly; unbalanced; tipsy
menakwisk *ii* wobbly; unbalanced; tipsy
mena:l'k *ta* remove; take off; pluck
menapaqam *ti* unscrew
menapaqq *ta* unscrew
mena:piyet *ai* remove (fish) from a net
menaq not yet (takes negative verb); never
menaqa carefully
menaqajewa:l'k *ta* do carefully
menaqajewa:tu *ti* do carefully
menaqajewey by rights! (an exclamation)
menaqajewo:kwet *ai* speak succinctly; speak carefully
menaqanaq *ii* weak
menaqanat *ai* weak
mena:qikwalk *ta* pry loose; scrape off
mena:qikwatm *ti* pry loose; scrape off
mena:qikwet *ai* pull up vegetables or weeds
menastatm *ti* break off a spruce bough [SH]
menastet *ai* break off spruce boughs [SH]
me: na: tami somewhere or someplace else [SH]
mena:taquk *ai* harvest (a garden)
menata:t *ai* sensitive
mena:tu *ti* remove; take off; pluck
menawjit *ai* cold-blooded; sensitive to the cold
menepqa:l'k *ta* strip off; rip off
menepqa:tu *ti* strip off; rip off
mene:smat *ai* {e:s} dig for clams [SH]
menikna:sit *ai* undress [BC]
menikwalk *ta* pry out or remove (with hands or tool)
menikwatm *ti* pry out or remove (with hands or tool)
meni:kwet *ai* strip off (birch) bark
menikwet *ai* grow off
menina:l'k *ta* rip or tear off (or out)
menina:tu *ti* rip or tear off (or out)
menipka:l'k *ta* remove by stripping; rip off
menipka:tu *ti* remove by stripping; rip off
menipku:sit *ai* {pku} collect spruce gum [BC]
menipqwa:l'k *ta* {pqwa:w} take off or remove bark [SH]
menipqwa:tu *ti* {pqwa:w} take off or remove bark [SH]
menipqwa:wet *ai* {pqwa:w} remove bark (from a tree) [SH]

menjapskek *ii* dome shaped; half round; door knob

menjapsk'sit *ai* dome shaped; half round

menja:sit *ai* get up or rise (from a prone position)

menjipukuwejk post

menkaq *ta* take off (using the foot); rub off

menkm *ti* take off (using the foot); rub off

menkosa:qanatpat *ai* become bald [BC]

menoqwam sun dog (small rainbow seen next to sun at sunrise and sundown) [BR]

menp'k *ta* bite off

mens'k *ta* cut out

mensm *ti* cut out

mente:k *ta* knock off; remove by striking

mente:m *ti* knock off; remove by striking

mente:maq *ta (do)* deflower

ment'k *ta* bite off

mentm *ti* bite off

menuweke:k *ta* need; able to use

menuweket *ai* required; needed

menuweketu *ti* need; able to use

me: pa anyhow

meptoqopsk'set *ai* big and round [PEI]

mesa:l'k *ta* swallow

mes-amu:k *ii* murky (of liquids) [SH]

me:sapjete:k *ta* fumble

me:sapjete:m *ti* fumble

mesa:tamit *ai* swallow

mesatkwa:l'k *ta* place against

mesatkwa:tu *ti* place against

mesatkwi·ksma:l'k *ta* {kesma:l'k} push up against [BR]

mesatkwi·ksma:tu *ti* kesma:tu} push up against [BR]

mesa:tu *ti* swallow

mese:k *ai (an)* of one piece [BC]; intact; whole

meseket *ai* swallow

mesekit (mesekijik) *ai (an)* cook (also used in reference to a housewife)

me:si unable; can not (used with non negative verb)

mesi:k *ta* infect; influence; affect

mesi:kowik *ii* change (of the weather) for the worst [CB]

mesiktaqanat *ai (an)* a gourmand [BC]

mesimk *ta* tell on; inform on

me:si-pmiyet *ai* {pemiyet} incapable of walking

me:situkwi:k (me:situkwi:m) *ai* incapable of running

mesiyapoq'k *ta* stir

mesiyapoqm *ti* stir

mesiyapoqte:k *ta* stir (with an instrument)

mesiyapoqte:m *ti* stir (with an instrument)

meskata:suwaqan sorrow

meske:k *ai* sorry

meski:k *ii* big

meski:kji:jit *ii* somewhat big; medium-sized

meskilk *ai* big

mesk'k (meskm) *ai* in one's prime

mesn(')k *ta* receive; get; catch hold of

mesna:l'k *ta* mend; repair [SH]

mesna:tu *ti* mend; repair [SH]

mesni:s'k *ta* patch; mend; sew [SH]

mesni:sm *ti* patch; mend; sew [SH]

mesn'm *ti* receive; get; catch hold of

meso:tamit *ai* swallow [BC]

mespit *ai* all there; a virgin

mesp'k *ta* taste

mespo:qek *ii* flooded

mespo:qet *ai* flooded

mesqana:l'k *ta* lay or put down

mesqana:sit *ai* go down (after being shot)

mesqanatelaq *ta* take down with a shot [CB]

mesqana:tu *ti* lay or put down

mesqanepit *ai* crouch

mesqani:telaq *ta* take down with a shot

mesqaniyet *ai* collapse from fatigue; pass out

mesqolit *ai* pierced (as in the hand or foot)

messa:l'k *ta* miss making connection with; miss an appointment or rendez-vous with

messa:tu *ti* miss making connection with; miss an appointment or rendez-vous with

mess'teskaq *ta* arrive too late for

mess'teskm *ti* arrive too late for

mess'teskmat *ai* arrive too late

mestm *ti* taste

mesuktaqanat *ai* crave

me: tale:n How are you (feeling)?

me: tali-w'le:n {wele:k} How are you? [BR]

metaqapit *ai* half naked; half bare

metaq-apja:l'k *ta* grab or take barehanded

metaq-apja:sit *ai* catch barehanded

metaq-apja:tu *ti* grab or take barehanded

metaq-apjit *ai* barehanded
metaqaptiyat *ai* barebottomed
metaqatek *ii* half naked; half bare
me:ta:teket *ai* do wonders [BR]
me:te:k *ta* strike
me:telaq *ta* hit (with a bullet or arrow)
me:tel'm *ti* hit (with a bullet or arrow)
me:te:m *ti* strike
metete:ket *ai* heard pounding
metetoqsit *ai* heard calling, groaning or moaning; heard cawing [SH]; heard quacking [SH]
metewaqsink *ai* heard flapping or fluttering
metewaqs'k *ii* heard flapping or fluttering
metewa:sit *ai* heard moving about
metewatalk *ai* heard eating
metewa:toq (metewa:tu) *ai* heard making a noise
metewe:k *ai* heard stirring or bustling about
metewenk (metewen'm) *ai* heard talking
metew-enmit *ai* overheard laughing
metewi-jikmit *ai* heard growling (as a dog)
metewiluwa:t *ai* overheard talking in anger; heard bellowing (as a moose)
metewintoq (metewintu) *ai* heard singing
metewo:kwet *ai* overheard talking
metewoqsink *ai* heard snoring or grunting
metkatat *ai* {nkat} barefooted
met'ki everywhere [SH]
metkwat *ai* bareheaded; hatless
metkwa:tat *ai* have an erection
metkwe:k *ai, ii* stiff
metla:s a'ikl (pl) ten dollars
metla:sipuna:t *ai* ten years old
metla:sipunq'k ten years
metla:siska:q ten times
metlu:sit *ai* smoke; smoky
metlu:tek *ii* smoke; smoky
meto:kwet *ai* heard talking [PEI]
meto:mt'k (meto:mtm) *ai* heard crying
metoqiyaq *ii* descend to the low ground or flat; go south
metoqiyet *ai* descend to the low ground or flat; go south
metoqwa:l'k *ta* take down to the flat; take south
metoqwa:tu *ti* take down to the flat; take south
metoqwiwsit *ai* move down to the flat
meto:temit *ai* heard crying

met'pna:kiyaq Red Bank [RB]
metu-amu:k *ii* look bad
metu-amuksit *ai* look bad
metuk aside [BR]
metukuna:q *ii* stormy
metu:na:q *ii* stormy
metu:pet *ai* stingy with one's drinks
metu:qamiksit *ai* hard to get along with; have a bad disposition
metuwatqek *ii* hard going (through a thicket) [CB]
metuwe:k *ii* difficult; hard to do; bad
metuwi-kisk'k *ii* a bad day
metuwima:q *ii* taste bad; smell bad
metuwima:t *ai* taste bad; smell bad
me: wen (me: wenik) *an* someone (else)
mewisit *ai* pick berries
mewlijoqo na honestly!; seriously! [SH]
mewli-na:kwekewey dinner (noon meal)
mija:kaj *an* vein
mi:jan *an* excrement; faeces
mi:jane:kmuti bowels
mi:janimat *ai (an)* a jealous mate [BC]; faeces smeller
mi:jano:kuti outhouse [SH]
mi:jano:kuwom outhouse
mijikwek *ii* ingrown
mijikwet *ai* ingrown
mijimij *an* buttocks; rump
mijimijqanaw (mijimijqanaq) *an* butterfly (with picture of ace of spades on wings, a good luck charm)
mijipjewey food
mijisit *ai* eat [BR] [NB]
mijisultimk meal [SH]
mijjako:kwej *an* moose bird [RB]
mijjit *ai* eat [BC]
mijjuwaqan mealtime
mijuwa:ji:j *an* baby
mijuwa:ji:juwe:k *ai* act like a baby
mi: kiju (voc) *an* grandmother! (from Big Cove) [PEI]
mikjako:kwej *an* Canada Jay; moose bird
mikjikj (mikjikjik) *an* turtle
mi:km *an* wood fairy; Maliseet word for a Micmac
mi:kma:ki land of the Micmac people
mi:kmaw (mi:kmaq) *an* Micmac

mi:kmawi:sit *ai* speak Micmac

mikmuwessu *an* person who has supernatural powers; Trickster

mikmuwessuwe:ket *ai* possessed by a mikmuwessu

mikpa:q *ii* weak tide

mikulltiyat *ai* experience (as a male) pregnancy symptoms (as a result of having caused a woman to become pregnant); become irritated (as a first child) when the mother carries her second child

mikustaq *ta* overhear; hear by happenstance

mikustm *ti* overhear; hear by happenstance

mikuteket *ai* plane (as in carpentry)

mikuteskaq *ta* bump into; run over

mikuteskm *ti* bump into; run over

mikutiyat *ai* whiney [PEI]

mikuwa:l'k *ta* find satisfactory

mikuwa:tu *ti* find satisfactory

mikwije:maqan fork; (food) utensil

mikwi-te:l'mk *ta* {tel-te:l'mk} remember; call to mind; recall [PEI]

mikwi-te:tm *ti* {tel-te:tm} remember; call to mind; recall [PEI]

mil-amu:k *ii* all kinds of; variety of

mil-amuksit *ai* all kinds of; variety of

mila:sit *ai* play

mila:suwalk *ta* play around with; toy with

mila:suwatm *ti* play around with; toy with

mila:teket *ai* mischievous; a practical joker

milatuwat[1] *ai* pasture

milatuwat[2] *ai* speak many languages

milesit *ai* rich

milikjetesink *ai* wiggle

milikjetesk *ii* wiggle

miliksnqwat *ai* hard to please; fussy

milipusit *ai* squirm around

mili-ta:sit *ai* {tel-ta:sit} think about all kinds of things

militaw (militaq) *an* hummingbird; birthmark

miliwisik *ii* have many names

miliwisit *ai* have many names

mili-wi:t'k *ta* {ewi:t'k} call by all kinds of names; have many names for

mili-wi:tm *ti* {ewi:tm} call by all kinds of names; have many names for

milkusit *ai* have all kinds of dreams (as when one is feverish)

milkwija:sit *ai* consider all kinds of possibilities

mil-lukwet *ai* {elukwet} do different kinds of work

miloqsawet *ai* make all kinds of pastry; make all kinds of food

miloqs'k *ta* cook all kinds of ways; carve

miloqsm *ti* cook all kinds of ways; carve

milpekitk *ii* flow in all directions

milqamikek *ii* {maqamikew} uneven; hilly (of the ground or floor)

mils'k *ta* whittle; carve on

milsm *ti* whittle; carve on

miltoqsit *ai* blab; talk about this and that

mimajik *ii* alive; live

mimajit *ai* alive; live

mimajiwaqan life; living; livelihood

mimajiwinu *an* human being; person

mima:kwa:l'k *ta* grease the face of (e.g., a pan)

mima:kwa:taqan greaser (for a pan)

mima:kwa:tu *ti* grease the face of (e.g., a pan)

mima:l'k *ta* grease; annoint

mimatpa:l'k *ta* grease the head of

mima:tu *ti* grease; annoint

mime:k *ai, ii* greasy

mimey oil; grease

mi:mije:maqan toadstool

mimikej *an* butterfly [SH]

mimikes *an* butterfly

mimkwaqan perfume; acorn; hair oil [BR]

mimkwaqanimusi oak tree [BR]; beech tree [SH]

mimkwat *ai* have on perfume, lotion or oil

mim'ntawa:l'k *ta* twist [SH]

mim'ntawa:tu *ti* twist [SH]

mimsit *ai* covered with grease and oil (as a mechanic)

mimtoqopskek *ii* round [BR]

mimtoqopsk'sit *ai* round [BR]

mimukwalk *ta* hide; conceal

mimukwasit *ai* hide

mimukwatu *ti* hide; conceal

minijk berry [SH]; fruit [PEI]

minik *ii* a good crop or harvest; grow in abundance

minit *ai* a good crop or harvest; grow in abundance

minjinikej *an* crab [CB]

minkna:sit *ai* change clothes
minu:nsit *ai* resurrected
minu:p'sk *ta* {eps'k} reheat
minu:p'sm *ti* {epsm} reheat
minuwa:l'k *ta* revive; duplicate
minuwa:tu *ti* revive; duplicate
minuwitaqan reproduction
minuwi:tm *ti* {ewi:tm} repeat (what is said)
minuwoqs'k *ta* re-cook
minuwoqsm *ti* re-cook
mi:poq *an* semen
mi:saqatp animal skull [SH]
miseknuj rag
Mise:l *an* Michael (Fr *Michele*)
misimijqanaw (misimijqanaq) *an* butterfly [SH]
misimimqanaw (misimimqanaq) *an* locust [SH]
misissiyaq *ii* get raggedy
misissiyet *ai* get raggedy
mi:soqo up to; as far as; until; between
mi:soqo me:j even still [BC]
mistun ace of spades
misuwes *an* ringworm
miti *an* poplar; aspen
miti:s *an* tree
mittoqopqa:l'k *ta* pinch [BC]
mittoqopqa:tu *ti* pinch [BC]
mittukwalk *ta* visit
mittukwatm *ti* visit
mittukwet *ai* visit
mi:walk *ta* thankful for; thank
mi:wat(i)mkewey na:kwek Thanksgiving Day
mi:watm *ti* thankful for; thank
miwsn load [SH]
miyamuj for sure! (an interjection)
miyawe:k (loc) between; in the middle
miyawitpa:q *ii* in the middle of the night
miyawj cat (familiar form) [SH]
miyaw-la:kewey dinner [SH]
miyaw-la:kwek *ii* noon; midday; the middle of the day
miyaw-na:kwek *ii* noon; midday [BR] [SH]
mjikapu dirty water; used (scrubbing) water [SH]
mjikapu:lkw sink; trough [SH]
mjikey {mejike:k} dirt [BR]
mj'key dirt
mkat awti footpath [BR]
m'kekn hide; leather; skin

mkikn hook; fish hook
mkikun hook [SH]
mklu:tew smoke
mkosaqanatpa:t *ai* get bald
mk'sn *an* {n'muksn} shoe
mk'snapi *an* {n'muksn} shoestring; shoelace
mkumi {mekunik} ice
mkumi:kn icicle
mkumi:knik *ii* icy (in patches)
mkumi:knit *ai* icy (in patches)
mkumiye:j *an* horseshoe
mkumiye:ja:q (mkumiye:ja:m) *ai* have on horseshoes
mkuniye:jo:tlk *ta* shoe (a horse)
mkwa:taqan {mekwe:k} rouge [SH]
m'lakej *an* milk [SH]
m'lakejk (pl) *an* milk
m'lakeju:mi butter
m'lakejuwa:tat *ai* add milk (to one's tea or coffee)
m'lakejuwo:q *an* milk pitcher or pail
m'lasisuwa:tat *ai* add molasses (to pancakes)
m'lasisuwa:tu *ti* put molasses on (Fr *mélasse*)
m'litaw (m'litaq) *an* birthmark [BC]
m'ljetkw burl
m'lkiknewinu *an* {melkiknaq} strong man or woman
m'lkiknoti {melkiknaq} strength; power
m'lsekna:ti Big Cove, N.B.
m'lsuwapu strong brew
m'lumkewej *an* ground hog; woodchuck [RB]
m'napskw's *an* chub [RB]
m'nawa:sit *ai* enter the water (by watercraft)
m'niku island
m'ni:maqanu:min suet [EG]; tallow [EG]
m'nnoqon *an* yellow birch
m'no:man grain of wild rice
m'nqwan rainbow [SH]
m'ntawa:l'k *ta* twist
m'ntawaqalk *ta* twist with a quick motion; wring out quickly
m'ntawaqtu *ti* twist with a quick motion; wring out quickly
m'ntawa:tu *ti* twist
m'ntmu *an* oyster

m'ntn *an* mountain
m'ntoqopsqa:l'k *ta* pinch
m'ntoqopsqa:tu *ti* pinch
m'ntu *an* devil
m'ntuwa:ki hell
m'ntuwit *ai* devilish
m'ntu wutmaqan (an interjection) the devil's
    pipe!
m'nuti bag [BR]; sack [BR]
mo not (a negative particle)
moqopa:q wine
moqsa:l'k *ta* build or set a fire (in a stove or
    furnace)
moqsa:tat *ai* use as fuel [SH]
moqsa:teket *ai* make a fire [SH]
moqsa:tu *ti* build or set a fire (in a stove or
    furnace)
moqwa no
moqwa: koqwey nothing; none
moqwa: wen (wenik) *an* nobody; no one
moqwe koqowey nothing [BR]; none [BR]
moqwe wen (wenik) nobody [BR]; no one [BR]
mowpek *ii* bloated; swollen
mowpet *ai* bloated; swollen
mpo:qon bed
mqatawapu black duck; cormorant
mqwan(ji:j) *an* spoon [SH]
msamu *an* shad
msaqa:kw (msaqakkw) *an* crust of bread
msaqtaqt floor
msiku hay [SH]; grass [SH]
msikuwe:j *an* sparrow
msikuwe:kati hay field
msikuwe:ket *ai* make hay; collect sweetgrass
msikuwiku:s May
msi:kw (msi:kuk) *an* hailstone; sleet
mskikuwe:ket *ai* make hay [SH]; cut grass [SH]
mskikuwom hay den [SH]
msk'tkw deadwater; eddy [SH]
m'skuto:kuk Muskadabit [SH]
ms'soq *an* horsefly [RB]
ms't all
ms't koqwey everything
ms't tami everywhere
ms't wen *an* everybody
m'ta because

mtaqtnej *an* an unidentified bird
mtasoq ledge; cliff; slate
mtawekn flag
mta:y *an* green (undressed) hide [SH]
mtesan *an* youngest or last born
mteskm (mteskmuk) *an* snake; reptile
mtijin an inch
mtl'n ten (in counting) [SH]
mtl'newa:j *an* tenth person
mtl'newey *an* in tenth (one)
mtl'n jel ne:kwt eleven (in counting) [BR]
mtl'n te:s pituwi-mtlnaqan ten thousand (in
    counting)
mtlu:tew {metlu:sit} smoke [BR]
mtnn ten [EG]
mto:kn mast [CB]
mtukunoqt {metukna:q} storm; blizzard
mtukunoqtnukwet *ai* act like a storm is
    approaching (said of a horse)
mtu:noqt {metuwe:k} hard times
mtuwi:kan rafter; gable
mu not (a negative particle)
mujkajewey the very best!
mujkajuweyji:j the very little best!
mujpe:j *an* porpoise [BR]
mujpej *an* mink [BR]
mukuteskaq *ta* bump into; run over
mukuteskm *ti* bump into; run over
mulin machine; engine; mill (Fr *moulin*)
mulinji:j sewing machine
mulqalk *ta* dig out
mulqatm *ti* dig out
mulqet *ai* dig
mulqwekn digging tool; hoe [SH]; shovel
mulumkwej *an* ground hog
munkwaqanemusi beech tree [PEI]
mu nnim not too much
munnte:j little sack
munnti bag; sack
munqwan-amuksit *ai* sky blue [SH]
munsapit *ai* strain to look
munsa:t *ai* insistent [SH]
munsayaq *ta* coax [SH]
munsi·ksma:l'k *ta* {kesma:l'k} try to push [SH]
munsi·ksma:tu *ti* {kesma:tu} try to push [SH]
munsi·ksmeket *ai* {kesmeket} forcefully shove

munsi-sapa:l'k *ta* struggle to get through; struggle to survive; strive to save

munsi-sapa:tu *ti* struggle to get through; struggle to survive; strive to save

munso:tm *ti* coax [SH]

munumkwej *an* woodchuck [ESK]

musapunit *ai* hairy (of the head) [SH]

musika:l'k *ta* skin; strip; clean

musikapskek *ii* smooth and round

musikapsk'sit *ai* smooth and round

musika:sit *ai* undress

musika:tu *ti* skin; strip; clean

musike:k *ai, ii* bare; empty; clear

musikiskw sky

musikn moss

musiknatkuk Big Cove

musik'nja:tm *ti* strip bare

musiko:l'k *ta* strip

musiko:tlk *ta* undress; untrim

musiko:tu *ti* strip

musikp'k *ta* {jikp'k} eat clean (leaving no leftovers)

musikte:ket *ai* clear the brush or thicket

musiktm *ti* {jikpm} eat clean (leaving no leftovers)

musikunnkete:ket *ai* weed; cultivate

musikwatm *ti* smooth out [PEI]

muskansk'pit *ai* protrude [SH]

muskask'pit *ai* protrude; stick out; penetrate; exposed

muskask'tek *ii* protrude; stick out; penetrate; exposed

muski:pit *ai* run out in the open (from the thicket)

muskulkukumat *ai* uncomfortable (in the body) from the presence of a foreign or intrusive object

muskumk *ta* lick

muskusi *an* creosote; chimney flue

muskwatamit *ai* lick

muskwatm *ti* lick

muskwje:j *an* couch [BC]

musoq *an* horsefly

muspusi *an* chimney flare; soot [BR]

musqun-amu:k *ti* dark bluish [SH]

musqun-amuksit *ta* dark bluish [SH]

mussa:t *ai* coax

mussayaq *ta* coax; persuade

musse:j a little piece or bit

mussew (mussal) piece (Fr *morceau*)

mussewji:j small piece

musso:tm *ti* coax; persuade

musswan-amuksit *ai* sky blue [BR]

musuwalk *ta* lonesome for

musuwet *ai* miss; long for; lonesome

musuwey handkerchief (Fr *mouchoir*)

muta because

mutkul-pa:sit *ai* {epa:sit} kneel down

mutkul-pukuwa:sit *ai* genuflect

mutputi chair

muwin (muwinaq) *an* bear

muwine:j *an* bear cub

muwine:skw (muwi:ne:skwaq) *an* she-bear

muwinewqamiksit *ai* behave or act like a bear

muwino:mi bear grease or fat

N

na:'ikjaqan *an* glove

naji-ilajit *ai* start to pack; go get prepared or
ready

na:jijjaqan *an* glove [EG] [NB]

najijjikwat *ai* {mejjikwat} defecate; go to the
toilet

na:jikat¹ *ai* crave; desire

na:jikat² *ai* fussy (eater, dresser)

na:jikjaqan *an* glove

naji·ktanteket *ai* {ketanteket} start out to hunt and
kill [CB]

naji-m'nk'te:mat *ai* {menk'te:mqaq} go get a
haircut [BC]

naji-ne:yamk *ta* go visit

naji·npat *ai* {nepat} go to sleep

naji·ntuksiktmat *ai* {netuksikmat} set out to hunt
provisions [BR]

naji·ntukulit *ai* {netukulit} set out for provisions
[BR]

naji-puktaqane:j *an* bat (the animal)

naji-tiya:muwe:ket *ai* set out to hunt moose

naji·tko:tk (naji·tko:tm) *ai* {teko:tk} start off to
church

naji·wsket *ai* {wesket} start out to fish

naj-kluluwet *ai* {keluluwet} go ask permission (of
fiancee's parents) to get married

na:ku:set *an* {na:kwew} sun

na:ku:setewey watch; clock

na:ku:setewik *ii* sunny

na:ku:wa:sik *ii* dawn [BR]

na:kwek *ii* day; daylight

na:kwekewa:q (nakwekewa:m) *ai* paid by the
day

na:kwew day

nalakit *ai* aggressive

nalko:sit *ai* comb one's hair with a fine tooth
comb

nalqo:n *an* comb [SH]

nalsi:k'k *ta* curry; comb

nalsi:km *ti* curry; comb

namek'te:ket *ai* hoe [BC]

namek'te:kn(ey) hoe [BC]

na ms't that's all; the end

na:n five (in counting)

nanama:l'k *ta* rock (a baby)

nanamiyaq *ii* rock; swing

nanamiyaqan swing [NB]

nanamiyaqawey rocking chair; swing

nanamiyemkewey rocking chair [SH]

nanamiyet *ai* rock; swing

nanamo:qiyaq *ii* rock to and fro

nanamo:qiyet *ai* rock to and fro

nana:n food (baby talk)

na:naq (pl) *an* pair of fives (in cards)

na:newa:j *an* fifth person; five-card

na:newey *an* in fifth one

na:nijik *ai* five

nanijik *ai* five [BR]

na:nikn food (baby talk) [SH]

naninska:q *ii* fifty (in counting) [SH]

nanipunq'k *ii* five years

naniska:ql (pl) *ii* fifty

naniskeksijik (pl) *ai* fifty

nankl *ii* five

nankmiw immediately; right away

nanko:n *an* fine-tooth comb

nanko:sit *ai* comb one's hair with a fine-tooth
comb

nankwe:ket *ai* card (moose hair or wool)

nankwenawejit (nankwenawejijik) *an* baboon

nankwenawet *ai* groom; delouse

nankwenk *ta* groom; delouse

nanma:l'k *ta* rock

nanma:tu *ti* rock

nanmo:qiyaq *ii* sway

nanmo:qiyet *ai* sway

nanntunawet *ai* feel about; feel around

nanntunk *ta* feel around for

nanntun'm *ti* feel around for

nanntuwat *ai* hunt eel

nanoqoskl (pl) *ii* five in a row

nanoqosmiya:tijik (pl) *ai* five lying in a row

nanoqsijik (pl) *ai* five cylindrical shaped objects
[BR]

nanoqskekl (pl) *ii* five cylindrical shaped objects
[BR]

nanukuna:q *ii* five days

nanupe:j *an* quintuplet

napapikwa:t *ai* blind

na:pasit *ai* strung (up)

na:pas'k *ii* strung (up)

na:pawet *ai* string (beads) [BC]

napemekw (napemaq) *an* male fish [BR]

nape:w *an* rooster [BR]; male animal

nape:wi:skw *an* female animal [BR]; female fowl [SH]

napiklej *an* hook-nosed salmon (male) [RB]

na:piptme:k *ta* track

napiyoq *an* male animal [BR]

napkwetu *ti* copy

naploqqatultijik (pl) *ai* go single file; follow one another in a straight line

na:po:qon forked stick

napto:sit *ai* break even (as in gambling)

na:puktaqan snare [BR]

napu-wi:kikemkewey {ewi:kiket} camera

napu-wi:kiket *ai (an)* {ewi:kiket} draw or trace pictures; take pictures; a photographer

napu-wi:kikn *an* {ewi:kiket} photograph; picture

napu-wi:k'k *ta* {ewi:k'k} draw; trace; take a picture of

napu-wi:km *ti* {ewi:km} draw; trace; take a picture of

naqa:l'k *ta* bring to a halt; stop

naqalk *ta* leave behind

naqamasa:l'k *ta* put where it can easily be found

naqamasa:tu *ti* put where it can easily be found

naqamase:k *ii* easy (to do)

naqamasi-ikatu *ti* put where easily found [PEI]

naqana:mat *ai* drink an alcoholic beverage

naqana:pet draw water from a well

naqana:q (naqana:m) *ai* dip out

naqani:ket *ai* bail; scoop out

naqank *ta* hold back; restrain

naqan'm *ti* hold back; restrain

naqanu:salk *ta* {nusalk} wean

naqanu:set *ai* {nuset} babysit

naqap (naqapaq) *an* slave; servant

na:qapa:l'k *ta* easily fool [ESK]

naqa:sit *ai* halt; stop

naqasu:putuwalk *ta* blow out; extinguish

naqasu:putuwatm *ti* blow out; extinguish

naqasuwa:l'k *ta* extinguish; put out

naqasuwa:m *ti* douse or put out (a fire) with a water hose

naqasuwa:tu *ti* extinguish; put out

naqasuwete:k *ta* beat out (a fire)

naqasuwete:m *ti* beat out (a fire)

naqasuweteskaq *ta* stamp out (a fire)

naqasuweteskm *ti* stamp out (a fire)

naqasuwi-putuwalk *ta* blow out (with breath) [SH]

naqa:tu *ti* bring to a halt; stop

naqji:sit *ai* underweight; light [PEI]

na:qokum (na:qokumaq) *an* (ice) skate

na:qoqum *ti* put on; don

naqsi-nijkik *ii* heal quickly

naqsi-nijkit *ai* heal quickly

naqsi·npat *ai* {nepat} sleep easily or without trouble

naqsi-o:pla:l'k *ta* easily hurt or harm

naqsi-o:pla:tu *ti* easily hurt or harm

naqsi·pkisink *ai* {pekisink} arrive early; arrive ahead of time

naqsi-tetapuwa:l'k *ta* easily please; easily or quickly correct

naqsi-tetapuwa:tu *ti* easily please; easily or quickly correct

naqsun *an* mat [SH]; mattress [SH]; bedsheet

naqte:k *ta* bring to a halt; stop (by nudging); interrupt

naqte:m *ti* bring to a halt; stop (by nudging); interrupt

naqtm *ti* leave behind

na:qum *an* (ice) skate

nasa:l'k *ta* put on; don

na:sapa:qam *ti* screw on [SH]

nasapaqam *ti* groove [SH]

nasapaqq *ta* groove [SH]

nasapaqtesink *ai* entangled

nasapaqtesk *ii* entangled

nasapaqteskm *ti* catch a tune [BR]

nasaqomkikwat *ai* fit a handle in or on (an axe or hammer)

nasa:tu *ti* put on; don

naseket *ai* fasten

nasiyet *ai* plate (Fr *l'assiette, une assiette*)

naskaq *ta* wear

naskm *ti* wear

nasko:l'k *ta* store; put away [SH]; divide (in bulk)

naskoqte:k *ta* split lengthwise (with a heavy blow)

naskoqte:ket *ai* split wood

naskoqte:m *ti* split lengthwise (with a heavy blow)

naskoqwa:l'k *ta* split (with the hand)

naskoqwa:tu *ti* split (with the hand)

nasko:tu *ti* store; put away [SH]; divide (in bulk)

naskwa:l'k *ta* halve; divide in half

naskwa:tatijik (pl) *ai* share
naskwa:tu *ti* halve; divide in half
naskwina:l'k *ta* split; tear
naskwina:tu *ti* split; tear
naskwine:k *ai, ii* split
naskwoqs'k *ta* slice in half
naskwoqsm *ti* slice in half
nasoqwa:taqan ring
naspit *ai* attached; enmeshed
nasplutaq *ta* repeat after
nassaputaqan earring
nassi:k'k *ta* scrape; curry; comb
nassi:km *ti* scrape; curry; comb
nassi:kwalk *ta* scrape (as a frying pan)
nassi:kwatm *ti* scrape (as a frying pan)
nassikwet *ai* go check traps
nastaqo:tlk *ta* hitch up (a horse)
nastek *ii* attached; enmeshed
nastesmk *ta* catch by hook or gill net; jig
nastestu *ti* catch by hook or gill net; jig
nasuwoqkaq *ta* straddle
nasuwoqkat *ai* astraddle
nasuwoqkm *ti* straddle
nasuwoqpa:sit *ai* get astride or astraddle
nasuwoqpit *ai* sit or set astride
nasuwoq-pukuwa:sit *ai* stand astride or astraddle
nasuwoqtek *ii* sit or set astride
nata:-lukwet *ai* {elukwet} good worker
nata:matnakket *ai* {matnakket} know how to fight
na tami somewhere
natanku:sit *ai* go selling or peddling
natankuwat *ai* go buying
nata:n'mat *ai* a handyman; a jack of all trades
natapuluwit *ai* go moose hunting [ESK]
na:taqama:l'k *ta* bring ashore
na:taqama:sit *ai* go ashore
na:taqama:tu *ti* bring ashore
nata:suteket *ai (an)* a good advier
nata:tawet *ai* {etawet} know how to beg
nata:toqtet *ai* {etoqtet} know how to bake
natawa:q (natawa:m) *ai* know how to swim
natawa:qa:l'k *ta* know how to do or handle; competent in
natawa:qa:tu *ti* know how to do or handle; competent in

natawatuwet *ai* know how to make a speech
natawe:k *ai* know how to get by; know one's way around; wordly wise; clever
natawinsku:mat *ai* always have an answer
natawintoq (natawintu) *ai* know how to sing; a good singer
nata:wisuwateket *ai* {ewisuwateket} know how to cook
natawi·tplu:teket *ai* {teplu:tm} have sound judgement
natawoqsawet *ai* know how to cook
na te:l over there [CB]
nat·kimk *ta* {ekimk} send for; order
nat·kiteket *ai* {ekiteket} order; send for
nat·kitm *ti* {ekitm} send for; order
nat koqwey something
na tliyaq *ii* {teliyaq} so be it; amen
na tmk first of all; in the beginning
na to:q it is said (that); it shall be so; all right; OK.
natqa:l'k *ta* remove from the water
natqapilawet *ai* pull out of the water by a rope or fish line
natqapilk *ta* reel or rope in (from the water)
natqapil'm *ti* reel or rope in (from the water)
natqa:piyet *ai* pull a net from the water
natqa:sit *ai* get out of the water
natqa:tu *ti* remove from the water
nat-telaq *ta* start off to buy or purchase
nat-tel'm *ti* start off to buy or purchase
natteskaq *ta* go after; chase
natteskm *ti* go after; chase
na tujiyu at that time
na tumk at first; in the beginning [CB]
natuptu *ti* go lug
natuptulk *ta* go lug
nat wen someone
nawaka:l'k *ta* halve [SH]
nawaka:tu *ti* halve [SH]
naw'n'k *ta* fail to reach
naw'n'm *ti* fail to reach
naw'nsewk *ta* carry for
nawska:l'k *ta* divide in half [SH]
nawswoqwa:t *ai* split open [SH]
nekapakwe:k *ai* blind [SH] [NB]
nekapikwa:l'k *ta* blind (with a light)
nekapikwa:t *ai* blind

nekapikwe:k *ai* blind [BC]
nekaqan *an* measure; ruler
ne:kaski:kn log (before being cut into specified lengths)
ne:kaw always [SH]
ne:kayiw always [CB]
neket those
ne:ki·ksma:l'k *ta* {kesma:l'k} push all the way
ne:ki·ksma:tu *ti* {kesma:tu} push all the way
nekkw'l *ii* four
nekla those; that (obviative)
nekm he; she; him; her
nekmewey *an* in his; hers; its
nekmow they; them
nekmowowey *an* in theirs
nekoqpit *ai* lie underneath [SH]
nekoqtek *ii* lie underneath [SH]
ne:kow all the time; always
nekulpit *ai* sit or set in the bottom of a canoe [BR]
nekulq'pit *ai* sit or set in a canoe [BR]
nekulq'tek *ii* sit or set in a canoe [BR]
nekultek *ii* sit or set in the bottom of a canoe [BR]
nekwasa:l'k *ta* put underneath [BR]
nekwa:satu *ti* put underneath [BR]
nekwi·ksma:l'k *ta* {kesma:l'k} push underneath [SH]
nekwi·ksma:tu *ti* {kesma:tu} push underneath [SH]
ne:kwt one (in counting) [BR]
nekwt one (in counting) [BR]
nekwta:'ik *ii* one dollar [BR]
nekwta'ikewey one-dollar bill [SH]
nekwtapskek *ii* one (of something round and solid) [BR]
nekwtapsk'sit *ai* one (of something round and solid) [BR]
nekwte:jit *ai* one [BR]; alone [BR]
nekwte:jk *ii* one [BR]; alone [BR]
nekwti-kisk'k one day [BR]
nekwtinska:q ten (in counting) [BR]
nekwtipuna:t *ai* one year old [BR]
nekwtitpa:q *ii* one night [BR]
nekwtmalsewk *ta* interpret [BR]
nekwtmalsewuti interpretation [BR]
nekwt sa:q once long ago; once upon a time [SH]
nekwtukna:q *ii* one day [BR]

ne:le:k *ai* inquisitive; meddlesome
nemakwe:kn hoe [SH]
nemaqt hill [SH]
nemaqt'ji:j hummock [SH]
nemijkami: (voc) gramps (term of respect for an old man)
nemi:k *ta* see
nemiskaq *ta* go get; fetch
nemiskm *ti* go get; fetch
nemiteket *ai* see; have eyesight
nemitu *ti* see
nemja:sit *ai* rise (from a prone position) [BR]
nem'k'te:ket *ai* furrow or drill
nemkwet *ai* have a drink (of an alcoholic beverage)
nenaq *ta* know; recognize
nenaqa:sit *ai* hurry off; hurry up
nenaqe:k *ai* in a hurry
nenaqji:jit *ai* light (in weight)
nenaqji:jk *ii* light (in weight)
nenestawe:k *ai, ii* delicate; timid; sickly
nenja:sit *ai* rise (from a prone position) [SH]
nenk'tesink *ai* tremble; shiver; vibrate
nenk'tesk *ii* tremble; shiver; vibrate
nen'm *ti* know; recognize
nenmuwe:k *ai, ii* damp
nenuwi-te:l'mk *ta* {tel-te:l'mk} respect [BR]; aware of; know and respect [BC]
nenuwi-te:tm *ti* {tel-te:tm} respect [BR]; aware of; know and respect [BC]
nepa:ji:jit *ai* take a nap
nepa:l'k *ta* put to sleep
nepapikwa:t *ai* blind [SH]
nepapimk insomnia [BC]
nepapit *ai* have insomnia [BC]
ne:pa:q *ta* kill
nepaq *ii* sleep; asleep
nepaqt'k (nepaqtm) *ai* stingy
nepasma:sit *ai* lie down to sleep
nepat *ai* sleep; asleep
ne:patat *ai (an)* a slaughterer; a butcher
ne:pateket *ai (an)* a murderer
ne:patu *ti* earn wages; obtain meat
nepe:k *ai* temperamental; touchy; easily agitated or offended; thin-skinned; delicate in health; nervous
nepilk *ta* cure; heal

nepiteket *ai (an)* a curer or healer
nepitm *ti* cure; heal
nepjit *ai* dead (a domestic animal) [BC]
nepk *ai* dead
nepm'kewey alame:s funeral mass [BC]
nepsluwat *ai* have a raised tail
neps'tkwa:l'k *ta* raise or lift up; bring up (a child)
neps'tkwa:tu *ti* raise or lift up; bring up (a child)
nepuwitewey alames funeral mass
nesa'ikl three dollars
nesalsit *ai* frightened of the dark [BC]
nesamuqawat *ai* drink
nesapskekl (pl) *ii* three round (globular) objects
nesapsk'sijik (pl) *ai* three round (globular) objects
nesa:ql (pl) *ii* three round (cylindrical) objects
nesaqpijik (pl) *ai* three flat (sheetlike) objects
nesaqtekl (pl) *ii* three flat (sheetlike) objects
nesawet *ai* timid [SH]; easily frightened
nesikateskmaq *ta* trip
nesi-kisk'k *ii* three days [BR]
nesinska:q jel si:st thirty-three (in counting) [BR]
nesipunqek *ii* three years
ne:sisijik *ai* three (of them)
nesiska:q je si:st thirty-three (in counting)
ne:siskl *ii* three (of them)
nesitpa:q *ii* three nights
neskaq *ta* console
neska:wet dance Indian style; dance and chant ceremonially [PEI]
neskawet *ai* offer condolences; join in the bereavement; console
nesoqsijik (pl) *ai* three round (cylindrical) objects
nespatalk (nespatal) *ai* eat (while otherwise occupied)
nespatejimk *ta* drag along with
nespatejitu *ti* drag along with
nespit *ai* temporarily substitute or fill in for; babysit or look after for; act as a caretaker
nespiw at the same time [CB]
nespnk *ta* take along
nespn'm *ti* take along
nessapoqwat *ai* lap (up)
nessaputaqan earring [BC]
nessasit *ai* frightened of the dark
nesssutmasewk *ta* interpret; speak for
nestaq *ta* understand

nestasit *ai* understand [BC]
nest'k (nestm) *ai* understand
nestmalsewet *ai (an)* an interpreter [BC]
nestmalsewuti interpretation [SH]
nestu:tesink *ai* come back to one's senses
nestuwapukuwet *ai* speak the truth (as a preacher)
nestuwe:k *ai* normal; sensible; of sound mind
nestu:wet[1] *ai* mature; grow into maturity
nestu:wet[2] *ai* regain consciousness
nestuwimk *ta* talk sense to; offer counsel to
nestuwita:sit *ai* recollect; remember
nesukna:q *ii* three days
nesu-nemi:k *ta* take or have three of a kind
nesupe:j *an* triplet
nesutmalsewk *ta* interpret for
nesutmalsewuti interpretation; translation
netajit *ai* lonesome; homesick [SH]
netaka:l'k *ta* embarrass
netaka:sit *ai* ashamed; embarrassed
netake:k *ai* shy; bashful
netako:qona:l'k *ta* shame
ne:tapit *ai* sharp-sighted; nosey
netaqasit *ai* shameful [SH]
netaqe:k *ai* ashamed [SH]
neta:sumk *ta* manage; direct
neta:sutm *ti* manage; direct
ne:tata:sit *ai* wise; a quick thinker
ne:tata:suwaqan wisdom
netawe:k *ai* clever
netawet *ai* a good talker
netawi-a:tukwet *ai* know how to tell stories
netawi-toqtet *ai* {etoqtet} know how to cook [BR]
ne:te:k *ai* aware
netlu:sit *ai* smoky [BC]
netlu:tek *ii* smoky [BC]
ne:tma:sit *ai* make oneself the center of attention
neto:tmuwet *ai* interrupt
netuk-siktmat *ai* kill for provisions [BR]
netukulimk provisioning [BR]
netukulit *ai* get provisions; provide [SH]
netukuluwe:set *ai* provision with porcupine [BR]; provision with fowl [SH]
netukuluwo:mi hunting ground; market place [SH]
netutmat *ai* ask for money owed

netuwiskalk *ta* sell (as a pimp)

netuwisket *ai (an)* a seller; a salesman

netuwisketu *ti* sell

netuwiskewkw *ta* sell for someone (as a sales representative)

netuwoqsawet *ai* know how to cook

ne:w four (in counting)

newapalk *ta* cool off (with water)

newapatm *ti* cool off (with water)

newapskekl (pl) *ii* four solid, round (globular) objects

newapsk'sijik (pl) *ai* four solid, round (globular) objects

newasit *ai* frightened of the dark

newek *ii* cool and breezy (of the weather)

ne:wijik *ai* four

ne:wijit *ai* four [BR]

newikata:t *ai* four-legged

newinska:q forty (in counting) [BR]

newinskekipunq'k *ii* forty years [SH]

newiska:q forty (in counting)

newjoqaluwesmk *ta* air out in the wind

newjoqaluwestu *ti* air out in the wind

newjoqwa:l'k *ta* air out

newjoqwa:tu *ti* air out

newkt one (in counting)

newkta'ik *ii* one dollar

newkw'l *ii* four [BR]

new'lasink *ai* frosted (from the cold) [SH]

new'lask *ii* frosted (from the cold) [SH]

ne:wowa:j *an* fourth one; four-card

ne:wowey fourth one; Thursday

news'k *ii* breezy; draughty

newt one (in counting)

newta'ik one dollar

newtalqikwat *ai* one-eyed

newt-amu:k *ii* one color; a flush (in poker)

newt-amuksit *ai* one color; a flush (in poker)

newtanqasit *ai* one (of something thin and flat)

newtanqek *ii* one (of something thin and flat)

newtapskek *ii* one (of something round and solid)

newtapsk'sit *ai* one (of something round and solid)

newte: one (with inanimate nouns)

newte:jit *ai* one; alone

newte:jk *ii* one; alone

newtikata:lukwet *ai* stand or slide on one leg

newtikatat *ai* have one leg or foot

newtikit *ai* an only child [CB]

newti·nqana:mat *ai* {naqana:mat} drink alone

newtiptnat *ai* {npitn} have one hand

newtipuk *ii* all winter; one winter

newtipunqek *ii* one year

newtiska:qawa:j *an* tenth person; ten-card

newt-nemi:k *ai* one kind

newtoqsit *ai* one (of something long and narrow, cylindrical)

newtuko:pj *an* loner

newtukwa:lukwet *ai* {elukwet} alone; a bachelor; single

newtumqwanet *ai* drink a beverage; drink an alcoholic beverage

newtu-nemi:kl (pl) *in* of one kind

newtu-nemiksijik (pl) *an* of one kind

newtunk *ta* have one

newtuwi:kasit *ai (an)* have a single mark; ace card

newtuwi:kas'k *ii* have a single mark; ace card

newukulasink *ai* moist underneath

ne:yamk *ta* check up on; call upon (for a visit)

ne:yamklek *ii* appear as or in a blaze

ne:yamklet *ai* appear as or in a blaze

ne:yamukwa:l'k *ta* make or cause to appear

ne:yamukwa:tu *ti* make or cause to appear

ne:yaptm *ti* check up on; call upon (for a visit)

ne:yapukuwa:sit *ai* make a brief appearance (on foot)

ne:yaseniket *ai* shine through (as the sun)

neyasiskowey marie copain (a medicinal salve)

ne:ya:sit *ai* appear; show up

ne:ya:s'k *ii* appear; show up

ne:ya:ta:q *ai* shine through [SH]

nijinj (nijinjik) *an* roe; seed; pit

nijkik *ii* heal

nijkit *ai* heal

nikana:sit *ai* walk ahead

nikani·kjitekewinu *an* {kejiteket} prophet [BC]

nikani·ksma:l'k *ta* {kesma:l'k} push ahead

nikani·ksma:tu *ti* {kesma:tu} push ahead

nikani-kuwiyaq *ii* {kewiyaq} fall forward [BR]

nikani-kuwiyet *ai* {kewiyet} fall forward [BR]

nikani-ta:suwinu *an* {tel-ta:sit} seer

nikani-te:tm *ti* {tel-te:tm} have foresight; think ahead about
nikanpit *ai* ahead
nikan-pukuwit *ai (an)* leader [CB]
nikantek *ii* ahead
nikant'ko:sit *ai* comb one's hair
nikantuk (loc) in front
nikantuko:n *an* large-toothed comb
nikattuko:n *an* large-toothed comb [SH]
nike: now
nikik *ii* sprout
nikit *ai* sprout
nikiyajiw *an* calf moose [SH]
nikjapnkwewj *an* grasshopper [BC]
nikoq eel spear [BR]
nikoqji:j[1] *an* a slim person [BC]
nikoqji:j[2] small two-pronged spear
nikoqji:j wikatat *ai* {nkat} bow-legged
nikoqol eel spear
niktu:sit *ai (an)* the human crotch [BR]
niktuwa:l'k *ta* separate; form into a crotch
niktuwa:sit *ai* form a crotch; divide
niktuwa:s'k *ii* form a crotch; divide
niktuwa:taqan separation
niktuwa:tijik (pl) *ai* separate; go separate ways
niktuwa:tu *ti* separate; form into a crotch
niktuwe:k *ai, ii* divided; separated; forked
niktuwikit *ai* shaped like a crotch
niktuwikk *ii* shaped like a crotch
niktuwoqonej *an* spike-horn bull (two points) [SH]
nikwenk *ta* grow; raise
nikwen'm *ti* grow; raise
ni:laje:k *ai* approachable; personable; friendly [BC]; open [BC]
ni:n *an* me
ninen we (exclusive); us (exclusive)
ninenewey *an, in* ours (exclusive)
ni:newey *an, in* mine
ninnjin-jakej *an* saltwater crab (used as a fertilizer for potatoes) [RB]
nipapit *ai* stay awake all night
nipi *an* leaf (of a tree); leaf (of paper); vegetable leaf
nipi-alasutmamk midnight mass [SH]
nipi-a:sutmamk midnight mass
nipisoqon brush; switch [BC]
nipitkwe:kn (table) fork [SH]

nipk *ii* summer
nipn last summer
nipniku:s *an* June
nipnuk next summer
nipukt forest; woods
nipuktukewe:sn *an* woodsman
nisa:kwa:sit *ai* bend head down [BC]; stoop down
nisa:l'k *ta* take down; bring down
nisaqalk *ta* throw down [BR]; shove down
nisaqan weir [SH]
nisaqtu *ti* throw down [BR]; shove down
nisa:sit *ai* descend
nisateja:lukwet *ai* slide down
nisa:tu *ti* take down; bring down
niseka:l'k *ta* pull down
niseka:tu *ti* pull down
niseket *ai* hurl down
nisi·ksma:l'k *ta* {kesma:l'k} push down
nisi·ksma:tu *ti* {kesma:tu} push down
nisimisqanaw (nisimisqanaq) *an* cocoon [BC]
nisiyaq *ii* fall down
nisiyet *ai* fall down
Niskam *an* God; Lord
niskusuwa:'it *ai* descend [SH]
niskusuwa:sit *ai* descend [SH]
niskusuwet *ai* climb down; descend
nisnk *ta* hoist down
nisn'm *ti* hoist down
nisnusit *ai* lower self (by hand); stoop; squat
niso:piyet *ai* swing down
nisoqpit *ai* point down (something of length)
nisoqtek *ii* point down (something of length)
nispilk *ta* lower (by rope)
nispil'm *ti* lower (by rope)
nissink *ai* land; descend
niss'k *ii* land; descend
nistelaq *ta* shoot down
nistel'm *ti* shoot down
nitapji:j *an* little (male) friend (also an exclamation of surprise)
ni:taqa:t *ai* recuperate
niwa:l'k *ta* dry out
niwa:sit *ai* get or become dry; evaporate
niwa:s'k *ii* get or become dry; evaporate
niwa:tu *ti* dry out
niwe:k *ai, ii* dry

niwetek *ii* dry tide
niwi-ka:s'k *ta* wipe dry
niwi-ka:sm *ti* wipe dry
niwi·pskuna:t *ai* {epskuninet} crave fluid
niwoqsit *ai* dried out (from heat)
niwoqtek *ii* dried out (from heat)
niya:sikowey a kind of salve
n'kaqan *an* ruler; tape measure
n'ke: now
nkijewiktuk (loc) on the maternal side
nklu:tew smoke
n'ku: now
nkuta:pewj *an* a solitary person [BC]
nkutey too; also; just like; same as; specifically
nkutilj *an* bachelor; spinster
nkuto:pj: *an* loner; solitary one; bachelor
nkutuko:pj *an* loner; bachelor; recluse
n'me:j *an* fish
n'me:ji:j *an* herring; any small fish
n'me:j'kowinu *an* fisherman
n'me:juwet *ai* fish [SH]
n'me:juwo:q *an* fish tank or bowl
nmi: (kiju:) (voc) granny! (also used as a term of affection for an older woman)
n'mispaqan switch
n'mispaqan-te:k *ta* beat with a switch
n'mispaqan-te:m *ti* beat with a switch
n'm'k'te:kn hoe
n'm'ntawa:l'k *ta* twist
n'm'ntawa:tu *ti* twist
n'm'ntoqopqa:l'k *ta* pinch
n'mtawa:tu *ti* pinch
n'mtm-jakej *an* crab
n'mtm'tqa:luwe:l (pl) pincers
n'mtm'tqa:luwet *ai* pinch
nmu:j (nmu:jik) *an* dog
nmu:ji:jmit *ai* have pups
nmu:ju:pa:q *ii* neap tide; dog tide
nnaqanatkw handle; axe handle
nnim too much! (an exclamation)
n'nkaqan measurement
n'nkatikn pound (of weight)
nnu *an* Indian
nnu a:sutmamk Indian mass
nnu saqamaw (nnu saqamaq) *an* Indian chief
nnu:skw *an* Indian lady

nnutesink *ai* dance Indian style
nnuwe:kati Indian village (reserve)
nnuweyey pertaining to Indians
nnu wipi Indian paddle [CB]
nnuwi:sit *ai* talk Indian; talk Micmac
nnu-wi:tm *ti* {ewi:tm} call, say in Micmac (in Indian)
nnuwoqta:w *an* (human) statue
no:q'q (no:qm) *ai* cough
noqt'k (noqtm) *ai* gag (as on food); choke
notqwi-jijikwe:jit *ai* insufficiently narrow
notqwi-jijikwe:jk *ii* insufficiently narrow
npisoqon switch (from a tree) [SH]
npisun medicine
npo:qon {nepat} bed
npuwaqan {nepk} death
npuwinu *an* {nepk} corpse
npuwinu'ulkw {nepk} hearse
npuwowin *an* shaman [CB]
nqana:paqsun *an* {naqana:pet} well bucket [NB]
nqani:kn *an* {naqani:ket} scoop; dip net
nqani:kuwom shelter; stable
nqano:pati {naqana:pet} well (of water)
nqa:sit *ai* {naqa:sit} stop
nqa:s'k *ii* {naqa:s'k} stop
nsa:mskw (nsa:mskuk) *an* three-year-old beaver [BR]
nsanoqon danger
nsanoqonik *ii* dangerous
nsanoqonit *ai* dangerous
nska:waqan {neskawet} ceremonial dance [BC]
ns'tnaqan *an* orphan
nsukwi: (voc) aunty!
n't who? (a question particle)
ntaqo:pj *an* {netaqe:k} a shy person (pejorative)
ntaqo:qon {netaqe:k} shame; disgrace
ntlu:tew smoke [BR]
ntuksuwinu *an* {netukulit} hunter; provider [SH]
nu: (voc) father! [BR]
nuja:kitteket *ai (an)* a sawyer
nuj-aknutmewinu *an* {aknutmaq} lawyer
nuja:q (nuja:m) *ai (an)* a swimmer
nujatejo:l'k *ta* pull; twitch (in logging)
nujatejo:ta:sit (nujatejo:ta:sijik) *ai (an)* a twitcher (person who, with a horse, pulls a log from the woods to a sawmill)
nujatejo:tasit *ai* delivery man

nujatejo:teket *ai* twitch or pull (logs)
nujatejo:tu *ti* pull; twitch (in logging)
nujeyaq *ta* in charge of; responsible for; handle
nuji·pskutuwe:muwet *ai (an)* {peskutuwe:k} a shaver [BC]
nuji·wsiket *ai (an)* {wesiket} a fortune-teller [SH]
nuji-alapit *ai (an)* a watchman; one who moves about
nuji-amalkat *ai (an)* a dancer
nuji-asiketk (nuji-asiketm) *ai (an)* a teamster
nuji-elutuwet *ai (an)* {elutaq} an imitator; an impersonator
nuji-ewjo:l'k *ta* haul
nuji-ewjo:tasit (nuji-ewjo:tasijik) *ai (an)* hauler
nuji-ewjo:teket *ai* haul
nuji-ewjo:tu *ti* haul
nuji-ilsuteket *ai (an)* a judge
nuji-keluwet *ai (an)* {keluluwet} a matchmaker [SH]
nuji:kik (pl) *ta* make professionally
nuji-kina:muwet *ai (an)* a teacher; an educator
nuji-kina:muwo:kuwom school [NB]
nuji-k'luluwet *ai (an)* {keluluwet} a matchmaker [BC]
nuji-koqqwa:luwet *ai (an)* koqqwa:l'k} a wrestler [SH]; a repossesser
nuji·ksmoqja:teket *ai (an)* {kesmoqja:tu} a foreman
nuji·ktu:muwet *ai (an)* {ketu:k} an entertainer (with musical instrument)
nuji·kwsiket *ai (an)* {kwesiket} a fortune-teller
nuji·kwtapet *ai (an)* {kwetapet} a diver [BR]
nuji-mattaqa:teket *ai (an)* a (church) bell ringer [BC]
nuji-milamukwa:teket *ai (an)* a magician; the one who puts things in every direction; a painter
nuji-milapulkikwa:teket *ai (an)* an illusionist
nuji-mila:teket *ai (an)* a joker, prankster or jester
nujimk *ta* an advisor to; the one who advises
nuji-m'mk'te:muwet *ai (an)* {memk'te:maq} a haircutter [BC]; barber [BC]
nuji-m'napita:teket *ai (an)* {menapita:teket} a dentist; take out teeth [PEI]
nujimuwet *ai (an)* an advisor
nuji-ne:pateket *ai (an)* an executioner
nuji·nket (nuji·nkejik) *ai (an)* {enket} a scaler (in lumbering)

nuji·npisuniket *ai (an)* {npisun} a charmer
nuji·npiteket *ai (an)* {nepiteket} a healer
nuji·ns'pit *ai (an)* {nespit} a babysitter; a housekeeper
nujintoq (nujintu) *ai (an)* a singer
nujintus *an* person who is barren or sterile
nuji·ntuwisket *ai (an)* {netuwisket} a peddler; a salesman
nuji·nutmaqaneket *ai (an)* {nutmat} a tattletale; a gossiper; a storyteller
nuji-pejo:l'k *ta* conduct; chauffeur [SH]
nuji-pestunk *ai (an)* a preacher
nuji-pipukwet *ai (an)* a musician; a whistler; a horn blower
nuji:pit *ai (an)* a runner (professional)
nuji-pi:tupet *ai (an)* a bartender
nuji-pkwateliket *ai (an)* {pekwateliket} a buyer or purchaser
nuji-postewit *ai (an)* a marriage (or divorce) broker; the one who acts as a go-between (in marriage or divorce)
nuji-putaqiket *ai (an)* a butcher
nuji-sa:se:wamukwa:teket *ai (an)* a magician; the one who changes things or colors
nujitat *ai* suck
nuji-tmastaqte:muwet *ai (an)* {temastaqte:muwet} a hairdresser [BC]
nuji-toqtet *ai (an)* {etoqtet} a baker (professional)
nujitu *ti* make professionally
nuji-wsuwa:teket *ai (an)* {wesuwa:teket} a policeman (the one who takes hold of you)
nujjewiktuk (loc) on my paternal side
nujkima:q *ii* melt [SH]
nujkma:q *ii* melt
nujkma:t *ai* melt
nujkmoqsit *ai* melt (through heating)
nujkmoqs'k *ta* soften; melt
nujkmoqsm *ti* soften; melt
nujkmoqtek *ii* melt (through heating)
nujo:teket *ai (an)* a witness (at a wedding)
nujo:tm *ti* in charge of; responsible for; handle; foretell (the weather) [CB]
nujumu *an* person who has gastric tuberculosis
nujumuwit *ai* have gastric tuberculosis
nukjaqa:l'k *ta* squash
nukjaqa:tu *ti* squash
nukjaqteskaq *ta* stomp to bits

nukjaqteskm *ti* stomp to bits
nuksaqatew (nuksaqatal) charcoal
nuks'k *ta* cut into pieces
nuksm *ti* cut into pieces
nukte:k *ta* smash to bits
nukte:m *ti* smash to bits
nukteskaq *ta* crush or soften (with the feet)
nukteskm *ti* crush or soften (with the feet)
nuktoqtejkwej *an* maid; servant; housemate [SH]
nukumi: (voc) granny!
nukwa:kipulk *ta* grind; tenderize
nukwa:kittu *ti* grind; tenderize
nu:kwa:l'k *ta* burn
nukwa:l'k *ta* soften; crumble [BR]
nukwaltukwo:sit *ai* comb one's hair with a coarse tooth comb
nukwa:luwejkewey cattail
nu:kwa:q *ii* burn
nu:kwa:qewey inflammable substance
nu:kwa:t *ai* burn
nu:kwa:tu *ti* burn
nukwa:tu *ti* soften; crumble [BR]
nukwe:k *ai, ii* soft
nunalk *ta* suck
nunaqapem *an* servant
nunat *ai* suck; suckle
nunatm *ti* suck
nune:s *an* freak
nune:sm *an* homosexual
nunmaqek *ii* incline; slope
nunmaqet *ai* incline; slope
nunmi-p'sit *ai* {epsit} lukewarm
nunmi-p'tek *ii* {eptek} lukewarm
nunu:n *an* nipple
nunuskwet *ai* breast-feed [BC]
nusalk *ta* suckle (an infant)
nuse:kn poker (for fireplace)
nuseskwet *ai (an)* a nurser; a breastfeeder
nuset *ai* breast-feed
nusknikn bread [PEI]
nussaqiket *ai (an)* a clerk
nuta:lutewey tugboat
nuta:lutm *ti* tow (by boat)
nutamk *ta* observe [BC]
nutanteket *ai (an)* a hunter; a killer; a hater [SH]
nutapit *ai* scout (around)

nutapteket *ai (an)* an observer [BC]; a coroner
nutaptm *ti* observe [BC]
nutaq *ai* hear
nutateji:pulk *ta* deliver
nutateji:putasit *ai (an)* a delivery man
nutateji:puteket *ai (an)* a delivery man
nutateji:putu *ti* deliver
nutatijo:tasit *ai (an)* a twitcher [PEI]
nutaw'lalk *ta* backpack
nutaw'latm *ti* backpack
nu:te:n'maqan campfire
nutkul-papatiket *ai* scrub (on one's hands and knees)
nutkul-pa:sit *ai* {epa:sit} kneel down
nutkul-pit *ai* {epit} kneel
nutkul-pukuwa:sit *ai* genuflect
nutm *ti* hear
nutmat *ai* hear about; hear tell
nutnawet *ai (an)* assist at mass; an altar boy
nutpet *ai (an)* tend bar; a bartender
nut-pipnet *ai (an)* {epipnet} a baker
nutputi chair
nutqwa:l'k *ta* put in an insufficient amount of; give an insufficient amount of
nutqwa:tu *ti* put in an insufficient amount of; give an insufficient amount of
nutqwe:k *ai* immature; undeveloped; a minor; naive
nutqwelk *ai, ii* inadequate; insufficient [SH]
nutsa:qaniket *ai (an)* the one who discharges or fires someone
nutsuteket *ai (an)* a director [BC]; a manager
Nuwel *an* Christmas (Fr *Noël*)
Nuwelewimk Christmas Day [SH]
Nuwelewumk Christmas Day (Fr *Noël*)

o:piyamiw way over

o:pl-aknutmajik (pl) *ai* have a disagreement

o:pla:l'k *ta* do wrong

opla:sik *ii* go wrong

opla:sit *ai* go wrong

o:platalk *ai* eat wrong; eat improperly; eat unappetizing food

o:pla:teket *ai* do wrong

o:pla:tu *ti* do wrong

o:ple:k *ai* do wrong; become pregnant (out of wedlock)

o:pli-mijisit *ai* eat improperly [SH]

o:plisqatesink *ai* sprained; disjointed

o:plisqatesk *ii* sprained; disjointed

o:plisqatestu *ti* sprain

o:pli-w'naqto:sit *ai* {wenaqto:sit} skip wrong [SH]

o:pl-te:k *ta* hit wrong; chop wrong

o:pl-te:m *ti* hit wrong; chop wrong

o:pl-wi:t'k *ta* {ewi:t'k} say or name wrong

o:pl-wi:tm *ti* {ewi:tm} say or name wrong

oqolumkwa:sit *ai* bend from the waist; get into a prone position

oqomk *ta* take leave of [SH]

oqon faggot; bundle of sticks (used for fuel) [SH]

oqonaliyaq *ii* snow-covered

oqonaliyet *ai* snow-covered

oqoniskwa:l'k *ta* cover

oqoniskwa:tu *ti* cover

oqonisqopilk *ta* wrap; cover

oqonisqopil'm *ti* wrap; cover

oqonitpaqiyaq *ii* get dark

oqono-qopisaqan {qopisun} wrapper; bundle (for an infant)

oqono-qopiso:tlk *ta* {qopisun} place a hood on (an infant)

oqopekiyaq salt water scum

oqopisaqan wrapper; bundle (for an infant) [SH]

oqopisit *ai* wrapped up; bundled (as an infant)

oqoskijikuwek *ii* cling; stick

oqoskijikuwet *ai* cling; stick

oqote:tut (voc) friends! (a greeting) [CB]

oqoti (voc) dear! (term of affection between husband and wife); friend!; that which clings or sticks

oqotqomk *ta* tease (about a member of the opposite sex); accuse of being an accomplice

oqotuwalk *ta* cling to [BC]

oqotuwatm *ti* cling to [BC]

oqpi:kanjek Eel River Bar [RB]

oqtatqa:tu *ti* put into drydock [SH]

oqtuwet *ai* cling [BC]

oqwa:q *ii* arrive; land; dock

oqwasa:tu *ti* beach (a canoe) [CB]

oqwa:t *ai* arrive; land; dock

oqwatk *ii* northwind

oqwatn north

oqwatqikan lean-to [SH]

oti (voc) friend!

P

pa'itepeka:sit *ai* overflow
pa'itepeka:s'k *ii* overflow
pajiji-klulk *ii* {kelu:lk} extremely good or nice; the best [SH]
pajiji-klu:sit *ai* {kelu:sit} extremely good or nice; the best [SH]
pajiji-ksma:l'k *ta* {kesma:l'k} push too hard
pajiji-ksma:tu *ti* {kesma:tu} push too hard
pajiji-piley *an, in* newest one
pajiji-winjik *ii* extremely bad; the worst [SH]
pajiji-winjit *ai* extremely bad; the worst [SH]
pajit-peka:sit *ai* overflow [SH]
pajit-peka:s'k *ii* overflow [SH]
pajjaqamat *ai* exaggerate; overdo; boast; brag
pa:ke:k *ai* sober
Pa:kewimk Easter [SH]
Pa:kewumk Easter (Fr *Pâques*)
pa:kitnet *ai* have a nosebleed [PEI]
pako:si waterlily (type of) [PEI]
pakwejk *ii* shallow water
pa:le'ewe:l (pl) barley
palltaqan gunwale (of a boat)
pa:mikli *an* a kind of tree (related to the ash; grows near the water)
pa na even so; just so
pana same as; just like; just so
pana:l'k *ta* open
pana:sit *ai* open up
pana:s'k *ii* open up
panatqa:sit *ai* come out of the woods
pana:tu *ti* open
panawijqanawet *ai* search
pane-kiskiyaq *ii* clear up (of clouds or fog)
paneta:q *ii* open or clear up (of the sky)
paniyanuk (loc) at the end of the snow period; next summer [PEI]
paniyaq *ii* end of the snow period
panjaskiyet *ai* fall back with legs outspread
pansaqam *ti* unlock
pansaqq *ta* unlock
pans'k *ta* cut open; operate on
pansm *ti* cut open; operate on
panta:l'k *ta* open up
panta:tu *ti* open up
pantepit *ai* open
pantetek *ii* open
pantuna:sit *ai* {ntun} open one's mouth

pantunepit *ai* {ntun} have one's mouth open
papewo:kwet *ai* talk nonsense; tell jokes
papimk joking
papit *ai* amuse oneself; joke
papitaqan toy
papitaqane:kati festival grounds (present Restigouche territory)
papka:l'k *ta* take to the east
papka:lukwet *ai* go downstream
papka:sit *ai* go east
papka:tu *ti* take to the east
papke:k down east
papke:kewa:j *an* down-easter
papkoqsikn jam; fruit preserve
papk'semk *ta* draw on (a pipe) [BR]; light up [SH]
papk'setmat *ai* light up (to smoke) [BR]
papk'smk *ta* draw on (a pipe) [BR]; light up [SH]
papkupsit *ai* gamble
papn-ji:j *an* spool; bobbin (Fr *bobine*)
papnsit *ai* pack a pipe [BR]
papqwa:tu *ti* strip off birchbark [SH]
papuwaqan celebration
pa:qala'ik *ai* surprised; amazed
pa:qala'imk amazement [CB]
pa:qala'iwaqan surprise; surprising news
paqa:l'k *ta* bite
paqa:luwet *ai* bite
pa:qapukuwa:l'k *ta* give confession to
pa:qapukuwatm *ti* confess
pa:qapukuwet *ai* confess
pa:qapukuwo:ti confession
paqaqamk behind; in the rear [SH]
paqasa:l'k *ta* put in the water (river)
paqasaqalk *ta* throw in the water; launch
paqasaqtu *ti* throw in the water; launch
paqasa:sit *ai* enter the water br
paqasa:tu *ti* put in the water (river)
paqasiyet *ai* drown [SH]; fall in the water
paqaste:m *ti* launch
pa:qastmat *ai* easily pick up news and gossip
paqa:tu *ti* bite
pa:qe:k downhill
paqiyatkwe'itesink *ai* stumble and fall
paqiyatkwe'itesm'k *ta* slam or throw down
paqiyatkwe'itestu *ti* slam or throw down

paqo:si water root (eaten by moose); a type of waterlily; seaweed (sometimes used as a cold remedy medicine by boiling it)

paqsikpetelaq *ta* kill instantly [PEI]

paqsikpetemit *ai* {atkitemit} burst into tears [PEI]

paqsipke'itelaq *ta* kill instantly (with a gun or bow and arrow)

paqsipk-elmit *ai* burst out laughing

paqsip-kimt'k (paqsip-kimtm} *ai* {kimtemit} burst out crying [BR]

paqsipkitemit *ai* {atkitemit} burst out crying

paqtaqamiktuk (loc) deserted area; echo place

paqtaqawa:q *ii* make an echo

paqtasit *ai* shining bright

paqtasm (paqtasmk) *an* wolf

paqtatek *ii* shining bright

paqtlusk'tek *ii* very low tide

paqt'sm (paqt'smuk) *an* wolf [BR]

paqtune'itesink *ai* fall flat on one's face

pasaltukwat *ai* have thick hair

pasapit *ai* nearsighted; have poor eyesight

pasatpat *ai* thick-headed

pase:k *ai, ii* thick

pasik only [CB]; just [CB]

pasi:tukwat *ai* have thick body or facial hair [SH]

pasi:tuwat *ai* have thick whiskers

pas'k only; just

paska:l'k *ta* crush

paskaq *ta* sit on

paska:tu *ti* crush

paske:k *ai, ii* crushed or shattered

paskesa:l'k *ta* light up; start afire

paskesa:tu *ti* light up; start afire

paskija:l'k *ta* squeeze; flatten

paskija:tu *ti* squeeze; flatten

paskina:l'k *ta* tear or rip

paskina:tu *ti* tear or rip

paskine:k *ai, ii* ripped or torn

paskinete:k *ta* split [SH]

paskinoqsit *ai* cracked (from excessive heat)

paskinoqtek *ii* cracked (from excessive heat)

paskipiyasit *ai* split or cracked (from dryness)

paskm *ti* sit on

paskoqjink *ai* cracked or split (from excessive cold)

paskoqsikn jam [BC]

paskoqsit *ai* pierced (from the heat)

paskoqtek *ii* pierced (from the heat)

paskoqt'k *ii* cracked or split (from excessive cold)

pask'semk *ta* draw on (a pipe); light up (a pipe)

pask'setmat *ai* light up; smoke

pa:sk'tek *ii* explode (a dry log on a fire, popcorn)

paskukjat *ai* cranky [SH]

paspit *ai* thick; dense; piled deep

pasp'k *ta* crush with the teeth

passoqsawet *ai* make jam

passoqsikn jam

passoqs'k *ta* make into jam

passoqsm *ti* make into jam

pastek *ii* thick; dense; piled deep

pastesink *ai* burst

pastesk *ii* burst; heavy snowfall

pastm *ti* crush with the teeth

pastun U.S.A. ("Boston")

pastunkewa:j *an* American (male)

pastunkewa:ki U.S.A.

pastunkewi:skw *an* American (female)

patalap *an* cross-eyed person

patalapit *ai* cock-eyed; cross-eyed

pataluti table [BR]

patanapjit *ai* hold on the left side

patanjuwey left hand

patank (patan'm) *ai* lefthanded

patanmit *ai* lefthanded

pata:taqan sin

pata:teket *ai* sin

pata:tekewinu *an* sinner

patatuj left side

patatujke:l toward the left

patatujo:q *an* a southpaw

pata'uti table

patkwi-alasutmaqan altar [CB]

patliks'te:wumk Saint Patrick's Day

patliya:s *an* priest (Fr *patriarche*)

patliya:si:skw (patliya:si:skwaq) *an* nun

patliyatji:j *an* cardinal (bird) [SH]; brother (religious)

pawalk *ta* want; desire; need

pawa:sit *ai* move slowly

pawa:s'k *ii* move slowly

pawatm *ti* want; desire; need

pawe:k *ai* a slowpoke; a malingerer

paw-natqa:sit *ai* get out of the water slowly

pe: hold on! (an interjection).
pe:(l) apukjik in a little while [BC]
pe: ap ta:n tujiyu some other time
pe'ikitnet *ai* have a nosebleed; bleed from the nostril
pe'ikwapit *ai* see all around
pe'ikwaqatk (pe'ikwaqatm) *ai* stay here and there
pe'ikwatek *ii* see all around
peji-jink'ja:lek *ta* squeeze unintentionally
peji-jink'ja:tu *ti* squeeze unintentionally
peji-kiskiyaq ceiling
pejikitnet *ai* bleed from the nostril
peji-kluluwet *ai* {keluluwet} arrange marriages
peji-ku:te:m *ti* {kewte:m} chop down unintentionally
pejila:'it: *ai* arrive unannounced or unexpectedly or by surprise
pejila:sit *ai* arrive unexpectedly
pejili·ksalk *ta* {kesalk} honour
peji-nuks'k *ta* slice up accidentally
peji-nuksm *ti* slice up accidentally
peji:pit *ai* come on the run
pejipuk *ii* winter arrives
pejipunmit *ai* experience winter
pejipunsit *ai* settle in for the winter
peji-sikte:k *ta* kill accidental; come to kill
peji:taqamat *ai* trip (over)
peji:taqane:'ite:k *ta* slap (on the back of the head or neck
peji:taqanete:k *ta* slap on the back of the head [PEI]
peji-tms'k *ta* {tems'k} cut (in two) accidentally
peji-tmsm *ti* {temsm} cut (in two) accidentally
pejiwsit *ai* move in to settle down
pejo:l'k *ta* bring; haul or deliver here in bulk
pejoqs'k *ta* burn unintentionally
pejoqsm *ti* burn unintentionally
pejo:tu *ti* bring; haul or deliver here in bulk
peju *an* cod
pejuwe:ket *ai* fish for cod
pejuwey cooked codfish
pekaja:l'k *ta* do neatly
pekaja:teket *ai* do correctly
pekaja:tu *ti* do neatly
pekaje:k *ai, ii* neat

pekajeyaq *ta* keep in good shape or condition
pekajo:tm *ti* keep in good shape or condition
peka:q *ii* long and straight
pekaqanqayaq *ii* grimy
pekaqanqayet *ai* grimy
pekayet *ai* shed (hair) [BC]
pekije:k *ii* a long time
pekiji-eskmalk *ta* wait a long time for
pekiji-eskmatm *ti* wait a long time for
pekijipnet *ai* suffer from a long term illness
pekisink *ai* arrive; get there
pekisitu *ti* bring or arrive with
pekisk *ii* arrive; get there
pekisulk *ta* bring or arrive with
pekisutu *ti* arrive with
pekitapek *ii* long lasting [SH]
pekitapeksik *ii* long lasting
pekitapemk *ta* use for a long time
pekitapetm *ti* use for a long time
pekita:wey map
pekitawsit *ai* live a long life
pekitewo:kwet *ai* talk a long time
pekitne:min sweetgrass ceremony [CB]
peki:t'pet *ai* tend bar [BR]
pekitqatk (pekitqatm) *ai* stay for a long time
pekittemit *ai* {atkitemit} cry for a long while
pekittoq (pekittu) *ai* arrive late
pekn'k *ii* dark (without light)
pekoqsit *ai* long and straight
pekte:s'k *ii* southwind
peku:laks the day before yesterday [BR]
pekuwik *ii* gummy; sticky
pekuwiptnat *ai* {npitn} sticky-fingered; a thief
pekuwit *ai* gummy; sticky
pekwaja:l'k *ta* dress or gut (as a fish, chicken)
pekwa:m *ti* peel
pe:kwamk *ta* see again after a long separation or absence; reminded of [PEI]
pe:kwaptm *ti* see again after a long separation or absence
pekwa:q *ta* peel
pekwatelaq *ta* buy; purchase
pekwateliket *ai* purchase; buy
pekwatel'm *ti* buy; purchase
pekwatoq (pekwatu) *ai* at fault; the cause
pekwikwalk *ta* budge; pry loose
pekwikwatm *ti* budge; pry loose

pe:kwi-n'mi:k *ta* nemi:k} seldom see
pe:kwi-n'mitu *ti* {nemitu} seldom see
pekwi:s'k *ta* patch
pekwi:sm *ti* patch
pe:l for now
pelakwet *an* parrot (Fr *perroquet*)
pela:l'k *ta* miss connecting with
pela:tu *ti* miss connecting with
peljaqan *an* mitten [SH]
pelkoqa:l'k *ta* peel by hand
pelkoqa:tu *ti* peel by hand
pelko:qiket debark
pelkoqsawet *ai* peel
pelkoqsewet *ai* peel [BR]
pelkoqsikn peeling
pelkoqs'k *ta* peel with a knife
pelkoqsm *ti* peel with a knife
pelkoqte:k *ta* strip off with an axe
pelkoqte:m *ti* strip off with an axe
Pelonik *an* Veronica (Fr *Véronique*)
pelqa:l'k *ta* peel; husk
pelqa:tu *ti* peel; husk
pelqoqte:kniket *ai* scrape the ground [SH]
pelsit *ai* pour thickly
peltek *ii* thick (as of liquids, porridge); pour thickly
pe:l tmk before all else
pema:l'k *ta* carry
pemamkuwat *ai* barter (for food) [PEI]
pemamkwe:ket *ai* pole along
pemank *ta* start to do away with
pemankuwat *ai* peddle along
peman'm *ti* start to do away with
pemapaqtesink *ai* streaked
pemapaqtesk *ii* streaked
pemapekit *ai* crawl along
pemapilawet *ai* carry by means of a rope or handle; carry by the scruff of the neck (as a cat)
pemapilk *ta* carry along in the hand (by means of rope, strap, handle, etc.)
pemapil'm *ti* carry along in the hand (by means of rope, strap, handle, etc.)
pema:q (pema:m) *ai* swim along
pemaqsink *ai* fly along
pemaqs'k *ii* fly along
pemaqteket *ai* sail along
pematalk (pematal) *ai* eat on the move
pematejimk *ta* drag along

pematejitu *ti* drag along
pema:teket *ai* a pallbearer
pematkwetesink *ai* move along nodding one's head
pematpe:pit *ai* run along with head abobbing
pematpetesink *ai* move along nodding one's head
pematqayet *ai* go through the thicket
pema:tu *ti* carry
pemaw'lalk *ta* carry along on one's back or shoulder
pemaw'latm *ti* carry along on one's back or shoulder
pemeyaq *ta* operate
pemi-jajika:sit *ai* move or walk along the shore
pemi-jajikisukwit *ai* paddle along the shore
pemi-ji:met *ai* paddle or row along
pemikate:pit *ai* {nkat} trot along
pemi-kekwi:pit *ai* run along slowly [SH]
pemikp'ta:q *ii* {elikp'ta:q} puff or smoke along
pemikp'ta:t *ai* {elikp'ta:t} puff or smoke along
pemi:kwe:k (pemi:kwe:m) *ai* swim along [SH]
pemi·mkwik *ii* {mekwik} swell [BR]
pemi·mkwit *ai* {mekwit} swell [BR]
pemi·mqapskek *ii* maqapskek} become large and round [SH]
pemi·mqapsk'sit *ai* {maqapsk'sit} become large and round [SH]
pemi·ms'ki:ka:sit *ai* {meski:k} get bigger [SH]
pemintoq (pemintu) *ai* sing along
pemi:pit *ai* run along
pemi·pqamik *ii* slide; coast or skate along
pemi·pqamit *ai* slide; coast or skate along
pemi:pukwet *ai* stagger along
pemi:puluwet *ai* ride along on horseback
pemi-qama:sit *ai* {kaqama:sit} get to one's feet [SH]
pemi-siyaw-i:pukwet *ai* {siyawiyet} stagger along by [BR]
pemi-siyaw-qo:qwek *ii* {siyawa:sit} float by [BR]
pemi-siyaw-temit *ai* {atkitemit} pass by crying [BR]
pemi·sqoqi-tukwi:k (pemi·sqoqi-tukwi:m) *ai* {so:qiyet} run up hill
pemisukwit *ai* paddle along
pemitk *ii* flow along
pemi·tke:k *ii* {teke:k} get cold (of the weather)

pemi·tkiyaq *ii* {tekiyaq} get chilly
pemi·tkiyet *ai* {tekiyet} get chilly
pemi-tma:sit *ai* {tema:sit} start to break [BR]
pemi-tma:s'k *ii* {tema:s'k} start to break [BR]
pemi-tqoju:tukwi:k (pemi·tqoju:tukwi:m) *ai*
  {toqjuwitukwi:k} run up hill; run upstairs
pemi-wikwa:smukwet *ai* whistle along [BR]
pemi-wisqi:pit *ai* sprint along [BR]
pemiyaq *ii* go or move along
pemiyet *ai* go or move along
pemja:t *ai* leap along; hop along
pem-ji:malk *ta* paddle or row along
pem-ji:matm *ti* paddle or row along
pem-ji:met *ai* paddle or row along
pe:m'k (pe:m'm) *ai* glide along in the water
pemkaq *ta* go past; pass; go over the head of
  someone in authority; promote over
pemk'k *ta* go or kick past (in time) [SH]
pemkm *ti* go past; pass; go or kick past (in time)
  [SH]; go over the head of someone in authority;
  promote over
pemkwi:tm *ti* steer along
peml'ka:t *ai* walk along [BR]
pemn'kalk *ta* carry on the shoulder
pemn'katm *ti* carry on the shoulder
pemn'ket *ai* shoulder pack
pemo:tm *ti* operate
pempa:q *ii* rise (of the tide)
pempaqto:sit *ai* splash along
pem·pa:sit *ii* {epa:sit} start to sit down
pempeka:s'k *ii* start to rise (of the tide)
pempekitk *ii* flow along
pempilk *ta* tow along
pempil'm *ti* tow along
pem-piskiyaq *ii* become twilight
pem-p'tek *ii* {eptek} start to get hot
pem-pukuwa:sit *ai* start to get back on one's
  feet; start to recover from bad times
pem-qama:sit *ai* {kaqama:sit} get to one's feet
pemqo:kwet *ai* float or drift along
pemqo:qwek *ii* float or drift along
pemsaqas'k *ii* wall
pemsaqiyaq *ii* (in) a partition [SH]
pemse:k (loc) precipice
pemsink *ai* pass by (in the air)
pem-siyaw-aqteket *ai* sail along by

pem-siyawa:sit *ai* pass by
pem-siyaw-elmit *ai* pass by laughing
pem-siyaw-qo:qwek *ii* float by
pems'k *ii* pass by (in the air)
pemta:q *ii* go by making a noise
pemtaqayet *ai* slither along
pemtemit *ai* {atkitemit} cry along
pemteskaq *ta* kick along; pass by; chase after
pemteskm *ti* kick along; pass by; chase after
pemto:kwek *ii* drift along; drift off (to sleep);
  pass out (from drinking)
pemto:kwet *ai* drift along; drift off (to sleep);
  pass out (from drinking)
pemtoqsit *ai* prattle or gab along
pem-tukwi:k (pem-tukwi:m) *ai* run along
pem-tulkomit *ai* carry concealed under the arm
pemukkwalk *ta* follow
pemukkwatm *ti* follow
pemulkwalk *ta* follow [BC]
pemulkwatm *ti* follow [BC]
penatk (penatm) *ai* lay (eggs)
peneskwit *ai* have pups [BC]; have kittens [BC]
pene:sukwa:t *ai* drool
pene:sukwati drool
penetkwit *ai* calve; foal [BC]
penikl(ewey) vinegar
penoqwe:k *ai* act disgracefully; ill-mannered;
  regarded with distain
penoqwi-te:l'mk *ta* {tel-te:l'mk} discriminate
  against; put down
penoqwitelsit *ai* act humbly; act diffidently
penoqwi-te:tm *ti* {tel-te:tm} discriminate against;
  put down
pent (pentik) *an* paint
penta:l'k *ta* paint
penta:tekewk *ta* paint for
penta:tu *ti* paint
pentoqsit *ai* make sounds; quack [SH]
pepka:'ipulk *ta* grind down; cut thin
pepka:kittu *ti* grind down; cut thin
pepka:l'k *ta* thin out (a liquid)
pepkatpat *ai* thin-headed; intelligent
pepka:tu *ti* thin out (a liquid)
pepke:jit *ai* thin
pepke:jk *ii* thin
pepkijatpat *ai* flat-headed; Pole

pepk'te:maq *ta (do)* cut someone's hair thin; crop (hair)
pepsikiyaq *ii* flexible
pepsikiyet *ai* flexible
pepsitelket *ai* rude; disrespectful
pepsi-te:l'mk *ta* rude; discourteous to
pept'skna:'it *ai* put on shoes and socks [SH]
pept'skna:sit *ai* put on shoes and socks [SH]
pepuweket *ai* shake (something)
pepuwetesink *ai* shake; tremble; vibrate
pepuwetesk *ii* shake; tremble; vibrate
pepuwetestu *ti* shake off
peqanqasita:teket *ai* get flat feet; get flatfooted [SH]
pesa:ji:jk *ii* light snow
pesa:l'k *ta* skin a fish
pesanakik *ii* snow mist [BR]
pesaq *ii* snow
pesaqanatkw moss
pesaqopska:sit *ai* let slip from the hand
pese:k *ta* smell
pesemk *ta* smell
pesetm *ti* smell
pesetu *ti* smell
pesi:k *ta* channel
pesikte:ket *ai* trim (tree branches); split wood
pesi:kukwet *ai* river drive
pesikwe'ite:k *ta* slap in the face
pesikwete:k *ta* slap in the face [PEI]
pe:sit *ai* have something in one's eye
pesitm *ti* channel
peska:l'k *ta* lead or take off the trail or road
peska:sit *ai* leave or go off the trail or road
peska:tu *ti* lead or take off the trail or road
peske:mat *ai* shave [SH]
pe:skewey gun
pe:skikek *ii* shoot
pe:skiket *ai* shoot
pe:sk'k *ta* shoot at (with a gun)
pe:skm *ti* shoot at (with a gun)
peskmat *ai* ejaculate
peskmewey *an* crucifix [SH]; holy picture or medal [SH]
pesk'tek *ii* lead off to (as a path)
pe:sk'tek *ii* fired (as a gun)
peskunatek nine (in counting)
peskunatek-te:sinska:q ninety (in counting) [BR]

peskutuwe:k *ta* shave
peskutuwe:m *ti* shave
peskutuwe:maq *ta (do)* shave [BC]
peskutuwe:mat *ai* shave [BC]
peskutuwo:sit *ai* shave oneself
peskwatalk *ai* graze (as a cow or horse)
peskwete:kemkewey sickle
peskwiyet *ai* moult; shed
peslu:teket *ai* talk high language [BR]
pesoqanatkw moss
pesoqopsk'te:k *ta* fumble; partially block; miss (in swinging at or striking at); hit a foul ball
pesoqopsk'te:m *ti* fumble; partially block; miss (in swinging at or striking at); hit a foul ball
pesoqte:k *ta* fail to hit (something aimed at)
pesoqtelaq *ta* miss (in shooting at)
pesoqtel'm *ti* miss (in shooting at)
pesoqte:m *ti* fail to hit (something aimed at)
pesoqteskaq *ta* miss; fail to meet or come into contact with
pesoqteskm *ti* miss; fail to meet or come into contact with
pesoqteskmat *ai* stumble; trip
pesqa:'ipusit *ai* chafed
pesqa:'iputek *ii* chafed
pesqa:l'k *ta* skin (an animal)
pesqate:k *ta* scrape (with an instrument)
pesqate:m *ti* scrape (with an instrument)
pesqatesm'k *ta* scrape (e.g. one's knee)
pesqatestu *ti* scrape (e.g. one's foot)
pesqayet *ai* peel (as from sunburn); shed hair [BC]
pesqojikuwek *ii* sticky [SH]
pesqojikuwet *ai* sticky [SH]
pesqojukuwek *ii* sticky
pesqojukuwet *ai* sticky
pesqojukuwiptnat *ai* {np'tn} have sticky fingers [BC]
pesqo:l'k *ta* pluck (as a chicken)
pe:s'sit *ai* burst into flame
pess'k *ta* slice or cut accidentally
pess'm *ti* slice or cut accidentally
pessmkewey *an* holy picture or medal; crucifix
pestaqa:l'k *ta* strain; pull a muscle
pestaqa:tu *ti* strain; pull a muscle
pe:s'tek *ii* burst into flame

pestiye:wa:taqatimk ceremony (honouring elders) [CB]

pestiye:wa:timk ceremony (honouring elders) [CB]

pestiye:wimk feast day [SH]

pestiye:wumk feast day

pestmat *ai* starve

pestmo:qon starvation

pestunk (pestun'm) *ai* preach; make a speech

petaptu:sit *ai* {aptu:n} come with a cane

petaqan pie

petaqanji:j (petaqanji:tl) piece of pie

petasenmat *ai* come with a light or torch

petasit *ai* blinded (by a glare of light or the sun)

petatejimk *ta* drag here

petatejitu *ti* drag here

petaw'lalk *ta* lug or carry (on the back)

petaw'latm *ti* lug or carry (on the back)

petaw'let *ai* lug here (on the back)

petkimk *ta* pacify; calm down

petknejik (pl) *ai* arrive at their destination

petkute:k *ta* knock out

petkwe:k *ai* stiff [BC]

petkwete:k *ta* knock out [BR]

petley (petleyaq) *an* peddler

pe: tmk first of all

petna:s'k *ii* a gust of cool wind

petqwasit *ai* deny

pette:k *ta* strike or hit accidentally

pette:m *ti* strike or hit accidentally

pettemit *ai* arrive crying

pettepit *ai* present by chance [CB]

petteskaq *ta* accidentally bump into

petu:kun cape

petu:niyaq *ii* {u:n} get foggy [BR]

petuptu *ti* lug here (on the shoulder)

pewalk *ta* need; want

pewa:m *ti* sweep

pewaqs'te:ket *ai* thrash (as of wheat)

pewaqs'te:kney thrasher (used in farming)

pewaqtesm'k *ta* shake off

pewaqtestu *ti* shake off

pewat *ai* dream

pewatm *ti* need; want

pewi:k *ta* dream about

pewi:ket *ai* sweep

pewitaqan dream

pewiteket *ai* dream

pewitu *ti* dream about

pija:l'k *ta* put in

pija:sit *ai* go underneath; go in

pija:tu *ti* put in

pijeket *ai* throw under; throw in

piji-jink'ja:l'k *ta* squeeze or press in

piji-jink'ja:tu *ti* squeeze or press in

pijikatat *ai* {nkat} long-legged

pijikiyaq *ii* curve in

pijikiyet *ai* curve in

pijik'njit (pijik'njijik) *an* mosquito [SH]; giraffe [SH]

piji-ksma:l'k *ta* {kema:l'k} push in

piji-ksma:tu *ti* {kesma:tu} push in

pijikwek *ii* grow in

pijikwet *ai* grow in

pijimaqan funnel

pijipkwiyaq *ii* cave in

pijipkwiyet *ai* cave in

pijiptnat *ai* {np'tn} have a long reach

pijisqonat *ai* {nsisqon} long-nosed

pijistaqanat *ai* long-eared [SH]

pijiyaq *ii* fall in; drop in

pijiyet *ai* fall in; drop in

pijjaqan *an* mitten; mitt

pijkwej *an* night hawk

pijoqosuti button [BC]

pi:k (pi:kaq) *an* spade (in cards) (Fr *pique*)

pikaqan *an* rib (of a splint basket) (Maria)

pikkw (pikkwik) *an* flea

pikkwit *ai* have fleas

piklewji:j *an* lamp globe

piksapekiyaq *ii* steam [EG]

piksa:q *ii* dusty; steamy

piksa:t *ai* dusty; steamy

piktit *ai* fart

piktu:n fart

pi:kun *an* feather

pi:kw *an* night hawk [NB]

pi:kwatikn shed hair

pi:kwatiknmit *ai* shed (hair)

pikwelk *ai, ii* several [SH]; many [BR]; much [BR]

pikweln'k *ta* have plenty of [BR]

pikweln'm *ti* have plenty of [BR]

pilekn new cloth

pile:sm (pile:smuk) *an* novice; rookie

piley new
piley jijjawiknej *an* "grass" widow
pili-jilta:sik *ii* newly blazed [BR]
pilikan new house; new camp
pilikana:qamikt new campsite or development
  [SH]
piliman *an* new potato
piljaqan *an* mitt [BC]
pilse:k¹ *ai* guilty [SH]
pilse:k² *ai* numb
pilse:k³ *ai, ii* unsalted
pilsimk *ta* speak falsely of
piltuwamk *ta* see something strange in; look
  strange or different to; look at differently
piltuwaptm *ti* see something strange in; look
  strange or different to; look at differently
piltuwa:sit *ai* turn out unexpectedly
piltuwa:s'k *ii* turn out unexpectedly
piltu-wi:t'k *ta* {ewi:t'k} call by a different name
piltu-wi:tm *ti* {ewi:tm} call by a different name
piluwamukwiyaq *ii* change colour; become
  dusk
piluwamukwiyet *ai* change colour; become
  dusk
piluwasit *ai* foolish; erratic
piluwe:k *ai, ii* changed; different
piluwowey bullet
pi:mat *ai* hunt waterfowl
pipanikesit *ai* ask or enquire about
pipanimk *ta* ask
pi:pi *an* peevee hook
pipnaqan bread
pipnaqane:ji:j caraway seed [BR]
pipqoqsitan corn (on the foot) [SH]
piptoqopsit *ai* round (cylindrical, tubular)
piptoqopskek *ii* round (globular)
piptoqopsk'sit *ai* round (globular)
piptoqwa:q *ii* round (cylindrical, tubular)
piptukwakik *ii* round (circular)
piptukwakit *ai* round (circular)
pipukwaqan wind instrument; horn; musical
  instrument
pipukwaqane:j *an* bugler
pipukwaqanji:j whistle
pipukwes¹ *an* fish scale
pipukwes² *an* sparrow hawk; chicken hawk [BR]

pipukwet *ai* make music on a horn or wind
  instrument
pipuwa:smukwet *ai* blow a whistle or horn [BR]
pis *an* flea [BR]
pi:san diaper
pi:sanatkw leichen
pi:sano:tlk *ta* put a diaper on
pisaqqan bubble [SH]
pisew foam; suds
pisewiyaq *ii* foamy; in a lather
pisewiyet *ai* foamy; in a lather
pisewtuna:t *ai* {ntun} foam at the mouth
pisit *ai* inside
piskiyaq *ii* get dark; become twilight
piskwa:l'k *ta* bring or take in; let in; put in time
  [CB]
piskwapa:sit *ai* peek in
piskwapit *ai* look in (from outside)
piskwa:q *ii* enter
piskwa:t *ai* enter
piskwa:tu *ti* bring or take in; let in; put in time
  [CB]
piskw-ekimk *ta* invite in
piskwe:putu *ti* bring in [SH]
piskwikiyaq *ii* curve inward
piskwikiyet *ai* curve inward
piskwi:putu *ti* bring in quickly
piskwiwkwalk *ta* follow in
piskwiwkwatm *ti* follow in
piskw'laq *ii* rain inside
piskw-paniks'k *ii* drift inside (snow)
piskw-wije:w'k *ta* accompany inside
piskw-wije:w'm *ti* accompany inside
pismuti mattress
pi:snalk *ta* pack (a pipe) with tobacco
pi:snsit *ai* pack a pipe
pisoqosuti button
pisoqotalk *ai* eat much; eat a lot
pisoqqowiyeksit *ai* greedy; gluttonous
pisqa:taqanapi chain
pisqoqowet *ai* take in the laundry [BC]
pissaqqutnat *ai* have a numb mouth
pisse:k *ai* numb
pissiyet *ai* become numb
pistamit *ai* sop up (e.g., gravy, molasses) with
  bread

pistamun bread spread or sop (fat, molasses, etc.); main course of the meal (fish, pork, etc.) [RB] [CB]

pisu-ilsutmaq *ta (do)* accuse falsely

pisu-ilsutmaqan false accusation

pisuwaq *an* indian dress [CB]

pisuwimk *ta* slander

pitalqek *ii* a deep hole

pitamkletesink *ai* flare up (toward inside)

pitamkletesk *ii* flare up (toward inside)

pitansk'pit *ai* penetrate [SH] [PEI]

pitansk'tek *ii* penetrate [SH] [PEI]

pitapekit *ai* crawl underneath

pita:q *ii* tall; long

pitaqan arrow pouch [SH]

pita:qawe:l (pl) trousers

pitaqawey'mk'l (pl) trousers [CB]

pitask'pit *ai* penetrate; stick in

pitask'tek *ii* penetrate; stick in

pi:taw upstream; west

pi:tawa:l'k *ta* take to the west

pi:tawa:sit *ai* go west

pi:tawa:s'k *ii* go west

pi:tawa:tu *ti* take to the west

pi:tawe:k (loc) in the west

pi:tawkowa:j *an* westerner

pitek *ii* inside

pi:tisikn-te:k *ta* caulk

pi:tisikn-te:m *ti* caulk

pitiyasit *ai* aglow; suffused with light; lit up; bright

pitiyatek *ii* aglow; suffused with light; lit up; bright

pitkimk *ta* send; dispatch; mail

pitkitm *ti* send; dispatch; mail

pitkmalk *ta* stuff; load; fill up

pitkmatm *ti* stuff; load; fill up

pitkmewk *ta* load up for

pitlan finger splint; quiver

pitlanji:j *an* string bean

pi:tmat *ai* stuff or pack a pipe

pitna:taq *ta* give a sniff to

pitna:tat *ai* sniff

pitnewey sniff

pito:qiptnat *ai* {np'tn} long-armed

pitoqna:q *ii* long [BR]

pitoqna:t *ai* long [BR]

pitoqoluwajit (pitoqoluwajijik) *ai (an)* animal with a long neck; crane; giraffe

pitoqoluwat *ai* long-necked [PEI]

pitoqoluwewj *an* a long-necked animal

pitoqona:q *ii* cylindrical; long [BR]

pitoqona:t *ai* cylindrical; long [BR]

pitoqpit *ai* sit (set) underneath

pitoqsit *ai* tall; long

pitoqtek *ii* burn underneath; penetrate beneath; sit (set) underneath

pi:t'pet *ai* pour in

pitqasawaqan ramrod

pitqasawet *ai* arm a gun; load (a gun) with gunpowder and ramrod

pitqonat *ai* {nqon} have (on) high heels

pi:ts (pi:ts'k) *an* beet [BR]

pittalu *an* lion

pittaqapekisk *ii* long enclosed structure

pittaqpisit *ai* tethered; hitched by a long rope

pittaqq *ii* long

pittaqsit *ai* long

pitto:tulltimk auction forty-five (a card game)

pitu:kun cape

pitu: n'mijkamij *an* great-grandfather

pitu: nuji:j *an* great-grandchild

pitupet *ai* tend bar [SH]

pituweka:l'k *ta* line (as a coat)

pituweka:taqan lining

pituweka:tu *ti* line (as a coat)

pituwi·mtlnaqan {metla:s-} thousand (in counting) [BR]

pituwi·ptnnaqan a thousand (in counting)

pi:wej *an* yearling beaver [BR]

pi:wetiknit *ai* feathery; downy

piwetm (animal) hair [BR]

piwetmit *ai* hairy (of the body) [BR]

piwikes *an* fish scale

piwiyaq *ii* left over; a remainder; surplus

piwsaw (piwsaq) *an* slice or slab of meat [BC]

piwsikn scrap of cloth or paper; wood shaving

piwsmik *ii* bushy; fluffy-haired; hairy

piwsmit *ai* bushy; fluffy-haired; hairy

piwtikn peeling (of a fruit or vegetable); food scrap

piyami·ksalk *ta* {kesalk} prefer

piyami·ksatm *ti* {kesatm} prefer

piyami-te:l'mk *ta* {tel-te:l'mk} think more of

piyami-te:tm *ti* {tel-te:tm} think more of
piyamiw more than; over; in excess (of)
piyamiyaq *ii* leftover; surplus
piyamiyet *ai* leftover; surplus
piyam-klu:lk *ii* {kelu:lk} better than
piyam-klu:sit *ai* {kelu:sit} better than
piyeskman corn [BR]
piyeskmin corn
pjila:si {pejila:sit} welcome!
pka:w *an* clay [SH]
pkekn hide (of skin) [SH]
pkenikn fertilizer; manure
pkesikn piece of cloth
pkesikn-ji:j small piece of cloth
pkijoqikn cork; plug (button) [SH]
pkijoqosuti button [SH]
p'kikwe:l (pl) eyeglasses [SH]
pkikwe:l (pl) eyeglasses
pku *an* gum; pitch
pkuman blueberry
pkuman-apu blueberry juice
pkumanaqsi blueberry branch or bush
pkumane:ket *ai* go after blueberries
pkumaqan weapon [BC]
pkuwiptnat *ai (an)* {npitn} sticky-fingered; a
  kleptomaniac
pkwiman blueberry
plamu *an* salmon
plamuj *an* tommy cod
plamukwet *ai* fish for salmon
Plansuwe Frank [BR]; Francis [BR]
Plasuwa Frank; Francis (Fr *François*)
plawej *an* partridge
plawe:si:s *an* young partridge
plawe:sis *an* chicken [SH]
pleku nail (Fr *les clous?*)
pleku:j tack
pleku:ji:j small nail
ples *an* pigeon
p'lkoq *an* fiancé(e) (male or female)
pl'mskw (pl'mskuk) *an* three or four-year-old
  beaver
plos brush (Fr *brosse*)
plu:jaqamat *ai* look in a mirror
plu:jaqamati mirror
pmetuk aside; on the side
p'mtn mountain [BR]

pnamujuwiku:s *an* January
pnasu:lkw vessel; ship [SH]
pnatmuwiku:s *an* {penatk} April; egg-laying
  month
pnekwiyaqal fragments [SH]
pne:sukwati {pene:sukwat} drool; saliva
poj *an* purse; wallet; pouch (Fr *poche*)
pokkwitewey buckwheat
pokoman a kind of berry; foxberry [SH]
po:kwin lagoon
po:laks (po:laksik) *an* Pole
ponjin puncheon [PEI]
ponjn *an* oversized (molasses) barrel
po:qiket *ai* drill; bore
po:qikn auger
poqji-atk'temit *ai* begin to cry
poqji-ktapekiyet *ai* {ketapekiyet} start to sing [BR]
poqji-kwitmet *ai* {ekwitmet} start off to fish [SH]
poqji-kwitna:q (poqji-kwitna:m) *ai* {kwitn} start
  off by canoe [SH]
poqjiluwa:t *ai* get angry
poqjimk *ta* deal harshly with [BR]
poqji-m'mkatpa:t *ai* {memkatpa:t} start to bald
  [BR]
poqji-newek *ii* start to get cool
poqjinntimk the onset of war
poqjintoq (poqjintu) *ai* start to sing
poqji-psaq {pesaq} start to snow [ESK]
poqjipu:k become winter [ESK]
poqjit *ai* elope [BR]
poqjiwsit *ai* start to move or vacate (a house,
  camp)
poqji-wsket *ai* {wesket} begin or start to fish
poqji-ws'kewe:k (poqji-ws'kewe:m) *ai*
  {weskwewe:k} start to laugh [BR]
po:q'k *ta* drill; bore
po:qm *ti* drill; bore
poqomaqan'skw cattail [SH]
poqomati weapon [CB]
poqonaqaluskw wikwam pole (to hold down
  covering) [SH]
poqtamka:l'k *ta* start to carry away or take along
poqtamka:sit *ai* start off
poqtamka:tu *ti* start to carry away or take along
poqtamkiyaq *ii* begin; start out
poqtamkiyet *ai* begin; start out
poqtamkwe:ket *ai* start off poling (in a boat)

poqtapa:teket *ai* start to scratch
poqtatejimk *ta* start to drag
poqtaw'lalk *ta* start to lug
poqtaw'latm *ti* start to lug
poqtaw'let *ai* start to lug [CB]
poqtewo:kwet *ai* begin to speak [BR]
poqtikimk *ta* send off
poqtisukwit *ai* start off by boat; paddle off
poqtiwkwalk *ta* start to follow
poqtiwkwatm *ti* start to follow
poqt'teskaq *ta* chase; start after
poqt'teskm *ti* chase; start after
poqtuktu *ti* start to backpack
poqwaji-te:l'mk *ta* {tel-te:l'mk} find distasteful; find unsavory; hate [BR]; mistrust
poqwaji-te:tm *ti* {tel-te:tm} find distasteful; find unsavory; hate [BR]; mistrust
poqwa:lamkewey chokecherry
poqwa:lat *ai* dry-throated
poqwas'tiyey thimble
poqwasutiyej *an* thimble [SH]
poqwatikn umbrella
postewit *ai (an)* a matchmaker; gossip; scout (Fr *poste*)
Po:tlo:tek Chapel Island [CB]
Potlotek Chapel Island
ppijoqwa:l'k *ta* button
pp'joqosuti button
pqalmawj (pqalmawjik) *an* black salmon
pqa:lu:skw clay
pqamk *an* fisher (of the weasel family) [RB]
pqan nut [BR]
pqasqaqan sack [SH]
pqojiw *an* amateur; beginner
pqoqt knurl; knot (on a tree) [SH]
pqoqte:kn deadfall (a kind of trap) [SH]
pqotnanj *an* bastard; illegitimate person
pqwamk coconut
pqwan'm den; lair [SH]
pqwasaw'l boneless eel [SH]
pqwa:w bark (of a tree) [SH]; peeled bark
pqwawlu:skw clay
psa:mun brisket
psan {pesaq} snowfall
psanji:j light snowfall
psaqa:kw bark; rind; crust

pse:s's *an* onion [SH]
psetkun knot (of a tree); branch [BR]
psetkunatkw dead (dried out) tree branch [SH]
psew gunpowder
p'si *an* wigwam pole [SH]
psi:kikwaqan river drive [BC]
psiktiyej a kind of ant (a derogatory expression)
psi:kukwaqan river drive
psikuwiku:s *an* July [BC]
psikweta:w *an* organ taken from a pig to predict the weather
psitn channel
psitnu:j small channel (of a river)
psk'san foreshoulder (of an animal) [SH]
p'skukun necklace
ps'kuwiku:s *an* July
pskweso:qon scythe
p'te:j broth
p'tew broth
p'tewey tea
p'tewey e:mat *ai* take tea; have a tea break
p'teweyo:q *an* teapot
pu:kewit *ai* gummy
pukkwana:l'k *ta* smoke (a fish, etc.) (Fr *boucane*)
pukkwana:taqan place, apparatus or utensil for smoking meat
pukkwana:ta:sit n'me:j *an* smoked fish
pukkwana:teket *ai* smoke (food)
pukkwana:tu *ti* smoke (a fish, etc.) (Fr *boucane*)
pukkwanaw (pukkwanaq) *an* smoked fish (e.g. herring) or ham
pukliye:wey boil; pimple
pu:kowij *an* balsam sap
puksaqatew (puksaqatal) ember of firewood
puksetew coal [BR]; soot
puksetewik *ii* sooty
puksikna:qewit *ai* hairy (of an animal) [BR]
puksuk firewood
puksukey epsaqtejk wood stove
puktaqan snare [BR]
puktew (puktal) fire
puktewijk whiskey; firewater
puktewikan hearth [BR]
puktewit *an* comet; meteorite
puktewulkw steamboat; steamship

puk'tli:kej *an* starling ("black robin") [ESK]
pukto:kuwom chimney
pukto:kuwome:j *an* cricket; chimney beetle
puku:kewij balsam sap [PEI]
pukulatmu:j dwarf; troll
pukuluwan *an* kidney
pukumaqan weapon
pukuna:w *an* fluffy or hairy animal
pukunesit *ai* bushy; hairy (of an animal); fluffy
puku:skw *an* dead and dry yellow birch
pukwaja:l'k *ta* dress (an animal)
pukwales *an* swallow
pukwatqasik *ii* bushy; whiskered
pukwatqasit *ai* bushy; whiskered
pukwatqek thicket
pu:kwe:l (pl) eyeglasses
pukwelijuwik *ii* flow extensively
pukwelijuwit *ai* flow extensively
pukwelikanik *ii* have many buildings; well-populated
pukweliket *ai* live together in a group
pukweliku:niyet *ai* bleed profusely
pukweliyaq *ii* in good supply; plenty
pukweliyet *ai* in good supply; plenty
pukwelk *ai, ii* lots; several; many; much
pukwenn'k *ta* have plenty of
pukwenn'm *ti* have plenty of
pukwey piece; chip; part
pukwistikna:qewit *ai* hairy (of the body) [SH]
pukwi:tuwat *ai* {nitu} whiskered [BC]
pullja'in train [SH]
pullja'in awti railroad track [SH]
pulljikn connecting rod (automobile)
punajeyaq *ta* stop doing; leave alone
punajimk *ta* stop lecturing or berating
punajo:tm *ti* stop doing; leave alone
puna:l'k *ta* quit; leave; desert; abandon
punalltijik (pl) *ai* separated; divorced
punamu *an* tomcod; a kind of salmon [BR]
punamujuwiku:s *an* January [CB]
puna:newit *ai* give the New Year's greeting [BC] (Fr *Bonne Année*)
puna:newumk New Year's Day
punatalk (punatal) *ai* cease eating
puna:tu *ti* quit; leave; desert; abandon
pun-el'mit *ai* stop laughing [SH]

punewenk (punewen'm) *ai* stop talking
pun-ewistoq (pun-ewistu) *ai* stop lecturing or preaching
pun-ewo:kwet *ai* cease lecturing
pun-lukwewk *ta* {elukwewk} stop working for
punqatk (punqatm) *ai* cease living there
puntalk *ta* hex; cast a spell on
puntat *ai* conjure; cast a spell; curse
puntatm *ti* hex; cast a spell on
puntemit *ai* {atkitemit} stop crying
pusik *ii* embark
pusit *ai* embark
pusk-elmit *ai* laugh repeatedly; laugh a lot
puski-alaknutk (puski-alaknutm) *ai (an)* go around spreading rumours; a rumour monger
puski-aliks'ta:kwet *ai (an)* go around free-loading; a free loader
puski-awannta:sit *ai* forgetful
puski·ksatmap *ti* {kesatm} used to like
puski-maqatuwi:ket *ai* generous
puskimt'k *ai* cry repeatedly; cry all the time
puski-weniyet *ai* absent-minded
puski-wiskuwa:teket *ai* {wiskuwet} blabbermouth [ESK]
puski·wjipilkwet *ai* {wejipilkwet} take frequent fits [PEI]
puski·wjipulkwet *ai (an)* {wejipilkwet} an epileptic
pustemit *ai* cry repeatedly; cry all the time
pusu:l greetings!; Hello! (Fr *Bonjour!*)
pusu:lewiktaq *ta* greet; shake hands with
pusu:lewit *ai* give greetings
pusu: puna:ne Happy New Year! (Fr *Bonjour!*, *Bonne Année!*)
pu:taliyewey basket [BR]
pu:talqank *ta* feel inside of (with the hand)
pu:talqan'm *ti* feel inside of (with the hand)
pu:tapa:sit *ai* peer into a hollow; peek through
pu:tapit *ai* peek into
putaqiket *ai* butcher
putaqq *ta* butcher
pu:taska:tu *ti* poke into
pu:taskilk *ta* urinate into
pu:taskitm *ti* urinate into
pu:tasknk *ta* poke at
pu:taskn'm *ti* poke at
pu:tasqi:ket *ai* poke around
putawiyaq *ii* bloated [SH]

pu:tay *an* bottle; jar (Fr *bouteille*)
putewiskwa:sit *ai* blister [SH]
putewiskwa:s'k *ii* blister [SH]
putlaq *ii* seep in [SH]
pu:tlaqan wood shaving
putmat *ai* miss; lose out on; come out empty-
   handed
put'p *an* whale
put'pe:j *an* small whale
put'peka:sit *ai* blister
put'peka:s'k *ii* blister
put'pekiyaq *ii* swell up; bloat
put'pekiyet *ai* swell up; bloat
putukte:mat *ai* fiddle or drum up a storm
putuktesink *ai* dance; shake without cease
putu:suwinu *an* lawyer [BC]
putuwalk *ta* blow on
putuwatamit *ai* blow; spout
putuwatm *ti* blow on
putuwesk *ii* a mild wind (the southwest wind that
   precedes a thunderstorm)
putuwet *ai* break wind
putuwiskwa:sik *ii* blister; fester [BR]
puwalk *ta* want; desire; need [SH]
puwatm *ti* want; desire; need [SH]
puwesu bushel (Fr *boisseau*)
puwi:kn *an* broom
puwi:kn-ji:j *an* whisk broom; Puerto Rican
puwi:kn-ji:je:skw *an* Puerto Rican woman
puwowin (puwowinaq) *an* shaman
puwowina:teket *ai* act like a puwowin
puwowinujkwej *an* witch
puwowinuti medicine bag

qalaputi shovel [SH]
qalipilk *ta* shovel
qalipit *ai* shovel
qalipitm *ti* shovel
qalipu *an* caribou
qalipu:sitat *ai* a jealous mate [BC]
qaliputi shovel
qame:k (loc) Campbellton; on the opposite side
qapsku:j little waterfall
qapskuji:j tiny waterfall
qapskw waterfall
qapskwamkitk *ii* rapids [BR]
qasawo:q iron
qasawo:qey lapuwey'lji:j iron pan
qasawo:qu:j knitting needle
qasko:tm *ti* take or withdraw in small amounts
qaskusi *an* cedar
qaskusi-a:qamikt cedar grove; Tide Head; Flatlands
qaskwatalk *ai* snack; nibble; eat between meals
qaskweyaq *ta* take or withdraw in small amounts
qa:skwit *ai* gallop
qasqe:j small board [SH]
qasqey board [SH]
qast'k *an* hemlock [BC]
qastulastu *an* branch of an evergreen tree (used for breaking a fever)
qata'ik (loc) half way
qolomqwa:sit *ai* droop (the head)
qones *an* seed beer; Restigouche term for a Micmac from Big Cove (pejorative); male witch [BR]; shank of meat [BR]; snowshoe moccasin [SH]
qonitpaq-amukwiyaq *ii* get dark
qopisun *an* infant
qopisune:k *ai* act like an infant
qopisunikn swaddling clothes [BC]; cradle [BC]
qoptm'n land area surrounding the Restigouche Reserve
qoqwejimuj *an* mud hen [SH]
qospem lake
qotaqani·kjipilaqan {kejipil'm} muffler; scarf [SH]
qotaqani·kjipilo:qon {kejipil'm} necktie [SH]
qoti pole for hanging dried meat inside wikwam [SH]
qo:tlo:mek market [SH]

qotoqonokj *an* conger eel [RB]

Sa:k *an* James [BC] (Fr *Jacques*)
Sa:ke:j *an* Jimmy [BC]
sa:l shawl (Fr *châle*)
salawapu salt water
salawa:tat *ai* add salt
salawe:k *ai, ii* salty
salawey salt (Fr *sel*)
salite(wey) contribution [BC] (Fr *charite*)
salitewa:taqatimk contribution raffle (following a wake) [ESK]
salitewa:teket *ai* give for charity; make a contribution [BC]
salite:wit *ai* solicit; beg; ask for charity (Fr *charité*)
sallpo:k ship [CB]; vessel [CB]; sailboat [CB]
sallpo:l ship; sailboat [CB]
sallpo:lku:j small sailboat [CB]
sama:l'k *ta* touch
samamk *ta* catch a glimpse of
samaptm *ti* catch a glimpse of
sama:tu *ti* touch
samoqo:tlk *ta* water (e.g. a horse)
samqwan water
samqwan-apuwa:q *ii* watery
samqwani:j *an* toad; a heavy drinker
samqwanik *ii* watery
samqwank *ii* watery
samqwano:q *an* water pitcher; pail
samte:k *ta* tap; touch slightly
samte:m *ti* tap; touch slightly
samteskaq *ta* graze; brush against
samteskm *ti* graze; brush against
Samuwel *an* Samuel
Sa:n *an* John (Fr *Jean*)
Sanet *an* Janet
sankewa:l'k *ta* do slowly and carefully; do gently
sankewa:sit *ai* cruise along; saunter along
sankewa:s'k *ii* cruise along; saunter along
sankewa:tu *ti* do slowly and carefully; do gently
sankew-ewo:kwet *ai* talk softly; talk slowly
sankewi-ankita:sit *ai* think slowly
sankewi:sit *ai* talk slowly
sankewi-te:l'mk *ta* {tel-te:l'mk} trust
sankewi-te:tm *ti* {tel-te:tm} trust
sankewsawet *ai* trim slowly; plow slowly
sante: mawiyo:mi a holy gathering

sapa:l'k *ta* save (from mishap); help through; resussitate
sapalqate:k *ta* pierce
sapalqate:m *ti* pierce
sapalqek *ii* pierce through; pass through (as a tunnel)
sapan paste; mush; batter
sapanewey dumpling
sapaqqate:k *ta* stab
sapate:mekw grampus whale [SH]
sapatis *an* jack (in cards) [SH]
Sapatis *an* Jean-Baptiste
sapa:tu *ti* save (from mishap); help through; resussitate
sapawsit *ai* survive
sape:k *ai* survive [SH]; saved
sape:wik *ii* holy; blessed; redeemed
sape:wik kesp'tek Holy Saturday
sape:wik ne:wowey Holy Thursday
sape:wit *ai* holy; blessed; redeemed
sa:pikn awl [SH]
Sapiye:l *an* John Peter (Fr *Jean-Pierre*)
sa:p'k *ta* pierce; penetrate
sa:pm *ti* pierce; penetrate
sapo:nuk tomorrow
sapoqo:tlk *ta* water (e.g. a horse [SH]
sapoqwan (sweet) water [SH]
sapoqwanij *an* bullfrog [SH]
sapoqwani-pako:sit lily root [SH]
saptaqjink *ai* chill through
sapte:k *ta* sting
sapte:m *ti* sting
sapun[1] hair
sapun[2] *an* contrary person
saputalqatm *ti* dig through
saputaqatm *ti* last or stay through; endure
saputa:sit *ai* pass through; go through
saputa:s'k *ii* pass through; go through
saputaskiyaq *ii* penetrate through
saputaskiyet *ai* penetrate through
saputa:t *ai* have diarrhea [SH]
saputawsit *ai* recover (from an illness); survive
saputete:k *ta* pierce through; cut or knock through (with a tool)
saputetelaq *ta* penetrate or pierce through (with bullet or arrow)

saputetel'm *ti* penetrate or pierce through (with bullet or arrow)

saputete:m *ti* pierce through; cut or knock through (with a tool)

saputeteskaq *ta* kick through; run through

saputeteskm *ti* kick through; run through

sa:puwejit *an* dragonfly

sa:q long ago

saqaliyaq *ii* sprout

saqaliyet *ai* sprout

saqalo:pi *an* hair ribbon

saqama:j *an* young gentleman

saqama:skw (saqama:skwaq) *an* woman of high rank; woman chief; lady

saqamaw (saqamaq) *an* chief; big shot; gentleman

saqamti district (of a chief) [CB]

saqamu:kuwet *ai* chew

saqaniyaq *ii* melt or thaw (of the snow)

saqanqapit *ai* seated or set on the ground

saqanqatek *ii* seated or set on the ground

sa:qati *an* needle

sa:qatiju:waq *ii* needly, prickly (of a limb); numb (of a limb)

sa:qatiyej *an* dragonfly [BC]

saqatuwetesink *ai* slip

sa:qawejjuwey old or worn out article

sa:qawey *an, in* something that is old

sa:qawikan old camp [BR]

saqpe:k *ai, ii* wet

saqpikjat *ai* wet-bottomed

saqpiku:n teardrop

saqpiku:niyet *ai* shed tears

saqpi·psaq *ii* {pesaq} wet snow

saqpi:sit *ai* speak wet; a Montagnais

saqpit *ai* flat

saqpiyaq *ii* get damp

saqpiyet *ai* get damp

saqsikwemkewey torchlight

saqsikwet *ai* torch fish or hunt [PEI]

saqtat *ai* light up and smoke

saqte:k *ai, ii* flat

saqtek flat

sasap *an* jellyfish

sa:se:wa:l'k *ta* exchange

sa:se:wa:sik *ii* change

sa:se:wa:sit *ai* change

sa:se:wa:tu *ti* exchange

sa:se:wikna:sit *ai* change clothes [BC]

sa:se:wikno:tlk *ta* change (a baby's) diaper [PEI]

sa:se:wi:sit *ai* change language

sa:se:wit *ai* exchange; swap

sa:se:wi:t'k *ta* {ewi:t'k} change the name of

sa:se:wi:tm *ti* {ewi:tm} change the name of

saska:kwit *an* large cooking pot

sas'ki:k *ai* barefooted

sa:slji:j *an* saucer

sasqa:kwiji:jit *an* small pot (for cooking)

sasqa:kwit (sasqa:kwijik) *an* pot (for cooking)

sasqale:s *an* scallop [BC]

sasqapit *ai* flat

sasqasitat *ai* flatfooted

sasqatek *ii* flat

sasqatesink *ai* fall flat on one's belly; belly flop

sasqatu *an* flying squirrel

sasqayejit (sasqayejijik) *an* crab

sasqe:k *ai, ii* flat; smooth

sasqikatat *ai* flatfooted

sasqitnat *ai* {nitn} pug-nosed

satamk in the stern [BC]

sata:sit *ai* step aside

sa'ukwat *ai* wear hair to the shoulders (of a man)

sawepit *ai* slouched over; hunched over; hung or drooped over

sa:wes (sa:westl) rain hat

sawetek *ii* slouched over; hunched over; hung or drooped over

sawiptn {npitn} deformed or crippled hand or arm

sawiptnat *ai* have a deformed or crippled hand or arm

sawkwatepit *ai* sit astraddle [BR]

sawtaqa:l'k *ta* tow

sawtaqa:taqan barge; raft; trailer

sawtaqa:tu *ti* tow

se:k somewhere; elsewhere

sekewa:t *ai* rise (sun or moon)

sekewe:ket *ai* have an illegitimate child

sekewey (sekewe:k) *an* illegitimate child

seki:kn *an* sail

sekilsit *ai* urinate oneself [BC]

sekit *ai* urinate

sekkapja:sit *ai* clasp with hands [PEI]

sekkapjit *ai* hold on tightly (with hands) [PEI]

sekki-kln'k *ta* {keln'k} hold tight [PEI]

sekkipilk *ta* tie tight

sekkipil'm *ti* tie tight

sekkiyap'sqa:tu *ti* {kepsaqa:tu} close tightly [PEI]

sekkw *ai, ii* sweet

sekkwewey sweetener

sekwiska:l'k *ta* break up; break in (a horse) [CB]

sekwiskina:l'k *ta* rip or tear up [BR]

sekwiskina:tu *ti* rip or tear up [BR]

sekwiskiyaq *ii* shred; come apart; break up [CB]

sekwiskiyet *ai* shred; come apart; break up [CB]

sekwiste:k *ta* pound or hack to bits

sekwiste:m *ti* pound or hack to bits

sekwistesmk *ta* smash [BR]

sekwistestu *ti* smash [BR]

sekwisto:kwek *ii* smashed; broken

sekwisto:kwet *ai* smashed; broken

semqaluk table ('case') knife

senusaqt'k *ii* southwest wind [SH]

senusaqtn southwest [SH]

sepapjit *ai* hold in concealment

sepay early this morning [SH]

sepey early this morning

sepikwa:sit *ai* close one's eyes

sepikwet *ai* have one's eyes closed

sepiljenk *ta* hold enclosed in one's hand [BC]

sepiljen'm *ti* hold enclosed in one's hand [BC]

sepitja:l'k *ta* grip; grasp

sepitja:tu *ti* grip; grasp

sepp'saqa:l'k *ta* penetrate

sepp'saqapit *ai* penetrated into

sepp'saqa:sit *ai* penetrate

sepp'saqa:s'k *ii* penetrate

sepp'saqatek *ii* penetrated into

sepp'saqa:tu *ti* penetrate

sepulkomat *ai* armpit [SH]

sepulkomit *ai* hold under the arm

sepusa:l'k *ta* bring to a point; seal

sepusa:tu *ti* bring to a point; seal

sepusepilk *ta* close by tying with a rope or string

sepusepil'm *ti* close by tying with a rope or string

sepusepit *ai* closed up

sepusetek *ii* closed up

sepusi:s'k *ta* seam; darn; sew closed the gap of a pointed article (such as a sock or mitt)

sepusi:sm *ti* seam; darn; sew closed the gap of a pointed article (such as a sock or mitt)

sepuwijjenk *ta* hide or conceal in the hand

sepuwijjen'm *ti* hide or conceal in the hand

sesaki:k (sesaki:m) *ai* barefoot; shoeless

se:sa:l'k *ta* spread out

se:saltukwat *ai* have messy hair [PEI]

se:saltukwepit *ai* have messy hair

sesaqtoqsit *ai* cackle [SH]

se:sa:sit *ai* spread out

se:sa:s'k *ii* spread out

se:sa:tu *ti* spread out

se:siketijik (pl) *ai* live apart [PEI]

se:sikwalk *ta* spread around

se:sikwatm *ti* spread around

se:siyaqawey buckshot

se:skwalk *ta* holler at [SH]; scream at [SH]

seskwalk *ta* holler at; scream at

seskwe:k *ai* lively; smart; active; a hard worker; ambitious

seskwet *ai* holler; scream; shout

sespa:sit *ai* restless; fidgety; squirm

sespe:k *ai, ii* noisy

sespemk *ta* disturb or bother (by talking about)

sespena:q *ii* create a commotion; noisy

sespenoqsit *ai* create a commotion; noisy

sespeta:q *ii* make continuous noise; talk continuously

sespete:l'mk *ta* worry about

sespete:tm *ti* worry about

sespetoqsit *ai* make continuous noise; talk continuously

sespewo:kwet *ai* talk on and on

sespeyaq *ta* bother with hands; chase after; seduce

sespo:teket *ai (an)* cheat (in love); act the playboy; into everything (as a baby)

sespo:tm *ti* bother with hands; chase after; seduce

sespumk *ta* nag about; fuss about

sesputm *ti* nag about; fuss about

Se:sukuli Jesus Christ

sesupa:lukwet *ai* slip

sesupe:k *ai, ii* slippery

Se:sus Jesus

seta:l'k *ta* put aside

setamk (loc) in the rear or stern (of a boat) [BR]

Se:ta:n *an* Sainte-Anne
Se:ta:newimk Sainte-Anne's Day [SH]
Se:tanewumk Sainte-Anne's Day
seta:sit *ai* step aside
seta:su *an* squid [SH]
seta:tu *ti* put aside
sete:su *an* squid
sewa:tat *ai* sweeten
sewiska:l'k *ta* break up; break in (a horse)
sewiska:tu *ti* break up; break in (a horse)
sewiskoqsit *ai* break up (in a fire)
sewiskoqtek *ii* break up (in a fire)
sewistamit *ai* gnaw
sewisto:kwek *ii* break up (through the action of the water)
sewisto:kwet *ai* break up (through the action of the water)
sewl'k *ai, ii* sour
sewlukowey (sewlukowe:k) *an* rhubarb
sewpet *ai* have a hangover [BC]
sewtiya:t *ai* have a stomach ache [SH]
seyekn dry goods
seyekn-ji:j piece of material
seytun *an* blabbermouth; gossiper
sika:lat spawn [SH]
sika:law (sika:laq) *an* spawn [SH]
si:kaq *ta* irritate; bother; make uncomfortable
si:kasit *ai* uncomfortable
sika:tat *ai* spawn [SH]
si:kewiku:s March
sikkw *ii* springtime [BR]
sikkwe:l about or toward spring [BR]
siklati *an* shark [SH]
sikn stocking; sock
sikniktewa:kik New Brunswick
siknntaq *ta* baptize; make use of (for the first time)
siknntasit *ai* baptized
siknntm *ti* baptize; make use of (for the first time)
sikowiku:s March
sikowiyet *ai* have spring fever
siksuti ankle length sock
sikte:k *ta* strike dead
siktelaq *ta* shoot dead
siktesink *ai* killed (in an accident)
siktewa:l'k *ta* tire out with talk

sikto:kwet *ai* killed; dispatched
sik'to:nqek Dalhousie
sikun last spring
sikune:ji:j *an* spring-born animal
sikuniyaq *ii* turn spring [SH]
sikuniyej *an* orphaned (spring-born) animal [BR]
sikunuk next spring
sikupaqte:kn buttermilk
siku:skw (siku:skwaq) *an* widow
siku:skwe:j *an* young widow
sikuwa:l'k *ta* empty (out)
sikuwap (sikuwapaq) *an* widower
sikuwapatikn rinse (water)
sikuwapji:j *an* young widower
sikuwaqs'te:kn straw
sikuwa:tu *ti* empty (out)
sikuwe:k *ai, ii* empty
si:kuwik *ai* irritate
simtuk right away; immediately
sina:l'k *ta* pack down (to make more room)
sinapska:teket *ai* take a break (for liquid refreshment)
sina:tu *ti* pack down (to make more room)
sineket *ai* drink up
si:niket *ai* bail out (a boat)
si:nikn (water) bailer
si:n'm *ti* bail (water from a boat)
sin'mkw *an* wild goose [BR] [RB] [SH]
sintesm'k *ta* drink in one gulp
sintestu *ti* drink in one gulp
sinutesink *ai* regain one's senses [BR]
sinu:wet *ai* back to one's senses (after drinking)
sinuwoqpa:sit *ai* sit up straight [BC]
sipela:l'k *ta* spread out [BR]
sipeleka:l'k *ta* spread out [BR]
sipeleka:tu *ti* spread out [BR]
sipiki:taqan whetstone
sipikpa:q *ii* supple; flexible
sipikpa:t *ai* supple; flexible
sipipka:q *ii* flexible [BC]
sipipka:t *ai* flexible [BC]
sipiska:sutiyo:q ash tray
sipistaqano:suti *an* safety pin
sipit *ai* stretch and yawn
sipitaqan hide-stretcher [BR]
sipke:k *ai (an)* a slowpoke; methodical

sipleka:l'k *ta* spread out; stretch out
sipleka:tu *ti* spread out; stretch out
sipma:m *ti* seal; baste; hemstitch
sipn'ma:m *ti* bring to a point (as in knitting a sock or a mitt)
sipn'ma:q *ta* bring to a point (as in knitting a sock or a mitt)
sipn'mi:ket *ai* join together (to make a point)
siptaqa:l'k *ta* stretch
siptaqa:sit *ai* stretch
siptaqa:s'k *ii* stretch
siptaqa:tu *ti* stretch
siptaqesink *ai* stretched out
sipu river
sipu e:s *an* (freshwater) mussel
sipu:ji:j brook
siputaqan whetstone; sharpener; file [SH]
si:sikn awl
sisip *an* bird; waterfowl
sisku mud
sisku apu muddy (dirty) water
siskuwik *ii* muddy
sisla:kwa:l'k *ta* fry (English *sizzle*)
sisla:kwa:taqan pancake; fried cake
sisla:kwa:temkewey frying pan
sisla:kwa:tu *ti* fry (English *sizzle*)
sismo:qon sugar
sismo:qon apu sugar water (for babies)
sismo:qone:j *an* sugar ant
sismoqonima:q *ii* sweet [BR]
sismo:qono:q sugar bowl
sismoqwan sugar [BR]
sisqallpo:qiyaq *ii* slimy
sisqallpo:qiyet *ai* slimy
sisqa:taq *ta* circumcise; stretch out
sisqa:tuj *an* one who has been circumcised
si:st three (in counting)
si:staq (pl) *an* pair of treys (in cards)
sistek foreskin
si:stewa:j *an* third one; trey (in cards)
si:stewa:juwit *ai* the third person
si:stewey third one; Wednesday
sisuwa:qataq *ii* chime
sisuwa:qate:kn bell clapper
sisuwa:qi:kn chime; bell
sisuwey blaze (of fire)
sitm shore; beach

siwa:l'k *ta* frustrate
siwamk *ta* fed up with; bored with
siwaptm *ti* fed up with; bored with
siwa:teket *ai (an)* a pest
siwe:k *ai* lonesome
siwikna:t *ai* ill; listless
siwinkutukwa:lukwet *ai* {nkutuko:pj} bored (with being alone)
siwi·skmat *ai* {eskmat} tired of waiting
siwiyet *ai* frustrated; bored
siwkewiku:s March [CB]
siwkw spring [BR] [CB]
siw'noqikwatm *ti* smooth out
siwoqtaq *ta* lonesome for
siwoqtm *ti* lonesome for
siw-pmiyet *ai* {pemiyet} tired of moving along
siws'taq *ta* {jiks'taq} tired of hearing about; tired of listrening to
siyawa:l'k *ta* continue with
siyawa:sit *ai* keep going; continue
siyawa:s'k *ii* keep going; continue
siyawa:tu *ti* continue with
siyawiw continuous [BR]
siyawiyet *ai* keep going [SH]
siyawkumiyet *ai* keep on coasting (on the river)
siyoqiyaq *ii* cave in; collapse; fall apart
siyoqiyet *ai* cave in; collapse; fall apart
s'kepn *an* a type of root; wild potato; Indian potato [SH]
s'kepne:kati wild potato place; Shubenacadie
skilmin seed [SH]
skinmin seed
skmukuwalaw spruce gum [SH]
skniman seed [BR]
sk'te:kmuj *an* ghost
sku:l school
sku:lltaqa:m *an* educated athlete; amateur [SH]
sku:lma:stl *an* schoolmaster
sku:s *an* weasel [RB]
skuti urine
skwesm *an* bitch
skwesmuj *an* bitch (dog)
skwe:w female fowl [SH]
skweyoq *an* female mammal
slapn low-bottomed wagon
slaps (slapsik) *an* slab (of wood)
sma:knis *an* soldier

sma:knisuwey na:kwek Veteran's Day
sma:knisuwit *ai* become a soldier
sma:tewa:sit *ai* act or do smartly; smarten up
sma:tewit *ai* smart; alert; fine
s'mkwati fishing pole [CB]
smtuk right away; immediately
snawey hard rock maple
s'nkatikn (log) boom; raft
s'nkatikna:taqan raft (of logs)
s'nkatikna:teket *ai* raft; work on a raft
s'nkatikna:tekewinu *an* a rafter
sno:pi stern paddle; sculling oar [NB]
so:kwistaqan yeast
soppey couch; sofa
so:qiyaq *ii* go north; go up (in altitude); go inland
so:qiyet *ai* go north; go up (in altitude); go inland
soqomkwewj (soqomkwewjik) *an* grasshopper; job hopper
so:qomu:j *an* minnow; gudgeon; sardine
so:qotemit *ai* vomit
so:qotmun vomit
soqowiyet *ai* go inland
soqpit *ai* close by
soqp'k *ta* chew
soqqwat *ai* an eclipse
soqqwet *ai* an eclipse [BC] [PEI]
soqtamit *ai* chew
soqtek *ii* close by
soqte:ket *ai* chew (as a cud); mastigate
soqtm *ti* chew
so:qwa:l'k *ta* take to the north; take up (in altitude)
so:qwa:t *ai* go up
so:qwa:tu *ti* take to the north; take up (in altitude)
spa:suwe:kati purgatory
sqana:kw steel
sqapantiyej beginner; rookie; amateur; klutz
sqato:min *an* raisin
sqno:pitij Burnt Church [BC]
sqolj (sqoljik) *an* pollywog [SH]; tadpole [SH]; frog [SH]
sqoljuwi:kan mushroom
sqoljuwiku:s May
sqolu:skuji:j small lead pellet; beebee

sqolu:skw lead; gunshot; sinkers (pl)
sqomu:kuwalaw spruce gum
sq'sikwetestaqan {saqsikwet} match [SH]
squ *an* leach [SH]
s'ta:l'k *ta* move aside
s'tapukuwa:l'k *ta* set aside
s'tapukuwa:tu *ti* set aside
s'ta:sit *ai* move aside
s'ta:s'k *ii* move aside
s'ta:tu *ti* move aside
st'ke: just like; same as
stoqon *an* fir or balsam tree; palm frond; tree [BC]
stoqon-amu:k *ii* fir-color; dark green
stoqon-amuksit *ai* fir-color; dark green
stoqonaqsi *an* spruce, fir or balsam tree [SH]
stoqone:ket *ai* search for fir boughs
sukul'kaq *ii* rotten
sukul'kat *ai* rotten
sukul'kma:q *ii* taste or smell rotten
sukul'kma:t *ai* taste or smell rotten
Suliyan *an* William; Julian
suliyewey money; silver
suliyewiye:j *an* daddy-long legs (spider)
sulmin *an* rosary [SH]
sulnalji:j bulletin (Fr *journal*) [SH]
sulumkw *an* wild goose
sumalki cent; copper [RB]
sumokati spear; pole [SH]
su:n cranberry
sune:wimk fast day
sune:wit *ai* fast (Fr *jeûne*)
sunmun *an* rosary
sunnalji:j bulletin (Fr *journal*)
supiki:taqan whetstone [SH]
suppin *an* pint; dipper; cup (Fr *chopine*)
suspanikn soap; detergent
suwam'k *ta* tired of seeing
suwekaw *an* tidal bore [SH]
suwel almost; hardly [CB]
suwitis candy ("sweets")
suwoman beech nut
suwo:musi beech [RB]

ta'im'n (ta'im'naq) *an*   diamond card
tajike:k *ai, ii*   healthy
tajiktuk   on the shore
takala:l'k *ta*   anger
takaliyet *ai*   feel anger
takli:j *an*   domestic goose or duck
tal amkiyaq *ii*   how full (of grain)? [BC]
tal amkiyet *ai*   how full (of grain)? [BC]
tal amu:k *ii*   what color?
tal amuksit *ai*   what color?
tal awtik *ii*   how much (in price)?
tal awtit *ai*   how much (in price)?
tal e:k *ii*   what time?; what date?
tal kis   how come?
tal ma: of course!
talpek *ii*   how full (of liquid)? [BC]
talpet *ai*   how full (of liquid)? [BC]
taluwekaq *ii*   what used for?
taluweket *ai*   what used for?
tami   where?
tam pas'k tami   just anywhere
ta:n (ta:nik) *an*   the one who [BC]
ta:n   when?
tanaps (tanaps'k) *an*   turnip [SH]
ta:n koqwey   something; whatever; what
tan ma   of course!
ta:n pa teken   either (one)
tansiyewe:l (pl) *in*   plant leaf (unidentified, used in medicine)
ta:n te:s   anytime; each time
ta:n te:sit *ai*   everybody; everything [SH]
ta:n te:s'k *ii*   everybody; everything [SH]
ta:n tett   wherever
ta:n tlinqase:k   as soon as
ta:n tlipkije:k {telipkijiyaq}   as long as
ta:n tujiw   whenever; when
ta:n wen *an*   somebody; whoever
tapaqan   sleigh; sled [BR]
tapatat *an*   potato (Fr *des patates*) [SH]
tapi *an*   bow
Ta:pit *an*   David
tapiya:'iji:jte:ket *ai*   fiddle
tapiya:jijk   fiddle [SH]
tapiya:jijk api *an*   fiddle string [SH]
tapiya:jijke:j *an*   fiddler; violinist [SH]
tapiya:jijke:juwit *ai*   fiddle [SH]
tap'tan *an*   potato (Fr *des patates*)

tap'tane:j *an*   potato bug
tap'taney   potato basket
ta:pu   two (in counting)
tapu a'ikewey   two-dollar bill [SH]
tapu a'ikl   two dollars
tapu:kl (pl) *ii*   two of them
tapukna:q *ii*   two days
tapu nemi:k *ta*   have two pairs (of a kind)
tapunkik (pl) *ta*   have two (of)
tapunmann (pl) *ti*   have two (of)
tapusijik (pl) *ai*   two of them
tapuwapjimkewey *an, in*   tool or object requiring use of both hands
tapuwapskekl (pl) *ii*   two (of something globular or round in shape)
tapuwapsk'sijik (pl) *ai*   two (of something globular or round in shape)
ta:puwaq *an*   pair of deuces
tapuwinska:q   twenty (in counting) [BR]
tapuwinska:qewa:j *an*   the twentieth one [BR]
tapuwipuna:t *ai*   two years old
tapuwipunqek   two years
tapuwiska:q   twenty (in counting)
tapuwiska:qal (pl) *ii*   twenty (persons or objects)
tapuwiskeksijik (pl) *ai*   twenty (persons or objects)
tapuwitpa:q *ii*   two nights
tapuwoqsijik (pl) *ai*   two (of something cylindrical in shape)
tapuwoqskekl (pl) *ii*   two (of something cylindrical in shape)
ta:puwowa:j *an*   the second one; deuce
ta:puwowey   the second one; Tuesday
taqale:k *ai*   grouchy; irritable
taqamk *ta*   hit; jab; punch
taqamoqi·ksma:l'k *ta*   {kesma:l'k} push from the side; push across
taqamoqi·ksma:tu *ti*   {kesma:tu} push from the side; push across
taqamoqi·sma:sit *ai*   {elsma:sit} lie down crossways or across
taqamoqpit *ai*   lie across or athwart
taqamoqtek *ii*   lie across or athwart
taqate:l *an*   currant
taqawaja:l'k *ta*   sadden (by one's departure)
taqawaje:k *ai*   feel lonely; feel depressed; feel despondent

taqawan *an* grilse
taqawan api *an* grilse net
taqawanji:j *an* grilse (type of fish)
taqtatoq *an* salamander [SH]
taqtm *ti* hit; jab; punch
ta:s ajiyet *ai* what time?; how much movement?
ta:sipuna:t *ai* how old?
ta:sit *ai* how much?
ta:sitpa:q *ii* how many nights?
ta:s'ji:jit *ai* a portion; a bit
ta:s'ji:jk *ii* a portion; a bit
ta:s'k *ii* how much?
ta:sunk *ta* have how much (many) of?
ta:ta daddy! (baby talk)
tata:t (voc) father!
tatuje:k *ai* how old?
tatuji(w) how much?; to what extent?; how far?
ta'uje:k *ai* how old?
ta'utna:l'k *ta* open (someone's mouth) wide
ta'utna:sit *ai* open (the mouth) wide
ta'utna:tu *ti* open (someone's mouth) wide
teka:l'k *ta* cool off
teka:tu *ti* cool off
teke:k *ii* cold (of the weather)
tekele:jk *ii* an insufficient amount or number
teken which?
tekik *ii* cold
tekikatat *ai* {nkat} have cold feet
teki-kisk'k *ii* a chilly day
tekiptnat *ai* {npitn} have cold hands
tekismit *ai* swim
tekistu *ti* cool off
tekit *ai* cold
tekle:jit *ai* an insufficient amount or number
teklo:qiyaq *ii* chilly evening
tekniyaq *ii* sweat
tekniyet *ai* sweat
teko:tm *ti* aware of; go to church; in close touch with
tekpa:q *ii* cold (of a liquid)
tekpaqikit *ai* straight; true (as in carpentry) [CB]
tekpaqikk *ii* straight; true (as in carpentry) [CB]
teks'k *ii* west wind
tekteskaq *ta* kick
tekteskawet *ai* kick [BR]
tekteskm *ti* kick
tekusuwet *ai* climb [BR]

tekwaqti:jk *ii* short [BR]
tekweyaq *ta* aware of; in close touch with
tela:kipulk *ta* saw
tela:kittu *ti* saw
telakumk *ta* related to as such
telakutijik (pl) *ai* related as such
tela:l'k *ta* do in such a way
telalsit *ai* at fault
telapetesink *ai* take a glance at
telap'lkikwa:l'k *ta* mesmerize; hypnotize
telap'lkikwa:sit *ai* see a mirage; see an imaginary thing
telapskek *ii* big and round or oval shaped
telapsk'sit *ai* big and round or oval shaped
tela:q *ii* have such a circumference
tela:sit *ai* behave or act in such a manner
telask'tek pointed in all directions
tela:tekek *ii* do (something) in such a way; the reason why; at fault
tela:teket *ai* do (something) in such a way; the reason why; at fault
tela:tu *ti* do in such a way
tel awtik *ii* worth so much
tel awtit *ai* worth so much
tele:k *ai, ii* happen; take place; act like that; pregnant; such time
teleyaq *ta* treat so; treat as such
teli:k *ta* make as such; make so
telikit *ai* shaped like; dressed as such
telikk *ii* shaped like; dressed as such
teliksukk *ii* weigh such an amount
teliksukulk *ai* weigh such an amount
telima:q *ii* have such a taste [SH]; have such a smell
telima:t *ai* have such a taste [SH]; have such a smell
telimk *ta* tell
teli·pkijiyaq *ii* {pekije:k} last; endure
teli·pkitqatm *ai* {pekitqatm} stay such a length of time
telisqataq *ta* obey
telistaqanewa:sit *ai* imagine one hears something
telitu *ti* make as such; make so
teliyaq *ii* true; happen; seems as such
tel-kisutnat *ai* sound (the voice) in such a manner

tel-kne:kek after a while
tel-lukwek *ii* {elukwet} do such and such work
tel-lukwet *ai* {elukwet} do such and such work
tel-m'naqanaq *ii* {menaqanaq} so weak
tel-m'naqanat *ai* {menaqanat} so weak
teloqsit[1] *ai* have such a circumference
teloqsit[2] *ai* cooked thus; cooked in such a manner
teloqs'k *ta* cook thus; cook in such a manner
teloqsm *ti* cook thus; cook in such a manner
teloqtek *ii* cooked thus; cooked in such a manner
telo:tm *ti* treat so; treat as such
tel-pita:q *ii* have such a length or height
tel-pitoqsit *ai* have such a length or height
telp'k *ta* gnaw on
telqamiksit *ai* act thus; act in such a manner
tels'k *ta* cut into
telsm *ti* cut into
tels'taq *ta* hear sound like
tels'tm *ti* hear sound like
tels'tmat *ai* hear tell
telta:q *ii* sound like; sound so
tel-ta:sit *ai* think (so)
telte:k *ta* cut or chop
tel-te:l'm(')k *ta* think about; think so [CB]; believe so [CB]
telte:m *ti* cut or chop
tel-te:qan opinion [PEI]
tel-te:tm *ti* think about; think so [CB]; believe so [CB]; have an opinion about [PEI]
teltm *ti* gnaw on
teltoqsit *ai* sound like; sound so
teluwekek *ii* used so
teluweket *ai* used so
teluwet *ai* say
teluwisik *ii* named or called
teluwisit *ai* named or called
teluwi:t'k *ta* {ewi:t'k} call by such a name
teluwi:tm *ti* {ewi:tm} call by such a name
tema:kipulk *ta* saw down
tema:kittu *ti* saw down
tema:l'k *ta* break in two
temaluwa:l'k *ta* break off at the tail or rear end
tema:luwat *ai* bobtailed
temaluwa:tu *ti* break off at the tail or rear end

temaluweket *ai* snap off at the tail [BR]
temaluwetesm'k *ta* break off at the tail end (by slamming) [BR]
temapsk'sk *ta* cut into segments or chunks
temapsk'sm *ti* cut into segments or chunks
temaqjo:tu *ti* tuck in the flaps (in basket making) [SH]
tema:sit *ai* broken off
tema:s'k *ii* broken off
temasqa:l'k *ta* break off
temasqa:tu *ti* break off
tema:tu *ti* break in two
temawikna:t *ai* a hunchback
temeket *ai* snap in two
temik *ii* deep
temikale:m mid lent (Fr *des mi-carêmes*)
temikatat *ai* one-legged [PEI]; have a foot or or leg cut off
temina:l'k *ta* tear or rip off or up
temina:tu *ti* tear or rip off or up
temine:k *ai, ii* ripped off
temi-piya:st fifty cents (Fr *demi-piastre*)
temiptnat *ai* {npitn} have a hand or arm cut off
temiskipeket *ai* snap off at the neck
temisqona:l'k *ta* {nsisqon} break off at the (nose) end
temisqona:tu *ti* {nsisqon} break off at the (nose) end
temkwa:l'k *ta* break off at the neck
temkwe:k *ai, ii* headless
temkwepk *ta* bite the head part off
temkwesk *ta* cut or slice off at the neck
temkwesm *ti* cut or slice off at the neck
temkwete:k *ta* chop off at the neck
temkwete:m *ti* chop off at the neck
temp'k *ta* bite off
temsaqas'k partition; wall
tems'k *ta* slice; sever (by knife)
temsm *ti* slice; sever (by knife)
temte:k *ta* knock off; chop off [CB]
temte:m *ti* knock off; chop off [CB]
temtesink *ai* broken in two
temtesk *ii* broken in two
temteskaq *ta* break by kicking or stomping on [BR]
temteskm *ti* break by kicking or stomping on [BR]
temtesmk *ta* break; fracture

temtestu *ti* break; fracture
temtm *ti* bite off
tepa:l'k *ta* put aboard
tepaqan sleigh; sled; vehicle
tepaqapit *ai* fit; the right size
tepaqatek *ii* fit; the right size
tepa:sit *ai* get on; get aboard
tepatat *an* potato (Fr *des patates*) [BR]
tepa:te tart [SH]; pâté (Fr *des pâtés*)
tepa:tu *ti* put aboard
tepaw near; handy
tepawtik *ii* worth the price
tepawtit *ai* worth the price
tepi:ketu *ti* distribute
tepiknaq *ii* strong enough
tepiknat *ai* strong enough
tepi-m'lke:k *ai, ii* {melke:k} hard enough
te:pineklewey vinegar (Fr *des vinaigres*)
tepine:s *an* bedbug (Fr *des punaises*)
tepipana:mk maturity
tepipunamk maturity
tepipuna:t *ai* mature
te:pisawa:tat *ai* add pepper
te:pisawey pepper (Fr *des épices*) [PEI]
te:pisewey pepper
tepi:timk welfare day
tepiyaq *ii* enough; sufficient; adequate
tepiyet *ai* enough; sufficient; adequate
tepkik night (period between midnight and dawn)
tepkisa:l'k *ta* set (sit) apart; separate
tepkisa:tu *ti* set (sit) apart; separate
tepkise:k *ai (an)* a loner
tepkispit *ai* apart (from others)
tepkistek *ii* apart (from others)
tepknuset (tepknusejik) *an* moon; month [BR]
tepkunset (tepkunsejik) *an* moon; month
tepkunsetewey wi:katikn calendar
tepkunsetewik *ii* moonshine
te:plj (te:pljik) *an* goat (Fr *des boucs?*)
te:plma:sewey cheese (Fr *des fromages*)
teplma:sewey cheese
teplumk *ta* promise (Fr *des promesses?*)
teplutm *ti* promise (Fr *des promesses?*)
tepne:k *ta* catch up with
tepne:m *ti* catch up with
tepn'k *ta* reach
tepn'm *ti* reach

tepot *an* rubber boot (Fr *des bottes*) [ESK]
tepo:tasit *ai* loaded up
tepo:tas'k *ii* loaded up
teppilk *ta* hoist aboard; haul or rope aboard
teppil'm *ti* hoist aboard; haul or rope aboard
teppit *ai* aboard; on or in a vehicle
tepplma:sewey cheese (Fr *des fromages*) [SH]
tepplma:sikewey cheese
tepqatk (tepqatm) *ai* married
teptek *ii* aboard; on or in a vehicle
tep'tuk instead
te:pulj (te:pulj'k) *an* goat (Fr *des boucs*)
tepu:sit *ai* get in or on (a vehicle) [SH]
te:s every time
te:si-kisk'k every day
tesipiyet *ai* itch [RB]
te:sipow *an* horse (Fr *des chevaux*)
te:sipow aluktesk *ii* form (as a cloud) in the shape of a horse
te:sipowa:q (te:sipowa:m) *ai* go by horse
te:sipowi:skw (te:sipowi:skwaq) *an* mare
te:sipow kumaqan horse whip
te:sipowmann (pl) oats
te:sipuk every winter [BR]
te:sipuna:t *ai* so many years old
te:sit *ai* so much (many)
te:sitpa:q *ii* every night
te:sitwa:q {toqwa:q} every fall
te:s'k *ii* so much (many)
te:sunemi:k *ii* so many kinds
te:sunemiksit *ai* so many kinds
te:sunk *ta* have so much or so many
te:sun'm *ti* have so much or so many
tetapu so happens
tetapu:qamikset *ai* act correctly
tetapu:s'k *ta* cut right or correctly
tetapu:sm *ti* cut right or correctly
tetapuwa:l'k *ta* treat right; do right by; satisfy; please
tetapuwa:teket *ai* do the right way
tetapuwa:tu *ti* treat right; do right by; satisfy; please
tetapuwi:s'k *ta* sew right or correctly
tetapuwi:sm *ti* sew right or correctly
tetapuwi-wsuwa:tu *ti* {wesuwa:tu} take the right or proper way
tetaqa:sit *ai* hurry

tetaqi-te:l'mk *ta* anxious about
tetaqi-te:tm *ti* anxious about
tetaqulkuni *an* king bird [SH]
te:tipja:l'k *ta* roll
te:tipja:tu *ti* roll
te:tipjiyet *ai* tumble
te:tipjo:l'k *ta* roll a cigarette; roll (something long and round) over
te:tipjo:tu *ti* roll a cigarette; roll (something long and round) over
te:tipoqja:l'k *ta* put one's arm around the waist of; hug; embrace
te:tipoqja:tu *ti* put one's arm around the waist of; hug; embrace
tetkuwek *ii* in the way
tetkuwet *ai* in the way
tetpaqa:l'k *ta* straighten [PEI]
tetpaqam *ti* weigh
tetpaqa:tu *ti* straighten [PEI]
tetpaqik *ii* straight; true (in carpentry) [CB]
tetpaqikit *ai* straight; true (in carpentry) [CB]
tetpaqikn scale
tetpaqopit *ai* sit straight
tetpaqpit *ai* straight; flush (in carpentry)
tetpaqq *ta* weigh
tetpaq-qama:l'k *ta* {kaqama:l'k} place straight
tetpaq-qama:tu *ti* {kaqama:tu} place straight
tetpaq-qamik *ii* {kaqamik} stand straight up
tetpaq-qamit *ai* {kaqamit} stand straight up
tetpaqsit *ai* straight
tetpaqs'k *ta* cut straight
tetpaqsm *ti* cut straight
tetpaqtek *ii* straight; flush (in carpentry)
tetpitsaq square; cube
tet'piyet *ai* roll over [SH]
te:t'pjiyet *ai* roll over
tett right here
tettaq *ta* owe
tettawaqan debt [PEI]
tettuwet *ai* owe a bill; in debt
tetuje:k *ai* so many years old; have such an age
tetuji·ntake:k *ai* {netake:k} so bashful
tetutki:k *ii* {meski:k} so big
tetutkilk *ai* {meskilk} so big
tetuwipskuna:t *ai* rumble (inside the stomach) [SH]
te'uje:k *ai* so many years old; have such an age

tewajjiyeket *ai* throw out
tewa:kwe'iteskaq *ta* kick out
tewa:l'k *ta* take or put out
tewalqa:l'k *ta* take out of; remove from [SH]; release
tewalqatesink *ai* dislocated [SH]
tewalqatesk *ii* dislocated [SH]
tewalqatesm'k *ta* shake out [SH]; dislocate
tewalqatestu *ti* shake out [SH]; dislocate
tewalqa:tu *ti* take out of; remove from [SH]; release
tewalqe:k *ii* dislocated [SH]
tewalqiyaq *ii* ooze out [SH]
tewalqiyet *ai* ooze out [SH]
tewapit *ai* look out (from inside)
tewaqji:jit *ai* short [BR]
tewaqji:jk *ii* short [BR]
tewaqpit *ai* stick out
tewaqqa:l'k *ta* take out; release
tewaqqatesm'k *ta* shake out
tewaqqatestu *ti* shake out
tewaqqa:tu *ti* take out; release
tewaqtek *ii* stick out
tewask'teskaq *ta* chase out [SH]
tewatalk *ai* eat outside; eat in a restaurant
tewatejimk *ta* drag out
tewatejitu *ti* drag out
tewatteskaq *ta* chase out
tewa:tu *ti* take or put out
teweket *ai* throw out
tewikiyaq *ii* curve outward
tewikiyet *ai* curve outward
tewi·ksma:l'k *ta* {kesma:l'k} push out
tewi·ksma:tu *ti* {kesmatu} push out
tewi·tk'teskaq *ta* {tekteska:q} kick out
tewi·tpaqatk (tewi·tpaqatm) *ai* {tepaqatk} married out (off the reserve)
tewiwsit *ai* vacate; move out
tewiyet *ai* go outside; exit
tewje·k *ai, ii* have a hole
tewlamit *ai* {kamlamit} exhale
tew-lukwet *ai* {elukwet} work out; work away from home
tew-maliye:wit *ai* marry out
tewopit *ai* look out (from inside) [SH]
tewoqpit *ai* stick out
tewoqtek *ii* stick out

tew-pukuwa:sit *ai* step outside
tew-pukuwit *ai* stand outside the door
tewukkwalk *ta* follow outside
tewukkwatm *ti* follow outside
ti:kitlo:q *an* teakettle
ti:ls (ti:lsik) *an* plank (Eng *deal*)
ti:tikli *an* great horned owl [SH]
titiyes *an* bluejay [SH]
tiya:m (tiya:muk) *an* moose
tiya:mi:skw *an* female moose [BR]; cow moose
tiya:mu:j *an* calf moose
tiya:mukwet *ai* hunt moose
tiya:mu:mi {mimey} moose fat or tallow
tiya:muwapi moose thong
tiya:muwe:ket *ai* hunt moose [BR]
tiya:muwekn moosehide
tiya:muwey moosemeat
tiya:muwimi {mimey} moosefat or tallow [BR]
tiya:muwi:sit *ai* moose-call; speak moose
tiya:muwi:suti moose caller [BR]
tiyom charm
tkesn {teks'k} west
tkeya:tat *ai* {teke:k} have a cold; take cold
tkniyewati {tekniyet} bead of sweat
tknu {tekniyaq} sweat
tk'poq spring water
tk'sn {teks'k} west
tk'snukowa:j *an* {teks'k} westerner
tku *an* wave
tkulmi:s *an* runt
tkupoq bubbling spring
tkuwik *ii* wavy (of the sea)
tlansu twenty-five cents; a sling (Fr *trente-sous*)
tlaqan *an* maple syrup siphon
tla:sij {tela:sit} Let him be!
tlawo:q *an* butcher knife; bread knife; hunting knife
tlawo:qs'k *ta* knife; strike with a knife
tlawo:qte:k *ta* stab; spear
tlawo:qte:m *ti* stab; spear
tle:yawit *ai* {tele:k} originate from; domiciled at
tli:suti {teluwi:sik} language
tma:kittaqan {tema:kittu} saw
tmaqan *an* pipe (for smoking)
tmaqanapskw pipestone
tmaqani *an* shell bird [SH]

tmaqanikju:waq *ii* loaded to the brim; overloaded
tmaqanikju:wet *ai* loaded to the brim; overloaded
tmato:s *an* tomato
tmawey tobacco
tmawiknessu *an* hunchback
tmem'napskek *ii* blunt
tmem'napsk'sit *ai* blunt
tmikalmji:jk (pl) *an* little people who live in caves [SH]
tmi:kn axe
tmi:knatkw axe handle
tmi:kn-te:k *ta* strike with an axe
t'mkewa:j *an* aborigine
t'mkwatiknej *an* crane
tm'letji:j glass tumbler
tmoqta:w (tmoqta:q) *an* beam [SH]; log [SH]
tmoqta:we:ket *ai* cut beams; cut logs [SH]
tmsaqatew (tmsaqatal) hot coal or log [SH]
t'mtmu *an* oyster
tm'tqe:kn pair of scissors
tm'tqe:kne:l (pl) pair of scissors [SH]
tnuwan *an* sinew; tendon; cord
tnuwanoq *an* sirloin; tenderloin [SH]
toqanqajat *ai* paired up (in stud poker)
toqi-mimejik (pl) *ai* co-habit [SH]
toqju:kimk *ta* send up
toqju:kitm *ti* send up
toqju:pilawek *ii* hoist
toqju:pilawet *ai* hoist
toqju:pilewet *ai* hoist [SH]
toqju:pilk *ta* hoist up
toqju:pil'm *ti* hoist up
toqju:teskaq *ta* chase upstairs
toqjuwapekit *ai* {pemapekit} crawl up
toqjuwa:q *ii* go up (stairs); mount (stairs)
toqjuwa:t *ai* go up (stairs); mount (stairs)
toqjuwe:k (loc) up above
toqjuwi-tukwi:k (toqjuwi-tukwi:m) *ai* {pem-tukwi:k} run upstairs [SH]
toq-mimajijik (pl) *ai* co-habit
toqo so; then [CB]
toqojiyu and then
toqo-lukwejik (pl) {elukwet} work in pairs; work in tandem
toqo na is that so?

toqonasit *ai* live common-law; share the load
toqopaqji:jit *ai* {tewaqji:jit} short (in length)
toqopaqji:jk *ii* {tewaqji:jk} short (in length)
toqopskek *ii* short and round (globular)
toqopskikatat *ai* {nkat} short-legged
toqopsk'ji:jit *ai* short and round; stout
toqopsk'sit *ai* short and round (globular)
toqo-pukuwa:l'kik (pl) *ta* stand together; marry
toqo-pukuwa:lltimk marriage
toqosinkik (pl) *ai* sleep together
toqo t'lisip so then [CB]
toqpijik (pl) *ai* {epit} sit together [BC]
toqqatu in spite of
toqtesinkik (pl) *ai* collide; dance
toqwa:majik (pl) *ai* stay or live together
toqwanqapit *ai* bent over double; doubled up
toqwanqapultijik (pl) *ai* go in double file; go two by two; go in pairs
toqwanqiskat *ai* double-jointed
toqwa:q *ii* fall; autumn
toqwaqji:jit *ai* short (in height)
toqwaqji:jk *ii* short (in height)
toqwe:kik (pl) *ai* together
tpi:tnewey {tepi:timk} welfare
tpi:tn ewqwan distribution blanket
tpi:tn ewqwan relief blanket; distribution blanket
t'pkwan gravel
t'pkwanalltimk Ash Wednesday
t'pkwanatpalltimk Ash Wednesday [BC]
t'pkwani·ptaqan *an* {petaqan} ash pan [SH]
t'pkwano:q *an* ash bin
tplutaqan {teplumk} law
tp'te:sn south
tp'te:snukowa:j southerner
tqamuwewey "old ladies" [CB]
tqatikn *an* harpoon [RB]
tqojuwan hill; incline
tqolj *an* toad [SH]
tqonasu *an* {toqonasit} person who lives common-law
tqo:nuk {toqwa:q} next fall
tqope:j *an* {toqwe:kik} twin
tqoq {toqwa:q} last fall
tqoqwe:j *an* domestic cat [BR]
tqoqwej *an* wild cat; bobcat [BR]
t'ssawiyaqan {essawiyalk} dye [SH]

tujiw at that time
tukwa:l'k *ta* wake up
tu:kwesmun pillow; cushion
tukweyaq *ta* wake up (by shaking)
tukwipnn'k *ta* wake up roughly
tukwiyet *ai* wake up; awaken
tukwteskaq *ta* wake (by making a loud noise)
tulijewe:l (pl) rice (Fr *du riz*)
tulkowey cannon
tune:l legendary strong man with supernatural powers (Fr *tonnerre*)
tupi *an* alder [SH]
tupik *ii* frosted (as a tree branch)
tupsi *in* alder twig [SH]; *an* alder tree (scrapings mixed with alum to make a grey dye)
tu:s (voc) daughter! girl! (term of affection)
tusati house extension; porch; shed
tutji:j (voc) little daughter! (term of affection for a child)
tu:waqan *an* {teweket} ball [BC] [RB]
tu:waqanatkw baseball bat
tu:wat *ai* {teweket} play ball
tuwi:kn Canso Strait, N.S.
tuwitn narrows [SH]; bay
tuwop'ti {tewiyiet} window

U

u:j *an* fly
u:je:s *an* blackfly
ujikan abandoned camp; wikwam; house [SH]
ujikana:qamikt old camp site or settlement [BR]
ukumejepit *ai* tipped over
ukumejetek *ii* tipped over
ukumejik *ii* lopsided
ukumejikit *ai* lopsided
ukumujjin eight (in counting) [EG]
ukumuljin eight (in counting)
ukumuljin-te:sinska:q eighty (in counting)
ula this [SH]
ula: tet right here! [BR]
u:n {ew'ne:k} fog
unama:ki Cape Breton
u:nik *ii* foggy
unikan portage trail [SH]
u:niyaq *ii* {ew'niyaq} get foggy
u:npekw rainbow (in the bay); fog eater [SH]
upmetuk on the side
u:t this
utan town
utank up mission

W

wa'isis *an* animal [RB] [BR]
waju:pa:q *ii* high (full) tide
waju:peka:l'k *ta* fill up (with a liquid)
waju:peka:tu *ti* fill up (with a liquid)
wajuwa:l'k *ta* fill up (with a non-liquid)
waju:waq *ii* full
waju:waq wennji:kuwom *ii* full house (in poker)
wajuwa:tu *ti* fill up (with a non-liquid)
wajuwejk blossom (of fruit or vegetable) [SH]
waju:wet *ai* full
wajuwiyaq *ii* full [SH]
wajuwiyet *ai* full [SH]
wa:kw (wa:kuk) *an* louse
wali:j *an* snowball
wali:kik (pl) *an* snowdrift
waljiks'k *ta* gouge; hollow out (with a knife) [SH]
waljiksm *ti* gouge; hollow out (with a knife) [SH]
waljikte:k *ta* gouge; hollow out (with an axe)
waljikte:m *ti* gouge; hollow out (with an axe)
walkwe:taqan nape (of the neck) [BR]
walkwi:taqanat *ai (an)* nape (of the neck)
walne:k (loc) up the mission [SH] [BR]
walnoqsitat *ai* have an instep or arch [BR]
walqopaqtek a puddle [ESK]
walqusk *ta* groove
walqusm *ti* groove
walqwan *an* rainbow
walqwe:k *ii* a hollow
walqwiyaq *ii* hollowed out; caved in
walqwiyet *ai* hollowed out; caved in
waltes *an* wooden plate used in dice game [SH]
waltestaqan *an* round bone or die used in dice game [SH]
waltestat *ai* play dice; play waltes
waltesta:timk dice game playing
walumkwej *an* lobster [BR]
wa:naw (wa:naq) *an* part of animal between ribs and belly; diaphram
wanna:sit *ai* go up the mission
wanne:k (loc) up the mission; at the cove
wanney cove
wannoqsit *ai* concave; curved inward
wannoqs'k *ii* concave; curved inward
wansit *ai* tame; gentle; quiet (of animals) [RB]
wantaqe:k *ai* calm; serene; quiet
wantaqpa:q *ii* calm water
wantaqpekitk *ii* still water

wantaqpit *ai* sit quietly; stay quiet
wantaqtek *ii* sit quietly; stay quiet
wantuwit *ai* clever [RB]
wap-amu:k *ii* look white
wap-amuksit *ai* look white
wapa:sit *ai* turn white; open one's eyes
wapa:s'k *ii* turn white; open one's eyes
wape:jik *ii* whitish
wape:jit (wape:jijik) *ai* whitish
wape:jk flour
wape:k *ai, ii* white
wapi *an* swan
wapiklej *an* large, hook-nosed male salmon
wapikneksit *ai* light complected
wapi·npat *ai* {nepat} sleep with eyes open
wapi-stoqon-amu:k *ii* {stoqon} pale green
wapit *ai* awake; have one's eyes open
wapk *ii* dawn; daylight
wapkwan grey or white hair
wapkwat *ai* have white hair
wapn daylight; dawn
wapn-amukwiyaq *ii* become dawn; daybreak
wapnapit *ai* stay up all night; see the break of dawn
wapnintoq (wapnintu) *ai* sing until dawn
wapnntesink *ai* dance until dawn
wapnuksit *ai* sleep until dawn [SH]
wapoqsit *ai* faded (from the sun)
wapoqtek *ii* faded (from the sun)
wapskw a kind of rock [BR]; coal [SH]
wap'staqapewit *ai* look pale
wap'staqe:q *ai* pale
wap'stoqon-amuksit *ai* pale green
wapt'k *ii* early morning frost
wapunkusit *ai* sleep until dawn
wapus *an* rabbit
wapusuwekn rabbit skin
wapusuwey rabbit meat
waqa:'anikn crooked knife [PEI]
wa:qa'ikikn crooked knife [RB]
wa:qa'ikn crooked knife
wa:qalopsk'saw marble [SH]
waqalo:pskw'saw marble [BR]
waqalusan fort
waqama:l'k *ta* clean
waqama:tu *ti* clean

waqame:k *ai, ii* clean
waqamitk *ii* clean flowing water
waqamn'mat *ai* neat; tidy
waqam'tkuk Nyanza, N.B.; Bonaventure, Québec
wa:qan knife; blade
waqan (butter) knife; blade [BR] [RB]
wa:qan-ji:j jackknife
waqanntew (waqanntal) bone
waqanntewatpat (waqanntewatpajik) *an* skull; skeleton
wa:qans'k *ta* knife; cut with a knife
wa:qansm *ti* knife; cut with a knife
waqa:qanikn crooked knife [SH]
waqasit *ai* hyperactive; jumpy
waqatask northern lights
waqayew pus
waqayewiyaq *ii* full of pus
waqju:pit *ai* crooked
waqju:tek *ii* crooked
waqjuwika:l'k *ta* bend
waqjuwika:sik *ii* droop
waqjuwika:sit *ai* droop
waqjuwika:tu *ti* bend
waqjuwikit *ai* bent; crooked; dishonest [RB]
waqjuwikk *ii* bent; crooked; dishonest [RB]
waqqat-amu:k *ii* frail; delicate
waqqat-amuksit *ai* frail; delicate
waqtiyan gizzard; intestines [RB]
wasamoqsit *ai* overcooked [PEI]
wasapa:q *ii* crystal-clear water [BR]
wasapeklaw (wasapeklaq) *an* spruce gum
wasapun white hair [SH]
wa:sis *an* animal [SH]
wa:so:q heaven
wasoqek *ii* light (of hue)
wasoqon light [SH]
wasoqonawek *ii* radiate; give off light
wasoqonawet *ai* radiate; give off light
wasoqonk *ta* illuminate; put light on
wasoqon'm *ti* illuminate; put light on
wasoqonmaqan candle; lamp; lantern
wasoqonmaqanatk candle stick
wasoqonmat *ai* illuminated
wasoqote:k *ta* polish; shine
wasoqote:m *ti* polish; shine
wasoqotesink *ai* lightning; sparkle

wasoqotesk *ii* lightning; sparkle
wasoqowi:j *an* firefly
wasoqwa:l'k *ta* light up
wasoqwa:taqan taper
wasoqwa:toqan diamond ring [BC]
wasoqwa:tu *ti* light up
wasoqwetesk *ii* lightning [BR]
waspu *an* seal
wastew fallen snow
wastewt'k *ii* frost; frosty
wastew tu:waqan {tu:wat} snowball [RB]
wasuwek *ii* blossom
wasuweka:tat *ai* menstruate
wasuweko:q flower pot; vase
wasuwet *ai* blossom
wataptek *ii* greyish; slate colored; yellow [BR]
wata:s'k *ii* become a cataract (of the eye)
wate:k *ii* cataract (of the eye)
wa:tukwaw (wa:tukwaq) *an* blood clot
wa:tukwawa:s'k *ii* clot
wa:tuwow blood clot [PEI]
wa:w egg
wa:wa:q *an* eggman [SH]
wa:we:j *an* eggman
wa:wiket *ai* lay eggs [SH]
wayekn cloth [BR]; wool [CB]
wayo:pskw bead
wayo:pskwe:kati bead place [BR]
we'ita:q *ii* shrink
we'ita:t *ai* shrink
we'i-teja:l'k *ta* drive from; test-drive
we'i-teja:tu *ti* drive from; test-drive
weja:l'k *ta* buy from; get or bring from
wejamoqsuwalk *ta* embrace; hug and kiss [RB]
wejankuwat *ai* buy from there
wejaqama:l'k *ta* boil
wejaqama:temkewey boiling kettle
wejaqama:tu *ti* boil
wejaqamiyaq *ii* boil
wejaqamiyet *ai* boil
weja:tekemk from there on
weja:tekemkek from that time on
weja:teket *ai* get a spouse from there
weja:tu *ti* buy from; get or bring from
wejeyaq *ta* try out; test
wejeyatijik (pl) *ai* quarrel
we:ji:k *ta* find; come upon; discover

weji:k *ta* make from; make out of
weji·kjiji:k *ta* {keji:k} come to know about
weji·kji:tu *ti* {kejitu} come to know (from such a
  source)
wejiknemk *ta* challenge (physically)
weji-koqqwa:l'k *ta* rescue by grabbing
weji·ksitesink *ai* {kesitesink} get injured
weji·ktalqa:l'k *ta* {ketalqa:l'k} take out from
  (underneath)
weji·ktalqa:tu *ti* {ketalqa:tu} take out from
  (underneath)
wejimk *ta* make out with; try out (sexually)
wejimoqsuwalk *ta* embrace
weji-nisa:l'k *ta* bring down from there
weji-nisiyaq *ii* fall from there
weji-nisiyet *ai* fall from there
wejinntijik (pl) *ai* fight over (something)
wejipek *ii* east or northeast wind; northeast wind
  [CB]
wejipewe:k *ii* an easterly breeze
wejipilkwet *ai* take a fit [PEI]
weji·psemk *ta* {pesemk} sniff
weji·psetm *ti* {pesetm} sniff
weji·psetmit *ai* {pesetemit} sniff
wejipulkwa:s'k *ii* have a cramp
wejipulkwet *ai* have a fit
weji-qolomkwi-pmiyet *ai* {qolomqwa:sit} move
  along with drooping head
we:jitaqan *an* foundling
weji-tepn'k *ta* try to reach (with the hand)
weji-tepn'm *ti* try to reach (with the hand)
wejitu *ti* make from; make out of
we:jitu *ti* find; come upon; discover
we:ji:wet *ai* find (said of a woman when she
  bears a child)
wejiyaq *ii* come from there
wejiyet *ai* come from there
wejjelamit *ai* take in and let out a long deep-
  sounded breath (as a result of boredom,
  disturbance, etc.)
wejkapa:q *ii* incoming or rising tide [RB]
wejkiyemkewey chicken pox; scabbiness
wejkiyet *ai* scabby
wejku:jink *ai* bent toward
wejku-pukuwit *ai* stand facing toward
wejkutemit *ai* {atkitemit} come crying

wejkutukwi:k (wejkutukwi:m) *ai* {elltukwi:k}
  come running
wejku:waq *ii* approach; come
wejku:wet *ai* approach; come
wejkuwijink *ai* bent toward [BR]
wejkuwiyaq *ii* approach [SH]; come [SH]
wejkuwiyet *ai* approach [SH]; come [SH]
wejkwajepit *ai* sit or set facing toward
wejkwajetek *ii* sit or set facing toward
wejkwa:l'k *ta* bring or come with
wejkwa-paneta:q *ii* clear up (of the sky)
wejkwapa:q *ii* incoming or rising tide
wejkwapit *ai* sit facing
wejkwapniyaq *ii* {wapn} daybreak
wejkwaqteket *ai* {alaqteket} come sailing on
wejkwateja:sit *ai* come in this direction; hurry
  this way
wejkwateja:s'k *ii* come in this direction; hurry
  this way
wejkwatejimkwet *ai* come riding on or in
wejkwatpo:jink *ai* bent toward (from the head)
wejkwa:tu *ti* bring or come with
wejkwi-kwitna:q (wejkwi-kwitna:m) *ai* come by
  canoe
wejkwi-na:taqamisukwit *ai* paddle toward shore
wejkwi:puluwet *ai* come on horseback
wejkwi-qolomkopit *ai* {qolomkwa:sit} approach
  with head hanging down
wejkwisikwit *ai* come paddling toward [CB]
wejkwistepit *ai* sit humped over facing toward
wejkwisukwit *ai* come rowing or paddling toward
wejkwitpa:q *ii* approach or come nightfall
wejkwitu:kwe:pit *ai* come with pounding feet
wejkwitukwi:k (wejkwitukwi:m) *ai* come on the
  run [BR]
wejkwitu:kwi:k (wejkwitu:kwi:m) *ai* come
  running
wejo:tasit *ai* trade or do one's business there
wejo:tm *ti* try out; test
we:ju:lkw *an* explorer; discoverer
weju:s'k *ii* windy
wejuwaqateskaq *ta* near; approach [BR]
wejuwaqateskm *ti* near; approach [BR]
wejuwe:k *ai* have a close call
wejuwow close by; recent(ly)
wejuwowita:sit {tel-ta:sit} absent-minded; have
  a short memory

weka'ik *ai* angry
weka'iya:l'k *ta* anger
weka'iyuktaq *ta* angry with; mad at
weka'iyuktm *ti* angry with; mad at
wekamk *ta* anger (through speech) [RB]
we:kaw until then
weket these; this (obv)
wekilalk *ta* bark at
wekilat *ai* bark
wekla these; this (obv)
weklams'k *ii* gusty (of the wind)
we:kopekitk Truro, N.S.
we:koqoma:q Whycogamagh, N.S.
we:kow until
we:kwa:maq *ta* best in an argument or duel of words; defeat in debate; outargue
we:kwamk *ta* follow (with one's eyes) until out of sight
we:kwamkuk where the waterway ends at the falls
we:kwamkwe:ket *ai* pole (a boat) as far as the waterway permits
we:kwanqe:ket *ai* walk or talk in one's sleep
we:kwapskw falls end
we:kwaptm *ti* follow (with one's eyes) until out of sight
we:kwa:sit *ai* go as far as
we:kwa:s'k *ii* go as far as
we:kwata:l'k *ta* scare; frighten
we:kwata:sit *ai* scared; frightened
we:kwi-ji:met *ai* row to the end
we:kwi-kewisink *ai* famished [ESK]
we:kwi-klu:sit *ai* {kelu:sit} extraordinarily good looking [ESK]
we:kwimk *ta* insult [RB]
wela:kw evening; dusk; night
wela:kwe:k last night
wela:kwe:l toward evening
wela:kwewey supper
wela:lin Thank you!
wela:l'k *ta* do well by; please; do a favor for
wela:luwet *ai* charitable; welcome; generous
welamk *ta* attracted to [BC]; like the looks of
welapemk *ta* obtain a favor or something good from; benefit from [PEI]
welapetm *ti* obtain a favor or something good from; benefit from [PEI]

welapetmuwet *ai* obtain a (religious) favor
welaptm *ti* attracted to [BC]; like the looks of
wela:q *ii* fit well
welaqapit *ai* feel good (from drinking)
welasek *ii* well lit; shiny
welaset *ai* well lit; shiny
wela:sit *ai* feel good (from being ill); turn out well; recovered (from being ill)
wela:s'k *ii* feel good (from being ill); turn out well; recovered (from being ill)
welat *ai* burp; belch
wela:tu *ti* do well by; please; do a favor for
wel-awtik *ii* good or reasonable (in price)
wel-awtit *ai* good or reasonable (in price)
wele:k *ai* fine; well; healthy
welekisk *ii* a nice breeze
weleyaq *ta* take good care of
weli-ankamkusit *ai* pretty [BC]
weli-a:su:na:q (weli-a:su:na:m) *ai* well-dressed
weli-eksitpu:k nice morning
weliket *ai* live in a good location
weli-kisk'k nice day
welikit *ai* have a nice shape
welikk *ii* have a nice shape
welikpa:q *ii* strip or split well
welikpa:t *ai* strip or split well
welikwek *ii* grow well
welikwenmat *ai* have a good crop [PEI]
welikwet *ai* grow well
welikwetutk (welikwetutm) *ai* have a nice countenance; wear a smile
welima:q *ii* smell good
welimasit *ai* have a nice odor
welima:t *ai* smell good
welimatek *ii* have a nice odor
welimk *ta* give good advice to
welina:q *ii* well-grooved
welina:t *ai* well-grooved
weli·nqana:mat *ai* {naqana:mat} drink moderately
weli-piyasit *ai* well-dried; kiln-dried
weli-piyatek *ii* well-dried; kiln-dried
welipot rowboat [SH]
weli·pteskna:q (weli·pteskna:m) *ai* {pepteskna:sit} have nice shoes or boots
welipuk *ii* a nice winter
welipunsit *ai* have a nice winter

welitpa:q *ii* nice evening or night

weli·tpa:sit *ai* {tepa:sit} happen unexpectedly and pleasantly; serendipitous happening

weli·tpa:s'k *ii* {tepa:s'k} happen unexpectedly and pleasantly; serendipitous happening

welitpima:q *ii* {telima:q} have a certain (nice) smell

welitpima:t *ai* {telima:t} have a certain (nice) smell

weli·wsuwa:tu *ti* {wesuwa:tu} take well; accept

weliyaq *ii* move well; useful; good

weliyet *ai* move well; useful; good

weljaqajewa:teket *ai* take it easy [SH]

weljaqam *ti* do nicely or smoothly

weljaqk *ta* do nicely or smoothly

weljemajkewe:l (pl) sweetgrass; lilacs

weljema:qewe:l (pl) sweetgrass [RB]; lilacs

weljepit *ai* feel good (from drinking)

weljesink *ai* happy

wel-jijikwe:jit *ai* narrow enough [BR]

wel-jijikwe:jk *ii* narrow enough [BR]

welkamit *ai* nice and fat [RB]

welkaq *ta* fit well; chance upon

wel-kijjet *ai* {ekijjet} read properly or well

welkm *ti* fit well; chance upon

wel-kna:q (wel-kna:m) *ai* {kekna:sit} nicely dressed

wel-knesit *ai* {keknesit} well-dressed

wel-knu:tmaq *ta* {keknu:tmaq} teach well; teach what is proper

wel-k'snet *ai* {mk'sn} well-shoed

wel-kutat *ai* well-dressed [SH]

welkwija:l'k *ta* put in good humour; make more confident

welkwijimk *ta* encourage

welkwijink *ai* in good humour

wel-lu:walk *ta* praise (Fr *louer*)

wel-lu:watm *ti* praise (Fr *louer*)

welma'ita:sit *ai* sad; suffer (in spirit); in mourning [BC]

welmaje:k *ai* suffer; grief stricken

welm'toq (welm'tu) *ai* kind-hearted

welnat *ai* have a good hand (in cards) [RB]

wel-ne:patat *ai* have a good catch [PEI]

wel-newek *ii* nice and cool (of the air)

welnuksik *ii* smooth

welnuksit *ai* smooth

weloqotalk *ai* have supper

weloqsit *ai* fit well; good and round in size; well-cooked [RB]

weloqtek *ii* well-cooked [RB]

welo:tm *ti* take good care of

wel-paspit *ai* nice and thick [RB]

wel-pastek *ii* nice and thick [RB]

wel-pesuk *ii* good and far; quite a distance

welpisit *ai* well-dressed

wel-pistamit *ai* have a good snack (on bread)

welpit *ai* nice; well-placed

wel-pmiyaq *ii* {pemiyet} go or move well

wel-pmiyet *ai* {pemiyet} go or move well

wel-p'sit *ai* {epsit} nice and warm

wel-p'sk *ta* {eps'k} heat up properly

wel-p'sm *ti* {epsm} heat up properly

wel-p'smat *ai* {epsmat} have a well-heated house

wel-p'tek *ii* {eptek} nice and warm

welqamiksit *ai* have a good disposition or character; good-natured

welqatmit *ai* have nice surroundings

welqwanet *ai* wear proper clothes (for the season)

welseksit *ai* well-supplied; well-furnished

wels'taq *ta* {jiks'taq} like the sound of

wels'tm *ti* {jiks'tm} like the sound of

weltamit *ai* eat one's favorite dish; eat well; good-eating; feast

weltamultimk Friday

welta:q *ii* have a good sound (music)

weltaqsit *ai* a good length (e.g. of rope)

wel-ta:sit *ai* happy; glad

wel-ta:suwalk *ta* happy to see; welcome

wel-ta:suwatm *ti* happy to see; welcome

welte:k *ta* hit well; meet up with

weltek *ii* nice; well-placed

wel-te:l'mk *ta* {tel-te:l'mk} approve of

wel-te:lsit *ai* worthy [BC]

welte:m *ti* hit well; meet up with

weltesink *ai* a good fit

weltesk *ii* a good fit

welteskaq *ta* meet up with (on foot); please (by one's presence)

welteskm *ti* meet up with (on foot)

wel-te:teket *ai* joyful; in good humor

wel-te:tm *ti* approve of

welto:qsit *ai* cut well
weltoqsit *ai* have a good sound (music)
wemsami-apje:jk *ii* too small [BR]
wen (wenik) *an* who?
wenakiyet *ai* resurrected
wenaqala:maq *ii* rain heavily [PEI]
wenaqa:l'k *ta* pick up; lift up
wenaqa:sit *ai* rise
wenaqa:s'k *ti* rise
wenaqa:tu *ti* pick up; lift up
wenaqeket *ai* throw up in the air; flip
wenaqiyalk *ta* jump (over)
wenaqiyaq *ii* jump
wenaqiyatm *ti* jump (over)
wenaqiyet *ai* jump
wenaqja:t *ai* skip
wenaqje:wj (wenaqje:wjik) *an* grasshopper [SH]
wena:q'k *ta* pry loose; lift up [RB]
wena:qm *ti* pry loose; lift up [RB]
wenaqpilk *ta* hoist (by rope or cable)
wenaqpil'm *ti* hoist (by rope or cable)
wenaqpmaqan lacrosse stick [SH]
wenaqteskasit *ai* spring
wenaqteskat *ai* flush (as a bird)
wenaqto:sit *ai* move up (in the world); skip rope [SH]
we:neweyaq *ta* distract
weniyet *ai* forgetful
wenmajita:sit *ai* mourn [BC]
wennat *ai* have a good hand (in cards)
wen net who's this?; who's that?
wennji:kuwom house
wennji-tiya:m (wennji-tiya:muk) *an* cow
wennju-a:p'tew {p'tew} pea soup
wennjujkwej *an* Frenchwoman; Englishwoman; queen card
wennjuksnan *an* {mk'sn} shoe; boot [SH]
wennju:-plawej *an* hen [BR]
wennju:-plawe:ji:j *an* chick [BR]
wennju:-s'kepn *an* turnip [BC]
wennjusknan *an* shoe; boot
wennju:-s'pekn *an* turnip [BC]
wennju:-sukapun *an* turnip
wennju:-su:n {su:n} apple
wennju:-su:n apu apple juice; apple cider
wennju:-su:naqsi apple tree

wennju:-tiya:m (wennju-tiya:muk) *an* cow [BR] [BC]
wennjuwa:'it *ai* act funny [RB]; act like a Frenchman [RB]
wennju:wet *ai* act foolishly
wennjuwipk tobacco leaf
wennjuwi:sit *ai* speak French
wennjuwi:skw *an* Frenchwoman [BC]
wen n't who's this?; who's that? [SH]
wenqaje:k *ii* regrettable [PEI]
wen tana who's this?; who is he?
wenuj *an* Frenchman
wenuji:skw *an* Frenchwoman [SH]; white woman [SH]
wepskuninet *ai* have dry tuberculosis [SH]
wesama:maq *ta* overcharge
wesama:sit *ai* overdo [BC]
wesamatalk *ai* overeat
wesamelk *ai, ii* too much
wesami-apje:jk *ii* too small
wesami-jijikwe:jk *ii* too narrow
wesami-kske:k *ii* {keske:k} too wide
wesami-twaqji:jit *ai* {tewaqji:jit} too short
wesamkamit *ai* too fat
wesamki:k *ii* {meski:k} too big
wesamkilk *ai* {meskilk} too big
wesam-klu:lk *ii* {kelu:lk} too good
wesam'la:maq *ta (do)* overload (someone's) plate
wesamoqsit *ai* {etloqs'k} overcooked
wesamoqs'k *ta* overcook
wesamoqsm *ti* overcook
wesamoqtek *ii* overcooked
wesamqwat *ai* drink too much of; drain [SH]
wesaqalk *ta* shoot dead [BR]
wesase:k *ii* slippery [BC]
wesawa:l'k *ta* put on to boil
wesawa:q *ii* hang over or on the edge; sink in [BR]
wesawa:t *ai* hang over or on the edge; sink in [BR]
wesawa:tu *ti* put on to boil
wesawey projection; point (of land)
wesekewa:nek (loc) {sekewa:t} where the sun rises (a religious expression); east [CB]
wesemuwit *ai* {nsmu} have a pair of horns
wesikalk *ta* tell the fortune of

wesiket *ai* foretell; tell fortunes
wesikwat *ai* scar-faced; scarred
wesimit *ai* flee [SH]; get away [SH]
weskaqal'm'k *ta* kiss
weskaqaltm *ti* kiss
weskemk fishing
wesket *ai* fish
weskewa:nek (loc) east [CB]
weskewe:k *ai* laugh
weskewikwetutk (weskewikwetutm) *ai* grin
weskewina:q *ii* happy, joyful or pleasureable (place) [SH]
weskewinoqsit *ai* joyful; jolly
weskijinuwa:l'k *ta* bring to life; give birth to
weskijinuwit *ai* born; surface
weskijiyama:l'k *ta* coat; paint; smear over
weskijiyama:tu *ti* coat; paint; smear over
weskit (weskijik) *an* vest
weskitmaskut (weskitmaskujik) *an* overcoat
weskit·pa:suwalk *ta* {epa:suwalk} set atop
weskit·pa:suwatm *ti* {epa:suwatm} set atop
weskitpeka:sit *ai* flow over
weskitpeka:s'k *ii* flow over
weskitpekiyaq *ii* coated
weskitpekiyet *ai* coated
weskitpit *ai* sit or set on top
weskitqo:wek *ii* float atop
weskitqo:wet *ai* float atop
weskittek *ii* sit or set on top
wesko:tm *ti* have [SH]; possess [SH]; handle; fondle
weskowa:sit *ai* stay, live or situated at
weskowa:s'k *ii* stay, live or situated at
weskowikwa:sit *ai* smile
wesku:mk *ta* talk business with [SH]; talk about
wesku:p'k *ta* cook for
wesku:tm *ti* talk business with [SH]; talk about
weskweyaq *ta* have [SH]; possess [SH]; handle; fondle
weskwimk *ta* converse with [BR]
wesma:sit *ai* overdo [BC]
wesmi:pulk *ta* run off with; kidnap
wesmi:putu *ti* run off with; kidnap
wesmoqjewalk *ta* embrace; hug
wesmukwat *ai* escape
wesmuwit *ai* {nsmu} have horns
wespayaq *ta* keep awake; disturb (the sleep of)

wessmuktaq *ta* escape from
wessmuktm *ti* escape from
wessmukwat *ai* escape from there
westawi:k *ta* save; redeem
westawit *ai* safe and sound
westawitu *ti* save; redeem
westaw'let *ai* gifted [SH]
westawu:lkw (westawu:lkwaq) *an* Savior; redeemer
wesumukwat *ai* run away
wesutqa:l'k *ta* pull; pull in (to dance)
wesutqa:tu *ti* pull; pull in (to dance)
wesuwa:kwa:l'k *ta* hug [PEI]
wesuwa:l'k *ta* take (hold of)
wesuwa:q *ii* sink in [BR]
wesuwaskiyaq *ii* sink in
wesuwaskiyet *ai* sink in
wesuwa:t *ai* sink in [BR]
wesuwatejimk *ta* drag
wesuwatejitu *ti* drag
wesuwa:teket *ai* haul in the pot (in a poker game)
wesuwa:tu *ti* take (hold of)
wesuwejo:qa:l'k *ta* tackle
wesuwejo:qa:tu *ti* tackle
wesuweket *ai* jerk
wesuwelamit *ai* inhale
wesuwepilk *ta* pull in (by rope)
wesuwepil'm *ti* pull in (by rope)
wesuwi-sepilasit *ai* {sepiljenk} gather tightly
wesuwi-sepilas'k *ii* {sepiljenk} gather tightly
wetajikwet *ai* scowl
wetakutijik (pl) *ai* of common descent
wetakutk (wetakutm) *ai* related through descent
wetapaqamit *ai* spring from; originate from [SH]
wetapeksit *ai* descend from
wetapsunik *ii* useful
wetapsunit *ai* useful
wetapulk *ta* chastise [RB]; scold
wetaqama:sit *ai* eat (archaic)
wetaqanikatm *ti* hit with a club [BR]
wetayaq *ta* quiet [SH]; frighten off
wetew-elmit *ai* overheard laughing [SH]
wetewi-jikmit *ai* heard growling [SH]
wetewiluwa:t *ai* bellow; low [SH]
wetewiluwat *ai* overheard bellowing [BR]

wetewintoq (wetewintu) *ai* heard singing [BR] [SH]

wetewoqsink *ai* heard snoring [SH]; heard grunting [BR]

weti *an* worm

wetlamit *ai* {kamlamit} breathe from

wetmamkewey pipe; cigarette; a smoke

wetmaq *ta (do)* give a smoke (cigarette) to

wetmat *ai* smoke [RB]

wetme:k *ai* busy

wetmeyaq *ta* use occasionally as needed; distract; disturb; pester [ESK]

wetmi-te:l'mk *ta* have need of; have use for; care for

wetmi-te:tm *ti* have need of; have use for; care for

wetmkuwet *ai* in the way

wetmo:taqan useful object or tool

wetmo:teket *ai (an)* a prankster

wetmo:tm *ti* use occasionally as needed; distract; disturb; pester [ESK]

wet-nasa:l'k *ta* try on there

wet-nasa:tu *ti* try on there

wet-nastek *ii* where hooked or attached

wetn'k *ta* pull; haul

wetn'm *ti* pull; haul

weto:mt'k (weto:mtm) *ai* heard crying [SH]

weto:temit *ai* bleat; cry [SH]; wail

wetp'k *ta* taste

wetqane:k *ii* mild (of the weather)

wetqani-kisk'k mild day [BR]

wetqapalk *ta* soak

wetqapalsit *ai* soak; bathe

wetqapatu *ti* soak

wetqolk *ta* forbid

wetqolsit *ai* abstain

wetqotm *ti* forbid

wettaqiya:tijik (pl) *ai* share a common descent

wettaqiyet *ai* related; of the same lineage

wet-telaq *ta* buy or purchase from there

wet-teliket *ai* buy from there

wet-tel'm *ti* buy or purchase from there

wetteniyaq *ii* blow from such direction

wet-tepne:k *ta* try to catch up with

wet-tepne:m *ti* try to catch up with

wett'k *ii* blow from such direction

wettm *ti* taste

wettm *ti* try the taste of

we:tunk *ta* feel; feel the weight of

we:tun'm *ti* feel the weight of

we:tu:tm *ti* feel

wetuwotm *ti* feel [SH]

wewkujan *an* red ochre

wija:qajim vein [PEI]

wijaw (wijaq) *an* maggot [BC]; fly

wije:s *an* fly [SH] [RB]

wije:wet *ai* tag along

wije:w'k *ta* accompany; go with

wije:w'm *ti* accompany; go with

wijey same

wijikimk *ta* have as a sibling [BR]

wijikitijik (pl) *ai* siblings [BR]; related as brothers or sisters [BR]; siblings

wijikmuwaluk iceberg [SH]

wijik'tijik (pl) *ai* siblings; related as brothers or sisters

wijikumk *ta* have as a relative

wijipoti *an* money belt (with pocket)

wijipo:ti *an* pouch (carried around the waist) [RB]; money belt

wiji·tko:tm *ti* {teko:tm} accompany; join

wiji·tkweyaq *ta* {tekweyaq} accompany; join

wijjustijik (pl) *ai* in-laws (sister's husband, brother's wife [BC]

wijkwe:j blister

wijkwe:tlaqan *an* birchbark dish or platter

wikamik *ii* lean [SH]; fat(ty)

wikamit *ai* lean [SH]; fat(ty)

wikapu:k *ii* taste good

wikapuksit *ai* taste good

wi:katikn paper; book; letter; newspaper

wi:katikne:ji:j piece of paper

wi:katiknipkw lettuce [SH]

wikew fat

wikewiku:s October

wikewit *ai* fat

wi:kikit *ai* encamped

wi:kikn *an* pen; pencil

wikimk *ta* call; invite; send for [SH]

wi:kipaltimk honouring ceremony [CB]

wikipjik soon

wikit *ai* reside or dwell there

wi:k ji:jat *ai* play house

wikk *ii* taste good [SH]; tasty

wiklatmu:j *an* dwarf; midget [SH]
wikmat *ai* a heavy smoker
wikpet *ai* like to drink (alcoholic beverages)
wikpe:tlaqan ash strip for making baskets
wikpi *an* elm [RB]
wikp'k *ta* like the taste of
wikplasit *ai* smoked (as meat)
wikplatek *ii* smoked (as meat)
wikplatewma:q *ii* smell smoky; smell of smoke
wikplatewma:t *ai* smell smoky; smell of smoke
wiktm *ti* like the taste of
wikumk *ta* call; invite; send for
wikumkewiku:s September
wikumkusimkewey invitation
wikun bean
wikupa:l'k *ta* give a feast for
wikupsit *ai* go for liquor
wi:kuwamk *ta* laugh at; find amusing; find funny
  in appearance
wi:kuwaptm *ti* laugh at; find amusing; find
  funny in appearance
wi:kuwe:k *ai, ii* queer; strange; weird
wikuwom dwelling; camp; wikwam [BR]
wikuwowiku:s October [CB]
wikwas-amu:k *ii* look pretty; look attractive
wikwas-amuksit *ai* look pretty; look attractive
wikwasapewit *ai* nice-looking; handsome;
  beautiful
wikwasmukwet *ai* whistle
wikwiyet *ai* collapse from exhaustion; faint
wili api umbilical cord
wilokamk *ta* catch full view of
wilokaptm *ti* catch full view of
wi:n marrow
winapewit *ai* ugly; homely
winapit *ai (an)* a voyeur; see poorly
wi:newey waqanntew marrow bone
wini-kisk'k a dirty day
winikit *ai* ugly; deformed; crooked [BR]
winikk *ii* ugly; deformed; crooked [BR]
winikwa:sit *ai* make a funny face; put on a face;
  scowl
winikwetaq *ta* squint at
winikwetuwet *ai* squint
wininuwit *ai* grouchy
winisqi tripe [SH]
winjik *ii* dirty; bad condition; a sin

winjinj (winjinjik) *an* roe [BR]; seed [SH]
winjit *ai* dirty; bad condition; a sin
winkutat *ai* poorly shod; poorly shoed
winnat *ai* make a poor selection; handle badly
winn'mat *ai* messy; sloppy
winpasit *ai* on the go; hustle
winpnet *ai* have a venereal disease
winqamiksit *ai* mean; have a bad character [BC]
winsit *ai* act bad or improperly
winsitat *ai* poorly shod [RB]
winsm (winsmuk) *an* filthy-minded person
winsmuwit *ai* filthy-minded
wintiku *an* wild man; cannibal [SH]
wipitmekw (wipitmaq) *an* shark [SH]
wipitmit *ai* have teeth
wipkoman pit; bud [SH]
wipskunk *ta* have only one of
wipskun'm *ti* have only one of
wipukjik soon [BR]
wisaw-amu:k *ii* yellowish
wisaw-amuksit *ai* yellowish
wisawe:k *ii* green; grayish [SH]; brownish [SH];
  yellow
wisawo:q copper pot [SH]
wisawo:qw copper; copper kettle
wisawow yellow jaundice; bile; appendix
wisaw suliyewey gold
wise:k *ai, ii* scarred
wisikat *ai* scar-faced; scarred
wi:sik'sit *ai* burn; feel as if on fire
wi:sik'tek *ii* burn; feel as if on fire
wi:sis *an* animal
wi:sisji:j *an* little animal
wi:s'kesit *ai* burn painfully
wi:s'ketek *ii* burn painfully
wiskipk stove ash; sand
wiskipko:q ashtray
wiskoq *an* black ash [RB]
wisku:p'k *ta* cook for
wiskuteskaq *ta* catch by surprise [PEI]
wiskuwet *ai* jealous
wiskwiya:teket *ai (an)* play the bagpipes;
  bagpiper
wismuti animal nest
wisnanaw (wisnanaq) *an* smelt [SH]
wisnaw (wisnaq) *an* perch
wisnuti animal nest [BR]

wisqan gall; gizzard; bile; bladder [RB]
wisqap'lkikwa:t *ai* snow-blinded; color-blind
wisqasaw (wisqasaq) *an* pine cone
wisqasoq *an* pine cone [RB]
wisqatenmat *ai* sun-blinded [PEI]
wisqateskaq *ta* take by surprise
wisqeket *ai* throw quickly
wisqi-jik'lsink *ai* {ejik'lsink} fly away quickly
wisqi-luwe:wit *ai* {eluwe:wit} quick-tempered
wisqi:pit *ai* sprint
wisqi·pkisink *ai* {pekisink} arrive suddenly
wisq'k *ii* bitter
wisqo:pit fang [SH]
wisqoq *an* ash tree; black ash [SH]
wisse:j nest
wissey nest
wissukwalk *ta* cook
wissukwat *ai* cook (for oneself)
wissukwatiket *ai* cook
wissukwatm *ti* cook
wissuwiknemk *ta* overcome; overpower; conquer
wissuwiknetm *ti* overcome; overpower; conquer
wisun name
wisunkalk *ta* call; name; christen
wisunkatm *ti* call; name
wisunkewk *ta* name
wisuwiknemk *ta* overpower (physically)
witpitaq *ta* sit with
witpitm *ti* sit with
witu:ji:tl (pl) pubic hair
wituwa:tijik (pl) *ai* partners in a boat (used in guiding)
wituwit *ai* whiskered
wiyaqiyaqal (pl) *ii* mixed
wiyaqiyejik (pl) *ai* mixed
wiyaqqatmu:tijik (pl) *ai* mix together
wiyu:ji:j piece of meat
wiyus meat
wiyuse:j *an* meat handler (cutter)
wja:law (wja:laq) *an* snot
wjijaqamiju:wet *ai* {njijaqamij} have a shadow
wjikapan incoming tide
wjiki scab; sore [BR]
wji:k'j tree stump
wjipen east

wjipenuk (loc) {wejipek} from the east [SH]
wjipenukowa:j *an* easterner
wjip'sk root
wjit for
wju:sn {weju:s'k} wind
wju:sney fan or propeller
wju:sniktuk (loc) in the wind
wkamlamun *an* heart (in cards)
wkat-awti footpath
wkatistuwik *ii* a twisted foot; a clubfoot
wktluwanipkaji:jit *an* a kind of leaf for medical purposes [SH]
wkwisit *ai* have a son
w'laku wela:gw} yesterday
w'lapetmuwaqan {welapetmuwet} favor obtained (religious)
w'laqan *an* plate [BR]; pan [BR]; dish [SH]
w'laqane:s *an* pan bullmoose [BR]
w'ljaqa carefully
w'ljikn lobster claw [BC]
w'lma'itasuwaqan {welma'ita:sit} sadness; sorrow
w'lmajita:suwaqan {welma'ita:sit} mourning [BC]
w'lo:nuk {wela:kw} tonight; this evening
w'loqotalk *ai* eat supper
w'lta:suti {welta:sit} gladness
w'lta:suwaqan {wel-ta:sit} happiness
w'ltestaqan *an* bone die (for dice game) [CB]
w'lukuni *an* yellow hammer woodpecker [SH]
w'lukwe:ket *ai* have a swollen gland or tonsil; have the mumps
w'lukwiyet *ai* have tonsilitus [SH]
w'misit *ai* have an older sister
w'naqapem *an* disciple
w'naqi:kn stove cover lifter [ESK]
wo:kumatijik (pl) *ai* related (as kin)
wow *an* pot
wowj *an* quicksand; bog [RB]; pit
wowkwis *an* fox
wpaqama:l'k *ta* back up; give support to
wpaqamk behind; in the rear of
wpi:kanj'k Eel River Bar, N.B.
wpitni:sawet *ai* sew (by hand) [SH]
wpitni:sewet *ai* sew (by hand)
wpmepikaj hip or side of one's body [BR]

wpmesink *ai* lie on one's side [BR]

wpmesma:sit *ai* lie down on one's side [BR]

wpmetuk (loc) on one's side [BR]

wpukikwa:l'k *ta* eye; watch [SH]

wpukikwe:l (pl) eyeglasses [SH]

wpukukwa:l'k *ta* eye; watch

wpukukwa:tu *ti* eye; watch

wpukukwe:l (pl) eyeglasses

wsaqatp human skull [SH]

wsitney stove pipe

wskewinu *an* {wesket} fisherman [BR]

wskijin *an* {weskijinuwit} person; gifted person (a Maliseet word)

wskijipnew *an* host (communion)

wskitwan {weskit} outer garment [BC]

wskma:taqanejk name of a portage trail located at present-day Micmac reserve [SH]

wskun liver

wskus *an* weasel

wskwipnek host (communion) [PEI]

ws'tqamu world; earth

ws'tqamuwa:l'k *ta* bear (a child); bring into the world

ws'tqamuwit *ai* born; come into the world

wtapsun useful object or person

wtapsunik *ii* useful

wtapsunit *ai* useful

wtejk (loc) in back; behind

wtejkewey *an, in* last one

wtewit *ai* have a dog [SH]

wti:t *ai* have a dog

wtmo:taqan {wetmo:tm} useful tool or object [SH]

wt'pi *an* a fine root used in basketry [SH]

wtqotalk *ta* bury

wtqotamk burial; funeral

wtqotaqan grave

wtqotaqane:kati graveyard

wtqotatm *ti* bury

wtqutaqan grave

wt'si bird nest [RB]

wtulit *ai* {ntul} have a vehicle

wtunapi bit [SH]; rein

wtune:l (pl) bridle and bit

wtutnuk (loc) in the east [SH]

wtuttemit *ai* have a totem or benefactor

wujjewit *ai* a father

wujjit *ai* have a father

- ENGLISH - MICMAC -

A

abandon puna:l'k *ta*, puna:tu *ti*; temporarily ~ eptoqalk *ta*, eptoqatm *ti*

abcess kluk (klukk) *an*

abdomen my ~ n'musti

abhor ketkite:l'mk *ta*, ketkite:tm *ti*

able kiskajiyet *ai*

aboard teppit *ai*, teptek *ii*; get ~ tepa:sit *ai*; hoist ~ teppil'm *ti*, teppilk *ta*; put ~ tepa:l'k *ta*, tepa:tu *ti*

aborigine t'mkewa:j *an*

abort kettiyalk *ta*

about coast ~ aliyo:qsat *ai* [ESK]; face ~ kinawaklapa:sit *ai* [CB]; sit all ~ allkopijik (pl) *ai*; skate ~ alipqamit *ai* [ESK]; what ~ ? katu

above k'p'tay; place oneself ~ emteski-te:l'mk *ta*, emteski-te:tm *ti*; up ~ ke:kwe:k

abscess my ~ nulukw *an*

absent-minded puski-weniyet *ai*; wejuwowita:sit *ai*

absolutely ketl etuk

abstain wetqolsit *ai*

abundance eat in ~ mekepk *ta*, meketm *ti*; grow in ~ minit *ai*, minik *ii*

accent speak with an ~ kesmi:sit *ai*

accept weliwsuwa:tu *ti*

accident die in an ~ ketemetesultijik (pl) *ai*

accidentally bump into ~ petteskaq *ta*; cut (in two) ~ peji-tms'k *ta*, peji-tmsm *ti*; kill ~ peji-sikte:k *ta*; slice up ~ peji-nuks'k *ta*, peji-nuksm *ti*; slice or cut ~ pess'k *ta*, pess'm *ti*; strike or hit ~ pette:k *ta*, pette:m *ti*

accompany wije:w'k *ta*, wije:w'm *ti*; wijitkweyaq *ta*, wijitko:tm *ti*; piskw-wije:w'k *ta*, piskw-wije:w'm *ti*

accumulate masqo:tasit *ai*

accusation false ~ pisu-ilsu:tmaqan

accuse ~ falsely pisu-ilsu:tmaq *ta*; ~ of being an accomplice oqotqomk *ta*

ace ~ card e:s (e:sik) *an*; newtuwi:kas'k *ii*, newtuwi:kasit *ai (an)*; ~ of spades mistun

ache kesinukuwik *ii*, kesinukuwit *ai*

acorn mimkwaqan

across a:sispit *ai*, a:sistek *ii*; fall ~ as'komoqtesk *ii* [BR]; asoqomoqtesk *ii*, asoqomoqtesink *ai*; go ~ as'koma:sit *ai* [BR]; lie ~ as'komoqtek *ii* [BR]; lie down

crossways or ~ taqamoqisma:sit *ai*; push ~ taqamoqiksma:l'k *ta*, taqamoqiksma:tu *ti*; wade ~ asoqomasukwet *ai*

act ~ correctly tetapu:qamikset *ai*; ~ funny wennjuwa:'it *ai* [RB]; ~ in such a manner telqamiksit *ai*

active seskwe:k *ai*

act up ew'nasa:sit *ai*; ikewkwet *ai* [PEI]

add ~ up mawkijjet *ai*

addition in ~ to atelk *ai*, *ii* [SH]

additional give an ~ amount to ankuwa:l'k *ta*, ankuwa:tu *ti*

adequate tepiyaq *ii*, tepiyet *ai*

adjust ila:l'k *ta*, ila:tu *ti*

admire kesite:l'm'k *ta*, kesite:tm *ti*

adopt an ~ -ed child kisikwenikn *an*

adoptee my ~ n'naqapem *an* [BC]

advance ~ in time ajiyet *ai*

advice give good ~ to welimk *ta*

advisor a good ~ nata:suteket *ai (an)*; nata:tawet *ai (an)*; an ~ to nujimk *ta (an)*; an ~ nujimuwet *ai (an)*

affect mesi:k *ta*

afire start ~ paskesa:l'k *ta*, paskesa:tu *ti*

afraid ~ of jipalk *ta*, jipatm *ti*

after look ~ anko:tm *ti*, ankweyaq *ta*; the day ~ tomorrow ktiki-sapo:nuk; ~ while apukjik

again apj [BR]; app

against lean ~ epatkupukuwik *ii*, epatkupukuwit *ai*; place ~ mesatkwa:l'k *ta*, mesatkwa:tu *ti*; push ~ epatkwiksma:l'k *ta*, epatkwiksma:tu *ti*; push up ~ mesatkwiksma:l'k *ta*, mesatkwiksma:tu *ti* [BR]; set ~ epatuwepit *ai*, epatuwetek *ii*; stand ~ kaqamutaq *ta*, kaqamutm *ti*

age have such an ~ tetuje:k *ai*; te'uje:k *ai*

agent Indian ~ e:jint (e:jintaq) *an*

aggravate askayaq *ta*, asko:tm *ti* [BC]; ki:kajeyaq *ta*, ki:kajo:tm *ti*

aggressive nalakit *ai*

agitated easily ~ or offended nepe:k *ai*

aglow pitiyasit *ai*, pitiyatek *ii*

ago a short while ~ kejikow; a while ~ atel; long ~ ki:s sa:q; sa:q

agree ~ on aknutmajik (pl) *ai*; ~ with keta:maq *ta* [BC]

agreement (formal) ~ keta:muweml [BC];
marriage ~ keluluwemk [BC]

ahead nikanpit *ai*, nikantek *ii*; arrive ~ of time
naqsipkisink *ai*; go ~ down in the water elmi-
nikanipqa:sit *ai* [BR]; push ~ nikaniksma:l'k
ta, nikaniksma:tu *ti*; run up ~ ikanitqa:sit *ai*
[SH]; think ~ about nikanite:tm *ti*; walk ~
nikana:sit *ai*

airs put on ~ me:kitutk *ai* [PEI]

alcoholic beverage drink an ~ beverage
newtumqwanet *ai*; want an ~
ketuktnukqwanet *ai*

alder tupi *an* [SH]; ~ tree tupsi *an* (scrapings
mixed with alum to make a grey dye); ~ twig
tupsi *in* [SH]

alert sma:tewit *ai*

alive mimajik *ii*, mimajit *ai*

all ms't; ~ the time ne:kow; ~ the same lpa
wijey; know ~ about kaqikjijitu *ti*, kaqikjiji:k
ta; own ~ of kaqi-alsumk *ta*, kaqi-alsutm *ti*
[BC]; stiff ~ over kaqi-petkwe:k *ai* [BC]; take
~ of kaqa:l'k *ta*, kaqa:tu *ti*; that's ~ na(:)
ms't

allow asite:l'mk *ta* [NB]; ikn'maq *ta (do)*

almost keket; suwel

alone nekwte:jk *ii*, nekwte:jit *ai* [BR]; newte:jit
ai, newte:jk *ii*; newtukwa:lukwet *ai*; drink ~
newtinqana:mat *ai*

alongside akmetuk (loc); jajikpit *ai*, jajiktek *ii*
[SH]; lie ~ jajikoqpit *ai*, jajikoqtek *ii*

Alphonse Allpo:s *an* (Fr *Alphonse*)

already ki:s

also elk; elp; elt; maw; nkutey

altar patkwi-alasutmaqan [CB]; an ~ boy
nutnawet *ai (an)*

alter ~ clothing apsi:s'k *ta*, apsi:sm *ti*

always ne:kow; ne:kaw [SH]; ne:kayiw [CB]

amateur pqojiw *an*; sku:lltaqa:m *an* [SH];
sqapantiyej

amaze pa:qala'ik *ai*

amazement pa:qala'imk [CB]

ambitious seskwe:k *ai*

ambush kimtelaq *ta*

amen na tliyaq *ii*

American pastunkewi:skw *an* (female);
pastunkewa:j *an* (male)

amount take or withdraw in small ~ -s
qasko:tm *ti*, qaskweyaq *ta*

amus-e malikeyaq *ta*, maliko:tm *ti*; ~ oneself
papit *ai*; find ~ -ing wi:kuwamk *ta*,
wi:kuwaptm *ti*

anal track my ~ np'siktiyem

anchor k'lpisun; kullpisun [CB]; ekuma:tu *ti*; ~
-ed ekumik *ii*, ekumit *ai*

ancient anqaney [BR]

and aqq

Andrew Antle *an* (Fr *André*)

angel ansale:wit (ansale:wijik) *an*

anger takala:l'k *ta*; ~ (through speech)
wekamk *ta* [RB]; weka'iya:l'k *ta*; feel ~
takaliyet *ai*

angry weka'ik *ai*; ~ with weka'iyuktaq *ta*,
weka'iyuktm *ti*; get ~ poqjiluwa:t *ai*

animal wa'isis *an* [RB][BR]; wa:sis *an* [SH];
wi:sis *an*; female ~ lape:wi:skw *an* [SH];
nape:wi:skw *an* [BR]; little ~ wi:sisji:j *an*;
male ~ nape:w *an*; napiyoq *an* [BR]; my
domestic ~ (e.g. a horse, cat, etc.) ntuwe:m
an; older ~ kisiku:sm (kisiku:smuk) *an*

Annapolis Valley kespukwitk [SH]

annoint amaqan'm *ti* [SH]; a:mekn'k *ta*,
a:meken'm *ti*; mima:l'k *ta*, mima:tu *ti*

annoy askayaq *ta*, asko:tm *ti*

another ktik *an*, *in*; again ~ apj kt'k [SH]; app
iktik; ~ one iktik *an*, *in*

answer always have an ~ natawinsku:mat *ai*

ant kilikwejit (kilikwejijik) *an* [SH]; a kind of ~
psiktiyej (a derogatory expression); sugar ~
sismo:qone:j *an*

antlers have nice shaped ~ or horns
kesi:wesmat *ai* [BR]; kesiw'lismat *ai* [BR]

anus my ~ nijimij; np'siktiyem

anxious ~ about tetaqite:l'mk *ta*, tetaqite:tm *ti*

anyhow me: pa

anything ~ else? me: koqwey

anytime ta:n te:s

anyway me:

anywhere just ~ tam pas'k tami

apart ~ from others tepkispit *ai*, tepkistek *ii*;
come ~ sekwiskiyaq *ii*, sekwiskiyet *ai*; fall ~
siyoqiyaq *ii*, siyoqiyet *ai*; live ~ se:siketijik

(pl) *ai* [PEI]; set (sit) ~ tepkisa:l'k *ta*, tepkisa:tu *ti*

apparition see or hear an ~ or ghost em'lsiktmat *ai*

appear amu:k *ii*, amuksit *ai*; ne:ya:s'k *ii*, ne:ya:sit *ai*; ~ in moving silhouette aluwasa:sit *ai*; make or or cause to ~ ne:yamukwa:l'k *ta*, ne:yamukwa:tu *ti*

appearance find funny in ~ wi:kuwamk *ta*, wi:kuwaptm *ti*; make a brief ~ (on foot) ne:yapukuwa:sit *ai*

appendix wisawow; my ~ nwisawo:m; nwisawe:m [SH]

apple wennju:-su:n; ~ juice wennju:-su:n apu; ~ tree wennju:-su:naqsi

approach wejku:waq *ii*, wejku:wet *ai*; wejuwaqateskaq *ta*, wejuwaqateskm *ti* [BR]; wejkuwiyaq *ii*, wejkuwiyet *ai* [SH]; ~ and listen jiks'tmakwet *ai* [SH]; ~ or come nightfall wejkwitpa:q *ii*; ~ with head hanging down wejkwi-qolomkopit *ai*

approachable ni:laje:k *ai*

approve ~ of wel-te:l'mk *ta*, wel-te:tm *ti*

April pnatmuwiku:s *an*

apron laqpisuti

arch have an instep or ~ walnoqsitat *ai* [BR]

Archangel kji-ansale:wit (ansale:wijik) *an*

argue ki:kaja:sit *ai*

argumentative ki:kaja:sit *ai*

arm[1] ~ a gun pitqasawet *ai*

arm[2] have large ~ -s maqo:qiptnat *ai*; have large upper ~ -s keskitlmaqanat *ai*; have small ~ -s apso:qiptnat *ai*; hold under the ~ sepulkomit *ai*; etulkomit *ai*; my ~ np'tnokom [SH]; put one's ~ -s around the neck of ke:kuluskwa:l'k *ta*

armpit sepulkomat *ai* [SH]

around chase each other ~ (in a circle) kitto:qateskatultijik (pl) *ai*; circle ~ kiwto:qwa:sit *ai*; see all ~ pe'ikwapit *ai*, pe'ikwatek *ii*; skip ~ iwtoqoto:sit *ai* [SH]; turn ~ kitto:qa:s'k *ii*, kitto:qa:sit *ai*; turn ~ to point in a different direction kitto:qaska:l'k *ta*, kitto:qaska:tu *ti*; turn one's head ~ kawaskulapa:sit *ai*

arouse massaqte:ket *ai*; sexually ~ -d or stimulated massaqiyet *ai*

arrive ika:q *ii*, ika:t *ai*; oqwa:q *ii*, oqwa:t *ai*; pekisk *ii*, pekisink *ai*; ~ with pekisulk *ta*, pekisutu *ti* ~ at their destination petknejik (pl) *ai*; ~ crying pettemit *ai*; ~ early naqsipkisink *ai*; ~ suddenly wisqipkisink *ai*; expected to ~ ketu:pkisink *ai*; ketuwipkisink *ai* [BR]

arrow majjoqtelikn *an*; mattelikn *an* [BR]

arrowhead l'tqa:mun *an*

as far as go ~ (to the limit) we:kwa:s'k *ii*, we:kwa:sit *ai*; pole (a boat) ~ the waterway permits we:kwamkwe:ket *ai*

ash[1] ~ bin t'pkwano:q *an*; ~ pan t'pkwaniptaqan *an* [SH]

ash[2] ~ strip (for making baskets) wikpe:tlaqan; ~ strip (for weaving baskets) likpete:knapi; black ~ wiskoq *an* [RB]; wisqoq *an* [SH]; pound ~ (to make basket splints) elikpete:ket *ai*; stove ~ wiskipk; strip ~ elikpetamit *ai* [SH]; (white) ~ (tree) likpeta:w *an*; ~ Wednesday t'pkwanatpalltimk [BC]; t'pkwanalltimk; ~ tree aqamoq *an* [SH]; wisqoq *an*

ashamed netaqe:k *ai* [SH]; netaka:sit *ai*

ashore bring ~ na:taqama:l'k *ta*, na:taqama:tu *ti*; go ~ na:taqama:sit *ai*

ashtray sipiska:sutiyo:q; wiskipko:q

aside anapiw, metuk [BR]; pmetuk; move ~ s'ta:l'k *ta*, s'ta:tu *ti*; s'ta:s'k *ii*, s'ta:sit *ai*; put ~ seta:l'k *ta*, seta:tu *ti*; set ~ s'tapukuwa:l'k *ta*, s'tapukuwa:tu *ti*; step ~ sata:sit *ai*; seta:sit *ai*

ask pipanimk *ta*; ~ for kelumk *ta*, kelutm *ti*; ~ of etamk *ta*; ~ (someone) to do something elulk *ta*

asleep nepat *ai*; nepaq *ii*

aspen miti *an*

assembly maw-nutmamk

assist apoqonmaq *ta*; ~ at mass nutnawet *ai* *(an)*

assistance apoqonmatimk; seek ~ from elulk *ta*

assume etlite:l'mk *ta*, etlite:tm *ti*

astraddle nasuwoqkat *ai*; get astride or ~ nasuwoqpa:sit *ai*

astride sit or set ~ nasuwoqpit *ai*, nasuwoqtek *ii*; stand ~ or astraddle nasuwoq-pukuwa:sit *ai*

athlete educated ~ skulltaqa:m *an*

athwart lie across or ~ taqamoqpit *ai*, taqamoqtek *ii*

atop get ~ ke:kwa:sit *ai*; land ~ ke:kutesink *ai*; lie ~ ke:koqpit *ai*, ke:koqtek *ii*; place ~ ke:ko:tu *ti*; set ~ weskitpa:suwalk *ta*, weskitpa:suwatm *ti*; sit ~ ewt'pa:suwalk *ta*, ewt'pa:suwatm *ti*; sit down ~ ewt'pa:sit *ai*; sit or set ~ ke:kupit *ai*, ke:kutek *ii*; stand ~ ke:ku-pukuwit *ai*; ke:kwi-pukuwit *ai* [SH]

attached naspit *ai*, nastek *ii*; ~ (as an integral part) mekwaspit *ai*, mekwastek *ii*; where hooked or ~ wet-nastek *ii*

attain kisapskn'm *ti*, kisapsknk *ta*

attention make oneself the centre of ~ ne:tma:sit *ai*

attract ~ -ed to welamk *ta*, welaptm *ti* [BC]

attractive kesite:wet *ai*; look ~ wikwasamuksit *ai*, wikwasamu:k *ii*

auction forty-five pitto:tulltimk (a card game)

auger po:qikn

August-September kisikwekewiku:s

aunt my ~ nsukwis *an*; nukumij *an* [BR]; my aunt (mother's sister) n'lis *an* [BC]

aunt and uncle my ~ nsukwisewijik (pl) *an* (aunt dominant)

aunty! nsukwi: (voc)

authority alsusuti [PEI]; assusuti

automobile kesikawiyaqewey [SH]

autumn toqwa:q *ii*

awake wapit *ai*; stay ~ all night nipapit *ai*; keep ~ wespayaq *ta*

awaken tukwiyet *ai*

aware ne:te:k *ai*; ~ of nenuwite:l'mk *ta*, nenuwite:tm *ti*; teko:tm *ti*, tekweyaq *ta*

away bent (head part) ~ ejiklako:jink *ai*; bent (at the waist) ~ ejiklu:jink *ai*; get ~ wesimit *ai* [SH]; lie facing ~ enmisink *ai*, enmisk *ii*; put ~ masqwa:l'k *ta*, masqwa:tu *ti*; nasko:l'k *ta*, nasko:tu *ti* [SH]; take ~ ejikla:l'k *ta*, ejikla:tu *ti*; throw ~ ejikleket *ai*; walk ~ enm'l'ka:t *ai*; work ~ from home tew-lukwet *ai*

awkward awane:k *ai*; lie ~ -ly ew'nasisink *ai*; do or perform ~ -ly

awl sa:pikn [SH]; si:sikn

axe tmi:kn; my ~ nutmi:kn; strike with an ~ tmi:kn-te:k *ta*

B

baboon nankwenawejit (nankwenawejijik) *an*

baby mijuwa:ji:j *an*; act like a ~ mijuwa:ji:juwe:k *ai*; expect a ~ ketu-w'njanit *ai*

babysit naqanu:set *ai*; ~ or look after for someone nespit *ai*

babysitter a ~ nujins'pit *ai (an)*

babytalk ka:kaka (said by a baby who is tired or in need of a change) [SH]

bachelor nkutuko:pj *an*; nkutilj *an*; nkuto:pj: *an*; a ~ newtukwa:lukwet *ai (an)*

back[1] animal that floats on its ~ atuwa:sa:kw *an* [BR]; my ~ npaqam; have a weak ~ malukunat *ai* [BR]; lie on one's ~ atuwa:skwesink *ai*; carry along on one's ~ or shoulder pemaw'lalk *ta*, pemaw'latm *ti*; carry around on the ~ alaw'lalk *ta*, alaw'latm *ti*; alaw'let *ai*

back[2] ~ from eating apatalk *ai* [ESK]; chase ~ apatte:k *ta*, apatte:m *ti*; come ~ apaja:sit *ai*; follow ~ apajukkwalk *ta*, apajukkwatm *ti*; in ~ wtejk (loc); move ~ eseta:sit *ai*; take ~ apajiksuwa:l'k *ta*, apajiksuwa:tu; walk or stride ~ apatl'ka:t *ai*; push ~ etekjiksma:l'k *ta*, etekjiksma:tu *ti*

back and forth pace ~ asu:set *ai*; walk ~ to asu:teskaq *ta*, asu:teskm *ti*

backbone my ~ no:kwin; nowikn [SH]

backpack nutaw'lalk *ta*, nutaw'latm *ti*; start to ~ poqtuktu *ti*

back up wpaqama:l'k *ta*

backward malja:t *ai*

backwards bring ~ esetekja:l'k *ta*, esetekja:tu *ti*; crawl ~ esetekjapekit *ai*; las'tikjapekit *ai* [SH]; do (something) in reverse order (e.g. skip rope ~ or paddle in reverse) apatto:sit *ai*; enter ~ eseti-pija:sit *ai*; fall ~ apatankiyet *ai* [PEI]; aputask'tesink *ai*; aputaskiyaq *ti*, aputaskiyet *ta*; atuwa:skwetesink *ai*; go in ~ esetekji-pija:sit *ai*; name ~ kiwaskiwi:tm *ti*; say ~ kawaskuwi:tm *ti*; stoop facing ~ enmikjo:kwet *ai*

bad metuwe:k *ii*; a ~ day metuwi-kisk'k *ii*; ~ condition winjik *ii*, winjit *ai*; extremely ~ pajiji-winjik *ii*, pajiji-winjit *ai*; feel ~ about

ansuwite:l'mk *ta*, ansuwite:tm *ti*; have a ~ character winqamiksit *ai* [BC]; have ~ breath eloqtnema:t *ai*; loqtnema:t *ai*; have a ~ disposition metu:qamiksit *ai*; look ~ metu-amuksit *ai*, metu-amu:k *ii*; pretty ~ mawi-winjik *ii* [SH]; maw-winjit *ai*, maw-winjik *ii*; smell ~ jijjema:q *ii*, jijjema:t *ai*; metuwima:q *ii*, metuwima:t *ai*; taste ~ metuwima:q *ii*, metuwima:t *ai*; too ~ ansuwe:k *ii*

badly ~ injured me:kiksitesink *ai* [SH]; handle ~ winnat *ai*; treat (people) ~ emeko:teket *ai (an)*

baffle maqana:l'k *ta*; ~ -d maqanat *ai*

bag m'nuti [BR]; munnti; medicine ~ puwowinuti

bagpipes play the ~ wiskwiya:teket *ai (an)*

bail naqani:ket *ai*; ~ out (a boat) si:niket *ai*; ~ (water) from a boat si:n'm *ti*

bailer (water) ~ si:nikn

bake etoqtalk *ta*, etoqtatm *ti*; etoqtet *ai*; ~ bread epipnet *ai*; know how to ~ nata:toqtet *ai*

baker a ~ nutpipnet *ai (an)*; a (professional) ~ nuji-toqtet *ai (an)*

balance illjo:qon'm *ti*, illjo:qonk *ta*; aptoqwet *ai*

bald memkatpat *ai* [SH]; become ~ menkosa:qanatpat *ai* [BC]; get ~ mkosaqanatpa:t *ai*; start to ~ poqji-m'mkatpa:t *ai* [BR]; ~ (-)headed

ball alje:maqan *an* [BR]; tu:waqan *an* [BC][RB]; play ~ ajje:mat *ai*; alje:mat *ai* [BR][BC]; tu:wat *ai*

balsam ~ sap puku:kewij [PEI]; fir or ~ tree stoqon *an*; spruce, fir or ~ tree stoqonaqsi *an* [SH]

bandage a:jijkopilaqan; a:jijkopil'm *ti*, a:jijkopilk *ta*

banish esa:q *ta*, esa:m *ti*; ese:k *ta*

bannock lusknikn

baptize sik'ntaq *ta*, sik'ntm *ti*; ~ -d sik'ntasit *ai*

bar tend ~ nutpet *ai (an)*; peki:t'pet *ai* [BR]

barber nuji-m'mk'te:muwet *ai (an)* [BC]

bare emisqe:k *ai, ii*; memke:k *ai, ii*; musike:k *ai, ii*; half ~ metaqapit *ai*, metaqatek *ii*; make ~ memkoqte:m *ti*; strip ~ musik'nja:tm *ti*

barebottomed metaqaptiyat *ai*

barefooted sesaki:k (sesaki:m) *ai*; sas'ki:k *ai*; metkatat *ai*

barehanded metaqapjit *ai*; catch ~ metaqapja:sit *ai*; do something ~ ketapja:sit *ai*; grab or take ~ metaqapja:l'k *ta*, metaqapja:tu *ti*; take ~ ketapsknk *ta*, ketapskn'm *ti*

bareheaded metkwat *ai*

barge sawtaqa:taqan

bark[1] wekilat *ai*; ~ at wekilalk *ta*

bark[2] psaqa:kw; peeled ~ pqwa:w [SH]; remove ~ (from a tree) menipqwa:wet *ai* [SH]; take off or remove ~ menipqwa:l'k *ta*, menipqwa:tu *ti* [SH]

barley pa:le'ewe:l (pl)

barn laqala:ns (Fr *la grange*); leklans (Fr *les granges*)

barrel malike:w *an*; equal or equivalent to a ~ malike:wa:t *ai*; oversized (molasses) ~ ponjn *an*

barren person who is ~ or sterile nujintus *an*

bartender nutpet *ai (an)*; nuji-pi:tupet *ai (an)*; nuji-pi:t'pet *ai (an)*

barter ~ for food pemamkuwat *ai* [PEI]

bashful netake:k *ai*; so ~ tetujintake:k *ai*

basket likpenikn; pu:taliyewey [BR]

bass jikaw *an*; ji:law (ji:laq) *an* [RB]

bastard pqotnanj *an*

baste sipma:m *ti*

bat[1] naji-puktaqane:j *an*

bat[2] baseball ~ tu:waqanatkw

bath take a ~ kesispalsit *ai*; take a sponge ~ kesispapalsit *ai*

bathe wetqapalsit *ai*

batter sapan

battle matnakkewaqan; mat'ntimk

bay tuwitn

be Let him ~ ! tla:sij; (it) has to ~ ! amujpa

beach[1] sitm

beach[2] ~ a canoe oqwasa:tu *ti* [CB]

bead wayo:pskw; ~ place wayo:pskwe:kati [BR]

beam tmoqta:w (tmoqta:q) *an* [SH]; cut ~ -s tmoqta:we:ket *ai*

bean wikun; string ~ pitlanji:j *an*

bear[1] muwin (muwinaq) *an*; ~ cub muwine:j *an*; she-~ muwine:skw (muwine:skwaq) *an*; ~ grease or fat muwino:mi; behave or act like a ~ muwinewqamiksit *ai*

bear[2] ~ a child ws'tqamuwa:l'k *ta*; finished ~ -ing or producing children kaqi-kwesmat *ai*

beat matte:k *ta*, matte:m *ti*; ~ (ash) into strips elanqate:m *ti*

beautiful wikwasapewit *ai*

beaver kopit (kopitaq) *an*; bank ~ e:tamkw (e:tamkwaq) *an* [RB]; extra large (bank) ~ ke:tamskw (ke:tamskuk) *an* [BR]; female ~ kopite:skw (kopite:skwaq) *an*; hunt or trap ~ kopitewe:ket *ai*; kitten ~ ijipanji:j *an* [SH]; kijipan(ji:j) *an* [RB]; old ~ kisiku:mskw *an*; three or four-year-old ~ pl'mskw (pl'mskuk) *an*; three-year-old ~ nsa:mskw (nsa:mskuk) *an* [BR]; yearling ~ pi:wej *an* [BR]

because m'ta; muta; lnim [CB]

become ~ or be a boy lpa:'ujuwit *ai*; ~ winter poqjipu:k [ESK]

bed mpo:qon; my ~ npo:qon; ntupun; ~ down (as an animal) elnaqsit *ai* [BC]; make the ~ elaqsensit *ai*

bedbug tepine:s *an* (Fr *des punaises*)

bedding anqono:simkewey [SH]

bedsheet naqsun *an*

bee amu *an*; amuwow (amuwaq) *an* [BR]; ~ hive amuwesusi

beebee sqolu:skuji:j

beech suwo:musi [RB]; ~ tree munkwaqanemusi [PEI]

beer seed ~ qones *an*

beet malltewiyejit *an* [SH]; mekwe:jit (mekwe:jijik) *an*; pi:ts (pi:ts'k) *an* [BR]

beetle kime:s *an*; kme:s *an* [SH]; kume:s *an* [PEI]; chimney ~ pukto:kuwome:j *an*

before keskm'naq; eskm'na:q (takes a negative verb form); ke:s mu (takes a negative verb form)

beg kiwiksit *ai* [CB]; salite:wit *ai*; ~ a favour etawet *ai*; ~ for etawaqtmaq *ta*; go about ~ -ging al-tawet *ai*; know how to ~ nata:-tawet *ai*

begin poqtamkiyaq *ii*, poqtamkiyet *ai*; ~ or start to fish poqjiwsket *ai*; ~ to cry poqji-atk'temit *ai*; ~ to speak poqtewo:kwet *ai* [BR]

beginner pqojiw *an*; sqapantiyej

beginning in the ~ na tmk; na tumk [CB]

behave keknu:qamiksit *ai*; ~ or act in such a manner tela:sit *ai*

behind paqaqamk; wpaqamk; wtejk (loc); leave ~ naqalk *ta*, naqtm *ti*; enqalk *ta*, enqatm *ti*; stand ~ e:taqaq *ta* [SH]

belch welat *ai*

belief my ~ nk'tlams'tmaqan [BC]; share the same ~ mawiktlams'tasultijik (pl) *ai* [BC]

believe etlite:l'mk *ta*, etlite:tm *ti*; ~ in ketlams'taq *ta*, ketlams'tm *ti*; ~ so tel-te:l'm'k *ta*, tel-te:tm *ti* [CB]

bell jejuwejk; jijuwejk; sisuwa:qi:kn; ~ clapper sisuwa:qate:kn; sleigh ~ jejuwejk'ji:j; ~ ringer (at church) nujimattaqa:teket *ai (an)* [BC]

bellow wetewiluwa:t *ai*; heard ~ **-ing** (as a moose) metewiluwa:t *ai*

belly have a big and round ~ maqapsk'tiyat *ai*; my ~ n'musti

belly button my ~ nili

belonging my ~ ntalikam; nutapsun

below epune:k; lame:k *ai, ii*; ~ deck lamulkuk (loc) [CB]

belt kispisun *an*; money ~ (with pocket) wijipoti *an*; wijipo:ti *an*

bend waqjuwika:l'k *ta*, waqjuwika:tu *ti*; ~ and show one's buttocks alikjo:kwet *ai*; ~ away from elmu:jink *ai* [SH]; ~ back facing in the opposite direction enmu:jink *ai*; ~ from the waist oqolumkwa:sit *ai*; ~ toward elu:jink *ai*

beneath ~ the surface elqanapit *ai* [BR]; enqanapit *ai*, enqanatek *ii*; penetrate ~ pitoqtek *ii*

benefactor have a totem or ~ wtuttemit *ai*

benefit ~ from welapemk *ta*, welapetm *ti* [PEI]

bent istuwik *ii*, istuwikit *ai*; waqjuwikk *ii*, waqjuwikit *ai*; ~ (at the waist) away ejiklu:jink *ai*; ~ toward (from the head) wejkwatpo:jink *ai*; ~ toward wejkuwijink *ai* [BR]

berat-e stop lecturing or ~ **-ing** punajimk *ta*

bereavement join in the ~ neskawet *ai*

berr-y minijk [SH]; a kind of ~ ka:to:min *an* [BR]; kawaqtejk, pokoman (pea-sized and green); pick **-ies** ewisit *ai* [CB]; thornbush ~ ko:kemin *an* [SH]; ko:kumin *an*

best ~ (in an argument or duel of words) we:kwa:maq *ta*; the ~ pajiji-klulk *ii*, pajiji-klu:sit *ai* [SH]; the very ~ ! mujkajewey; the very little ~ ! mujkajuweyji:j

better aji-klu:lk *ii*, aji-klu:sit *ai*; ~ than piyam-klu:lk *ii*, piyam-klu:sit *ai*

between lukwe:k [SH]; mi:soqo; miyawe:k (loc)

beverage drink a ~ newtumqwanet *ai*

beyond a:se:k (loc); a:sispit *ai*, a:sistek *ii*

big meskilk *ai*, meski:k *ii*; ~ and round meptoqopsk'set *ai* [PEI]; ~ in girth maqa:q *ii*, maqoqsit *ai*; ~ waves maqatkwik *ii*; have a ~ and round belly maqapsk'tiyat *ai*; have a ~ bowel movement maqijjikwat *ai*; have ~ buttocks maqikjat *ai*; have a ~ head maqatpat *ai*; have a ~ mouth maqtunat *ai*; have ~ shoulders kekitlmaqanat *ai* [PEI]; so ~ tetutkilk *ai*, tetutki:k *ii*; too ~ wesamkilk *ai*, wesamki:k *ii*; get ~ **-ger** pemims'ki:ka:sit *ai* [SH]

Big Cove (N.B.) m'lsekna:ti; elsipuktuk; lsipuktuk (loc); musiknatkuk

big shot saqamaw (saqamaq) *an*

bile wisawow; wisqan

bill my ~ ntettuwoqon'm

bin ash ~ t'pkwano:q *an*

bind elaqpa:l'k *ta*, elaqpa:tu *ti*; elaqpa:teket *ai*

binding laqpo:taqan

binoculars pair of ~ laputi:l

birch white ~ bark maskwi; dead and dry yellow ~ puku:skw *an*; ~ genus maskwe:simusi *an*; ~ grove maskwe:simanaqse:kati [SH]; yellow ~ m'nnoqon *an*; young ~ tree maskwe:s *an*

bird jipji:j *an*; sisip *an*; an unidentified ~ mtaqtnej *an*; have a voice like a ~ jipji:ju:kisutnat *ai*

birth give ~ to weskijinuwa:l'k *ta*

birthmark klitam; militaw (militaq) *an*; m'litaw (m'litaq) *an* [BC]; my ~ nklitam; nm'litam [BC]

biscuit kalkunawey [BC]; lusknikn

bishop kji-pa:tliya:s *an*

Bishop the ~ 's garment! kji-pa:tliya:s ewkwam (exclamation of surprise)

bit[1] wtunapi [SH]; bridle and ~ wtune:l (pl)

bit[2] ta:s'ji:jit *ai*; ta:s'ji:jk *ii*; a little ~ kijka:ji:jk

bitch[1] skwesmuj *an* (female dog)

bitch[2] skwesm *an*

bite paqa:l'k *ta*, paqa:tu *ti*; paqa:luwet *ai*; ~ off menp'k *ta*, mentm *ti*; ment'k *ta*, mentm *ti*; temp'k *ta*, temtm *ti*; ~ the head part off temkwepk *ta*

bits smash to ~ nukte:k *ta*, nukte:m *ti*

bitter wisq'k *ii*

blab miltoqsit *ai*; ~ away etlaqqisewet *ai*

blabbermouth seytun *an*; puski-wiskuwa:teket *ai* [ESK]

black maqtewe:k *ai, ii* [BR]; maqtawe:k *ai, ii*; ~ -ish maqtew-amuksit *ai*, maqtew-amu:k *ii*; ~ man kanntakwey *an* [PEI]

black-bearded maqtawi:tuwat *ai*

blackberry ajiyoqjimin *an* [SH]; kl'muwejimin *an* [BC]; maqtewiman *an*

black-bottomed maqtewikjat *ai*

blackfly u:je:s *an*

blackhead jujijuwikan [BC]

blacksmith klaptan *an*

bladder wisqan [RB]

blade waqan [BR][RB]; wa:q'n

blame ~ on elsu:tmaq *ta (do)*

blanket a:su:n; anqono:sun; distribution ~ etpi:tnewqwan; relief ~ tpi:tnewqwan

blaze[1] appear as or in a ~ ne:yamklek *ii*, ne:yamklet *ai*; ~ of fire sisuwey

blaze[2] ~ a trail keknukwatiket *ai*; newly ~ -d pili-jilta:sik *ii* [BR]; ~ (on a tree) knukwatikn *an*; ~ with a knife jiloqs'k *ta*, jiloqsm *ti*; ~ with an axe jiloqte:k *ta*, jiloqte:m *ti*; a trail ~ -r ikanawtiket (ikanawtikejik) *ai (an)*

bleat weto:temit *ai*

bleed etliku:niyet *ai*, malltewiyaq *ii*, malltewiyet *ai*; ~ as the result of a fall malltewtesk *ii*, malltewtesink *ai*; ~ down toward eli-nisku:niyet *ai* [BR]; ~ from the nostril pe'i:kitnet *ai*; pejikitnet *ai*; ~ profusely pukweliku:niyet *ai*; ~ toward eliku:niyet *ai*; ~ to death apjiku:niyet *ai*

bless elapalk *ta*, elapatu *ti*

blessed kji-sape:wit *an (an)*; sape:wik *ii*; sape:wit *ai*

blind[1] window ~ lekepilaqan

blind[2] napapikwa:t *ai*; nekapakwe:k *ai* [SH][NB]; nekapikwa:t *ai*; nekapikwe:k *ai* [BC]; nepapikwa:t *ai* [SH]; ~ -ed by a glare of light or the sun petasit *ai*; ~ with a light nekapikwa:l'k *ta*

blister putewiskwa:s'k *ii*, putewiskwa:sit *ai* [SH]; put'peka:sit *ai*, put'peka:s'k *ii*; putuwiskwa:sik *ii*; wijkwe:j

blizzard mtukunoqt

bloat put'pekiyaq *ii*, put'pekiyet *ai*; ~ -ed apita:q *ii*, apita:t *ai*; mowpek *ii*, mowpet *ai*; putawiyaq *ii* [SH]

block kepijoqwa:l'k *ta*, kepijoqwa:tu *ti*; ~ off the air from aptlama:l'k *ta*, aptlama:tu *ti*; partially ~ pesoqopsk'te:k *ta*, pesoqopsk'te:m *ti*; ~ -ed kepjoqpit *ai*, kepjoqtek *ii*; ~ -ed or plugged (of the ear or nose) kepe:k *ai, ii*

blood malltew; cut (so as to cause ~ to flow) malltews'k *ta*; malltewsm *ti*; get ~ on malltewa:l'k *ta*, malltewa:tu *ti*; hit (so as to cause ~ to flow) malltewte:k *ta*, malltewte:m *ti*; my ~ n'malltem; ~ -y malltewik *ii*, malltewit *ai*; get or make ~ -y malltewtesmk *ta*, malltewtestu *ti*

blossom wasuwek *ii*, wasuwet *ai*; ~ (of a fruit or vegetable) wajuwejk [SH]

blouse matlet; my ~ n'matletm [PEI]

blow putuwatamit *ai*; ~ a whistle or horn pipuwa:smukwet *ai* [BR]; ~ from such direction wetteniyaq *ii*; wett'k *ii*; ~ on putuwalk *ta*, putuwatm *ti*; ~ out (with breath) naqasuwi-putuwalk *ta* [SH]

blown ~ over keskiss'k *ii*

blue ew'ne:k *ii*; sky ~ munqwan-amuksit *ai* [SH]; turn ~ ew'niyaq *ii*

blueberry pkuman; pkwiman [BR]; ~ juice pkuman-apu; go after blueberries pkumane:ket *ai*

bluejay titiyes *an* [SH]

bluff ewsa:tu *ti*; ewsimk *ta*

bluish dark ~ musqun-amuksit *ta*, musqun-amu:k *ti* [SH]

blunt kesp'k *ii*; kesplk *ta*, kesp'tu *ti*; kesp'plk *ta*; t'mem'napskek *ii*, t'mem'napsk'sit *ai*

blurred keskmuksit *ai*, keskmu:k *ii*

blush mekwe:saqa:sit *ai*
board lasqo:plaw (lasqo:plaq) *an*; qasqey [SH]; small ~ qasqe:j [SH]
boast pajjaqamat *ai*
boastful kinuwet *ai*
boat old canoe or ~ kisiku:lkw [BR]; start off by ~ poqtisukwit *ai*
bob run along with head a ~ -bing pematpe:pit *ai*; run with one's hair ~ -bing up and down enmisa:kwatp'tesink *ai*
bobbin papn-ji:j *an* (Fr *bobine*)
bobcat tqoqwej *an* [BR]
bobtailed tema:luwat *ai*
bog wowj *an* [RB]
boil¹ kl'muwej *an*; kmuwej *an* [BR]; pukliye:wey; have ~ -s kmuweju:sit *ai* [PEI]
boil² kwejaqamiyaq *ii*, kwejaqamiyet *ai* [BR]; kwejaqama:l'k *ta*, kwejaqama:tu *ti* [BR]; wejaqamiyaq *ii*, wejaqamiyet *ai*; wejaqama:l'k *ta*, wejaqama:tu *ti*; ~ -ing kettle wejaqama:temkewey; put on to ~ wesawa:l'k *ta*, wesawa:tu *ti*
Bonaventure, Québec waqam'tkuk
bone waqnntew (waqnntal); marrow ~ kuwikn; round ~ or die (used in dice game) waltestaqan *an* [SH]
book wi:katikn
boom log ~ s'nkatikn
boost give a ~ kesmoqja:l'k *ta*; kesmoqja:tu *ti*; kesmoqjeket *ai*
boot wennjuksnan *an*; wennjuksnan *an* [SH]; wennjusknan *an*
bore po:qiket *ai*; po:q'k *ta*, po:qm *ti*; tidal ~ suwekaw *an* [SH]
bored siwiyet *ai*; ~ with siwamk *ta*, siwaptm *ti*; ~ with being alone siwinkutukwa:lukwet *ai*
boring jikawepit *ai*, jikawetek *ii*
born weskijinuwit *ai*; ws'tqamuwit *ai*; youngest or last ~ mtesan *an*
boss alsumk *ta*, alsutm *ti*; alsusit *ai (an)* [SH]; assusit *ai (an)*
Boston pastun (meaning the U.S.A.)
both kitk
bother lkowaqana:l'k *ta*, lkowaqana:tu *ti*; lukwaqana:l'k *ta*, lukwaqana:tu *ti*; si:kaq *ta*; ~ with hands sespeyaq *ta*, sespo:tm *ti*

bothersome lukowaqanit *ai*; lukowaqana:teket *ai*
bottle mamam (baby talk) [SH]; pu:tay *an*
bottom ~ of the river or lake lampo:q; sit or set in the ~ of a canoe nekulpit *ai*, nekultek *ii* [BR]; make the ~ part (of a basket) elikjepilawet *ai* [SH]; weave the ~ (of a basket) elikjipil'm *ti* [SH]
bow¹ ~ down matkwa:sit *ai*; ~ to matkwetaq *ta*, matkwetm *ti*
bow² api *an* [BR]; tapi *an*
bowel movement have a big ~ maqijjikwat *ai*
bowels mi:jane:kmuti
bowl lapol *an* (Fr *le bol*); sugar ~ sismo:qono:q
bow-legged nikoqji:j wikatat *ai*
box tool ~ lukowaqane:kmuti; quill ~ kawiyo:qolaqan [SH]
boy! kwi:s (voc) (term of affection)
boy lpa:tuj *an*; lpa:'uj *an*; become or be a ~ lpa:tujuwit *ai*; lpa:'ujuwit *ai*; small ~ lpa:tu:ji:j *an*
boyfriend my ~ nt'lpa:tu:sm *an* [PEI]; nt'lpa:tum *an* [SH]
brace ~ oneself (to keep one's balance or to slow down) elqamkwejat *ai*
brag pajjaqamat *ai*; kinuwet *ai*; ~ about kinuwalk *ta*, kinuwatm *ti*
braid kni:sikn [BC]; elisknuwalk *ta*, elisknuwatm *ti*; elisknuwet *ai*; ~ or strand lisknuwapi (Maria)
brain my ~ nt'p
branch psetkun [BR]; ~ of an evergreen tree (used for breaking a fever) qastulastu *an*; ~ used to hold a tea kettle over a fire to boil water kinipewa:j *an*; dead (dried out) tree ~ psetkunatkw
brassiere my ~ npuskuney
brave melkita:t *ai*
bread nuskniknn [PEI]; pipnaqan
break¹ eskutesm'k *ta*; eskwitesm(')k *ta* [BR]; temtesmk *ta*, temtestu *ti*; ~ in ewe:kiska:l'k *ta*, ewe:kiska:tu *ti*; ~ in a horse sekwiska:l'k *ta* [CB]; sewiska:l'k *ta*, sewiska:tu *ti*; ~ in two tema:l'k *ta*, tema:tu *ti*; ~ (a rope, string or chain) in two kesippeket *ai*; ~ off at the tail

or rear end temaluwa:l'k *ta*, temaluwa:tu *ti*;
~ off spruce boughs menastet *ai*; ~ off a
spruce bough menastatm *ti*; ~ wind
putuwet *ai*; start to ~ pemi-tma:s'k *ii*, pemi-
tma:sit *ai* [BR]

break² take a ~ atlasmu:teket *ai*; take a ~
(for liquid refreshment) sinapska:teket *ai*

breakfast eksitpu:kwowey; ~ food
eksitpu:kwatal'mkewey

breast have a large ~ or chest maqipskunat
ai; my ~ np'skun [BR]; npuskun

breast-feed nuset *ai*; nunuskwet *ai* [BC]; a ~
-**er** nuseskwet *ai (an)*

breath catch one's ~ ew'lamsit *ai*; have bad
~ eloqtnema:t *ai*; loqtnema:t *ai*; hold one's
~ aptluwat *ai*; lose one's ~ (in a gale)
aptlamsink *ai*; my ~ nkamlamuti;
nkamlamuti(m) [SH]; out of ~ (as a result of
having a tantrum) apjitoq (apjitu) *ai*; take in
and let out a long deep-sounded ~ (as a
result of boredom, disturbance, etc.)
wejjelamit *ai*

breath-e kamlamit *ai*; ~ from wetlamit *ai*; ~
hard or heavily kesikawlamit *ai*; stop ~ **-ing**
kaqalamit *ai*

breathless aptlamsink *ai*

breeze a nice ~ welekisk *ii*

breezy news'k *ii*; cool and ~ (of the weather)
newek *ii*

brew strong ~ m'lsuwapu

brick construct or build with ~ or cement
blocks et'l-seknk *ta*, et'l-sekn'm *ti*

bride-price ~ activity lu:sukwewa:timk

bridge as'kom'nkaqan [SH]; as'kommkaqan
[BR]; asoqommtaqan; railroad ~
asoqonnkaqan [SH]

bridle ~ and bit wtune:l (pl)

briefcase alapilawemkewey

bright kesasit *ai*, kesatek *ii*; pitiyasit *ai*,
pitiyatek *ii*; shining ~ paqtasit *ai*, paqtatek *ii*

bring pejo:l'k *ta*, pejo:tu *ti*; ~ in piskwe:putu *ti*
[SH]; ~ in bulk elo:l'k *ta*, elo:tu *ti*; ~ in quickly
piskwi:putu *ti*; get or ~ from weja:l'k *ta*,
weja:tu *ti*

bring up anko:tm *ti*, ankweyaq *ta*

brisket katewaqanntaqan [SH]; psa:mun

brittle kaqjek *ii*, kaqjet *ai*; menaje:jit *ai*,
menaje:jk *ii*

broad-beamed keskoqomaqasit *ai* [SH];
keskitlmaqasit *ai*

broad-hipped keskitlmaqasit *ai*

broad-shouldered keskiyaqasit *ai*

broken sekwisto:kwek *ii*, sekwisto:kwet *ai*; ~
in two temtesink *ai*, temtesk *ii*; ~ off
tema:s'k *ii*, tema:sit *ai*

broker a marriage (or divorce) ~ nuji-postewit
ai (an)

brood epitm *ti*

brook jipu:ji:j; sipu:ji:j

Brook Village, N.S. atupikej

broom puwi:kn *an*; whisk ~ puwi:k'nji:j *an*

broth p'te:j; p'tew

brother patliyatji:j *an* (in a religious order); my
older ~ nsis *an*; my younger ~ njiknam *an*

brother-in-law my ~ (female speaker) nilmus
an [BC][PEI]; my ~ (male speaker) n'magtam
an [BC]; my ~ (male speaker) nsukwis *an*
[PEI]

brother or sister-in-law my ~ n'maqtam *an*

brothers or sisters related as ~ wijikitijik (pl)
ai [BR]

brownish wisawe:k *ii* [SH]

brush nipisoqon; plos (Fr *brosse*); ~ against
samteskaq *ta*, samteskm *ti*

bubble pisaqqan [SH]; ~ along elmi-
pisaqqaniyet *ai* [SH]

bucket la:taqsun *an*; lessow *an* (Fr *les seaux*)
[BR]; well ~ nqana:paqsun *an*

buckshot se:siyaqawey

buckwheat pokkwitewey

bud wipkoman [SH]

budge pekwikwalk *ta*, pekwikwatm *ti*

bug juji:ji:j *an*; potato ~ tap'tane:j *an*

bugler pipukwaqane:j *an*

build eli:k *ta*, el-tu *ti*; ~ a fire within
mawksa:l'k *ta*, mawksa:tu *ti*; ~ a house
ewi:kat *ai*; ~ a house for ewi:kewk *ta*

building frame house or ~ kmu:ji:kan

buildings have many ~ pukwelikanik *ii*

bull iyap (iyapaq) *an* (moose, caribou, etc.)
[BR]; latto:law *an*; full-grown ~ moose, etc.)
ke:tiyap (ke:tiyapaq) *an* [SH]

bullet piluwowey

bulletin sulnalji:j (Fr *journal*) [BR]; sunnalji:j (Fr *journal*)

bullfrog a:taqali *an*; sapoqwanij *an* [SH]

bullmoose pan ~ w'laqane:s *an* [BR]

bum ~ dry jakeju:p'k *ta*

bump ~ into kesmteskaq *ta*, kesmteskm *ti*; mikuteskaq *ta*, mikuteskm *ti*; mukuteskaq *ta*, mukuteskm *ti*

bun hair ~ jaman [BC]; kni:sikn

bunched ~ together mawpit *ai*, mawtek *ii*

bundle oqono-qopisaqan; oqopisaqan (for an infant) [SH]; ~ up with a scarf elpiso:tulk *ta*; tied or ~ -d together mawpisit *ai*, mawpitek *ii*; ~ -d (as an infant) oqopisit *ai*

burdock kawiksaw (kawiksaq) *an*; kelikwet *an*; kesaluwejit (kesaluwejijik) *an*

burial wtqotamk

burl m'ljetkw

burn kaqs'k *ta*, kaqsm *ti*; nu:kwa:l'k *ta*, nu:kwa:tu *ti*; nu:kwa:q *ii*, nu:kwa:t *ai*; wi:sik'sit *ai*, wi:sik'tek *ii*; ~ painfully wi:s'kesit *ai*, wi:s'ketek *ii*; ~ unintentionally pejoqs'k *ta*, pejoqsm *ti*; ~ underneath pitoqtek *ii*; ~ -ed completely out ketmoqsit *ai*, ketmoqtek *ii*; ~ -ed out kaqoqsit *ai*, kaqoqtek *ii*; ~ -ed up or out kaqsit *ai*, kaqtek *ii*; ~ -ed out (as a stove) kaqamklek *ii*, kaqamklet *ai*; finish ~ -ing up kaqa-nu:kwa:l'k *ta*, kaqa-nu:kwa:tu *ti*

Burnt Church esknuwapatij [RB]; sqno:pitij [BC]

burp welat *ai*

burst pastesk *ii*, pastesink *ai*; ~ into tears paqsikpetemit *ai* [PEI]; ~ out crying paqsikpetemit *ai* [PEI]; paqsipkimt'k (paqsipkimtm) *ai* [BR]; ~ out laughing paqsipk-elmit *ai*

bury wtqotalk *ta*, wtqotatm *ti*

bush blueberry branch or ~ pkumanaqsi; gooseberry ~ kawaqtejkumusi; hazelnut ~ or tree malipqwanjmusi

bushel puwesu (Fr *boisseau*)

bushy elatqek *ii*; piwsmik *ii*, piwsmit *ai*; pukunesit *ai*; pukwatqasik *ii*, pukwatqasit *ai*

business talk ~ with wesku:mk *ta*, wesku:tm *ti* [SH]; trade of do one's ~ there wejo:tasit *ai*

busy wetme:k *ai*

but katu

butcher putaqiket *ai*; putaqq *ta*; a ~ ne:patat *ai (an)*; nuji-putaqiket *ai (an)*

butter m'lakeju:mi

butterfly mimikej *an* [SH]; mimikes *an*; mijimijqanaw (mijimijqanaq) *an*; misimijqanaw (misimijqanaq) *an* (with picture of ace of spades on wings, a good luck charm) [SH]

buttermilk sikupaqte:kn

buttocks mijimij *an*; my ~ nijimij; bend and show one's ~ alikjo:kwet *ai*; have big ~ maqikjat *ai*; have small ~ apsikjat *ai*; show one's ~ alikja:t *ai*; show one's ~ to (in an argument) alikje:yaq *ta* [SH]

button pijoqosuti [BC]; pisoqosuti; pkijoqosuti [SH]; pp'joqosuti; ppijoqwa:l'k *ta*;

buy pekwateliket *ai*; pekwatelaq *ta*, pekwatel'm *ti*; ~ from weja:l'k *ta*, weja:tu *ti*; ~ from there wejankuwat *ai*; wet-teliket *ai*; ~ or purchase from there wet-telaq *ta*, wet-tel'm *ti*; ~ the proper or right one keknu:telaq *ta*, keknu:tel'm *ti*; start off to ~ or purchase nattelaq *ta*, nattel'm *ti*; go ~ -ing natankuwat *ai*

buyer a ~ or purchaser nujipkwateliket *ai (an)*

by pass ~ pemsiyawa:sit *ai*; sail along ~ pemsiyawaqteket *ai*

by rights! menaqajewey (an exclamation)

C

cabinet china ~ eptaqano:kuwom

cackle sesaqtoqsit *ai* [SH]

calculate mawkiljet *ai* [SH]

calendar tepkunsetewey wi:katikn

calf ~ moose tiya:mu:j *an*; carry a ~ jesmuwit *ai*; give birth to a ~ jesmuwit *ai*; my ~ (of the leg) nkata:law (nkata:laq) *an* [SH]; ntatqa:lam *an*

call wikimk *ta*; wikumk *ta*; wisunkalk *ta*, wisunkatm *ti*; ~ by all kinds of names miliwi:t'k *ta*, miliwi:tm *ti*; ~ by such a name teluwi:t'k *ta*, teluwi:tm *ti*; ~ by a different name piltuwit'k *ta*, piltuwitm *ti*; ~ out to (for assistance) elkomiktaq *ta*; ~ together (pl) maw-kimk *ta*; maw-kitm *ti*; named or ~ -ed teluwisik *ii*, teluwisit *ai*

call upon ~ for a visit ne:yamk *ta*, ne:yaptm *ti*

calm wantaqe:k *ai*; ~ down petkimk *ta*; ~ down (as the wind) jena:s'k *ii*, jena:sit *ai*; ~ water epekwitk *ii*; ewipk *ii*; jiktek *ii* [PEI]; jiku:k *ii*; wantaqpa:q *ii*

calve jesmuwit *ai*; penetkwit *ai*

camera napuwi:kikemkewey

camp wikuwom; abadoned ~ ujikan; make a ~ or dwelling ewi:kat *ai*; new ~ pilikan; old ~ sa:qawikan [BR]

Campbellton, N.B. esiyamkek *ii*; qame:k (loc)

campfire nu:te:n'maqan

campsite new ~ or development pilikana:kamikt [SH]

Canada kanata

Canada Jay mikjako:kwej *an*

Canadian kanatiyes *an*; ~ woman kanatiyesuwi:skw *an*; young ~ man kanatiye:si:s *an*; young ~ woman kanatiyesuwi:skwe:j *an*

candle wasoqonmaqan; ~ stick wasoqonmaqanatk

candy kannti *an* [BC]; suwitis ("sweets")

cane aptu:n; come with a ~ petaptu:sit *ai*; my ~ ntaptu:n; walk with a ~ or crutch elapte:k (elapte:m) *ai*

cannibal wintiku *an* [SH]

cannon tulkowey

canoe kwitn; come by ~ wejkwi-kwitna:q (wejkwi-kwitna:m) *ai*; dirty ~ mejikulkw [BR];

go by ~ kwitna:q (kwitna:m) *ai*; old ~ or boat kisiku:lkw [BR]; red ~ mekwulkw [SH]; sit or set in a ~ nekulq'pit *ai*, nekulq'tek *ii* [BR]; small ~ kwitnu:j; start off by ~ poqji-kwitna:q (poqji-kwitna:m) *ai* [SH]

Canso kamso:k (loc) [SH]

Canso Strait, N.S. tuwi:kn

cape petu:kun; pitu:kun

Cape Breton unama:ki

captain kapiten *an* (Fr *capitaine*); keptin *an* [CB]

car my ~ nutepaqan

carbuncle kl'muwej *an*

carcass ma:qi

card[1] ~ (moose hair or wool) nankwe:ket *ai*

card[2] ~ playing ilaskukwaqan [SH]; ilaskuwaqan [BC]; laskukutimk; playing ~ ilaskw (ilaskuk) *an* [SH]; laskw (laskuk) *an*; play ~ -s elaskukwet *ai*; ilaskuwet *ai* [BC]; laskukwet *ai*; laskukwet *ai*; game of ~ -s laskukwaqan

cardinal patliyatji:j *an* (a bird) [SH]

care ~ for wetmite:l'mk *ta*, wetmite:tm *ti*; leave in ~ of somebody eptoqalk *ta*, eptoqatm *ti*; take ~ of anko:tm *ti*, ankweyaq *ta*; take good ~ of weleyaq *ta*, welo:tm *ti*

carefully kimu:tuk; menaqa; w'ljaqa; do ~ menaqajewa:l'k *ta*, menaqajewa:tu; do slowly and ~ sankewa:l'k *ta*, sankewa:tu *ti*; speak ~ menaqajewo:kwet *ai*

caretaker act as a ~ nespit *ai*

caribou kalipu *an* [RB]; qalipu *an*

Carlyle kalla'ink (loc)

carrot enmapej *an* [ESK]; enmapet (enmapejik) *an*

carry[1] ~ (pertaining to the voice) enmoqowet *ai*

carry[2] pema:l'k *ta*, pema:tu *ti*; ~ along in the hand (by means of rope, strap, handle, etc.) pemapilk *ta*, pemapil'm *ti*; ~ around ala:l'k *ta*, ala:tu *ti*; ~ around on the back alaw'lalk *ta*; alaw'latm *ti*; alaw'let *ai*; ~ by means of a rope or handle pemapilawet *ai*; ~ by the scruff of the neck (as a cat) pemapilawet *ai*; ~ for naw'nsewk *ta*; ~ or pack on the

shoulder eln'kalk *ta*, eln'katm *ti*; ~ toward on
one's back or shoulder eluktulk *ta*, eluktu *ti*;
~ with oneself ala:l'k *ta*, ala:tu *ti*; start to ~
away or take along poqtamka:l'k *ta*,
poqtamka:tu *ti*

carve amaliks'k *ta*, amaliksm *ti*; amaliksawet
ai; amaloqsawet *ai*; eloqs'k *ta*, eloqsm *ti*;
miloqs'k *ta*, miloqsm *ti*; ~ on mils'k *ta*, milsm
ti

casket l'sqi:kn

cast ~ a fishing line elapaqtesteket *ai*; ~ (as
in fishing) kwitamet *ai*

cat kajuwewj *an*; miyawj (familiar form) [SH];
domestic ~ tqoqwe:j *an* [BR]

cataract wate:k *ii*; become a ~ (of the eye)
wata:s'k *ii*

catch kisapskn'm *ti*, kisapsknk *ta*; ~ a tune
nasapaqteskm *ti* [BR]; ~ by hook or gill net
nastesmk *ta*, nastestu *ti*; ~ by surprise
keskuteskaq *ta*, keskuteskm *ti*; wiskuteskaq
ta [PEI]; ~ hold of mesn(')k *ta*, mesn'm *ti*; ~
on time keskuteskaq *ta*, keskuteskm *ti*; have
a good ~ wel-ne:patat *ai* [PEI]; try to ~
kwejiks'kuteskaq *ta*; wejiks'kuteskm *ti*; try to
~ up with wet-tepne:k *ta*, wet-tepne:m *ti*

caterpillar enkejit (enkejijik) *an*

Catherine Katli:n *an* (Fr *Cathérine*)

cattail nukwa:luwejkewey; poqomaqan'skw
[SH]

caught amjimoqtesk *ii*, amjimoqtesink *ai*

caulk pi:tisikn-te:k *ta*, pi:tisikn-te:m *ti*

cause the ~ pekwatoq (pekwatu) *ai*

cave ~ in pijipkwiyaq *ii*, pijipkwiyet *ai*;
siyoqiyaq *ii*, siyoqiyet *ai*; ~ -d in walqwiyaq
ii, walqwiyet *ai*

caw heard ~ -ing metetoqsit *ai* [SH]

cease ~ eating punatalk (punatal) *ai*; ~
lecturing punewo:kwet *ai*; ~ living there
punqatk (punqatm) *ai*

cedar qaskusi *an*; ~ grove qaskusi-a:qamikt

ceiling pejikiskiyaq

celebration papuwaqan

cellar lakka:p (Fr *la cave*); lekka:p (Fr *les
caves*)

cement construct or build with brick or ~
blocks et'l-seknk *ta*, et'l-sekn'm *ti*

cent sumalki

center in the ~ mekwa'ik

ceremony ~ honouring elders pestiye:wa:timk
[CB]; pestiye:wa:taqatimk [CB]; honouring ~
wi:kipaltimk [CB]

certain a ~ thing keknuwe:k *ai, ii*

certainly ketl etuk

chafed pesqa:'ipusit *ai*, pesqa:'iputek *ii*

chain pisqa:taqanapi

chair kutputi; mutputi; nutputi

challenge ~ physically wejiknemk *ta*

chance ~ upon welkaq *ta*, welkm *ti*; present
by ~ pettepit *ai* [CB]

change sa:se:wa:sik *ii*, sa:se:wa:sit *ai*; ~ a
baby's diaper sa:se:wikno:tlk *ta* [PEI]; ~
clothes minkna:sit *ai*; sa:se:wikna:sit *ai* [BC];
~ colour piluwamukwiyaq *ii*, piluwamukwiyet
ai; ~ direction (of the wind) kawask'tniyaq *ii*;
kinawskituniyaq *ii* [BR]; ~ (of the weather) for
the worse mesi:kowik *ii* [CB]; ~ language
sa:se:wi:sit *ai*; ~ one's place of residence
ejikliwsit *ai*; ~ position (while lying prone)
ilisma:sit *ai*; ~ the name of sa:se:wi:t'k *ta*,
sa:se:wi:tm *ti*; go ~ the diaper (of and infant)
atpi:sewk *ta*; the one who ~ -s things or
colors nuji-sa:se:wamukwa:teket *ai (an)*; ~
-d piluwe:k *ai, ii*

channel pesitm *ti*, pesi:k *ta*; psitn; small ~ (of
a river) psitnu:j

chant dance and ~ ceremonially neska:wet
[PEI]

Chapel Island Po:tlo:tek [CB]; Potlotek

character[1] ~ (used in writing Micmac)
komkwejuwi:kaqan

character[2] have a bad ~ winqamiksit *ai* [BC]

charcoal nuksaqatew (nuksaqatal)

charge in ~ of nujeyaq *ta*, nujo:tm *ti*

charged for awtit *ai*

charitable wela:luwet *ai*

charity ask for ~ salite:wit *ai* (Fr *charité*);
give for ~ salitewa:teket *ai*

charm tiyom

charmer nujinpisuniket *ai (an)*; a charmer
nujinpisuniket *ai (an)*

chase natteskaq *ta*, natteskm *ti*; poqt'teskaq *ta*, poqt'teskm *ti*; ~ after pemteskaq *ta*, pemteskm *ti*; sespeyaq *ta*; ~ back apatte:k *ta*, apatte:m *ti*; ~ each other around (in a circle) kitto:qateskatultijik (pl) *ai*; ~ home enm'teskaq *ta*; sespo:tm *ti*; ~ out tewask'teskaq *ta* [SH]; tewatteskaq *ta*; ~ toward elteskaq *ta*; ~ upstairs toqju:teskaq *ta*

chastise wetapulk *ta* [RB]

chauffeur nuji-pejo:l'k *ta* [SH]

cheap anawtik *ii*, anawtit *ai*

cheat kemutnek *ii*, kemutnet *ai*; ~ (in love) sespo:teket *ai (an)*

check ~ over iloqamk *ta* [BC]; ~ up on ne:yamk *ta*, ne:yaptm *ti*; go ~ traps nassikwet *ai*

checker a:tnaqan *an*; ~ board a:tnaqaney

checkered a:tnaqanwi:kas'k *ii*, a:tnaqanwi:kasit *ai*

checkers item or event pertaining to the game of ~ a:tnamkewey; play ~ a:tnat *ai*

cheek my ~ nijinuwan; nk'jinuwan [BR]; nkujinuwan [SH]; nujininuwan [BC]

cheese teplma:sewey; te:plma:sewey; tepplma:sikewey; tepplma:sewey (Fr *des fromages*) [SH]

cherished something or someone ~ or valued ksite:taqan

cherry maskwe:siman; ~ tree maskwe:simanaqsi *an*

chest have a large breast or ~ maqipskunat *ai*; my ~ np'skun; npuskun

chest protector my ~ (in baseball) npuskuney

chew alisqopk *ta*, alisqotm *ti*; saqamu:kuwet *ai*; soqp'k *ta*, soqtm *ti*; soqtamit *ai*; ~ (as a cud) soqte:ket *ai*; ~ and swallow mawkutamit *ai*; ~ on al-p'k *ta*, al-tm *ti*; ~ tobacco ja:wa:tat *ai*

chick wennju:-plawe:ji:j *an* [BR]

chickadee jik'tli:kej *an* [BC]

chicken kikli:kwej *an* [PEI]; koqoli:kwej *an*; plawe:sis *an* [SH]

chicken pox wejkiyemkewey

chief saqamaw (saqamaq) *an*; Grand ~ kji-saqamaw *an* [CB]; Indian ~ nnu saqamaw (nnu saqamaq) *an*; woman ~ saqama:skw (saqama:skwaq) *an*

child an only ~ newtikit *ai* [CB]; my ~ nijan *an*; n'nijan *an* [SH]; n'njan *an*; my foster (adopted) ~ nn'snaqan'm *an* [SH]

children my ~ nijink (pl) *an* [BR]

chill ~ through saptaqjink *ai*

chills have the ~ kewjiya:qiyet *ai*

chilly kewjiya:qiyet *ai*; a ~ day teki-kisk'k *ii*; ~ evening teklo:qiyaq *ii*; get ~ pemitkiyaq *ii*, pemitkiyet *ai*

chime sisuwa:qataq *ii*; sisuwa:qi:kn

chimney lasinamey (Fr *la cheminée*) [SH]; pukto:kuwom; ~ beetle pukto:kuwome:j *an*

china ~ cabinet eptaqano:kuwom

chip pukwey; ~ off a protuberance manapsk'te:m *ti*

chip in ~ together mawa:tajik (pl) *ai*

chipmunk amalpaqamej *an*; apalqaqamej *an*

choke kestuna:l'k *ta*; noqt'k (noqtm) *ai*; ~ on food elu:kwit *ai*

choke-cherry lluwiman [RB]; poqwa:lamkewey

choose meknk *ta*, mekn'm *ti*

chop cut or ~ telte:k *ta*, telte:m *ti*; ~ off at the neck temkwete:k *ta*, temkwete:m *ti*; ~ or push down toward eloqtesmk *ta*, eloqtestu *ti*

christen wisunkalk *ta*, wisunkatm *ti*

Christmas Nuwel *an* (Fr *Noël*); ~ Day Nuwelewimk [SH]; Nuwelewumk (Fr *Noël*)

chub m'napskw's *an* [RB]

chum my ~ nikmaq *an* [SH]; n'naqapem *an*

church alasutmo:kuwom [BR]; a:sutmo:kuwom; go to ~ teko:tk (teko:tm) *ti*; start off to ~ najitko:tk (najitko:tm) *ai*

cider apple ~ wennju-su:n apu

cigarette eloqo(n)maqa:taqan [BR]; iloqomoqwa:taqan [SH]; loqomoqa:taqan [SH]; wetmamkewey

circle ~ around kiwto:qwa:sit *ai*; follow one another in a ~ kitto:qakatultijik (pl) *ai*; sit around in a ~ kitto:qopiya:tijik (pl) *ai*; kitto:qopultijik (pl) *ai*

circumcise sisqa:taq *ta*; one who has been ~ -d sisqa:tuj *an*

circumference have such a ~ tela:q *ii*, teloqsit *ai*

city kjikan

claim put a ~ , deposit, retainer or down payment on kelte:k *ta*, kelte:m *ti*

clam e:s (e:sik) *an*

clams dig for ~ mene:smat *ai*; hunt for ~ e:se:ket *ai*

clansman my fellow ~ ntuttem *an*

clapper bell ~ sisuwa:qate:kn

clasp ~ with hands sekkapja:sit *ai* [PEI]

claw lobster ~ w'ljikn [BC]

clay pka:w *an* [SH]; pqa:lu:skw, pqwawlu:skw

clean musika:l'k *ta*, musika:tu *ti*; waqama:l'k *ta*, waqama:tu *ti*; waqame:k *ai, ii*; ~ flowing water waqamitk *ii*; ~ out jakeju:p'k *ta*; eat ~ (leaving no leftovers) musikp'k *ta*, musiktm *ti*

clear musike:k *ai, ii*; ~ out memkoqte:m *ti*; ~ the brush or thicket musikte:ket *ai*; ~ up (of clouds or fog) pane-kiskiyaq *ii*; ~ up (of the sky) wejkwa-paneta:q *ii*; crystal- ~ water wasapa:q *ii* [BR]; open or ~ up (of the sky) paneta:q *ii*; ~ -ed memke:k *ai, ii*

clearing make a ~ memkoqte:ket *ai*

clench aptluwajik (pl) *ai* (two dogs fighting or copulating)

clerk a ~ nussaqiket *ai (an)*

clever ke'itine:k *ai*; kejitme:k *ai* [BC]; natawe:k *ai*; netawe:k *ai*; wantuwit *ai* [RB]

cliff mtasoq

climb tekusuwet *ai* [BR]; ~ over a:sisapekit *ai*; ~ up elkusuwet *ai*; elqo:suwet *ai* [EG]

cling oqoskijikuwek *ii*, oqoskijikuwet *ai*; oqtuwet *ai* [BC]; ~ to keliket *ai*; oqotuwalk *ta*, oqotuwatm *ti* [BC]; that which ~ -s or sticks oqoti

clock na:ku:setewey

close[1] iltaqa:l'k *ta*, iltaqa:tu *ti* [BC]; kepsaqa:l'k *ta*, kepsaqa:tu *ti*; ~ (by tying with a rope or string) sepusepil'm *ti*, sepusepilk *ta*; ~ one's eyes sepikwa:sit *ai*; ~ tightly sekki-ap'sqa:tu *ti* [PEI]; ~ the drapes (on windows) elekepilawet *ai*; ~ down ilta:l'k *ta*, ilta:tu *ti*; ~ -d kepsoqpit *ai*, kepsoqtek *ii*; ~ -d up sepusepit *ai*, sepusetek *ii*; have one's eyes ~ -d sepikwet *ai*; sew ~ -d (the gap of a

pointed article, such as a sock or mitt) sepusi:s'k *ta*, sepusi:sm *ti*

close[2] ~ by kikjiw; soqpit *ai*, soqtek *ii*; wejuwow have a ~ call wejuwe:k *ai*

closet klo:kowey

clot wa:tukwawa:s'k *ii*; blood ~ wa:tukwaw (wa:tikwaq) *an*; wa:tuwow [PEI]

cloth atlawekn; atla:wekn; wayekn [BR]; new ~ pilekn; piece of ~ pkesikn; small piece of ~ pkesik'nji:j

clothe a:su:nkewk *ta*

clothes alikew (alikal); change ~ minkna:sit *ai*; sa:se:wikna:sit *ai* [BC]; swaddling ~ qopisunikn [BC]; wear dirty ~ mejikkumet *ai*; wear proper ~ (for the season) welqwanet *ai*

clothing alikew (alikal); my ~ nutapsun

cloud aluk [BR]; form (as a ~) in the shape of a horse te:sipow aluktesk *ii*; form into ~ -s awaluktesk *ii* [BR]

cloudy turn ~ alukiyaq *ii*

club[1] ~ (in cards) klap (klapaq) *an* [SH]; klep (klepaq) *an*

club[2] hit with a ~ wetaqanikatm *ti* [BR]

clubfoot a ~ wkatistuwik *ii*; have a ~ istuwikata:t *ai*; ~ -ed istuwikata:t *ai*

coal wapskw [SH]; kl'muweji-wapskw; puksetew [BR]; hot ~ or log tmsaqatew (tmsaqatal) [SH]

coast ~ about aliyo:qsat *ai* [ESK]; keep on ~ -ing (on the river) siyawkumiyet *ai*

coat weskijiyama:l'k *ta*, weskijiyama:tu *ti*; ~ -ed weskitpekiyaq *ii*, weskitpekiyet *ai*

coax mussayaq *ta*, musso:tm *ti*; munsayaq *ta*, munso:tm *ti* [SH]; mussa:t *ai*

cock ~ a gun ilsaqa:tu *ti*

cock-eyed patalapit *ai*

coconut pqwamk

cocoon nisimisqanaw (nisimisqanaq) *an* [BC]

cod peju *an*; fish for ~ pejuwe:ket *ai*; tommy ~ plamuj *an*

codfish cooked ~ pejuwey

coffin lesqe:kn; l'sqi:kn

co-habit toq-mimajijik (pl) *ai*; toqi-mimejik (pl) *ai* [SH]

coil eletqo:l'k *ta*, eletqo:tu *ti*; ~ -ed el'tqek *ii*, el'tqet *ai*

coincidentally a'itetapu; kestetapu [BC]

cold kewjik *ii*, kewjit *ai*; teke:k *ii* (of the weather); tekik *ii*, tekit *ai*; tekpa:q *ii* (of a liquid); extremely ~ (of the weather) a:munitke:k *ii* [PEI]; get ~ (of the weather) pemitke:k *ii*; have a ~ tkeya:tat *ai*; have ~ feet kewtaqsikit *ai*; tekikatat *ai*; have ~ hands kewjipnewjit *ai*; tekiptnat *ai*; somewhat ~ (of the weather) amitke:k *ii*; sensitive to the ~ menawjit *ai*; take ~ tkeya:tat *ai*

cold-blooded menawjit *ai*

collapse siyoqiyaq *ii*, siyoqiyet *ai*; ~ from exhaustion wikwiyet *ai*; ~ from fatigue mesqaniyet *ai*

collect mawte:k *ta*, mawte:m *ti*; mekete:k *ta*, mekete:m *ti*; meknk *ta*, mekn'm *ti*; ~ sweetgrass msikuwe:ket *ai*

collector a ~ mawo:tasit *ai (an)*

collide toqtesinkik (pl) *ai*

color an unpleasant (ugly) ~ kajj-amuksit *ai*, kajj-amu:k *ii*; change ~ piluwamukwiyaq *ii*, piluwamukwiyet *ai*; cream ~ -ed laklem-amuksit *ai*, laklem-amu:k *ii*; one ~ newt-amuksit *ai*, newt-amu:k *ii*; what ~ ? tal amuksit *ai*, tal amu:k *ii*

color-blind wisqap'lkikwa:t *ai*

comb nalqo:n *an* [SH]; fine-tooth ~ nanko:n *an*; large-toothed ~ nikattuko:n *an* [SH]; nalsi:k'k *ta*, nalsi:km *ti*; nassi:k'k *ta*, nassi:km *ti*; ~ one's hair nikant'ko:sit *ai*; ~ one's hair with a coarse tooth ~ nukwaltukwo:sit *ai*; ~ one's hair with a fine-tooth ~ nanko:sit *ai*; nalko:sit *ai*

come wejku:waq *ii*, wejku:wet *ai*; wejkuwiyaq *ii*, wejkuwiyet *ai* [SH]; bring or ~ with wejkwa:l'k *ta*, wejkwa:tu *ti*; ~ by canoe wejkwi-kwitna:q (wejkwi-kwitna:m) *ai*; ~ crying wejkutemit *ai*; ~ from there wejiyaq *ii*, wejiyet *ai*; ~ in this direction wejkwateja:s'k *ii*, wejkwateja:sit *ai*; ~ with pounding feet wejkwitu:kwe:pit *ai*; ~ on the run wejkwitukwi:k (wejkwitukwi:m) *ai* [BR]; ~ running wejkutukwi:k (wejkutukwi:m) *ai*; ~ sailing wejkwaqteket *ai*

comet puktewit *an*

come upon we:jitu *ti*, we:ji:k *ta*

common-law live ~ toqonasit *ai*; person who lives ~ tqonasu *an*

commotion create a ~ sespena:q *ii*, sespenoqsit *ai*

communion receive ~ kupniye:wit; receive holy ~ kmeniye:wit *ai*

compass lu:kwejk

competent ~ in natawa:qa:l'k *ta*, natawa:qa:tu *ti*

complected light ~ wapikneksit *ai*

completely burned ~ out ketmoqsit *ai*, ketmoqtek *ii*

concave wannoqs'k *ii*, wannoqsit *ai*

conceal aqawikalk *ta*, aqawikatm *ti*; mimukwalk *ta*, mimukwatu *ti*; carry ~ -ed under the arm pem-tulkomit *ai*; hide or ~ in the hand sepuwijjenk *ta*, sepuwijjen'm *ti*

concealment hold in ~ sepapjit *ai*

conceited ki:nujink *ai*

condolences offer ~ neskawet *ai*

condor klu *an*

conduct nuji-pejo:l'k *ta*

cone pine ~ wisqasaw (wisqasaq) *an*; wisqasoq *an* [RB]

conference maw-nutmamk

confess aknimk *ta*, aknutm *ti*; pa:qapukuwet *ai*; pa:qapukuwatm *ti*

confession pa:qapukuwo:ti; give ~ to pa:qapukuwa:l'k *ta*

confident make more ~ welkwija:l'k *ta*

confrontational ki:kaja:sit *ai*

confuse maqana:l'k *ta*; ~ -d ew'nasiyaq *ii*, ew'nasiyet *ai*; maqanat *ai*

congregate mawiyejik (pl) *ai*; ~ (to help each other) mawi-apoqonatultijik (pl) *ai* [BC]

conjure puntat *ai*

connect miss ~ -ing with pela:l'k *ta*, pela:tu *ti*

conquer wissuwiknemk *ta*, wissuwiknetm *ti*

consciousness regain ~ nestu:wet *ai*

consider ~ all kinds of possibilities milkwija:sit *ai*

console neskawet *ai*; neskaq *ta*

constable kast'pl *an*

constantly apji

constipated melk'jat *ai*

construct ~ or build with brick or cement blocks et'l-seknk *ta*, et'l-sekn'm *ti*

consume jikp'k *ta*, jiktm *ti*

continue siyawa:sit *ai*, siyawa:s'k *ii*; ~ with siyawa:l'k *ta*, siyawa:tu *ti*

continuous siyawiw [BR]

continuously talk ~ sespeta:q *ii*, sespetoqsit *ai*

contrary ~ person sapun *an*

contribution apankituwowey; salite(wey) [BC] (Fr *charité*); make a ~ salitewa:teket *ai* [BC]

control alsumk *ta*, alsutm *ti* [BC]

converse ~ with weskwimk *ta* [BR]

convert a (religious) ~ kawaska:sit *ai* [PEI]

convey ~ or drive home (in a vehicle) enmateja:l'k *ta*, enmateja:tu *ti*

cook etloqs'k *ta*, etloqsm *ti*; etoqtalk *ta*, etoqtatm *ti* [SH]; etoqtet *ai* [SH]; ewissukwateket *ai* [SH]; ewissukwalk *ta*, ewissukwatm *ti* [SH]; mesekit (mesekijik) *ai (an)* (also used in reference to a housewife); wissukwatiket *ai*; wissukwalk *ta*, wissukwatm *ti*; ~ all kinds of ways miloqs'k *ta*, miloqsm *ti*; ~ for oneself wissukwat *ai*; ~ for wesku:p'k *ta*; wisku:p'k *ta*; ~ in such a manner teloqs'k *ta*, teloqsm *ti*; ~ thus teloqs'k *ta*, teloqsm *ti*; know how to ~ netuwoqsawet *ai*; natawoqsawet *ai*; netawitoqtet *ai* [BR]; finished ~ -ing ki:s'k *ta*, ki:sm *ti*; ~ -ed etloqtek *ii*; already ~ -ed kisoqsit *ai*, kisoqtek *ii*; ~ -ed thus teloqsit *ai*, teloqtek *ii*

cool ~ and breezy (of the weather) newek *ii*; ~ off teka:l'k *ta*, teka:tu *ti*; tekistu *ti*; ~ off (with water) newapalk *ta*, newapatm *ti*; nice and ~ (of the air) wel-newek *ii*; start to get ~ poqji-newek *ii*; ~ -ish amitkik *ii*, amitkit *ai*

copper sumalki [RB]; wisawo:qw; ~ kettle or pot wisawo:qw [SH]

copulate etl-te:mat *ai*; majaqtat *ai*; ~ in a standing position kaqm'te:mat *ai*

copy napkwetu *ti*

cord[1] ntuwan *an*

cord[2] ~ of wood lakko:l (Fr *la corde*); equal or equivalent to a ~ of wood lakko:la:laq *ii*

cork kepjoqikn; pkijoqikn

cormorant mqatawapu

corn[1] piyeskman [BR]; piyeskmin

corn[2] pipqoqsitan (on the foot) [SH]

corner e:k [SH]; in the ~ ki:ke:k [SH]; the ~ keji:kas'k *ii*; kejikiyaq *ii*

coroner a ~ nutapteket *ai (an)*

corpse npuwinu *an*

corpulent mawkamik *ii*, mawkamit *ai*

correct easily or quickly ~ naqsi-tetapuwa:l'k *ta*, naqsi-tetapuwa:tu *ti*

correctly act ~ tetapu:qamikset *ai*; do ~ koqqaja:teket *ai*; pekaja:teket *ai*; live ~ keknuwe:k *ai, ii*; read properly or ~ keknu:kijjet *ai*; sew right or ~ tetapuwi:s'k *ta*, tetapuwi:sm *ti*; skip ~ koqqaji-w'naqto:sit *ai* [BR]; work ~ keknu:lukwet *ai*

couch muskwje:j *an* [BC]; soppey

cough no:q'q (no:qm) *ai*

counsel offer ~ to nestuwimk *ta*

count ejiljet *ai* [BR]; ekijjet *ai* [BR]; mawkijjet *ai*; ~ off ekimk *ta*, ekitm *ti*; ~ stick kitmaqan *an* (in waltes game) [CB]; include in the ~ maw-kimk *ta*, maw-kitm *ti*

countenance have a nice ~ welikwetutk (welikwetutm) *ai*

cousin my ~ no:kumaw (no:kumaq) *an*; my distant ~ (elder referring to a youth) no:kuma:j(i:j) *an*

cove wanney; at the ~ wanne:k (loc)

cover oqonisqopil'm *ti*, oqonisqopilk *ta*; oqoniskwa:l'k *ta*, oqoniskwa:tu *ti*

covering anqoni:kn

covet kesi-pawalk *ta* [BR]; kesi-pewalk *ta* [SH]; kesi-puwalk *ta*, kesi-puwatm *ti*

cow wennji-tiya:m (wennji-tiya:muk) *an*; wennju-tiya:m (wennju-tiya:muk) *an* [BR][BC]; ~ moose tiya:mi:skw *an*

crab jakej *an* [BR][SH]; minjinikej *an* [CB]; n'mtm-jakej *an*; sasqayejit (sasqayejijik) *an*; saltwater ~ ninnjin-jakej *an* (used as a fertilizer for potatoes) [RB]

cracked ~ from excessive heat paskinoqsit *ai*, paskinoqtek *ii*; ~ or split from excessive cold paskoqjink *ai*, paskoqt'k *ii*; split or ~ (from dryness) paskipiyasit *ai*

cradle jitlo:mukwaqan; kjitloqomuwaqan; qopisunikn [BC]

cradleboard ki:naqan
cramp have a ~ wejipulkwa:s'k *ii*
cranberry su:n
crane pitoqoluwajit (pitoqoluwajijik) *ai (an)*;
   t'mkwatiknej *an*
cranky paskukjat *ai* [SH]
crave mesuktaqanat *ai*; na:jikat *ai*; ~ fluid
   niwipskuna:t *ai*; ~ food, sex ketutamit *ai*
crawl ~ across as'komapekit *ai* [BR]; ~ along
   pemapekit *ai*; ~ backwards esetekjapekit *ai*;
   las'tikjapekit *ai* [SH]; ~ home elmapekit *ai*
   [BR]; ~ over a:sisapekit *ai*; ~ underneath
   pitapekit *ai*; ~ up toqjuwapekit *ai*
crazy eluwe:wiyaq *ii*, eluwe:wiyet *ai*
cream laklem (Fr *la crème*); ~ coloured
   laklem-amuksit *ai*, laklem-amu:k *ii*
crease ~ with a bullet or arrow kipoqtelaq *ta*,
   kipoqtel'm *ti*
create etlitu *ti*, etli:k *ta*
created Indians are ~ ! kisu:snik nnu:k
   (expression of surprise); you are ~ ! kisu:lk
   (expression of surprise)
creature crawling ~ jujij *an*
creosote muskusi *an*
crib jitlo:mukwaqan
cricket pukto:kuwome:j *an*
crochet amalisknuwet *ai*
crooked istuwik *ii*, istuwikit *ai*; istu:pit *ai*,
   istu:tek *ii*; istuwe:k *ai, ii* [BC]; waqju:pit *ai*,
   waqju:tek *ii*; waqjuwikk *ii*, waqjuwikit *ai*;
   winikk *ii*, winikit *ai* [BR]; istu-napuwi:k'k *ta*,
   istu-napuwi:km *ti*; do or make ~ istuwa:l'k
   ta, istuwa:tu *ti*; draw or trace unevenly or ~
   -ly
crop[1] a good ~ or harvest minit *ai*, minik *ii*;
   have a good ~ welikwenmat *ai* [PEI]
crop[2] ~ hair pepk'te:maq *ta (do)*
cross klujje:wey (Fr *crucifix?*) [BC]; kulje:wey
   [SH]; kuljiyewey [SH]; ~ oneself kuljewto:sit
   ai; make the sign of the ~ klujjewto:sit *ai*
   [BC]; skip the ~ (in jump rope)
   klujjewtaqto:sit *ai* [SH]
cross-eyed patalapit *ai*; ~ person patalap *an*
cross over asoqoma:s'k *ii*, asoqoma:sit *ai*
crotch form a ~ niktuwa:s'k *ii*, niktuwa:sit *ai*;
   form into a ~ niktuwa:l'k *ta*, niktuwa:tu *ti*; my

~ nsaski; the human ~ niktu:sit *ai (an)* [BR];
   shaped like a ~ niktuwikk *ii*, niktuwikit *ai*
crouch mesqanepit *ai*
crow ka:qaquj *an*
crucifix klujjewta:sit *an* [SH]; kuljewta:sit
   (kuljewta:sijik) *an*; pess'mkewey *an*;
   peskmewey *an* [SH]
cruise ~ along sankewa:s'k *ii*, sankewa:sit *ai*
crumble nukwa:l'k *ta*, nukwa:tu *ti* [BR]
crumple mawiseteskaq *ta*, mawiseteskm *ti*
crush paska:l'k *ta*, paska:tu *ti*; ~ or soften
   (with the feet) nukteskaq *ta*, nukteskm *ti*; ~
   with the teeth pasp'k *ta*, pastm *ti*; ~ -ed or
   shattered paske:k *ai, ii*
crust psaqa:kw; ~ of bread msaqa:kw
   (msaqakkw) *an*
crutch my ~ ntaptu:n
cry etl-temit *ai*; weto:temit *ai* [SH]; begin to ~
   poqji-atk'temit *ai*; paqsipkimt'k
   (paqsipkimtm) *ai* [BR]; ~ all the time
   puskimt'k *ai*; pustemit *ai*; ~ along pemtemit
   ai; ~ at length apjimt'k (apjimtm) *ai*; ~ for a
   long while pekittemit *ai*; ~ hard kesimt'k
   (kesimtm) *ai*; ~ inside kimtemit *ai*; ~
   repeatedly puskimt'k *ai*; make ~
   atkitemu:l'k *ta*; arrive ~ -ing pettemit *ai*;
   burst out ~ -ing paqsikpetemit *ai* [PEI];
   come ~ -ing wejkutemit *ai*; heard ~ -ing
   weto:mt'k (weto:mtm) *ai* [SH]; meto:mt'k
   (meto:mtm) *ai*; pass by ~ -ing pemi-
   siyawtemit *ai* [BR]
cube tetpitsaq
cubit lusniknekaluj *an* (a measurement) [ESK]
cucumber esk'tm'kewey
cultivate elkete:ket *ai*; elekete:ket *ai*;
   matkete:ket *ai*; musikunnkete:ket *ai*
cup kups'ji:j *an* [SH]; suppin *an* (Fr *chopine*)
cupboard eptaqano:kuwom
cure[1] nepilk *ta*, nepitm *ti*
cure[2] ~ wood etlipiyask *ta*, etlipiyasm *ti*; ~ -d
   wood etlipiyasit *ai*, etlipiyatek *ii*; ~ -d lumber
   kispasas'k *ii*, kispasasit *ai*
curer a ~ or healer nepiteket *ai (an)*
currant kawaqtejk; taqate:l *an*
current a swift ~ kesikawitk *ii*

curry nalsi:k′k *ta*, nalsi:km *ti*; nassi:k′k *ta*,
nassi:km *ti*

curse puntat *ai*

curtain lekepilaqan [SH]

curve ~ in pijikiyaq *ii*, pijikiyet *ai*; ~ inward
piskwikiyaq *ii*, piskwikiyet *ai*; ~ outward
tewikiyaq *ii*, tewikiyet *ai*; ~ -d inward
wannoqs′k *ii*, wannoqsit *ai*

cushion tu:kwesmun

cut ~ (so as to cause blood to flow)
malltews′k *ta*; malltewsm *ti*; ~ grass
mskikuwe:ket *ai* [SH]; ~ into tels′k *ta*, telsm
ti; ~ into segments or chunks temapsk′sk *ta*,
temapsk′sm *ti*; ~ into narrow strips aps′sm
ti, aps′sk *ta*; ~ into pieces nuks′k *ta*, nuksm
ti; ~ out mens′k *ta*, mensm *ti*; ~ or chop
telte:k *ta*, telte:m *ti*; ~ or knock through (with
a tool) saputete:k *ta*, saputete:m *ti*; ~ self
elsusit *ai* [BR]; ~ small aps′te:m *ii*; ~
someone′s hair thin pepk′te:maq *ta (do)*; ~
someone′s hair short or thin memk′te:maq *ta
(do)* [BR]; ~ well welto:ksit *ai*; ~ with a knife
wa:qans′k *ta*, wa:qansm *ti*

cylindrical pitoqona:t *ai*, pitoqona:q *ii*; five ~
shaped objects nanoqskekl (pl) *ii*, nanoqsijik
(pl) *ai* [BR]; six (of something ~ in shape)
as′kom-te:soqsijik (pl) *ai*

D

dab ~ or sprinkle self (with powder or perfume) amjaqto:sit *ai*

daddy! ta:ta (baby talk)

daddy my ~ nujjiji:j *an* [SH]

daddy-long-legs suliyewiye:j *an* (spider)

Dalhousie sik'to:nqek

damp nenmuwe:k *ai, ii*; get ~ saqpiyaq *ii*, saqpiyet *ai*

damper ilta:l'k *ta*, ilta:tu *ti*

danc-e amalkat *ai*; toqtesinkik (pl) *ai*; etl-tesk *ii*, etl-tesink *ai*; putuktesink *ai*; ceremonial ~ nska:waqan [BC]; ~ Indian style lnu:kwat *ai* [BC]; lnu:tesink *ai*, lnutesink *ai* [SH]; ~ until dawn wap'ntesink *ai*; a ~ -r <nuji-amalkat *ai*; ~ -ing et'ltesink

danger nsanoqon

dangerous ensanoqonik *ii*, ensanoqonit *ai*; nsanoqonik *ii*, nsanoqonit *ai*

dare ki:kajimk *ta* [BR]

dark pekn'k *ii* (without light); ~ complected maqtawikneksit *ai*; get ~ kiskiyaq *ii* [SH]; oqonitpaqiyaq *ii*; piskiyaq *ii*; qonitpaqamukwiyaq *ii*; ~ -ish maqtew-amuksit *ai*, maqtew-amu:k *ii*; ~ -ened maqtawoqsit *ai*, maqtawoqtek *ii*

darn sepusi:s'k *ta*, sepusi:sm *ti*

date what ~ ? tal e:k *ii*

daughter! ~ (or girl!) tu:s (voc) (term of affection); little ~ tutji:j (voc) (term of affection for a child)

daughter my ~ ntus *an*; my little ~ ntutji:j (dim) *an*

daughter-in-law act like a ~ lu:suweskwewit *ai*; my ~ ntlu:suwe:skum *an*; perform the duties of a prospective ~ lu:suweskwewa:sit *ai*

David Ta:pit *an*

dawn wapn; wapk *ii*; na:ku:wa:sik *ii* [BR]; become ~ wapn-amukwiyaq *ii*; dance until ~ wap'ntesink *ai*; see the break of ~ wapnapit *ai*; sing until ~ wapnintoq (wapnintu) *ai*; sleep until ~ wapnuksit *ai* [SH]; wapunkusit *ai*

day na:kwew; na:kwek *ii*; a bad ~ metuwi-kisk'k *ii*; a chilly ~ teki-kisk'k *ii*; a nice ~ weli-kisk'k; one ~ nekwtukna:q *ii* [BR]; one ~ nekwti-kisk'k [BR]; paid by the ~

na:kwekewa:q (nakwekewa:m) *ai*; the last ~ kiyaspi-kisk'k; the middle of the ~ miyaw-na:kwek *ii*; three ~ -s nesukna:q *ii*; two ~ -s tapukna:q *ii*

daybreak wejkwapniyaq *ii*; wapn-amukwiyaq *ii*

daylight wapn; wapk *ii*; na:kwek *ii*

dead nepjit *ai* (when referring to a domestic animal) [BC]; nepk *ai*; kaqiyaq *ii*, kaqiyet *ai* [BR]; shoot ~ siktelaq *ta*; wesaqalk *ta* [BR]; strike ~ sikte:k *ta*

deadfall pqoqte:kn (a kind of trap) [SH]

deadwater msk'tkw

deaf kepistaqanat *ai*; slightly ~ amistaqanat *ai*

deal atknawet *ai*; ~ cards atknewk *ta*; ~ for atkne:k *ta* [PEI]

dear! oqoti (voc) (term of affection between husband and wife)

dear something or someone held ~ ks'keltaqan

death npuwaqan

debark pelko:qiket

debt tettawaqan [PEI]; my ~ ntettuwoqon'm; in ~ tettuwet *ai*

deceased ketmenet (ketmenejik) *ai (an)*

December kesikewiku:s; kjiku:s *an*

decorate amal-lukwalk *ta*, amal-lukwatm *ti*; amaltaqa:l'k *ta*, amaltaqa:tu *ti*; kekna:l'k *ta*, kekna:tu *ti*

decoration amaltaqa:taqan; kna:taqan

decorative ~ object kna:taqan

deep espulqek *ii*; temik *ii*; wide and ~ (e.g., a canoe, chair) keskulq'k *ii*; a ~ hole pitalqek *ii*

deer lentuk *an*

defeat ~ in a game kespu:taq *ta*; ~ in debate we:kwa:maq *ta*

defecate najijjikwat *ai*; mejjikwat *ai*; ~ on oneself mejjilsit *ai*

defend ikalk *ta*, ikatm *ti*; ~ self ikalsit *ai*

defer ~ to elsutmaq *ta (do)* [BC]

deflower mente:maq *ta (do)*

deformed winikk *ii*, winikit *ai*; have a ~ or crippled hand or arm sawiptnat *ai*; ~ or crippled hand or arm sawiptn

delicate an'stawe:k *ai, ii*; menaje:jit *ai*, menaje:jk *ii*; nenestawe:k *ai, ii*;

waqqatamuksit *ai*, waqqatamu:k *ii*; ~ in
health nepe:k *ai*

deliver nutateji:pulk *ta*, nutateji:putu *ti*; haul or
~ here in bulk pejo:l'k *ta*, pejo:tu *ti*

delivery a ~ man nujatejo:tasit *ai (an)*;
ewjo:tat *ai (an)*; nutateji:putasit *ai (an)*;
nutateji:puteket *ai (an)*

delouse nankwenk *ta*; nankwenawet *ai*

den pqwan'm; hay ~ mskikuwom [SH]

dense paspit *ai*, pastek *ii*; ~ (as a thicket)
elatqek *ii*

dentist a ~ nuji-m'napita:teket *ai (an)*

deny petqwasit *ai*

depart ejikla:sit *ai*; elmiyet *ai*, elmiyaq *ii* [BR];
enmiyet *ai*, enmiyaq *ii*

depend ~ on elita:suwalk *ta*, elita:suwatm *ti*

dependent ~ on elita:sit *ai*

deposit put a claim, ~ , retainer or down
payment on kelte:k *ta*, kelte:m *ti*

depressed feel ~ taqawaje:k *ai*

desalinate kutapikwalk *ta*, kutapikwatm *ti*

descend nisa:sit *ai*; niskusuwa:sit *ai* [SH];
niskusuwet *ai*; niskusuwa:'it *ai* [SH]; niss'k *ii*,
nissink *ai*; ~ from wetapeksit *ai*; ~ into the
hollow elmi-walqwasiyet *ai* [CB]; ~ to the low
ground or flat metoqiyaq *ii*, metoqiyet *ai*

descent of common ~ wetakutijik (pl) *ai*;
related through ~ wetakutk (wetakutm) *ai*;
share a common ~ wettaqiya:tijik (pl) *ai*

desert puna:l'k *ta*, puna:tu *ti*

deserted ~ area paqtaqamiktuk (loc)

design amaltaqa:taqan; a mixed ~
amaltaqawi:kas'k *ii*; put a ~ on amaltaqa:l'k
ta, amaltaqa:tu *ti*

desire na:jikat *ai*; pawalk *ta*, pawatm *ti*;
puwalk *ta*, puwatm *ti*

despondent feel ~ taqawaje:k *ai*

detergent suspanikn

deuce ta:puwowa:j *an*

devil m'ntu *an*; the ~ 's pipe! m'ntu
wutmaqan (an interjection)

devilish m'ntuwit *ai*

dew kekpewisk *ii*; morning ~ keppewisk *ii*;
kikpewisk *ii* [PEI]

diamond ~ (in cards) ta'im'n (ta'im'naq) *an*

diaper pi:san; change a baby's ~
sa:se:wikno:tlk *ta* [PEI]; go change the ~ (of

and infant) atpi:sewk *ta*; put a ~ on
pi:sano:tlk *ta*

diaphram wa:naw (wa:naq) *an*

diarrhea have ~ kesaqtiyat *ai*; saputa:t *ai* [SH]

dice ~ (in game playing) waltesta:timk; play ~
waltestat *ai*

die¹ ~ in an accident ketemetesultijik (pl) *ai*; ~
from a disease ketemenejik (pl) *ai*

die² bone ~ (for dice game) w'ltestaqan *an*
[CB]; round bone or ~ used in dice game
waltestaqan *an* [SH]

different istuwe:k *ai, ii*; piluwe:k *ai, ii*; call by
a ~ name piltuwit'k *ta*, piltuwitm *ti*; look at ~
-ly piltuwamk *ta*, piltuwaptm *ti*

difficult metuwe:k *ii*

diffidently act ~ penoqwitelsit *ai*

dig mulqet *ai*; ~ out mulqalk *ta*, mulqatm *ti*; ~
through saputalqatm *ti*; ~ for clams
mene:smat *ai*

digestive tract my ~ tract ntalsuwikn

dinner mewli-na:kwekewey (noon meal);
miyaw-la:kewey [SH]

dip ~ out naqana:q (naqana:m) *ai*

dipper la:maqan *an*; suppin *an*

direct neta:sumk *ta*, neta:sutm *ti*

direction bend back facing in the opposite ~
enmu:jink *ai*; blow from such ~ wett'k *ii*;
come in this ~ wejkwateja:s'k *ii*,
wejkwateja:sit *ai*; face the other ~
enmejepit *ai*, enmejetek *ii*; lie facing in the
opposite ~ enmikjesink *ai*; the one who puts
things in every ~ nuji-milamukwa:teket *ai (an)*

director a ~ nutsuteket *ai (an)* [BC]

dirt mjikey [BR]; mj'key

dirty mejike:k *ai, ii*; winjik *ii*, winjit *ii*; a ~ day
wini-kisk'k; ~ canoe mejikulkw [BR]; ~ sink
mejiku:lkw [BR]; ~ water mjikapu; have a ~
face mejikapewit *ai*; have ~ hands
mejikiptnat *ai* [PEI]; look ~ mejik-amuksit *ai*;
wear ~ clothes mejikkumet *ai*

disagreement have a ~ o:pla:knutmajik (pl) *ai*

disappear keska:s'k *ii*, keska:sit *ai*; ~ in a
flash keskatesk *ii*, keskatesink *ai*; make ~
keska:l'k *ta*, keska:tu *ti*; keskma:l'k *ta*,
keskma:tu *ti*; make or or cause to vanish or
~ keskamukwa:l'k *ta*, keskamukwa:tu *ti*

disbelieve mektaq *ta*, mektm *ti*

discharge the one who ~ -s or fires someone nutsa:qaniket *ai (an)*

disciple w'naqapem *an*

discourteous to pepsite:l'mk *ta*

discover we:jitu *ti*, we:ji:k *ta*; ~ -er we:ju:lkw *an*

discriminate ~ against penoqwite:l'mk *ta*, penoqwite:tk *ti*

disease die from a ~ ketemenejik (pl) *ai*

disgrace ntaqo:qon

disgracefully act ~ penoqwe:k *ai*

dish eptaqan *an*; w'laqan *an* [SH]

dishonest istuwik *ii*, istuwikit *ai*; waqjuwikk *ii*, waqjuwikit *ai* [RB]

dish out ela:miket *ai* [SH]; ela:muwet *ai*

disjointed o:plisqatesk *ii*, o:plisqatesink *ai*

dislocate tewalqatesm'k *ta*, tewalqatestu *ti*; ~ -d tewalqe:k *ii* [SH]; tewalqatesink *ai*, tewalqatesk *ii* [SH]

disobedient elist'k *ai* [PEI]

disobey elistaq *ta*, elistm *ti*; elist'k (elistm) *ai* [PEI]

dispatch pitkimk *ta*, pitkitm *ti*; ~ -ed sikto:kwet *ai*

disposition have a bad ~ metu:qamiksit *ai*; have a good ~ or character welqamiksit *ai*

disrespectful pepsitelket *ai*

dissolve keskamukwa:l'k *ta*, keskamukwa:tu *ti*; ~ -d keskamukwa:s'k *ii*, keskmukwa:sit *ai*

distain regarded with ~ penoqwe:k *ai*

distance quite a ~ wel-pesuk *ii*

distant ~ relatives or relations knek wetakutijik (pl) *ai*; a little ways ~ amaseji:jk *ii*

distasteful find ~ poqwajite:l'mk *ta*, poqwajite:tm *ti*

distorted ~ (of sound) jijje:taq *ii*

distract we:neweyaq *ta*; wetmeyaq *ta*, wetmo:tm *ti*

distribute tepi:ketu *ti*

district ~ (of a chief) saqamti [CB]

distrust ansuwite:l'mk *ta*, ansuwite:tm *ti* [PEI]

disturb askayaq *ta*, asko:tm *ti*; wetmeyaq *ta*, wetmo:tm *ti*; ~ or bother (by talking about) sespemk *ta*; ~ the sleep of wespayaq *ta*

dive ketapetesink *ai*; ketapet *ai*; kwetapet *ai* [BR]

diver a ~ nujikwtapet *ai (an)* [BR]

divide niktuwa:s'k *ii*, niktuwa:sit *ai*; ~ in bulk nasko:l'k *ta*, nasko:tu *ti*; ~ in half naskwa:l'k *ta*, naskwa:tu *ti*; nawska:l'k *ta* [SH]; ~ -d elsaqtek *ii* [SH]; niktuwe:k *ai, ii*

divorced punalltijik (pl) *ai*

dizzy ew'naskwiyet *ai*; make ~ ew'naskwatpa:l'k *ta*; ~ (from a blow to the head) ew'naskwatpetesink *ai*

do ~ in such a way tela:l'k *ta*, tela:tu *ti*; ~ nicely or smoothly weljaqk *ta*, weljaqam *ti*; start to ~ away with peman'm *ti*, pemank *ta*; ~ back to asita:teket *ai*

dock oqwa:q *ii*, oqwa:t *ai*

doctor mallpale:wit (mallpale:wijik) *an*; look like a ~ mallpale:witewapewit; woman ~ mallpale:wi:skw (mallpale:wi:skwaq) *an*

dog lmu:j (lmu:jik) *an* [BR]; nmu:j (nmu:jik) *an*; have a ~ wtewit *ai* [SH]; wti:t *ai*; my ~ nti *an*

doll amsute:kan *an* [SH]; apsute:kan *an*

dollar one ~ nekwta:'ik *ii* [BR]; newkta'ik *ii*; one ~ bill nekwta'ikewey [SH]; ten ~ -s metla:sa'ikl (pl); three ~ -s nesa'ikl; two ~ -s tapu a'ikl

dome ~ shaped menjapsk'sit *ai*, menjapskek *ii*

domiciled ~ at tle:yawit *ai*

don na:qoqum *ti*; nasa:l'k *ta*, nasa:tu *ti*

door ka:qan; kaqani [BR]

double bent over ~ toqwanqapit; go in ~ file toqwanqapultijik (pl) *ai*; ~ -d up toqwanqapit *ai*

double-jointed toqwanqiskat *ai*

doubt mektaq *ta*, mektm *ti*

dough lusknikn

douse ~ or put out a fire with a water hose naqasuwa:m *ti*

down bend head ~ nisa:kwa:sit *ai* [BC]; bring ~ nisa:l'k *ta*, nisa:tu *ti*; bring ~ from there weji-nisa:l'k *ta*; climb ~ niskusuwet *ai*; force ~ with one's weight kewk'k *ta*, kewkm *ti*; go ~ (after being shot) mesqana:sit *ai*; knock ~ kewte:k *ta*, kewte:m *ti*; lay or put ~ mesqana:l'k *ta*, mesqana:tu *ti*; point ~ (something of length) nisoqpit *ai*, nisoqtek *ii*; shove ~ nisaqalk *ta*, nisaqtu *ti*; take ~

nisa:l'k *ta*, nisa:tu *ti*; take ~ to the flat
metoqwa:l'k *ta*, metoqwa:tu *ti*; take ~ with a
shot mesqanatelaq *ta* [CB]; mesqani:telaq
ta; throw ~ nisaqalk *ta*, nisaqtu *ti* [BR]

down-easter papke:kewa:j *an*

downhill pa:qe:k

down payment put a claim, deposit, retainer
or ~ on kelte:k *ta*, kelte:m *ti*

downstairs epune:k

downstream go ~ papka:lukwet *ai*

downtide ekiyaq *ii* [RB]

downy pi:wetiknit *ai*

doze ~ off kepskit *ai*

drag wesuwatejimk *ta*, wesuwatejitu *ti*; ~
along pematejimk *ta*, pematejitu *ti*; ~ along
with nespatejimk *ta*, nespatejitu *ti*; ~ here
petatejimk *ta*, petatejitu *ti*; ~ out tewatejimk
ta, tewatejitu *ti*; ~ over elatejimk *ta*, elatejitu
ti; start to ~ poqtatejimk *ta*

dragonfly sa:qatiyej *an* [BC]; sa:puwejit *an*

drain wesamqwat *ai* [SH]

drape laqpilaqan; close the ~ **-s** (on windows)
elekepilawet AI

draughty news'k *ii*

draw¹ napuwi:k'k *ta*, napuwi:km *ti*; ~ or trace
pictures napuwi:kiket *ai (an)*; ~ or trace
unevenly or crookedly istu-napuwi:k'k *ta*,
istu-napuwi:km *ti*

draw² ~ on a pipe papk'semk *ta* [BR];
papk'smk *ta* [BR]; pask'semk *ta*; ~ water
from a well naqana:pet

dream pewat *ai*; pewitaqan; pewiteket *ai*; ~
about pewitu *ti*, pewi:k *ta*; have all kinds of
~ **-s** (as when one is feverish) milkusit *ai*

drenched ~ by heavy seas ko:pukwet *ai* [BC]

dress¹ makot Indian ~ pisuwaqan [CB]; my
~ n'makkatem [BC]; ntoqon; ntoqwan [BR];
wear a ~ makota:q (makota:m) *ai*; ~
properly ilpilk *ta*, ilpil'm *ti*; ~ warmly
kisu:piso:tlk *ta*; ~ **-ed** keknesit *ai*; warmly
~ **-ed** kisu:k'k (kisu:km); fancily ~ **-ed**
kesmpisit *ai*

dress² ji:kate:k *ta*, ji:kate:m *ti*; ji:kate:ket *ai*;
kekno:tlk *ta*; ~ or gut (an animal) pukwaja:l'k
ta; pekwaja:l'k *ta*; ~ **-ed** wood ji:ka:taw
(ji:ka:taq) *an*; ~ **-ed** as such telikk *ii*, telikit *ai*

drift ~ along pemto:kwet *ai*, pemto:kwek *ii*; ~
inside (snow) piskw-paniks'k *ii*; ~ toward
ela:lukwet *ai* [BC] (waltes term); ~ **-ed** up
against el-paniks'k *ii*, el-paniksink *ai*

drill po:qiket *ai*; po:q'k *ta*, po:qm *ti*; construct
a furrow or ~ nem'k'te:ket *ai*

drink mamam; esamqwatm *ti* [BR];
esamuqwat *ai*; esapoqwat *ai* [SH];
esapoqwatm *ti* [SH]; nesamuqawat *ai*; ~
alone newtinqana:mat *ai*; ~ moderately
welinqana:mat *ai*; ~ up sineket *ai*; ~ too
much of wesamqwat *ai*; give a ~ to
esamuqo:tlk *ta*; esapoqo:tlk *ta* [SH]; have a
~ (of an alcoholic beverage) nemkwet *ai*;
like to ~ (alcoholic beverages) wikpet *ai*;
heavy ~ **-er** samqwani:j *an*; feel good (from
~ **-ing**) welaqapit *ai*

drip elikuwa:laq *ii*, elikuwa:lat *ai*

drive¹ ~ away ejikl-te:k *ta*, ejikl-te:m *ti*; ~ in (a
nail) ke'ipaqte:m *ti*; kejitapaqte:m *ti*

drive² ~ from we'i-teja:l'k *ta*, we'i-teja:tu *ti*; ~
to (in a vehicle) el-teja:l'k *ta*, el-teja:tu *ti*

drool pene:sukwati; pne:sukwati;
pene:sukwa:t *ai*

droop waqjuwika:sik *ii*, waqjuwika:sit *ai*; ~ the
head qolomqwa:sit *ai*; hung or ~ **-ed** over
sawepit *ai*, sawetek *ii*; move along with ~
-ing head weji-qolomkwi-pmiyet *ai*

drop eleket *ai*; ~ in pijiyaq *ii*, pijiyet *ai*

drown paqasiyet *ai* [SH]

drum jikmaqan [SH]

drumstick mawtejjuwey

drunk ketkiyet *ai*; ~ **-ard** kt'kiyewinuj *an*;
~ **-enness** kt'kiyewuti

dr-y etlipiyasit *ai*, etlipiyatek *ii*; etlipiyask *ta*,
etlipiyasm *ti*; kispasit *ai*, kispatek *ii*; kispask
ta, kispasm *ti*; niwe:k *ai, ii*; ~ out niwa:l'k *ta*,
niwa:tu *ti*; ~ tide niwetek *ii*; get or become
~ niwa:s'k *ii*, niwa:sit *ai*; wipe ~ niwika:s'k
ta, niwika:sm *ti*; ~ **-ied** out kaqjek *ii*, kaqjet
ai; kisipiyasit *ai*, kisipiyatek *ii*; ~ **-ied** out
(from the heat) niwoqsit *ai*, niwoqtek *ii*; ~
-ied out (of lumber) kispasas'k *ii*, kispasasit
ai

drydock put into ~ oqtatqa:tu *ti* [SH]

dryer kispasawemkewey;
  ksispa:tekemkewey

dry-throated poqwa:lat *ai*

dull jikawepit *ai*, jikawetek *ii*; kesp'k *ii*; kesplk
  ta, kesp'tu *ti*; kiwaje:k *ai*; get ~ kespiyaq *ii*

dumpling sapanewey

duplicate kinuwa:l'k *ta*, kinuwa:tu *ti* [SH];
  minuwa:l'k *ta*, minuwa:tu *ti*

dusk wela:kw; become ~ piluwamukwiyaq *ii*,
  piluwamukwiyet *ai*

dusty piksa:q *ii*, piksa:t *ai*

dwarf pukulatmu:j; wiklatmu:j *an*

dwell reside or ~ there wikit *ai*

dwelling wikuwom; enter a ~ enm'piskwa:t
  ai; enter ~ elm'piskwa(:)t *ai* [BR]; my ~ ni:k

dye t'ssawiyaqan [SH]; essawiyaqan;
  essawiyalk *ta*, essawiyatm *ti* [SH];
  essawiya:l'k *ta*, essawiya:tu *ti*; essawiyet *ai*
  [SH]; ess'k *ta*, ess'm *ti*; ~ -d essasit *ai*

E

eagle kitpu *an*

ear my ~ ns'tuwaqan; have large or long ~ **-s** maqistaqanat *ai* (Big Cove term for a Micmac from Restigouche)

early arrive ~ naqsipkisink *ai*; ~ this morning sepay [SH]; sepey

earn kaniye:wit *ai* (Fr *gagner*); ~ wages ne:patu *ti*

earring nassaputaqan; nessaputaqan [BC]

earth ws'tqamu

earthquake kiwkw *ii*

earwax kulkwikmk [SH]

easily ~ fool na:qapa:l'k *ta* [ESK]; ~ hurt or harm naqsi-o:pla:l'k *ta*, naqsi-o:pla:tu *ti*; put where ~ found naqamasi:katu *ti* [PEI]; put where it can ~ be found naqamasa:l'k *ta*, naqamasa:tu *ti*; sleep ~ or without trouble naqsinpat *ai*;

east wesekewa:nek (loc) [CB]; weskewa:nek (loc) [CB]; wjipen; down ~ papke:k; ~ or northwest wind wejipek *ii*; from the ~ wjipenuk (loc) [SH]; go ~ papka:sit *ai*; in the ~ wtutnuk (loc) [SH]; take to the ~ papka:l'k *ta*, papka:tu *ti*; ~ **-erner** wjipenukowa:j *an*; an ~ **-erly** breeze wejipewe:k *ii*;

Easter Pa:kewimk [SH]; Pa:kewumk (Fr *Pâques*)

easy ~ to do naqamase:k *ii*; take it ~ weljaqajewa:teket *ai* [SH]

eat etlatalk *ai*; malqomk *ta*, malqotm *ti*; mijisit *ai* [BR][NB]; mijjit *ai* [BC]; wetaqama:sit *ai* (archaic); ~ all of jikp'k *ta*, jiktm *ti*; ~ between meals qaskwatalk *ai*; ~ clean (leaving no leftovers) musikp'k *ta*, musiktm *ti*; ~ fussily emteskatalk *ai*; ~ ill-manneredly ketkatalk *ai*; ~ improperly emekwatalk *ai*; o:platalk *ai*; o:pli-mijisit *ai* [SH]; ~ in abundance mekepk *ta*, meketm *ti*; ~ little malatalk *ai*; ~ lunch ketaqama:sit *ai* [BC]; ~ much pisoqotalk *ai*; ~ on the move pematalk (pematal) *ai*; ~ one's favorite dish weltamit *ai*; ~ outside tewatalk *ai*; ~ plenty of mekepk *ta*, meketm *ti*; ~ poorly ettamit *ai*; matuwatalk *ai*; ~ raw esk'pk *ta*, esk'tm *ti*; ~ the faeces of jakeju:p'k *ta*; ~ the leftovers of matu:p'k *ta*, matu:tm *ti*; ~ the main course (fish, pork) epistamit *ai* [BC]; ~

what no one else would ketkatalk *ai*; ~ while otherwise occupied nespatalk (nespatal) *ai*; back from ~ **-ing** apatalk *ai* [ESK]; cease ~ **-ing** punatalk (punatal) *ai*; finished ~ **-ing** kisatalk *ai* [BR]; k'satalk *ai*; heard ~ **-ing** metewatalk *ai*

eavesdrop jikistaqanat *ai*

echo ke:skwaq [SH]; ~ place paqtaqamiktuk (loc); make an ~ paqtaqawa:q *ii*

eclipse an ~ soqqwat *ai*; soqqwet *ai* [BC][PEI]

eddy msk'tkw [SH]; form an ~ apskwitk *ii*

edge along the ~ jajikiw [SH]; along the ~ of a cliff enmipkowe:k

education kina:masuti; kina:matnewey

educator an ~ nuji-kina:muwet *ai (an)*

Edward Etuwe:l *an* (Fr *Edouard*)

eel ka:t (ka:taq) *an*; katew (kataq) *an* [BR]; boneless ~ pqwasaw'l; conger ~ qotoqonokj *an* [RB]; hunt ~ nanntuwat *ai*; go for ~ **-s** aji-kate:ket *ai* [NB]; hunt for ~ **-s** ka:tewe:ket *ai* [SH]; katewe:ket [BC]

Eel Ground, N.B. a:tukwaqanek (loc) [RB]

Eel River Bar, N.B. oqpi:kanjek [RB]; wpi:kanj'k

eelskin ka:tomi

effeminately act ~ e:pitewqamiksit *ai*

egg wa:w; lay ~ **-s** wa:wiket *ai* [SH]

egg-laying ~ month pnatmuwiku:s *an*

eggman wa:wa:q *an* [SH]; wa:we:j *an*

eight ~ (in counting) ukumujjin [EG]; ukumuljin

eighty ~ (in counting) ukumuljin-te:sinska:q

either ~ one ta:n pa teken

ejaculate peskmat *ai*

elbow my ~ nluskunikn'm *an*

elder ~ **-ly** person ami: (voc) *an* (term of respect and affection) [SH]

elegant asamaje:k *ai, ii*; do fancily or ~ **-ly** asamaja:l'k *ta*, asamaja:tu *ti*

eleven eleven (in counting) mtl'n jel ne:kwt [BR]

elm wikpi *an* [RB]

elope poqjit *ai* [BR]

else before all ~ pe:l tmk

elsewhere se:k

embankment water ~ kwe:kwiyamkek [CB]

embark pusik *ii*, pusit *ai*; ~ frequently or regularly i:pusit *ai*

embarrass netaka:l'k *ta*; ~ **-ed** netaka:sit *ai*
ember ~ of firewood puksaqatew (puksaqatal)
embossed ~ (of bead work) elapska:tasit *ai*
embrace te:tipoqja:l'k *ta*, te:tipoqja:tu *ti*; wejamoqsuwalk *ta*; wejimoqsuwalk *ta*; wesmoqjewalk *ta*
embroider amaltaqi:sawet *ai*; amaltaqi:s'k *ta*, amaltaqi:sm *ti*; ~ **-ed** amaltaqawi:kas'k *ii*
empty musike:k *ai, ii*; sikuwe:k *ai, ii*; ~ out sikuwa:l'k *ta*, sikuwa:tu *ti*
empty-handed come out ~ putmat *ai*
encamped wi:kikit *ai*
encase ankuna:l'k *ta*, ankuna:tu *ti*
encircled ~ with a halo (as the sun or moon) awiyalusink *ai*
enclose ~ with ankuna:l'k *ta*, ankuna:tu *ti*; hold ~ **-d** in one's hand sepiljenk *ta*, sepiljen'm *ti* [BC]
encourage ajipjulk *ta*, ajipjutu *ti*; welkwijimk *ta*
end kaqa:l'k *ta*, kaqa:tu *ti*; kaqa:teket *ai*; at the ~ of the snow period paniyanuk (loc); beak off at the (nose) ~ temisqona:l'k *ta*, temisqona:tu *ti*; the ~ of the snow period paniyaq *ii*; falls ~ we:kwapskw; reach the ~ kaqtaqayaq *ii*, kaqtaqayet *ai*; row to the ~ we:kwi-ji:met *ai*; the ~ kespiyaq *ii* [SH]; kiyaspiyaq *ii*; na(:) ms't; the ~ of the story (the sound) kespiyatoqsit *ai*; the ~ of the world kespaqami:k *ii*; ~ **-ed** kaqiyaq *ii*, kaqiyet *ai*; where the waterway ~ **-s** we:kwamkuk
endure saputaqatm *ti*; telipkijiyaq *ii*
engine mulin
England innklan [CB]
English speak ~ to aklasiyewimk *ta* [BR]; aqalasiyewimk *ta*; speak ~ aqalasiyewi:sit *ai*; aklasiyewi:sit *ai* [BR]
Englishman aklasiyew *an*; aqalasiyew *an* (Fr *anglais*)
Englishwoman wennjujkwej *an*
enjoyable kise:k *ai*
enlarge maqa:l'k *ta*, maqa:tu *ti*
enlist akase:wit *ai*
enmeshed naspit *ai*, nastek *ii*

enough tepiyaq *ii*, tepiyet *ai*; hard ~ tepi-m'lke:k *ai, ii*; narrow ~ wel-jijikwe:jk *ii*, wel-jijikwe:jit *ai* [BR]; strong ~ tepiknaq *ii*, tepiknat *ai*
enquire ask or ~ about pipanikesit *ai*
entangled nasapaqtesk *ii*, nasapaqtesink *ai*
enter piskwa:q *ii*, piskwa:t *ai*; ~ a dwelling enm'piskwa:t *ai*; elm'piskwa(:)t *ai* [BR]
entertainer an ~ (with musical instrument) nujiktu:muwet *ai (an)*
entrails read ~ ikanite:tm *ti* [SH]
entranceway kaqani
entwine elaqpa:l'k *ta*, elaqpa:tu *ti*
envious emteskit *ai* [BC]
Ephiphany eleke:wiya:timk
epilepsy kjipulkowey
epileptic an ~ puskiwkjipulkwet *ai (an)*; puskikjipulkwet *ai (an)*
erase keskamukwa:l'k *ta*, keskamukwa:tu *ti*
erection have an ~ metkwa:tat *ai*
erratic piluwasit *ai*
escape wesmukwat *ai*; ~ from wessmuktaq *ta*, wessmuktm *ti*; ~ from there wessmukwat *ai*
escapee an ~ alsumukwat *ai (an)*
especially! meluwij [ESK]
European apaqtukewa:j *an*
evaporate niwa:s'k *ii*, niwa:sit *ai*
even ~ (as in gambling) napto:sit *ai*; ~ so je tliya; lpa; pa na; not ~ lpa mu (takes negative verb form); not ~ je mu; jel mu (takes negative verb form) [BR]
evening wela:kw; chilly ~ teklo:qiyaq *ii*; nice ~ or night welitpa:q *ii*; this ~ w'lo:nuk; toward ~ wela:kwe:l
every e:ta:s [SH]; i:ta:s; ~ day te:si-kisk'k; ~ time te:s
everybody ms't wen *an*; ta:n te:sit *ai*, ta:n te:s'k *ii*
everything ms't koqwey; ta:n te:sit *ai*, ta:n te:s'k *ii* [SH]; into ~ (as a baby) sespo:teket *ai (an)*
everywhere met'ki [SH]; ms't tami
exactly ansma; assma

exaggerate pajjaqamat *ai*; ~ about ki:kat-akanutaq *ta*, ki:kat-akanutm *ti*; ~ to ki:kajimk *ta*

examine ilamk *ta*, ilaptm *ti*; ilapt'k *ta*, ilaptm *ti*

excess in ~ (of) piyamiw

exchange sa:se:wit *ai*; sa:se:wa:l'k *ta*, sa:se:wa:tu *ti*

excrement mi:jan *an*

executioner an ~ nuji-ne:pateket *ai (an)*

exercise ewe:kiska:l'k *ta*, ewe:kiska:tu *ti*; ewe:kiskalsit *ai*

exhale tewlamit *ai*

exit tewiyet *ai*

expect eskipetu *ti*, eskipe:k *ta*; ~ a baby ketu-w'njanit *ai*; ~ **-ing** a baby eskmaqtmat *ai*; ~ **-ed** to arrive ketu:pkisink *ai*; ketuwipkisink *ai* [BR]

expensive meko:tik *ii*, meko:tit *ai*

explode ~ (as a dry log on a fire, popcorn, etc.) pa:sk'tek *ii*

explorer we:ju:lkw *an*

exposed muskask'pit *ai*, muskask'tek *ii*

extension house ~ tusati

extensively flow ~ pukwelijuwik *ii*, pukwelijuwit *ai*

extent to what ~ ? tatuji(w)

extinguish naqasu:-putuwalk *ta*, naqasu:-putuwatm *ti*; naqasuwa:l'k *ta*, naqasuwa:tu *ti*

extraordinar-y perform ~ feats kina:teket *ai*; ~ **-ily** good looking we:kwi-klu:sit *ai* [ESK]

extremely ~ bad pajiji-winjik *ii*, pajiji-winjit *ai*; ~ cold a:munitke:k *ii* [PEI]; ~ good or nice pajiji-klulk *ii*, pajiji-klu:sit *ai*

eye my ~ np'kikw [BR][BC]; npukukw; npu:kw; wpukikwa:l'k *ta*, wpukukwa:l'k *ta*, wpukukwa:tu *ti*; close one's ~ **-s** sepikwa:sit *ai*; have large ~ **-s** maqalqikwat *ai*; have one's ~ **-s** closed sepikwet *ai*; have one's ~ **-s** open wapit *ai*; have small ~ **-s** apsalqikwat *ai*; have something in one's ~ **-s** pe:sit *ai*; have tiny ~ **-s** apsalkikwat *ai* [PEI]; apsalqikwa:ji:jit *ai*; open one's ~ **-s** wapa:s'k *ii*, wapa:sit *ai*; sleep with ~ **-s** open wapinpat *ai*

eyeball lamipkikwan [SH]; lamipkikwam [BR]

eyebrow my ~ n'mi:sikwan *an*

eyeglasses pkikwe:l (pl); p'kikwe:l (pl) [SH]; pu:kwe:l (pl); wpukikwe:l (pl) [SH]; wpukukwe:l (pl)

eyelash my ~ nitku *an*; n'msekun *an* [SH]; n'tku *an*

eyesight have ~ nemiteket *ai*; have poor ~ pasapit *ai*

F

fac-e my ~ nsiskw; have a dirty ~ mejikapewit *ai*; make a funny ~ winikwa:sit *ai*; put on a ~ winikwa:sit *ai*; ~ about kinawaklapa:sit *ai* [CB]; grease the ~ of (e.g., a pan) mima:kwa:l′k *ta*, mima:kwa:tu *ti*; slap in the ~ pesikwe′ite:k *ta*; pesikwete:k *ta* [PEI]; ~ away ejiklamukwiyet *ai*; ~ the other direction enmejepit *ai*, enmejetek *ii*; fall ~ first ketkwijetesk *ii*, ketkwijetesink *ii*; sit humped over ~ -**ing** toward wejkwistepit *ai*; sit ~ -**ing** wejkwapit *ai*; sit or set ~ -**ing** toward wejkwajepit *ai*, wejkwajetek *ii*; ~ -**d** toward elko:jink *ai*

fact a ~ ki:wajiyaq *ii*; ki:wajiyet *ai*

fade essawiyet *ai*; ~ out of sight keskapekiyaq *ii*; keskamukwiyaq *ii*, keskamukwiyet *ai*; ~ -**d** (from the sun) wapoqsit *ai*, wapoqtek *ii*

faeces mi:jan *an*; eat the ~ of jakeju:p′k *ta*; ~ smeller mi:janimat *ai (an)*; my ~ n′mi:jan *an*

faggot oqon

fail ~ to hit (something aimed at) pesoqte:k *ta*, pesoqte:m *ti*; ~ to meet or come into contact with pesoqteskaq *ta*, pesoqteskm *ti*; ~ to reach naw′n′k *ta*, naw′n′m *ti*

faint wikwiyet *ai*

fairy wood ~ mi:km *an*

fall[1] ~ across as′komoqtesk *ii* [BR]; asoqomoqtesk *ii*, asoqomoqtesink *ai*; ~ backwards apatankiyet *ai* [PEI]; aputask′tesink *ai*; aputaskiyaq *ti*, aputaskiyet *ta*; atuwa:skwetesink *ai*; ~ down nisiyaq *ii*, nisiyet *ai*; ~ face first ketkwijetesk *ii*, ketkwijetesink *ai*; ~ from there weji-nisiyaq *ii*, weji-nisiyet *ai*; ~ in pijiyaq *ii*, pijiyet *ai*; ~ in a heap mawisetesk *ii*, mawisetesink *ai*; stumble and ~ paqiyatkwe′itesink *ai*

fall[2] toqwa:q *ii*; last ~ tqoq; next ~ tqo:nuk; every ~ te:sitwa:q

falls ~ end we:kwapskw

falsely accuse ~ pisu-ilsu:tmaq *ta*; speak ~ of pilsimk *ta*

family my immediate ~ nikmaq *an*

famished we:kwi-kewisink *ai* [ESK]

fan ~ or propeller wju:sney

fancily ~ dressed kesmpisit *ai*; do ~ or elegantly asamaja:l′k *ta*, asamaja:tu *ti*

fancy little and ~ kelu:si:ji:jit *ai*

fang wisqo:pit [SH]

far amasek *ii*; knek *ii*; good and ~ wel-pesuk *ii*; how ~ ? tatuji(w)

far-sighted amasapit *ai*

fart piktu:n; piktit *ai*

fast[1] sune:wit *ai* (Fr *jeûne*); ~ day sune:wimk

fast[2] a ~ runner kji-kawa:suwinu *an*; ~ (as a sled, etc.) kesikaq *ii*, kesikat *ai*; go ~ kesikawiyaq *ii*, kesikawiyet *ai* [SH]; move ~ kesikawa:sik *ii*, kesikawa:sit *ai*

fasten naseket *ai*; kelapaqam *ti*, kelapaqq *ta*

fat wikew; my ~ (outer layer) nwikew′m; bear grease or ~ muwino:mi; my ~ (outer layer) nwikew′m; moose ~ kaqqamew; moose ~ or tallow tiya:mu:mi; pork ~ kulkwi:su:mi; kulkwi:suwimi; my inner ~ (around the kidneys) ntelkw; wikewit *ai*; nice and ~ welkamit *ai* [RB]; very ~ mawkamik *ii*, mawkamit *ai*; too ~ wesamkamit *ai*; -**ty** wikamik *ii*, wikamit *ai*

father! nu: (voc) [BR]; tata:t (voc)

father a ~ wujjewit *ai*; have a ~ wujjit *ai*; my ~ nujj *an*; our ~ kujjinu (inclusive)

father-in-law my ~ njilj *an*

Father's Day me:kite:l′manej kujjinaq

fault at ~ pekwatoq (pekwatu) *ai*; telalsit *ai*; tela:tekek *ii*, tela:teket *ai*

favorite eat one's ~ dish weltamit *ai*

favour ikalk *ta*, ikatm *ti*; ask for a ~ etawaqtmat *ai*; do a ~ for wela:l′k *ta*, wela:tu *ti*; ~ obtained (religious) w′lapetmuwaqan; obtain a ~ or something good from welapemk *ta*, welapetm *ti*; obtain a (religious) ~ welapetmuwet *ai*

fear jipalk *ta*, jipatm *ti*

feast kweltamit *ai*; weltamit *ai*; kweltanat *ai* [SH]; give a ~ for wikupa:l′k *ta*

feast day pestiye:wumk (Fr *fête*); pestiye:wimk [SH]

feather pi:kun *an*; ~ -**y** pi:wetiknit *ai*

February apukunajit *ai* [ESK]

fed up ~ with siwamk *ta*, siwaptm *ti*

feed esm(′)k *ta* [BR]; force ~ ki:kass′mk *ta*

feel wetuwotm *ti* [SH]; we:tunk *ta*, we:tu:tm *ti*; ~ about nanntunawet *ai*; ~ around nanntunawet *ai*; ~ around for aliskalk *ta*, aliskatm *ti*; ~ around for nanntunk *ta*, nanntun'm *ti*; ~ inside of (with the hand) pu:talqan'm *ti*, pu:talqank *ta*; ~ one's way around (as a blind man) al-nanntunawet *ai* [SH]; an-nanntunawet *ai*; ~ the weight of we:tunk *ta*, we:tun'm *ti*

feet[1] come with pounding ~ wejkwitu:kwe:pit *ai*; get to one's ~ pemi-qama:sit *ai* [SH]; have cold ~ kewtaqsikit *ai* tekikatat *ai*; have large ~ maqsitat *ai*; knock down with the ~ ejaqje'iteskaq *ta*; start to get back on one's ~ pem-pukuwa:sit *ai*

feet[2] leppiye (no plural) (in measurement), (Fr *les pieds*);

feign ~ sleep ewsinpat *ai*

feint ewsa:tu *ti*

fell ~ (by cutting) kews'k *ta*, kews'm *ti*

female ~ animal lape:wi:skw *an*; nape:wi:skw *an* [BR]; ~ fowl nape:wi:skw *an* [SH]; skwe:w; ~ mammal lkwetuk *an*; lukwetuk *an*; skweyoq *an*

fence llutaqan

ferry asoqommtaqan; as'kommkaqan; ~ across asoqomute:ket *ai*

fertilize epkenk *ta*, epken'm *ti*; ~ -r pkenikn; epkenikn

fester putuwiskwa:sik *ii* [BR]

festival ~ grounds (present Restigouche territory) papitaqane:kati

fetch nemiskaq *ta*, nemiskm *ti*; apiskaq *ta*, apiskm [NB]; go ~ app n'miskaq *ta*, app n'miskm *ti*

fetlock my ~ nsit *an* [SH]

fever epsimkewey

fiancé(e) fiancé(e) (male or female) p'lkoq *an*; my ~ np'lkoqom *an*; nte:pite:sm *an*

fib kluskapewit *ai*

fiddle tapiya:jijk [SH]; tapiya:jijke:juwit *ai* [SH]; tapiya:'iji:jte:ket *ai*; ~ or drum up a storm putukte:mat *ai*; ~ string tapiya:jijk api *an* [SH]; ~ -r tapiya:jijke:j *an*

fiddlehead ma:susi [RB]; apiya:jijkewatp [SH]

fidget fidgety sespa:sit *ai*

field hay ~ msikuwe:kati

fifth ~ person na:newa:j *an*; ~ one na:newey *an, in*

fifty naniska:ql (pl) *ii*, naniskeksijik (pl) *ai*; ~ (in counting) naninska:q *ii* [SH]

fifty cents temi-piya:st (Fr *demi-piastre*)

fight matnakket *ai*; mat'ntijik (pl) *ai*; ~ for ikalk *ta*, ikatm *ti*; ~ or struggle against matn'm *ti*, matnk *ta*; know how to ~ nata:matnakket *ai*; ~ over (something) wejinntijik (pl) *ai*; ~ -ing matnakkewaqan

figure mawkiljet *ai*

file siputaqan [SH]; la:kittaqan; esipulk *ta*, esiputu *ti*

fill ~ up pitkmalk *ta*, pitkmatm *ti*; ~ up (with a non-liquid) wajuwa:l'k *ta*, wajuwa:tu *ti*; ~ up (with a liquid) waju:peka:l'k *ta*, waju:peka:tu *ti*

filthy-minded winsmuwit *ai*; ~ person winsm (winsmuk) *an*

finally klapis

find we:jitu *ti*, we:ji:k *ta*; we:ji:wet *ai* (said of a woman when she bears a child)

fine wele:k *ai*; sma:tewit *ai*

finger my ~ ntluwikn; have sticky ~ -s pesqojukuwiptnat *ai* [BC]

fingernail my ~ nqosi *an*

finish kaq-kisa:l'k *ta*, kaq-kisa:tu *ti*; kaqa:teket *ai*; kaqa:l'k *ta*, kaqa:tu *ti*; ~ beating kiste:k *ta*, kiste:m *ti*; ~ burning up kaqa-nu:kwa:l'k *ta*, kaqa-nu:kwa:tu *ti*; ~ making kisitu *ti*, kisi:k *ta*; ~ off ketmete:k *ta*, ketmete:m *ti*; ~ off quickly (as in boxing or cards) jaqal-te:k *ta*, jaqal-te:m *ti*; ~ singing kisintoq (kisintu) *ai*; ~ with kaqo:tm *ti*; ~ working kaqa-lukwet *ai*; ~ -ed kaqi net [BC]; kaqiyaq *ii*, kaqiyet *ai*; ~ -ed bearing or producing children kaqi-kwesmat *ai*; ~ -ed being cooked kisoqsit *ai*, kisoqtek *ii*; ~ -ed cooking ki:s'k *ta*, ki:sm *ti*; ~ -ed eating kisatalk *ai* [BR]; k'satalk; ~ -ed off ketmete:mat *ai*

fir ~ or balsam tree stoqon *an*; search for ~ boughs stoqone:ket *ai*; spruce, ~ or balsam tree stoqonaqsi *an* [SH]

fir-color stoqon-amuksit *ai*, stoqon-amu:k *ii*

fire[1] puktew (puktal); build a ~ within mawksa:l'k *ta*, mawksa:tu *ti*; build or set a ~ (in a stove or furnace) moqsa:l'k *ta*,

moqsa:tu *ti*; make a ~ moqsa:teket *ai* [SH];
mawksa:teket *ai*

fire² esa:q *ta*, esa:m *ti*; ese:k *ta*

fired ~ (as a gun) pe:sk'tek *ii*

firefly wasoqowi:j *an*

firewater puktewijk

firewood puksuk

first amskwes [BR]; amkwes; at ~ na tumk;
~ of all na tmk; pe: tmk; the ~ one
amkwesewa:j *an*; amkwesewey *an, in*; the ~
person amkwesewa:juwit *ai*; the ~ work day
amkwes elukutimk

fish n'me:juwet *ai* [SH]; wesket *ai*; ekwitamet
ai [SH][BC]; n'me:j *an*; any small ~ n'me:ji:j
an; male ~ napemekw (napemaq) *an* [BR];
~ tank or bowl n'me:juwo:q *an*; begin or
start to ~ poqjiwsket *ai*; ~ for salmon
plamukwet *ai*; smoked ~ pukkwanata:sit
n'me:j *an*; start off to ~ poqji-kwitmet *ai* [SH];
start out to ~ najiwsket *ai*; ice ~ **-ing**
ekwitamemk; ~ **-ing** weskemk;
ekwitamemk [CB]; kwitamaqan [CB]; ~ **-ery**
kwitamaqan [BC]

fisher pqamk *an* (of the weasel family) [RB]

fisherman wskewinu *an*; n'me:j'kowinu *an*; an
unskilled ~ awaniwsket *ai*

fish-hawk eskwaqanik (eskwaqanikaq) *an*

fishnet a:pi *an*

fit¹ tepaqapit *ai*, tepaqatek *ii*; a good ~
weltesk *ii*, weltesink *ai*; ~ a handle in or on
(an axe or hammer) nasaqomkikwat *ai*; ~ a
handle on an axe eloqomkiyatm *ti*; ~ well
wela:q *ii*, weloqsit *ai*; welkaq *ta*, welkm *ti*;
trim to ~ eloqwalk *ta*, eloqwatm *ti* [BR]

fit² have a ~ wejipulkwet *ai*; take a ~
wejipilkwet *ai* [PEI]; take frequent ~ **-s**
puskiwijipilkwet *ai*

five ~ (in counting) na:n; nanijik *ai* [BR]; nankl
ii, na:nijik *ai*; ~ cylindrical shaped objects
nanoqskekl (pl) *ii*, nanoqsijik (pl) *ai* [BR]; ~
days nanukuna:q *ii*; ~ in a row nanoqoskl
(pl) *ii*; ~ lying in a row nanoqosmiya:tijik (pl)
ai; pair of ~ **-s** na:naq (pl) *an*; ~ **-card**
na:newa:j *an*

fix kisa:l'k *ta*, kisa:tu *ti*; elukwalk *ta*, elukwatm
ti; ila:l'k *ta*, ila:tu *ti*; ~ up kiskatte:k *ta*; ~ **-ed**
kisa:tasit *ai*, kisa:tas'k *ii*

flag mtawekn

flame burst into ~ pe:s'sit *ai*, pe:s'tek *ii*

flap (skin) door ~ ka:qanipsun; tent ~
ksuskwate:kn [SH]; heard ~ **-ping** or
fluttering metewaqsink *ai*, metawaqs'k *ii*

flare chimney ~ muspusi *an*; ~ up (toward
inside) pitamkletesk *ii*, pitamkletesink *ai*

flat sasqe:k *ai, ii*; saqte:k *ai, ii*; sasqapit *ai*,
sasqatek *ii*; esne:k *ai, ii*; saqpit *ai*, saqtek;
fall ~ on one's belly sasqatesink *ai*; fall ~ on
one's face paqtune'itesink *ai*; ~ and rigid
elsaqapit *ai*, elsaqas'k *ii*; get ~ feet
peqanqasita:teket *ai*; three ~ (sheetlike)
objects nesaqpijik (pl) *ai*, nesaqtekl (pl) *ii*

flatfooted sasqasitat *ai*; sasqikatat *ai*; get ~
peqanqasita:teket *ai* [SH]

flat-headed pepkijatpat *ai*

Flatlands qaskusi-a:qamikt

flatten paskija:l'k *ta*, paskija:tu *ti*

flax flax seed lapilas *an* (Fr *la filasse*)

flea pis *an* [BR]; pikkw (pikkwik) *an*; have ~ **-s**
pikkwit *ai*

flee wesimit *ai* [SH]; ~ toward elsumukwat *ai*

flesh ma:qi [SH]; my ~ na:qi; ntinin

flexible sipipka:q *ii*, sipipka:t *ai* [BC];
pepsikiyaq *ii*, pepsikiyet; sipikpa:t *ai*,
sipikpa:q *ii*; long and ~ eltaqpit *ai*, (ltaqtek *ii*

flint mals [SH]; ~ ed (as a gun) malsa:sik *ii*
[SH]

flip wenaqeket *ai*

float ekwijink *ai*, ekwitk *ii*; weskitqo:wek *ii*,
weskitqo:wet *ai*; ~ about ala:lukwek *ii*,
ala:lukwet *ai*; alqo:wek *ii*, alqo:wet *ai* [BR]; ~
around ala:lukwek *ii*, ala:lukwet *ai*; ~ or drift
along pemqo:qwek *ii*, pemqo:kwet *ai*;
animal ~ **-ing** on its back atuwa:sa:kw *an*
[BR]

flood flooded mespo:qek *ii*, mespo:qet *ai*

floodtide kispa:q *ii* [BR]

floor msaqtaqt

flounder anakwe:j *an*

flour wape:jk

flow ~ along pemitk *ii*; pempekitk *ii*; ~ away
enmitk *ii*; ~ extensively pukwelijuwik *ii*,
pukwelijuwit *ai*; ~ in all directions milpekitk
ii; ~ toward elitk *ii*; clean ~ **-ing** water
waqamitk *ii*

flower ~ pot wasuweko:q

flown ~ way ejiklsink *ai* [CB]; ~ over keskiss'k *ii*, keskissink *ai*

flue chimney ~ muskusi *an*

fluffy pukunesit *ai*; ~ or hairy animal pukuna:w *an*

fluffy-haired piwsmik *ii*, piwsmit *ai*

fluid crave ~ niwipskuna:t *ai*

flush a ~ (in poker) newtamuksit *ai*, newtamu:k *ii*; ~ (as a bird) wenaqteskat *ai*; ~ (in carpentry) tetpaqpit *ai*, tetpaqtek *ii*

flutter heard flapping or ~ **-ing** metewaqsink *ai*, metawaqs'k *ii*

fly[1] wijaw (wijaq) *an*; u:j *an*; wije:s *an* [SH][RB]

fly[2] ~ along pemaqsink *ai*, pemaqs'k *ii*; ~ away ejiklajija:sit *ai* [CB]; ~ away quickly wisqi-jik'lsink *ai*; ~ or glide around als'k *ii*, alsink *ai*; ~ over keskijaqsink *ii*, elaqsink *ai*; ~ toward elaqs'k *ii*, elaqsink *ai*

foal penetkwit *ai* [BC]

foam pisew; ~ at the mouth pisewtuna:t *ai*; ~ **-y** pisewiyaq *ii*, pisewiyet *ai*

fog u:n; fog eater u:npekw [SH]; ~ **-gy** u:nik; get ~ **-gy** ew'niyaq *ii* [SH]; petu:niyaq *ii* [BR]; u:niyaq *ii*

fold ~ right ilanqa:l'k *ta*, ilanqa:tu *ti*

follow pemukkwalk *ta*, pemukkwatm *ti*; pemulkwalk *ta*, pemulkwatm *ti* [BC]; majulkalk *ta*, majulkwatm *ti* [SH]; majukkwalk *ta*, majukkwatm *ti*; ~ along enmukkwalk *ta*, enmukkwatm *ti*; ~ around alukkwalk *ta*, alukkwatm *ti*; ~ back apajukkwalk *ta*, apajukkwatm *ti*; ~ home enmukkwalk *ta*, enmukkwatm *ti*; ~ in piskwiwkwalk *ta*, piskwiwkwatm *ti*; ~ one another in a circle kitto:qakatultijik (pl) *ai*; ~ outside tewukkwalk *ta*, tewukkwatm *ti*; ~ toward elukkwalk *ta*, elukkwatm *ti*; ~ (with one's eyes) until out of sight we:kwamk *ta*, we:kwaptm *ti*; start to ~ poqtiwkwalk *ta*, poqtiwkwatm *ti*

fond ~ of kesite:l'm'k *ta*, kesite:tm *ti*

fondle wesko:tm *ti*, weskweyaq *ta*

food mijipjewey; mamam; ~ (in baby talk) nana:n; na:nikn [SH]; make all kinds of ~ miloqsawet *ai*; my ~ ninu

fool eluwe:wa:l'k *ta*; amassit *ai* (foolish); act the ~ amassuwajit *ai*; easily ~ na:qapa:l'k *ta* [ESK]

foolish piluwasit *ai*; amassit *ai*; ewayatpat *ai* [SH]; act ~ ew'nasa:sit *ai*; act ~ **-ly** amatpesmat *ai*; wennju:wet *ai*

foot[1] my ~ nkat; a twisted ~ wkatistuwik *ii*; go toward on ~ elenqwe:set *ai*; go home on ~ elm'l'kat *ai*; have a ~ or leg cut off temikatat *ai*; have a small ~ aps'sitat *ai*; shove with the ~ kesmteskaq *ta*, kesmteskm *ti*

foot[2] ~ (of measurement, no plural) leppiye

footpath mkat awti [BR]; wkat awti

footprint make ~ **-s** jilaptoq (jilaptu) *ai*

footstep make the sound of ~ **-s** al-tuqwa:t *ai*

footwear wear out one's ~ kaqteskmat *ai*

for wjit

forbid wetqolk *ta*, wetqotm *ti*

force ki:kaja:l'k *ta*, ki:kaja:tu *ti*; ~ feed ki:kass'mk *ta*; ~ to go home ki:kajinmikimk *ta*

forcefully ~ shove munsiksmeket *ai*; use ~ **-ly** ki:kaji-e:w'mk *ta*

forearm my ~ np'ssan

forefront sit (set) in the ~ e:tmapit *ai*, e:tmatek *ii*; stand in the ~ e:tmapukuwit *ai*

forehead my ~ ntukwejan

foreleg my ~ nkajikn; np'ssanikat [SH]

forelimb my ~ np'ssan [SH]

foreman a ~ nujiksmoqja:teket *ai (an)*

foreshoulder ~ (of an animal) psk'san [SH]

foresight have ~ nikanite:tm *ti*

foreskin sistek

forest nipukt

foretell wesiket *ai*; kwesiket *ai* [SH]; ~ the weather nujo:tm *ti* [CB]

forever iyapjiw

forget awan-ta:sit *ai*; ~ about awan-ta:suwalk *ta*, awan-ta:suwatm *ti*

forgetful puski-awannta:sit *ai*; weniyet *ai*

forgive apiksiktaq *ta*

fork mikwije:maqan; (table) ~ nipitkwe:kn [SH]; ~ **-ed** niktuwe:k *ai, ii*

formal ~ meeting or gathering mawiyo:mi

fort waqalusan

fortune tell a ~ kwesiket *ai* [SH]; wesiket *ai*;
tell the ~ of wesikalk *ta*

fortune-teller a ~ nujikwsiket *ai (an)*;
nujiwsiket *ai (an)* [SH]

forty ~ (in counting) newinska:q [BR];
newiska:q; ~ years newinskekipunq'k *ii* [SH]

forward fall ~ nikani-kuwiyaq *ii*; nikani-
kuwiyet *ai* [BR]

foster my ~ (adopted) child nn'snaqan'm *an*
[SH]

foul hit a ~ ball pesoqopsk'te:k *ta*,
pesoqopsk'te:m *ti*

foundling we:jitaqan *an*

four nekkw'l *ii*, ne:wijik *ai*; ne:wijit *ai*, newkw'l
ii [BR]; ~ (in counting) ne:w; ~ solid, round
(globular) objects newapsk'sijik (pl) *ai*,
newapskekl (pl) *ii*

four-card ne:wowa:j *an*

four-legged newikata:t *ai*

fourth the ~ one ne:wowa:j *an*; ne:wowey

fowl female ~ skwe:w *an* [SH]; nape:wi:skw
an [SH]; provision with ~ netukuluwe:set *ai*
[SH]

fox wowkwis *an*

foxberry pokoman [SH]

fracture kelkwisketesm'k *ta*, kelkwisketestu *ti*;
temtesmk *ta*, temtestu *ti*; ~ -d kelkwiske:k *ii*

fragile menaje:jit *ai*, menaje:jk *ii*

fragments pnekwiyaqal [SH]

frail waqqatamuksit *ai*, waqqatamu:k *ii*

Francis Plansuwe [BR]; Plasuwa (Fr
François)

Frank Plansuwe [BR]; Plasuwa

freak nune:s *an*

freckle eptekwati; have ~ -s aptekwat *ai*,
eptekwat *ai*; ~ -d eptekwat *ai*

free loader a ~ puski-aliks'ta:kwet *ai (an)*

free-loading go around ~ puski-aliks'ta:kwet
ai (an)

French speak ~ wennjuwi:sit *ai*

Frenchman kniskwikn (slang); wenuj *an*; act
like a ~ wennjuwa:'it *ai* [RB]; overseas ~
almanntiyew *an*

Frenchwoman wennjuwi:skw *an* [BC];
wennjujkwej *an*; wenuji:skw *an* [SH]

frequent embark ~ -ly i:pusit *ai*;

Friday weltamultimk; Good ~ klujjewto:t
weltamultimk

fried cake sisla:kwa:taqan

friend! oqoti (voc); oti (voc); ~ -s! oqote:tut
(voc) [CB] (a greeting)

friend little (male) ~ nitapji:j *an* (also an
exclamation of surprise); my female ~
nitape:skw (nitape:skwaq) *an*; my male ~
nitap (nitapaq) *an*

friendly ni:laje:k *ai* [BC]

fright gripped with ~ aptapjiyet *ai*; stiff with ~
(from a nightmare) melkwiskat *ai*

frighten jipkaq *ta*; we:kwata:l'k *ta*; jipaqa:l'k
ta; ~ off wetayaq *ta*; ~ -ed jipasit *ai*;
we:kwata:sit *ai*; easily ~ -ed nesawet *ai*; ~
-ed of the dark nesalsit *ai* [BC]; nessasit *ai*;
newasit *ai*

frivolous kesnqo:we:k *ai*; ~ person ksno:qon
an [RB]

frog sqolj (sqoljik) *an* [SH]; atakali [SH]

from shrink ~ ketkite:l'mk *ta*, ketkite:tm *ti* [BC]

frond palm ~ stoqon *an*

front in ~ nikantuk (loc)

frost wastewt'k *ii*; early morning ~ wapt'k *ii*;
~ -y wastewt'k *ii*; ~ -ed (as a tree branch)
tupik *ii*; ~ -ed (from the cold) new'lask *ii*,
new'lasink *ai* [SH]

frozen kelt'k *ii* [ESK]; ~ ground keltaqamiktuk
[ESK]; ~ water kep't'k *ii*; half ~ kakwejink
ai, kakwetk *ii* [SH]

frugal matu:n'mat *ai*

fruit minijk [PEI]

frustrate siwa:l'k *ta*; ~ -d siwiyet *ai*

fry sisla:kwa:l'k *ta*, sisla:kwa:tu *ti* (English
sizzle); ~ -ing pan lapuwe:l *an* (Fr *la poêle*);
sisla:kwa:temkewey

fuel use as ~ moqsa:tat *ai* [SH]

full wajuwiyaq *ii*, wajuwiyet *ai* [SH]; waju:waq
ii, waju:wet *ai*; ~ house in poker waju:waq
wennji:kuwom *ii*; how ~ (of grain)? tal
amkiyaq *ii*, tal amkiyet *ai* [BC]; how ~ (of
liquid)? talpek *ii*, talpet *ai* [BC]

fumble me:sapjete:k *ta*, me:sapjete:m *ti*;
pesoqopsk'te:k *ta*, pesoqopsk'te:m *ti*

fun! lots of ~ kiso:qon (an interjection)

fun have ~ kise:k *ai*; make ~ of malikitm *ti*

funeral wtqotamk; ~ mass nepm'kewey
   alame:s [BC]; nepuwitewey alames
funnel pijimaqan
funny act ~ wennjuwa:'it *ai* [RB]; find ~ in
   appearance wi:kuwamk *ta*, wi:kuwaptm *ti*;
   make a ~ face winikwa:sit *ai*
fur anko:way [ESK]; ankuwowey
furrow ~ or drill nem'k'te:ket *ai*
furtively look at ~ kipoqamk *ta*, kipoqaptm *ti*
fuss ~ about sespumk *ta*, sesputm *ti*; eat ~
   -ily emteskatalk *ai*
fussy miliksnqwat *ai*; na:jikat *ai* (eater,
   dresser, etc.); a ~ eater emteskatalk *ai*

G

gable mtuwi:kan

Gabriel Kapliye:l *an* (Fr *Gabriel*)

gag elu:kwit *ai*; ~ (on food) noqt'k (noqtm) *ai*

gale ekulamsn *an* [BR]; ew'lamsn *an*; ~ force wind me:kiwju:s'k *ii* [SH]

gall wisqan

gallon kalun

gallop qa:skwit *ai*

gallows kestunepilaqan

gamble papkupsit *ai*

game my ~ ninu [BR]; nilu [ESK]

garden ika:taqan

garland amaltaqa:l'k *ta*, amaltaqa:tu *ti*

garment ewqwam; outer ~ wskitwan [BC]; the Bishop's ~ ! kji-pa:tliya:s ewkwam (exclamation of surprise)

garrot kestunepilk *ta*

gash deep wound or ~ la:qan

gasp enm'lamit *ai*

gaspereau kaspalaw *an* [RB]

gather meknk *ta*, mekn'm *ti*; mekete:k *ta*, mekete:m *ti*; mawiya:tijik (pl) *ai*; ~ tightly wesuwisepilasit *ai*; wesuwisepilas'k *ii*; ~ together mawita:jik (pl) *ai*; mawiyejik (pl) *ai*; ~ up mawo:l'k *ta*, mawo:tu *ti*; ~ -ed together mawe:kik (pl) *ai*

gatherer mawo:tasit *ai (an)*; a ~ mawo:tasit *ai (an)*

gathering a ~ for purposes of eating a meal in common and to extend New Year's greetings maw-mekisiw'ltimk pusu: puna:newimk; a holy ~ sante: mawiyo:mi; formal meeting or ~ mawiyo:mi

gauge lapasaqan (for making baskets)

generous puski-maqatuwi:ket *ai*; wela:luwet *ai*

gentle wansit *ai*

gentleman saqamaw (saqamaq) *an*; my ~ friend ntutem *an* [BC]; ntuttem *an* [SH]; my young ~ friend ntuttemji:j *an* [SH]; young ~ saqama:j *an*

gently do ~ sankewa:l'k *ta*, sankewa:tu *ti*

genuflect mutkupukuwa:sit *ai*; nutkul-pukuwa:sit *ai*

German alma *an* [SH] (Fr *Allemand*); almanntiyew *an*

get mesn(')k *ta*, mesn'm *ti*; go ~ nemiskaq *ta*, nemiskm *ti*

ghost sk'te:kmuj *an*

giant kukwes *an* [SH]; jenu *an*; kukwej *an* [BR]; wind ~ jenu *an*

giddy amatpat *ai* [ESK]

gifted westaw'let *ai* [SH]; kwestaw'let *ai* [BR]; ~ person wskijin *an* (a Maliseet word)

ginap stand like a ~ (a legendary warrior; a person of great strength) kin-pukuwit *ai*

giraffe pitoqoluwajit (pitoqoluwajijik) *ai (an)*; pijik'njit (pijik'njijik) *an* [SH]

girl! tu:s (voc) (term of affection)

girl act like a ~ e:pite:siwqamiksit *ai*; young ~ e:pite:ji:j *an*

girlfriend my ~ nte:pite:sm *an*

give ~ away ikn'muwetu *ti*; ~ to ikn'maq *ta (do)*

gizzard wisqan; waqtiyan

glad wel-ta:sit *ai*

gladness w'lta:suti

glance matuwapetesink *ai*; ~ at amalamk *ta*, amalaptm *ti*; take a ~ at telapetesink *ai*

gland kluk (klukk) *an*; have a swollen ~ or tonsil w'lukwe:ket *ai*; my ~ n'luk *an*

glasses my ~ npukukwe:l; npu:kwe:l (pl)

glide fly or ~ around als'k *ii*, alsink *ai*; ~ along in the water pe:m'k (pe:m'm) *ai*

glimpse catch a ~ of kipoqamk *ta*, kipoqaptm *ti*; samamk *ta*, samaptm *ti*

globe lamp ~ piklewji:j *an*

Glooscap kluskap *an* (a culture hero)

glove na:jikjaqan *an*; na:jijjaqan *an* [EG][NB]; la:jijjaqan *an* [NB]; na:'ikjaqan *an*

glue ~ on mekwasa:l'k *ta*, mekwasa:tu *ti*

gluttonous pisoqqowiyeksit *ai*

gnaw sewistamit *ai*; ~ on telp'k *ta*, teltm *ti*

go eliyaq *ii*, eliyet *ai*; ~ about ala:s'k *ii*, ala:sit *ai*; ~ after natteskaq *ta*, natteskm *ti*; ~ away ejikla:sit *ai*; ~ away quickly ejikl-ajija:sit *ai*; ~ with wije:w'k *ta*, wije:w'm *ti*; on the ~ winpasit *ai*

goad ki:kajimk *ta* [SH]; asimk *ta*

goat te:pulj (te:pulj'k) *an* (Fr *des boucs*); te:p'lj (te:p'ljik) *an* (Fr *des boucs*)

go-between the one who acts as a ~ (in marriage or divorce) nuji-postewit *ai (an)*
God Niskam *an*
godchild my ~ nklnikn *an* [CB][BC]; nknnikn *an*
godmother my ~ nkekkusk *an* [BC]
godparent kekkunawet *ai*; my ~ nkekkusk *an*; nkekkuni *an* [NB]; nkekunit *an* [CB]
gold wisaw suliyewey
golden-thread mali:japa:qawey (root)
good weliyaq *ii*, weliyet *ai*; kelu:lk *ii*, kelu:sit *ai*; extremely ~ or nice pajiji-klulk *ii*, pajiji-klu:sit *ai*; extraordinarily ~ looking we:kwi-klu:sit *ai* [ESK]; feel ~ (from drinking) weljepit *ai*; feel ~ (from being ill) wela:s'k *ii*, wela:sit *ai*; live in a ~ location weliket *ai*; pretty ~ mawi-klu:lk *ii*; maw-klulk *ii*, maw-klu:sit *ai*; keep in ~ shape or condition pekajeyaq *ta*, pekajo:tm *ti*; in ~ supply pukweliyaq *ii*, pukweliyet *ai*; have a ~ time kise:k *ai*; put in ~ humour welkwija:l'k *ta*
goodbye atiyu (Fr *adieu*, Basque *adiu*); say ~ atiyewit *ai*
good-eating weltamit *ai*
good-natured welqamiksit *ai*
goose domestic ~ or duck takli:j *an*; wild ~ sin'mkw *an* [BR][RB][SH]; sulumkw *an*
gooseberry kawaqtejk; ka:to:min *an*; kapaqtesk [RB]; ~ bush kawaqtejkumusi
gossip postewit *ai (an)*; lutmaqan; easily pick up news and ~ pa:qastmat *ai*
gossiper seytun *an*; a ~ nuji-nutmaqaneket *ai (an)*
gouge waljiks'k *ta*, waljiksm *ti*; waljikte:k *ta*, waljikte:m *ti*
gourmand a ~ mesiktaqanat *ai (an)* [BC]
government k'pnno:l *an* (Fr *gouverneur*)
gown my ~ nma:tletm
grab koqqwa:l'k *ta*, koqqwa:tu *ti*; rescue by ~ -bing weji-koqqwa:l'k *ta*
grain have a ~ (as of wood) elikuwaq *ii*
gramps nemijkami: (voc) (term of respect for an old man)
grandchild my ~ nuji:j *an*; great- ~ pitu: nuji:j *an*
granddaughter my ~ nkoji:j *an* [BR]

grandfather my ~ niskamij *an* [SH]; n'mijkamij *an*; n'niskamij *an* [EG][NB]; great- ~ pitu: n'mijkamij *an*;
grandmother! mi: kiju (voc) *an* [PEI] (from Big Cove); kiju:mi (voc) *an* [PEI]
grandmother my ~ niskamiji:skw *an*; n'lis *an* [BR]; n'niskamiji:skw *an*; nukumij *an*
granny! nukumi: (voc); nmi: (kiju:) (voc) (also used as a term of affection for an older woman)
granular elamkiyaq *ii*, elamkiyet *ai*
grasp sepitja:l'k *ta*, sepitja:tu *ti*; try to ~ kwejimsn'm *ti*, kwejimsnk *ta*
grass msiku [SH]; cut ~ mskikuwe:ket *ai* [SH]
grasshopper wenaqje:wj (wenaqje:wjik) *an* [SH]; nikjapnkwewj *an* [BC]; soqomkwewj (soqomkwewjik) *an*
grave wtqutaqan; wtqotaqan
gravel t'pkwan
graveyard wtqotaqane:kati
grayish wisawe:k *ii* [SH]
graze samteskaq *ta*, samteskm *ti*; ~ (as a cow or horse) peskwatalk *ai*
greas-e mimey; mima:l'k *ta*, mima:tu *ti*; covered with ~ and oil (as a mechanic) mimsit *ai*; ~ the face of (e.g., a pan) mima:kwa:l'k *ta*, mima:kwa:tu *ti*; ~ the head of mimatpa:l'k *ta*; ~ -er mima:kwa:taqan (for a pan); ~ -y mime:k *ai, ii*
great ~ (Christmas) month kjiku:s *an* [CB][BC]; ~ -grandfather pitu: n'mijkamij *an*; ~ -grandchild pitu: nuji:j *an*
greedy pisoqqowiyeksit *ai*; me:ka:sit *ai*, me:ka:s'k *ii*
green wisawe:k *ii*; eskik *ii*, eskit *ai* (as of foliage); dark ~ stoqon-amuksit *ai*, stoqon-amu:k *ii*; ~ twig eskikloqon [SH]; pale ~ wap'stoqon-amuksit *ai*, wapistoqon-amu:k *ii*
greet pusu:lewiktaq *ta*; kwe:maq *ta*
greeter (ceremonial) ~ kwetaluktuwet *ai (an)* [BC]
greetings! kwe: (obsolete [Iroquois?]); pusu:l; give ~ pusu:lewit *ai*
greyish wataptek *ii*
grilse taqawanji:j *an* (type of fish); taqawan *an*
grimy pekaqanqayaq *ii*, pekaqanqayet *ai*

grin weskewikwetutk (weskewikwetutm) *ai*

grind nukwa:kipulk *ta*, nukwa:kittu *ti*; esipulk *ta*, esiputu *ti*; ~ down pepka:'ipulk *ta*, pepka:kittu *ti*; ~ or scrape ela:kittu *ti*

grindstone ki:taqan

grip sepitja:l'k *ta*, sepitja:tu *ti*; have a strong ~ melkapjit *ai*

groan kesitewipnet *ai* [SH]; heard calling, ~ -**ing** or moaning metetoqsit *ai*

groin my ~ nplaqan

groom nankwenawet *ai*; nankwenk *ta*

groove walqusk *ta*, walqusm *ti*; nasapaqam *ti*, nasapaqq *ta* [SH]

grosbeak kniskwatkiyej *an*

grouchy taqale:k *ai*; wininuwit *ai*

ground maqamikew (maqamikal); frozen ~ keltaqamiktuk [ESK]; seated or set on the ~ saqanqapit *ai*, saqanqatek *ii*

ground hog m'lumkewej *an*; mulumkwej *an*

grounds festival ~ (present Restigouche territory) papitaqane:kati

ground-squirrel amalpaqamej *an* [CB]; apalqaqamej *an*

group live together in a ~ pukweliket *ai*

grove eletqek *ii*; birch ~ maskwe:simanaqse:kati [SH]; maple ~ jiyoqjimusi-a:qamikt [SH]

grow nikwen'm *ti*, nikwenk *ta*; kisikwen'm *ti*, kisikwenk *ta*; ~ in pijikwek *ii*, pijikwet *ai*; ~ off menikwet *ai*; ~ slowly malikwek *ii*, malikwet *ai*; ~ well welikwek *ii*, welikwet *ai*

growl jikmit *ai*; ~ at jikmuktaq *ta*, jikmuktm *ti*; heard ~ -**ing** (as a dog) metew-jikmit *ai*; wetewi-jikmit *ai* [SH]

grown full ~ kisikwek *ii*, kisikwet *ai*

grub ~ up kiwiksit *ai* [BR]

grunt heard ~ -**ing** wetewoqsink *ai* [BR]; heard snoring or ~ -**ing** metewoqsink *ai*

guard keliket *ai*

gudgeon so:qomu:j *an*

guide a ~ (by boat) a:lutasit *ai (an)*; ~ by boat a:lulk *ta*; ~ or direct (a horse) by the reins iltaqank *ta*; ~ or steer (by the head or bow) ilkwen'm *ti*, ilkwenk *ta*

guilty pilse:k *ai* [SH]; ~ by association ko:pukwet *ai* [BC]

gulp drink in one ~ sintesm'k *ta*, sintestu *ti*

gum pku *an*; my ~ nipitokom; spruce ~ skmukuwalaw [SH]; sqomu:kuwalaw; wasapeklaw (wasapeklaq) *an*

gummy pu:kewit *ai*; pekuwik *ii*, pekuwit *ai*

gun pe:skewey; kaqtukwewe:sn *an* [CB]

gunshot sqolu:skw

gunwale palltaqan

gust a ~ of cool wind petna:s'k *ii*

gusty ~ wind weklams'k *ii*; a:petna:s'k *ii*

gut[1] dress or ~ (as a fish, chicken) pekwaja:l'k *ta*; ~ a fish elukwalk *ta*, elukwatm *ti*

gut[2] my ~ niliksi; n'liksi

H

habit make a ~ of kiyaspiyet *ai*

hail kwe:maq *ta*

hailstone msi:kw (msi:kuk) *an*

hair sapun; cut someone's ~ short or thin memk'te:maq *ta (do)* [BR]; grey or white ~ wapkwan; (animal) ~ piwetm [SH]; have messy ~ se:saltukwat *ai* [PEI]; se:saltukwepit *ai*; have thick body or facial ~ pasi:tukwat *ai* [SH]; have thick ~ pasaltukwat *ai*; have white ~ wapkwat *ai*; my head ~ nusapun; shed ~ pi:kwatikn; run with one's ~ bobbing up and down enmisa:kwatp'tesink *ai*; wear ~ to the shoulders (of a man) sa'ukwat *ai*; white ~ wasapun [SH]

haircut get a ~ naji-m'nk'te:mat *ai* [BC]

haircutter a ~ nuji-m'mk'te:muwet *ai (an)* [BC]

hairdresser a ~ nuji-tmastaqte:muwet *ai (an)* [BC]

hairy piwsmik *ii*, piwsmit *ai*; ~ animal puksikna:qewit *ai* [BR]; pukunesit *ai*; ~ body piwetmit *ai* [BR]; pukwistikna:qewit *ai* [SH]; ~ head musapunit *ai* [SH]

half aqati [BR]; isey [BR]; aqata'ik *ii*; ~ shot (from drinking) a:qatapit *ai*; ~ way qata'ik (loc); slice in ~ naskwoqs'k *ta*, naskwoqsm *ti*

half-full aqtamkiyaq *ii*, aqtamkiyet *ai*

half-witted a:qatatpa:t *ai*

Halifax, N.S. jipuktuk

Haligonian jipuktukwewa:j *an*

Hallowe'en kap'ji: night (Fr *gabegie*); kemutna:timk [SH]

hallucinate keskmap'lkikwa:t *ai*

halt naqa:sit *ai*; bring to a ~ naqa:l'k *ta*; naqa:tu *ti*; naqte:k *ta*, naqte:m *ti*

halve naskwa:l'k *ta*, naskwa:tu *ti*; nawaka:l'k *ta*, nawaka:tu *ti* [SH]

hammer maltejjuwey [SH]; maltejuwey [BC][CB] (Fr *marteau*); mattejjuwey; ennmte:k *ta*; ennmte:m *ti*; ~ handle maltejjuweyatkw [SH]; ~ in elnmte:k *ta*, elnmte:m *ti* [BR]; ~ (of a flintlock gun) apuwaqaj [CB]

hand my ~ npitn; np'tn; my back of the ~ npaqamiptn; deformed or crippled ~ or arm sawiptn; have a deformed or crippled ~ or

arm sawiptnat *ai*; have a good ~ (in cards) welnat *ai* [RB]; wennat *ai*; have a ~ or arm cut off temiptnat *ai*; have cold ~ -s kewjipnewjit *ai*; tekiptnat *ai*; have large ~ -s maqiptnat *ai*; have one ~ newtiptnat *ai*; hide or conceal in the ~ sepuwijjenk *ta*, sepuwijjen'm *ti*; have small ~ -s or paws apsiptnat *ai*; have the ~ of an insect; jujiju:nat *ai* [BC]; clasp with ~ -s sekkapja:sit *ai* [PEI]; have dirty ~ -s mejikiptnat *ai* [PEI]; take with one's bare ~ -s ketapja:l'k *ta*, ketapja:tu *ti*

handkerchief musuwey (Fr *mouchoir*)

handle[1] apjun [SH]; lnaqanatkw; lnaqantkw; nnaqanatkw; axe ~ lnaqanatkw [BR]; lnaqanatkw [SH]; nnaqanatkw; tmi:knatkw; fit a ~ in or on (an axe or hammer) nasaqomkikwat *ai*; fit a ~ on an axe eloqomkiyatm *ti*; put a ~ on apjuna:tu *ti* [SH]; weave a ~ on elisqanpeka:tu *ti* [SH]

handle[2] ~ badly winnat *ai*; know how to do or ~ natawa:qa:l'k *ta*, natawa:qa:tu *ti*; operate or ~ poorly awaneyaq *ta*, awano:tm *ti*; nujeyaq *ta*, nujo:tm *ti*; wesko:tm *ti*, weskweyaq *ta*

handsome wikwasapewit *ai*

handy tepaw

handyman matu:-lukwet *ai (an)*; nata:n'mat *ai (an))*

hang kestunepilk *ta*; kaqa-pijink *ai*, kaqa-pitk *ii*; approach with head ~ -ing down wejkwi-qolomkopit *ai*; ~ over or on the edge wesawa:t *ai*, wesawa:q *ii*; ~ up kaqa-pija:l'k *ta*, kaqa-pija:tu *ti*

hangar clothes ~ klo:kowey [CB]

hangover have a ~ sewpet *ai* [BC]

happen teliyaq *ii*; tele:k *ai, ii*; ~ unexpectedly and pleasantly welitpa:s'k *ii*, welitpa:sit *ai*; so ~ tetapu

happenstance hear by ~ mikustaq *ta*, mikustm *ti*

happ-y weljesink *ai*; wel-ta:sit *ai*; ~ to see wel-ta:suwalk *ta*, wel-ta:suwatm *ti*; very ~ or pleased mawi-w'lta:sit *ai*; ~ -iness w'lta:suwaqan

hard melke:k *ai, ii*; breathe ~ or heavily kesikawlamit *ai*; cry ~ kesimt'k (kesimtm) *ai;* ~ enough tepi-m'lke:k *ai, ii;* ~ going (through a thicket) metuwatqek *ii* [CB]; ~ to do metuwe:k *ii;* ~ to get along with metu:qamiksit *ai;* have a ~ stool melk'jat *ai;* give a ~ time to kitn'meyaq *ta,* kitn'mo:tm *ti;* have a ~ time kitn'mat *ai;* a ~ worker seskwe:k *ai;* ~ times; mtu:noqt

harden melka:l'k *ta,* melka:tu *ti;* ~ **-ed** melka:s'k *ii,* melka:sit *ai*

hard-headed ekkatpat *ai* [BC]

hardly suwel [CB]

hardtack kalkunawey

hare apli:kmuj *an*

harm askayaq *ta,* asko:tm *ti;* easily hurt or ~ naqsi-o:pla:l'k *ta,* naqsi-o:pla:tu *ti*

harpoon tqatikn *an* [RB]; l'tqa:mun *an* [BR]; lutqamun *an* [SH]

harrow elkete:ket *ai;* elekete:ket *ai*

harsh deal ~ **-ly** with poqjimk *ta* [BR]

harvest ~ a garden mena:taquk *ai;* ~ roots or tubers (e.g. potatoes, carrots, turnips) ke:tipnet *ai;* potato picker or ~ **-er** ke:tipnewinu *an*

hat a:kusn; a:kwesn [BR]; rain ~ sa:wes (sa:westl)

hatch epitm *ti*

hate ketank *ta,* ketantu *ti;* ketanteket *ai;* maskel'mk *ta,* maskeltm *ti;* poqwajite:l'mk *ta,* poqwajite:tm *ti* [BR]; person who ~ **-s** ktantekewinu *an*

hater a ~ nutanteket *ai (an)* [SH]

hatless metkwat *ai*

hatred ktantaqan

haughty me:ke:k *ai*

haul nuji-ewjo:l'k *ta,* nuji-ewjo:tu *ti;* nuji-ewjo:teket *ai;* wetn'k *ta,* wetn'm *ti;* ~ back and forth ewjo:l'k *ta,* ewjo:tu *ti;* ~ in the pot (in a poker game) wesuwa:teket *ai;* a ~ **-er** nuji-ewjo:tasit (nuji-ewjo:tasijik) *ai (an)*

have kekkun'm *ti,* kekkunk *ta;* kelkunk *ta;* kenkunk *ta,* kenkun'm *ti;* kewkunk *ta;* wesko:tm *ti,* weskweyaq *ta* [SH]

hawk chicken ~ pipukwes *an* [BR]; night ~ pijkwej *an;* pi:kw *an* [NB]; sparrow ~ pipukwes *an*

hay msiku [SH]; ~ den mskikuwom [SH]; ~ field msikuwe:kati; make ~ msikuwe:ket *ai;* mskikuwe:ket *ai* [SH]

hazelnut malipqwanj; malimqwanj [BR]

he nekm

head my ~ n'nuji [SH]; nunnji; bend ~ down nisa:kwa:sit *ai* [BC]; bent (~ part) away ejiklako:jink *ai;* bent toward (from the ~) wejkwatpo:jink *ai;* bite the ~ part off temkwepk *ta;* dizzy from a blow to the ~ ew'naskwatpetesink *ai;* grease the ~ of mimatpa:l'k *ta;* have a small ~ apsatpat *ai;* have a big ~ maqatpat *ai;* ~ swamper ikanawtiket (ikanawtikejik) *ai (an);* lean one's ~ toward elatpo:jink *ai;* make someone's ~ turn ew'naskwatpa:l'k *ta;* move along nodding one's ~ pematpetesink *ai;* move along with drooping ~ weji-qolomkwi-pmiyet *ai;* move along nodding one's ~ pematkwetesink *ai;* rest one's ~ on etu:kwesmit *ai;* run fast with ~ bobbing kesikawatpi:pit *ai* [BR]; run along with ~ abobbing pematpe:pit *ai;* side of the ~ epme:tkwaj *an* [SH]; slap along the side of the ~ epme:tkwete:k *ta* [SH]; slap on the back of the ~ peji:taqanete:k *ta* [PEI]; stand at the ~ ikan-pukuwit *ai (an)* [SH]

head cheese matnukteskewey

headless temkwe:k *ai, ii*

heal nijkik *ii,* nijkit; nepilk *ta,* nepitm *ti;* ~ quickly naqsi-nijkik *ii,* naqsi-nijkit *ai;* a curer or ~ **-er** nepiteket *ai (an);* a ~ **-er** nujinpiteket *ai (an)*

healthy jajike:k *ai* [BR]; tajike:k *ai, ii;* wele:k *ai;* look ~ jajik-amuksit *ai*

heap fall in a ~ mawisetesk *ii,* mawisetesink *ai*

hear nutaq *ai,* nutm *ti;* ~ about nutmat *ai;* ~ by happenstance mikustaq *ta,* mikustm *ti;* ~ sound like tels'taq *ta,* tels'tm *ti;* ~ vaguely about ams'tmat *ai;* imagine one ~ **-s** something telistaqanewa:sit *ai;* hard of ~ **-ing** am-k'ppistaqanat; amistaqanat *ai* [SH]; tired of ~ **-ing** about siws'taq *ta*

heard ~ calling, groaning or moaning metetoqsit *ai;* ~ cawing metetoqsit *ai* [SH];

~ crying meto:temit *ai*; ~ crying meto:mt'k (meto:mtm) *ai*; ~ eating metewatalk *ai*; ~ flapping or fluttering metewaqsink *ai*, metawaqs'k *ii*; ~ making a noise metewa:toq (metewa:tu) *ai*; ~ moving about metewa:sit *ai*; ~ pounding metete:ket *ai*; ~ quacking metetoqsit *ai* [SH]; ~ singing metewintoq (metewintu) *ai*; wetewintoq (wetewintu) *ai* [BR][SH]; ~ snoring or grunting metewoqsink *ai*; ~ stirring or bustling about metewe:k *ai*; ~ talking meto:kwet *ai* [PEI]

hearsay lutmaqan

hearse npuwinu'ulkw

heart my ~ nkamlamun; ~ (in cards) ke:l (ke:laq) *an* [SH] (Fr *coeur*); wkamlamun *an*

heartburn have ~ epuktaqanat *ai*

hear tell nutmat *ai*; tels'tmat *ai*

hearth puktewikan [BR]

heat eps'k *ta*, epsm *ti*; give off ~ epsawek *ii*, epsawet *ai*; ~ up properly wel-p'sk *ta*, wel-p'sm *ti*; in ~ (said of a dog) ikekkwet *ai*

heaven wa:so:q

heavily rain ~ ma:munlaq *ii*; wenaqala:maq *ii* [PEI]; snow ~ ma:munipsaq *ii*

heavy keskukk *ii*, keskulk *ai*; carry a ~ load keskunasit *ai*; ~ seas maqatkwik *ii*; ~ snowfall e:pluwipsaq *ii* [ESK]

heel my ~ nqon *an*; have (on) high ~ **-s** pitqonat *ai*

heifer lkwetukji:j *an*

height have such a length or ~ tel-pitoqsit *ai*, tel-pita:q *ii*

hell m'ntuwa:ki

hello! pusu:l (Fr *Bonjour!*)

help apoqonmatimk; apoqonmaq *ta*; congregate to ~ each other mawi-apoqonatultijik (pl) *ai* [BC]; ~ self ela:mat *ai* [ESK]; ~ through sapa:l'k *ta*, sapa:tu *ti*; ~ oneself ketuwapsit *ai*; unable to ~ ejala:l'k *ta*, ejala:tu *ti*; ~ **-less** ejala:sit *ai* [SH]

hemlock ksu:skw (ksu:skuk) *an* [SH]; kastuk *an*; qast'k *an* [BC]

hemmorage etliku:niyet *ai*

hemstitch sipma:m *ti*

hen kikli:kwej *an* [BR]; kikli:wej *an* [SH]; koqoli:kwej *an*; wennju:-plawej *an* [BR]

her nekm

here right ~ ! ula: tett [BR]; tett

here and there stay ~ pe'ikwaqatk (pe'ikwaqatm) *ai*

herring n'me:ji:j *an*

hers nekmewey *an*, *in*

hew ji:kate:k *ta*, ji:kate:m *ti*

hex puntalk *ta*, puntatm *ti*

hiccough ejkwit *ai* [BC]

hidden aqupit *ai*, aqutek *ii*; ~ internally masqupit *ai*, masqutek *ii*

hide¹ mimukwasit *ai*; mimukwalk *ta*, mimukwatu *ti*; aqawikalk *ta*, aqawikatm *ti*; masqute:k *ta*, masqute:m *ti*; ~ or conceal in the hand sepuwijjenk *ta*, sepuwijjen'm *ti*

hide² m'kekn; pkekn [SH] (of skin); green (undressed) ~ mta:y *an* [SH]

hide-stretcher sipitaqan [SH]

high ask a ~ price me:kusit *ai*; have a ~ opinion of oneself me:kitelsit *ai*; have (on) ~ heels pitqonat *ai*; ~ up in rank espe:k *ai*; ~ (full) tide waju:pa:q *ii*; hold a ~ position esp'pukuwik *ii*, esp'pukuwit; stand up ~ esp'pukuwik *ii*, esp'pukuwit; sit (or set) up ~ esp'pit *ai*, esp'tek *ii*; think ~ **-ly** of me:kite:l'mk *ta*, mekite:tm *ti*; kesite:l'm'k *ta*, kesite:tm *ti*; use ~ -sounding language espi:sit *ai*; talk ~ language peslu:teket *ai* [BR]

High Mass espe:k *ai* [SH]

hill tqojuwan; nemaqt [SH]; atop a ~ kisoqek

hilltop ke:kupn

hilly milqamikek *ii* (of the ground or floor)

him nekm

hindquarter apuwaqaj

hindrance become a ~ a:jela:s'k *ii*, a:jela:sit *ai*

hint alo:stasit

hip my ~ ns'kun; nsukun; ~ or side of one's body wpmepikaj [BR]; his ~ upmepikaj [SH]

hire akase:wa:l'k *ta*, akase:wa:tu *ti*; elulk *ta*; ~ on akase:wit *ai*

his nekmewey *an*, *in*

hit taqamk *ta*, taqtm *ti*; ~ (so as to cause blood to flow) malltewte:k *ta*, malltewte:m *ti*; ~ well welte:k *ta*, welte:m *ti*; ~ with a bullet or arrow me:telaq *ta*, me:tel'm *ti*; ~ with a

club wetaqanikatm *ti* [BR]; ~ a foul ball
pesoqopsk'te:k *ta*, pesoqopsk'te:m *ti*; ~
wrong o:p'lte:k *ta*, o:p'lte:m *ti*
hitch ~ up a wagon iltaqotm *ti* [SH]; ~ up a
horse iltaqalk *ta* [SH]; nastaqo:tlk *ta*; ~ **-ed**
by a long rope pittaqpisit *ai*
hive bee ~ amuwesusi
hoarse kepiyet *ai*; have a ~ voice or throat
kepa:tat *ai*; speak ~ **ly** kepitnetoqsit *ai*
hoe lke:kn; mulqwekn [SH]; namek'te:kn(ey)
[BC]; nemakwe:kn [SH]; n'm'k'te:kn;
elekete:ket *ai*; elkete:ket *ai*; matkete:ket *ai*
[SH]; namek'te:ket *ai* [BC]
hoist toqju:pilewet *ai* [SH]; toqju:pilawek *ii*,
toqju:pilawet *ai*; ~ by rope or cable
wenaqpil'm *ti*, wenaqpilk *ta*; ~ down nisnk
ta, nisn'm *ti*; ~ up toqju:pil'm *ti*, toqju:pilk *ta*
hold kekkun'm *ti*, kekkunk *ta*; kelkunk *ta*;
keln'k *ta* [NB]; keltaqan'm *ti*, keltaqank *ta*;
kenkunk *ta*, kenkun'm *ti*; kenn'k *ta*, kenn'm
ti; kewkunk *ta*; ~ back naqan'm *ti*, naqank
ta; ~ down with one's body kelkaq *ta*, kelkm
ti; ~ enclosed in one's hand sepiljenk *ta*,
sepiljen'm *ti* [BC]; ~ in concealment sepapjit
ai; ~ (the family) together as a unit kelkaq
(pl) *ta*, kelkm *ti*; ~ tight sekki-kln'k *ta* [PEI]; ~
on tightly (with hands) sekkapjit *ai* [PEI]; get
~ of kisapskn'm *ti*, kisapsknk *ta*; ~ or pin
down by covering etulkomit *ai*; ~ back
(money) ewt'paskm *ti*
hold on! ke:s'k; pe: (an interjection)
hole elmalqey [BR]; enmalqey; enmaqqey; a
deep ~ pitalqek *ii*; a long ~ elalqek *ii*; have
a ~ tewje:k *ai, ii*; have a large ~ maqalqasit
ai; small ~ elmalqe:ji:j
holler seskwet *ai*; ~ at seskwalk *ta*;
se:skwalk *ta* [SH]; start to ~ or sing ketu:k
(ketu:m) *ai*; ketuk *ai* [BR]
hollow elltukne:k *ai*; walqwe:k *ii*; a ~
walqwe:k *ii*; ~ out with a knife waljiks'k *ta*,
waljiksm *ti* [SH]; ~ out (with an axe)
waljikte:k *ta*, waljikte:m *ti*; peer into a ~
pu:tapa:sit *ai*; round and ~ elltuknapskek *ii*,
elltuknapsk'sit *ai*; ~ **-ed** out walqwiyaq *ii*,
walqwiyet *ai*

holy sape:wik *ii*, sape:wit *ai*; a ~ gathering
sante: mawiyo:mi; ~ picture or medal
pess'mkewey *an*; peskmewey *an* [SH]; ~
water sprinkler lapatikn; lapaltnewey (Fr *le
baptême*)
Holy Saturday sape:wik kesp'tek
Holy Thursday sape:wik ne:wowey
homage pay ~ to kepmite:l'mk *ta*, kepmite:tm
ti
home beat it ~ enm'kate:pit *ai*; carry ~
enmaw'lalk *ta*, enmaw'latm *ti*; chase ~
enm'teskaq *ta*; convey or drive ~ (in a
vehicle) enmateja:l'k *ta*, enmateja:tu *ti*;
crawl ~ elmapekit *ai* [BR]; force to go ~
ki:kajinmikimk *ta*; go ~ elmiyaq *ii*, elmiyet *ai*
[BR]; enmiyet *ai*, enmiyaq *ii*; go ~ in a huff
enm'nqwe:set *ai*; hurry ~ enmateja:sit *ai*;
sail ~ elmaqteket *ai* [CB]; scoot ~
elmoqwe:set *ai* [CB]; send ~ elmikimk *ta*
[BR]; take or bring back ~ elma:l'k *ta*,
elma:tu *ti* [BR]; enma:l'k *ta*, enma:tu *ti*; want
or intend to go ~ ketu:lmiyet *ai*
homely winapewit *ai*
home made ~ item kisitaqan; kisiyaqan
homesick netajit *ai* [SH]
homosexual nune:sm *an*
honest ki:wajiyaq *ii*, ki:wajiyet *ai*
honestly! mewlijoqo na; meluwijoqo na
honorific kujjinu (used in addressing an old
man); kkijinu (used in addressing an old
woman or a chief's wife) [SH]
honour pejiliksalk *ta*; kepmite:l'mk *ta*,
kepmite:tm *ti*; ~ **-ed** me:kite:tasit *ai*,
me:kite:tas'k *ii* [BC]; ~ **-ing** ceremony
wi:kipaltimk [CB]
hood place a ~ on (an infant) oqonoqopiso:tlk
ta
hoof my ~ nqosi *an*; nsi *an* [SH]
hook catch by ~ or gill net nastesmk *ta*,
nastestu *ti*; fish ~ mkikn; mkikun [SH];
where ~ **-ed** or attached wet-nastek *ii*
hoop (basket) ~ lukwistaqan [SH];
loqwistaqan [BR]; wooden ~ support around
inside of wikwam laqpilaqan [SH]
hop ~ along pemja:t *ai*
hope etawet *ai*

hopper job ~ soqomkwewj (soqomkwewjik) *an*

horizon kwaptm'n

horn pipukwaqan; a ~ blower nuji-pipukwet *ai (an)*; blow a whistle or ~ pipuwa:smukwet *ai* [BR]; my (animal) ~ nsmu *an*; have ~ **-s** wesmuwit *ai*; have a pair of ~ **-s** wesemuwit *ai*

hornpow klatpetaw (klatpetaq) *an* (a kind of fish)

horse te:sipow *an* (Fr *des chevaux*); form (as a cloud) in the shape of a ~ te:sipow aluktesk *ii*; go by ~ te:sipowa:q (te:sipowa:m) *ai*; ~ whip te:sipow kumaqan

horseback come on ~ wejkwi:puluwet *ai*; ride along on ~ pemi:puluwet *ai*

horsefly ms'soq *an* [RB]; musoq *an*

horseshoe mkumiye:j *an*; have on ~ **-s** mkumiye:ja:q (mkumiye:ja:m) *ai*

hose ~ down kesispapal'k *ta*, kesispapatu *ti*

hospital ksnuko:kuwom

host (communion) ~ wskijipnew *an*; wskwipnek [PEI]

hot epsit *ai*, eptek *ii* (eptek is also used for the weather); start to get ~ pem-p'tek *ii*

house ujikan [SH]; wennji:kuwom; have a well-heated ~ wel-p'smat *ai*; my ~ ni:k; new ~ pilikan; play ~ wi:k ji:jat *ai*

housekeeper a ~ nujins'pit *ai (an)*; my ~ n'naqapem *an*

housemate nuktoqtejkwej *an* [SH]; my ~ nikmaj *an* [SH]

how are you? ~ (feeling)? me: tale:n

how come? tal kis

huff go home in a ~ enm'nqwe:set *ai*

hug te:tipoqja:l'k *ta*, te:tipoqja:tu *ti*; wesmoqjewalk *ta*; wesuwa:kwa:l'k *ta* [PEI]; ~ and kiss wejamoqsuwalk *ta* [RB]

human ~ being mimajiwinu *an*

humbly act ~ penoqwitelsit *ai*

hummingbird militaw (militaq) *an*

hummock nemaqt'ji:j [SH]

humour in good ~ wel-te:teket *ai*

humped sit ~ over facing toward wejkwistepit *ai*

hunchback a ~ temawikna:t *ai (an)*

hunched ~ over sawepit *ai*, sawetek *ii*

hundred kaskimtlnagan [BR]; kask'ptnnaqan; one ~ years old kaskimtlnaqanipuna:t [BR]; kask'ptnnaqanipuna:t *ai*

hungry kewisink *ai*; make ~ kewisina:l'k *ta* [CB]; somewhat ~ kewisinji:jit *ai*

hunt ketanteket *ai*; ~ for ketank *ta*, ketantu *ti*; ~ for clams e:se:ket *ai*; ~ for eels ka:tewe:ket *ai* [SH]; katewe:ket [BC]; ~ moose tiya:mukwet *ai*; tiya:muwe:ket *ai* [BR]; set out to ~ provisions najintuksiktmat *ai* [BR]; start out to ~ and kill najiktanteket *ai* [CB]; go moose ~ -ing natapuluwit *ai* [ESK]; ~ **-ing** ground netukuluwo:mi; ~ **-er** ktantekewinu *an*; ntuksuwinu *an*; a ~ **-er** nutanteket *ai (an)*

hurl ~ in ennmtesm'k *ta*, ennmtestu *ti*; ~ in (as a spear) elnmttesm(')k *ta* [BR]; ~ down niseket *ai*

hurricane ekulamsn *an*; ew'lamsn *an*

hurriedly pick up ~ ew'nasimknasit *i* [BR]

hurry in a ~ nenaqe:k *ai*

hurry ketaqa:sit *ai*; tetaqa:sit *ai*; ~ off enaqsit *ai* [CB]; nenaqa:sit *ai*; ~ up enaqsit *ai* [CB]; nenaqa:sit *ai*

hurt jile:k *ai*; kesa:l'k *ta*; kesinukuwik *ii*, kesinukuwit *ai*; get ~ badly (from a fall) kesitesink *ai*; ~ badly kesite:k *ta*; ~ by biting kesipk *ta*

husband my ~ nji:n'mum *an*; my ex- ~ nji:n'mumt'p

husk pelqa:l'k *ta*, pelqa:tu *ti*

husky have a ~ voice kepi:sit *ai*; speak with a deep or ~ voice maqi:sit *ai*

hustle winpasit *ai*; ~ about ew'nasa:sit *ai* [BR]

hyperactive waqasit *ai*

hypnotize telap'lkikwa:l'k *ta*

ic-e mkumi; ~ **-y** mekunik *ii*; ~ **-y** in patches mkumi:knik *ii*, mkumi:knit *ai*

iceberg wijikmuwaluk [SH]

ice skate na:qokum (na:qokumaq) *an*

icicle mkumi:kn

ill siwikna:t *ai*; fall suddenly ~ jaqalipnet *ai*

illegitimate have an ~ child sekewe:ket *ai*; ~ child sekewey (sekewe:k *an*; ~ person pqotnanj *an*

ill-mannered penoqwe:k *ai*; ketkaqamiksit *ai*; eat ~ **-ly** ketkatalk *ai*

illuminate wasoqonk *ta*, wasoqon'm *ti*; ~ **-d** wasoqonmat *ai*

illusionist an ~ nuji-milapulkikwa:teket *ai (an)*

imaginary see an ~ thing telap'lkikwa:sit *ai*

imagine ~ hearing something telistaqanewa:sit *ai*

imitat-e elutaq *ta*; speak or ~ the Restigouche dialect listukujewa:tuwat *ai*; an ~ **-or** nuji-elutuwet *ai (an)*

immature nutqwe:k *ai*

immediately nankmiw; simtuk; smtuk

impersonate elutaq *ta*

impersonator an ~ nuji-elutuwet *ai (an)*

important espe:k *ai*

impregnate kistelaq *ta*; kiste:k *ta*; kiskatte:k *ta* [SH]

improperly act ~ emekwe:k *ai*; eat ~ emekwatalk *ai*; o:platalk *ai*; o:pli-mijisit *ai* [SH]; pick up ~ ew'nasimkn'm *ti*, ew'nasimknk; act bad or ~ winsit *ai*

in bring or take ~ piskwa:l'k *ta*, piskwa:tu *ti*; caved ~ walqwiyaq *ii*, walqwiyet *ai*; curve ~ pijikiyaq *ii*, pijikiyet *ai*; follow ~ piskwiwkwalk *ta*, piskwiwkwatm *ti*; get ~ or on (a vehicle) tepu:sit *ai* [SH]; go ~ pija:sit *ai*; let ~ piskwa:l'k *ta*, piskwa:tu *ti*; look ~ (from the outside) piskwapit *ai*; push ~ pijiksma:l'k *ta*, pijiksma:tu *ti*; put ~ pija:l'k *ta*, pija:tu *ti*; squeeze or press ~ piji-jink'ja:l'k *ta*; piji-jink'ja:tu *ti*; take ~ the laundry pisqoqowet *ai* [BC]; throw ~ pijeket *ai*

inactive jikawepit *ai*, jikawetek *ii*

inadequate nutqwelk *ai, ii*; an ~ lover ketkiyet *ai*

incapable consider ~ malikite:l'mk *ta*, malikite:tm *ti*; ~ of running me:situkwi:k

inch mtijin (a measurement)

(me:situkwi:m) *ai*; ~ of walking me:sipmiyet *ai*

incite asimk *ta*

incline tqojuwan; an ~ nunmaqek *ii*, nunmaqet *ai*

include ~ in the count maw-kimk *ta*, maw-kitm *ti*; ~ in the repairs maw-lukwalk *ta*, mawlukwatm *ti*

inconsiderate me:ke:k *ai*

indecent ketke:k *ai*

Indian Inu *an* [BR]; nnu *an*; dance ~ style Inu:tesink *ai*; Inutesink *ai* [SH]; Inu:kwat *ai* [BC]; pertaining to ~ **-s** Inuweyey [BR]; nnuweyey; ~ village (reserve) Inuwe:kati [BR]; ~ woman Inuwi:skw *an* [BR]; talk ~ nnuwi:sit *ai*

indigestion my ~ ntalsuwikn

inexpensive anawtik *ii*, anawtit *ai*

infant qopisun *an*; act like an ~ qopisune:k *ai*

infect mesi:k *ta*

inflammable ~ substance nu:kwa:qewey

influence mesi:k *ta*

inform ekinuwa:l'k *ta* [SH]; keknuwa:taq *ta (do)*

inform on mesimk *ta*

ingrown mijikwek *ii*, mijikwet *ai*

inhale wesu-welamit *ai*

injured jile:k *ai*; badly ~ me:kiksitesink *ai* [SH]; get ~ wejiksitesink *ai*; where one got ~ et'ltesk *ii*, et'ltesink *ai*

inland go ~ so:qiyet *ai*, so:qiyaq *ii*; soqowiyet *ai*

in-laws ~ (sister's husband, brother's wife) wijjustijik (pl) *ai* [BC]

innards my ~ ntlamilu

inquisitive ne:le:k *ai*

insect juji:ji:j *an*; eln'ma:l'k *ta*, eln'ma:tu *ti*; have the hand of an ~ jujiju:nat *ai* [BC]

inside lame:k *ai, ii*; pisit *ai*, pitek *ii*; cry ~ kimtemit *ai*; drift ~ (of snow) piskw-paniks'k *ii*; feel ~ of (with the hand) pu:talqan'm *ti*, pu:talqank *ta*; ~ the house lamukuwomk (loc) [SH]; rain ~ piskw'laq *ii*

inside out skin ~ esetekjipsa:l'k, esetekjipsa:tu *ti* [SH]; turn ~ esetipsa:l'k *ta*

insinuate *ai* alo:stasit; ~ about elaqtaq *ta*

insistent munsa:t *ai* [SH]

insomnia nepapimk [BC]; have ~ nepapit *ai* [BC]

instance for ~ katu

instantly kill ~ paqsikpetelaq *ta* [PEI]; kill ~ (with a gun or bow and arrow) paqsipke'itelaq *ta*

instead aw na; tep'tuk

instep elsita:sit *ai (an)*; have an ~ or arch walnoqsitat *ai* [BR]

instigate asimk *ta*; asiketk (asiketm) *ai*; massaqte:ket *ai*

instrument[1] wind ~ pipukwaqan; make music on a horn or wind ~ pipukwet *ai*

instrument[2] scratch with an ~ kesipte:k *ta*, kesipte:m *ti*

insufficient nutqwelk *ai, ii* [SH]; an ~ amount or number tekele:jk *ii*, tekle:jit *ai*; give or put in an ~ amount of nutqwa:l'k *ta*, nutqwa:tu *ti*; ~ -ly narrow notqwi-jijikwe:jk *ii*, notqwi-jijikwe:jit *ai*

insult amsalimk *ta*; we:kwimk *ta* [RB]

intact mese:k *ai (an)*

intelligent kejiteket *ai*; ke'iteket *ai*; pepkatpat *ai*

intercourse have ~ with asite:l'mk *ta*; etl-te:k *ta*

interior the ~ (of a dwelling) lamikuwom; lamukuwom [SH]

internally hidden ~ masqupit *ai*, masqutek *ii*

interpret nekwtmalsewk *ta* [BR]; nesssutmasewk *ta*; ~ for nesutmalsewk *ta*; ~ -ation nesutmalsewuti; nestmalsewuti [SH]; nekwtmalsewuti [BR]; an ~ -er nestmalsewet *ai (an)* [BC]

interrupt naqte:k *ta*, naqte:m *ti*; neto:tmuwet *ai*; ~ (in conversation) ejoqjemk *ta*

intestines waqtiyan [RB]

invent kisite:l'mk *ta*, kisite:tm *ti*

invisible become ~ keska:s'k *ii*, keska:sit *ai*

invit-e wikimk *ta*; wikumk *ta*; ~ in piskwekimk *ta*; ~ -ation wikumkusimkewey

inward curve ~ piskwikiyaq *ii*, piskwikiyet *ai*

iron kasawo:q; qasawo:q; clothing ~ jitnaqi:kney [BC]; ~ pan qasawo:qey lapuwe:ji:j

Iroquois ~ Indian kwetej *an*

irresponsible amassit *ai*

irritable taqale:k *ai*

irritate si:kuwik *ai*; si:kaq *ta*; become ~ -d (as a first child) when the mother carries her second child mikulltiyat *ai*

island m'niku

it "it" (in tag game) kukwejuwit *ai*

itch tesipiyet *ai* [RB]

itchy kesipiyaq *ii*, kesipiyet *ai*; kesipkuwek *ii*, kesipkuwet *ai* (of a garment); ~ **ness** kesipiyemkewey

its nekmewey *an, in*

J

jab taqamk *ta*, taqtm *ti*

jack ~ (in cards) je:k *an*

Jack sapatis *an* [SH]

jacket je:kit *an* [SH]

jackknife wa:qan-ji:j

jack of all trades a ~ nata:n'mat *ai (an)*

jail laplusan (Fr *la prison*); ~ **-ed** masqwa:tasit *ai*

jam papkoqsikn; paskoqsikn [BC]; passoqsikn; make ~ passoqsawet *ai*; make into ~ passoqs'k *ta*, passoqsm *ti*

James Sa:k *an* (Fr *Jacques*) [BC]

Janet Sanet *an*

January pnamujuwiku:s *an*; punamujuwiku:s *an* [CB]

jar pu:tay *an* (Fr *bouteille*)

jaundice yellow ~ wisawow

jaw my ~ ntukwape:kn

jealous wiskuwet *ai*; a ~ mate mi:janimat *ai (an)* [BC]; qalipu:sitat *ai* [BC]

Jean-Baptiste Sapatis *an*

jellyfish sasap *an*

jerk wesuweket *ai*

Jesus Se:sus

Jesus Christ Se:sukuli

Jew lesuwi:p (lesuwi:paq) *an* (Fr *les Juifs*); lasuwi:p *an* (Fr *le Juif*) [SH]

jig nastesmk *ta*, nastestu *ti*; ~ fish ekwitamet *ai*

Jimmy Sa:ke:j *an* [BC]

job complete the ~ matawa:sit *ai* [BC]; do odd ~ **-s** matu:-lukwet *ai (an)*

John Sa:n *an* (Fr *Jean*)

John Peter Sapiye:l *an* (Fr *Jean-Pierre*)

join wijitkweyaq *ta*, wijitko:tm *ti*; ~ together (to form a point) sipn'mi:ket *ai*

jok-e papit *ai*; tell a ~ papewo:kwet *ai*; ~ **-ing** papimk

joker a practical ~ mila:teket *ai*

jolly weskewinoqsit *ai*

joyful wel-te:teket *ai*; weskewinoqsit *ai*; ~ time or occasion mawi-w'lta:suwaqan

judge ilsumk *ta*, ilsutm *ti*; a ~ nuji-ilsuteket *ai (an)*

judgement have poor ~ awanitplu:teket *ai*; have sound ~ natawitplu:teket *ai*

juice apple ~ wennju:-su:n apu; blueberry ~ pkuman-apu

Julian Suliyan *an*

July psikuwiku:s *an* [BC]; ps'kuwiku:s *an*

jump kwi:sit *ai* (used in reference to a fish only); wenaqiyaq *ii*, wenaqiyet *ai*; ~ over wenaqiyalk *ta*, wenaqiyatm *ti*

jumpy waqasit *ai*

June nipniku:s *an*

just ansma; assma; pasik [CB]; pas'k; ~ like nkutey; pana; ~ so pa na

just a minute! ke:s'k

just desserts get one's ~ (for cruelty committed) aniyamukwet *ai*

K

Kahnawake kakknawa:ki

keep on ~ going siyawa:sit *ai*, siyawa:s'k *ii*;
siyawiyet *ai* [SH]; ~ coasting (on the river)
siyawkumiyet *ai*

keg malike:w *an*

kerosene ko:layl

kettle jik'tlo:q (jik'tlo:qq) *an*; copper ~
wisawo:qw

key apt'sqi:kn; app'sqi:kn [BR]

kick tekteskaq *ta*, tekteskm *ti*; tekteskawet *ai*
[BR]; ~ along pemteskaq *ta*, pemteskm *ti*; ~
back and forth asu:teskaq *ta*, asu:teskm *ti*;
~ out tewa:kwe'iteskaq *ta*; tewitk'teskaq *ta*;
~ through saputeskaq *ta*, saputeskm *ti*;
break by ~ **-ing** or stomping temteskaq *ta*,
temteskm *ti* [BR]

kid[1] ewsimk *ta*

kid[2] luks'ji:j *an*

kidnap kimutna:l'k *ta*; kimutnalk *ta*;
wesmi:pulk *ta*, wesmi:putu *ti*

kidney pukuluwan *an*

kill ne:pa:q *ta*; ~ accidentally peji-sikte:k *ta*; ~
for provisions netuk-siktmat *ai* [BR]; ~
instantly (with a gun or bow and arrow)
paqsipke'itelaq *ta*; ~ instantly paqsikpetelaq
ta [PEI]; ~ **-ed** sikto:kwet *ai*; ~ **-ed** in an
accident siktesink *ai*

killer a ~ nutanteket *ai (an)*

killing make a quick ~ jaqallte:k *ta*, jaqallte:m
ti

kiln-dried weli-piyasit *ai*, weli-piyatek *ii*

kind one ~ newt-nemi:k *ai*; all ~ **-s** of
milamuksit *ai*, milamu:k *ii*; think about all ~
-s of things milita:sit *ai*; have all ~ **-s** of
dreams (as when one is feverish) milkusit *ai*;
make all ~ **-s** of food miloqsawet *ai*; so
many ~ **-s** te:sunemiksit *ai*, te:sunemi:k *ii*

kind-hearted welm'toq (welm'tu) *ai*

kindling make ~ aps'sqate:ket *ai*

king eleke:wit (eleke:wijik) *an*; ~ card
eleke:wit (eleke:wijik) *an* (Basque *errege*)

king bird tetaqulkuni *an* [SH]

kingfisher jik'tli:kej *an* [ESK]

kiss weskaqal'm'k *ta*, weskaqaltm *ti*

kit tool ~ lukowaqane:kmuti

kitten kajuwewji:j *an*; have ~ **-s** peneskwit *ai*
[BC]

kleptomaniac a ~ pkuwiptnat *ai (an)*

klutz sqapantiyej

knapsack alapilaqan

knead epipnatm *ti*; ~ dough elu:knawet *ai*
[PEI]; elusknawet *ai*

knee my ~ njikun *an*

kneel nutkul-pit *ai*; ~ down mutkul-pa:sit *ai*;
nutkul-pa:sit *ai*

knick ~ with a knife jils'k *ta*, jilsm *ti*

knife wa:q'n; bread ~ tlawo:q *an*; crooked ~
awa:qi:kn; waqa:'anikn [PEI]; wa:qa'ikikn
[RB]; wa:qa'ikn; waqa:qanikn [SH]; butcher
~ tlawo:q *an*; hunting ~ tlawo:q *an*; (butter)
~ waq'n; my ~ ntuwaqan; table ('case') ~
semqaluk; cut with a ~ wa:qans'k *ta*,
wa:qansm *ti*; tlawo:qs'k *ta*

knit apsisknuwet *ai*; elisknuwalk *ta*,
elisknuwatm *ti*; elisknuwet *ai*; eltnuwalk *ta*,
eltnuwatm *ti* [SH]; eltnuwet *ai*; ~ **-ting**
lisknuwaqan

knob door ~ menjapskek

knock ~ away ejikl-te:k *ta*, ejikl-te:m *ti*; ~
down jaqje'ite:k *ta*, jaqje'ite:m *ti*; jaqjete:k
ta, jaqjete:m *ti*; kewte:k *ta*, kewte:m *ti*; ~ off
mente:k *ta*, mente:m *ti*; temte:k *ta*, temte:m
ti; ~ down to the knees ejaqje'ite:k *ta*; ~
down with the feet ejaqje'iteskaq *ta*; ~ out
petkute:k *ta*; petkwete:k *ta* [BR]

knot ~ on a tree pqoqt [SH]; psetkun

know nenaq *ta*, nen'm *ti*; come to ~ about
wejikjiji:k *ta*; come to ~ (from such a source)
wejikji:tu *ti*; ~ about ke'itu *ti*; kejitu *ti*, keji:k
ta; ~ all about kaqikjijitu *ti*, kaqikjiji:k *ta*; ~
and respect nenuwite:l'mk *ta*, nenuwite:tm *ti*
[BC]; ~ one's way around natawe:k *ai*; ~ **-n**
ke'itmk *ii*; kejitmk *ii*

know how ~ to bake nata:-toqtet *ai*; ~ to beg
nata:-tawet *ai*; ~ to cook netuwoqsawet *ai*;
~ to get by natawe:k *ai*; ~ to swim
natawa:q (natawa:m) *ai*

knowledge have ~ of ke'itu *ti*; kejitu *ti*, keji:k
ta; ~ **able** ke'iteket *ai*; kejiteket *ai*

knurl pqoqt

L

labor attikna:s'k *ii*, attikna:sit *ai*

lac-e elaqpa:l'k *ta*, elaqpa:tu *ti*; elaqpa:teket
ai; ~ up elaqpo:l'k *ta*, elaqpo:tu *ti*; ~ -ing
laqpo:taqan

lacrosse ~ stick wenaqpmaqan [SH]

ladder lkusuwaqan

ladies "old" ~ tqamuwewey [CB]

ladle ela:miket *ai*; ela:muwet *ai*; la:maqan *an*

lady saqama:skw (saqama:skwaq) *an*; Indian
~ nnu:skw *an*; my ~ friend ntuttemi:skw *an*
[SH]; my young ~ friend ntuttemi:skwe:j *an*
[SH]

lagoon po:kwin

laid out ~ lengthwise eloqosk *ii*, eloqosink *ai*

lair pqwan'm [SH]

lake qospem

lamp wasoqonmaqan

land[1] maqamikew (maqamikal); cultivated ~
or field ika:taqan; go by ~ maqamikewa:sit
ai; ~ of the Micmac people mi:kma:ki

land[2] oqwa:q *ii*, oqwa:t *ai*; niss'k *ii*, nissink *ai*

language tli:suti; speak many ~ -s milatuwat
ai; use high-sounding ~ espi:sit *ai*

lantern lasiyantejk [SH]; wasoqonmaqan

lap[1] my ~ nplaqan

lap[2] ~ up nessapoqwat *ai*

lard kulkwi:suwimi [BR]; kulkwi:su:mi [SH]

larder my ~ ninu

large have a ~ boat maqiwtulit *ai* [BR]; have a
~ breast or chest maqipskunat *ai*; have a ~
tongue maqi-wilnuwit *ai*; have a ~ hole
maqalqasit *ai*; have a ~ stool maqijjikwat
ai; have ~ arms maqo:qiptnat *ai*; have ~
eyes maqalqikwat *ai*; have ~ feet maqsitat
ai; have ~ hands maqiptnat *ai*; have ~ legs
maqo:qonikata:t *ai*; have ~ or long ears
maqistaqanat *ai* (Big Cove term for a
Micmac from Restigouche); have ~ testicles
maqapskusuwat *ai*; have ~ upper arms
keskitlmaqanat *ai*; ~ and round kesi-
maqapsk'sit *ai*, kesi-maqapskek *ii*;
maqapsk'sit *ai*, maqapskek *ii*

last telipkijiyaq *ii*; ~ one wtejkewey *an*, *in*; ~
or stay through saputaqatm *ti*; ~ summer
ktiki-nipn; the ~ kiyaspiyaq *ii*; the ~ day
kiyaspi-kisk'k; the night before ~ ktiki-
w'la:kwe:k

last-born my ~ n'mtesan *an*

late arrive too ~ for mess'teskaq *ta*,
mess'teskm *ti*; mess'teskmat *ai*; arrive ~
pekittoq (pekittu) *ai*

lather in a ~ pisewiyaq *ii*, pisewiyet *ai*

laugh elmit *ai* [BR]; enmit *ai* [NB]; etl-elmit *ai*
[SH]; etl-enmit *ai*; weskewe:k *ai*; ~ at
malikitm *ti* [BC]; wi:kuwamk *ta*, wi:kuwaptm
ti; ~ at length apj-elmit *ai*; apt-elmit *ai*; ~ to
oneself kim-elmuktasit [SH]; ~ secretly
kim-elmit *ai* [BR]; start to ~ poqjiws'kewe:k
(poqjiws'kewe:m) *ai*; kim-enmit *ai* [SH];
burst out ~ -ing paqsipk-elmit *ai*; pass by ~
ing pemsiyaw-elmit *ai*; stop ~ ing pun-
el'mit *ai* [SH]

launch paqaste:m *ti*; paqasaqalk *ta*,
paqasaqtu *ti*

laundry do the ~ kestaqanewet *ai*; hang out
~ elqawet *ai* [BC]; elqowet *ai*; take in the ~
pisqoqowet *ai* [BC]

law tplutaqan

Lawrence Lola *an* (Fr *Laurent*)

lawyer nuj-aknutmewinu *an*; putu:suwinu *an*
[BC]

lay ~ down elsma:l'k *ta*, elsma:tu *ti*; ~ down
lengthwise eloqwa:l'k *ta*, eloqwatu *ti*; ~ on
top ke:kwisma:l'k *ta*, ke:kwisma:tu *ti*; ~ out
eleko:l'k *ta*, eleko:tu *ti*; ~ eggs penatk
(penatm) *ai*

layered elipqiyaq *ii*, elipqiyet *ai*; elsaqtek *ii*;
lipqamu:k

lazy male:k *ai*; mentally ~ malikwat *ai*

leach squ *an* [SH]

lead[1] sqolu:skw

lead[2] ~ off (as a path) pesk'tek *ii*; ~ to eltek
ii

leader ikanus *an* [SH]; a ~ ikan-pukuwit *ai* *(an)*
[SH][CB]

leaf a kind of ~ (for medicinal purposes)
wktluwanipkaji:jit *an* [SH]; ~ of paper nipi *an*;
~ of a tree nipi *an*; plant ~ tansiyewe:l (pl) *in*
(unidentified, used in medicine); tobacco ~
wennjuwipk; vegetable ~ nipi *an*

leak espek *ii*, espet *ai*

lean[1] alu:saq *ii*, alu:sat *ai*; wikamik *ii*, wikamit
ai [SH]

lean[2] ~ against epatkupukuwik *ii*,
epatkupukuwit *ai*; ~ one's head toward
elatpo:jink *ai*; ~ toward elikuwet *ai*
lean-to anapikan [BR]; anapi:kan; oqwatqikan
[SH]
leap ~ along pemja:t *ai*
learn keknu:tmasit *ai*; ~ (by holding on to
something) to walk aptoqwet *ai*; ~ **-ing**
kekina:matimkewey; kekina:matnewey [SH];
kina:matimk; kina:matnewey [SH]
lease akase:wa:l'k *ta*, akase:wa:tu *ti*
leash take (a dog) for a walk on a ~ al-
k'ltaqan'k *ta*
leather m'kekn
leave maja:sit *ai*; puna:l'k *ta*, puna:tu *ti*; ~
alone punajeyaq *ta*, punajo:tm *ti*; ~ behind
naqalk *ta*, naqtm *ti*; ~ or go off the trail or
road peska:sit *ai*; take ~ of oqomk *ta* [SH]
lectur-e cease ~ **-ing** punewo:kwet *ai*
ledge mtasoq
left hold on the ~ side patanapjit *ai*; ~ hand
patanjuwey; ~ side patatuj; toward the ~
patatujke:l
lefthanded patanmit *ai*; patank (patan'm) *ai*
leftover eskwiyaq *ii*, eskwiyet *ai*; piyamiyaq *ii*,
piyamiyet *ai*; piwiyaq *ii*; eat the ~ **-s** of
matu:p'k *ta*, matu:tm *ti*
leg have large ~ **-s** maqo:qonikata:t *ai*; have
one ~ or foot newtikatat *ai*; have small ~ **-s**
apso:qonikatat *ai*; stand or slide on one ~
newtikata:lukwet *ai*
legendary person a ~ of great strength kinap
an
legendary strong man a ~ with supernatural
powers tune:l (Fr *tonnerre*)
leichen pi:sanatkw
lend ~ (something) to maqata:q *ta (do)*; a ~
-er maqatuwi:ket *ai (an)*
length a good ~ (e.g. of rope) weltaqsit *ai*;
cry at ~ apjimt'k (apjimtm) *ai*; have such a ~
or height tel-pitoqsit *ai*, tel-pita:q *ii*; laugh at
~ apj-elmit *ai*; apt-elmit *ai*
lengthwise laid out ~ eloqosk *ii*, eloqosink *ai*;
throw ~ eloqeket *ai* [BR]; wrap up ~
eloqo(n)maqa:tu *ti* [BR]

Lent kale:m (Fr *carême*); kale:mewimk [SH];
kale:mewumk; mid ~ temikale:m (Fr *des
mi-carêmes*)
let go elaqalk *ta*, elaqtu *ti*
letter wi:katikn; ~ (of the alphabet)
knukwatikn *an*
lettuce wi:katiknipkw [SH]
lick muskumk *ta*, muskwatm *ti*; muskwatamit
ai
lie[1] ~ across as'komoqtek *ii* [BR]; ~ across or
athwart taqamoqpit *ai*, taqamoqtek *ii*; ~
atop ke:kwisink *ai*; ~ down elisma:sit *ai*
[BR]; elsma:sit *ai*; epasma:sit *ai* [CB]; ~
down crossways or across taqamoqisma:sit
ai; ~ down to sleep nepasma:sit *ai*; ~ facing
away enmisink *ai*, enmisk *ii*; ~ facing in the
opposite direction enmikjesink *ai*; ~ in the
way a:jelisink *ai*; ~ near kikjiw-eloqpit *ai*
[SH]; ~ on one's side wpmesink *ai* [BR];
wpmesma:sit *ai* [BR]
lie[2] eksuwo:qon; ks'pukuwa:taqan [PEI]; ~ to
eksupukuwa:l'k *ta*; kesipukwa:l'k *ta* [BR];
kespukuwa:l'k *ta* [BC]; tell a ~ eksuwet *ai*;
tell ~ **-s** ew'let *ai* [PEI]; kluskapewit *ai*
life mimajiwaqan; bring to ~ weskijinuwa:l'k
ta
lift ~ up wenaqa:l'k *ta*, wenaqa:tu *ti*; wena:q'k
ta, wena:qm *ti* [RB]; ~ off kepta:l'k *ta*,
kepta:tu *ti*; ~ out of ketaqqa:l'k *ta*,
ketaqqa:tu *ti* [BC]
lifter stove cover ~ w'naqi:kn [ESK]
light[1] naqji:sit *ai* [PEI]; ~ in weight nenaqji:jk
ii, nenaqji:jit *ai*; ~ snow pesa:ji:jk *ii*; ~ and
warm (of a breeze) epoqek *ii*
light[2] wasoqon [SH]; give off ~ wasoqonawek
ii, wasoqonawet *ai*; ~ complected
wapikneksit *ai*; ~ (of hue) wasoqek *ii*; ~ up
wasoqwa:l'k *ta*, wasoqwa:tu *ti*; put ~ on
wasoqonk *ta*, wasoqon'm *ti*; suffused with ~
pitiyasit *ai*, pitiyatek *ii*; walk around with a ~
alasenmat *ai*
lightning wasoqwetesk *ii* [BR]; wasoqotesk *ii*,
wasoqotesink *ai*; heat ~ kiwask *ii*
light up papk'semk *ta* [SH]; paskesa:l'k *ta*,
paskesa:tu *ti*; pask'setmat *ai*; ~ (a pipe)

pask'semk *ta*; ~ and smoke saqtat *ai*; ~ to smoke papk'setmat *ai* [BR]

like[1] kesalk *ta*, kesatm *ti*; ~ the looks of welamk *ta*, welaptm *ti*; ~ very much ma:muniksalk *ta*

like[2] act ~ that tele:k *ai, ii*; just ~ ankutey

lilacs weljema:qewe:l (pl); weljemajkewe:l (pl)

limber ilisqa:l'k *ta*, ilisqa:tu *ti*

limp askatesink *ai*; walk with a ~ aska:sit *ai*

lin-e[1] ~ a coat pituweka:l'k *ta*, pituweka:tu *ti*; ~ -ing pituweka:taqan; elapaqtesmk *ta*

line[2] pull out of the water by a rope or fish ~ natqapilawet *ai*; rope or fishing ~ a:papi *an*

lineage of the same ~ wettaqiyet *ai*

lion pittalu *an*

lip my ~ nsi

liquefy apu:s'k *ta*, apu:sm *ti*

liquid warm ~ eppa:q *ii*

liquor go for ~ wikupsit *ai*

listen approach and ~ jiks'tmakwet *ai* [SH]; ~ to jiks'taq *ta*, jiks'tm *ti*; tired of ~ -ing to siws'taq *ta*

listless kiwaje:k *ai*; siwikna:t *ai*

lit ~ up kesasek *ii*, kesaset *ai*; pitiyasit *ai*, pitiyatek *ii*; well ~ welasek *ii*, welaset *ai*

little one my ~ ni:naji:j (dim) *an* [SH]

live mimajik *ii*, mimajit *ai*; ~ a long life pekitawsit *ai*; ~ apart se:siketijik (pl) *ai* [PEI]; ~ in a good location weliket *ai*; ~ simply matu:-mimajit *ai*; ~ together mawe:kik (pl) *ai*

livelihood mimajiwaqan

lively seskwe:k *ai*

liver wskun; my ~ ntalsuwikn [NB]; ntuskun'm

lizard jujij *an*

load miwsn [SH]; pitkmalk *ta*, pitkmatm *ti*; ~ up for pitkmewk *ta*; ~ (a gun) with gunpowder and ramrod pitqasawet *ai*; ~ -ed to the brim tmaqanikju:waq *ii*, tmaqanikju:wet *ai*; ~ -ed up tepo:tas'k *ii*, tepo:tasit *ai*

loan maqatewey; emqatuwi:ketu *ti*; ~ to emqata:q *ta*; emqatuwi:k *ta*

lobster jakej *an*; walumkwej *an* [BR]; trap ~ -s jakejuwe:ket *ai*

located ~ at epit *ai*, etek *ii*; set, ~ or situated there etek *ii*

lock ~ in kepsoqk *ta*, kepsoqom *ti*; ~ up kepjoqiket *ai*; ~ up, in or out apt'sqa:m *ti*, apt'sqa:q *ta*; ~ up, in or out (quickly) apt'sqate:k *ta*, apt'sqate:m *ti*

locked ~ together aptluwajik (pl) *ai*

locust misimimqanaw (misimimqanaq) *an* [SH]

lodging prepare ~ for ilaji:kewk *ta*

log lo:ks (lo:ksik) *an*; ne:kaski:kn (before being cut into specified lengths); tmoqta:w (tmoqta:q) *an* [SH]; cut ~ -s tmoqta:we:ket *ai* [SH]

lonely feel ~ taqawaje:k *ai*

loner newtuko:pj *an*; nkuto:pj: *an*; nkutuko:pj *an*; a ~ tepkise:k *ai (an)*

lonesome musuwet *ai*; netajit *ai*; siwe:k *ai*; ~ for musuwalk *ta*; siwoqtaq *ta*, siwoqtm *ti*

long pita:q *ii*, pitoqsit *ai*; pitoqona:t *ai*, pitoqona:q *ii* [BR]; pittaqq *ii*, pittaqsit *ai*; a ~ time pekije:k *ii*; as ~ as ta:n tlipkije:k; have a ~ reach pijiptnat *ai*; live a ~ life pekitawsit *ai*; ~ and cylindrical eloqpit *ai*, eloqtek *ii*; ~ and flexible eltaqpit *ai*, (ltaqtek *ii*; ~ and straight peka:q *ii*, pekoqsit *ai*; ~ enclosed structure pittaqapekisk *ii*; ~ lasting pekitapeksik *ii*; ~ or yearn for kiwajeyaq *ta*, kiwajo:tm *ti*; stuffer from a ~ term illness pekijipnet *ai*; use for a ~ time pekitapemk *ta*, pekitapetm *ti*; ~ lasting pekitapek *ii* [SH]; wait a ~ time for pekiji-eskmalk *ta*, pekiji-eskmatm *ti*; once ~ ago nekwt sa:q; ~ for musuwet *ai*

long-armed pito:qiptnat *ai*

long-eared pijistaqanat *ai* [SH]

long-legged pijikatat *ai*

long-necked pitoqoluwat *ai* [PEI]; a ~ animal pitoqoluwewj *an*

long-nosed pijisqonat *ai*

long time no see! je pe:kwamuksin

look ~ after anko:tm *ti*, ankweyaq *ta*; ~ around alapit *ai*; ~ around for alamk *ta*, alaptm *ti*; ~ for kwilaq *ta*, kwil'm *ti* ~ at ankamk *ta*, ankaptm *ti*; ~ dirty mejik-amuksit *ai*; ~ healthy jajik-amuksit *ai*; ~ in (from outside) piskwapit *ai*; ~ out (from inside) tewapit *ai*; tewopit *ai* [SH]; ~ over ilamk *ta*, ilaptm *ti*; ilapt'k *ta*, ilaptm *ti*; ~ so amu:k *ii*, amuksit *ai* [SH]; ~ strange or weird kesmapewit *ai*; strain to ~ munsapit *ai*; ~ toward elapit *ai*; take a quick ~ at amalamk *ta*, amalaptm *ti*

looking glass ankamsuti(yey) [SH]

look like ~ rain kikpesan-amukwiyaq *ii*; ~ a doctor mallpale:wit ewapewit *ai*

loon kwimu *an* [CB]; kwinu *an* [SH]

loose apkwa:'ik *ii*, apkwa:'it *ai*

loosen ewe:ka:l'k *ta*, ewe:ka:tu *ti*; ~ up ewe:kiskalsit *ai*

lopsided ukumejik *ii*, ukumejikit *ai*

Lord Niskam *an*

lose e:n'k *ta*, e:n'm *ti*; entu *ti*, e:n'k *ta*

lose out putmat *ai*

lost keska:t *ai*

lot eat a ~ pisoqotalk *ai*; laugh a ~ pusk-elmit *ai*

lotion have on perfume, ~ or oil mimkwat *ai*

lots pukwelk *ai, ii*

loud a ~ mouth kintoqsit *ai* [EG]; make a ~ crack kesikawlusit *ai*; make a ~ noise kesikawta:q *ii*; make a ~ noise (with the voice) kesikawtoqsit *ai*; make a ~ noise or report kesikawtesiket *ai*; make a ~ rapport (as a cannon or gun) kesikawtewesikek *ii*, kesikawtewesiket *ai*; sound or talk ~ jakwek *ii*, jakwet *ai*; speak ~ **-ly** kesikawewo:kwet *ai*

louse wa:kw (wa:kuk) *an*

lov-e kesalk *ta*, kesatm *ti*; kesaluwet *ai*; ksaltimkewey; ~ **-ing** ksaltimkewey

low[1] esne:k *ai, ii*

low[2] wetewiluwa:t *ai* [SH]

lower ~ by rope nispil'm *ti*, nispilk *ta*; ~ self (by hand) nisnusit *ai*

luck apattek *ii* [SH]

lucky lokowit *ai*; get ~ keskmsit *ai*

lug go ~ natuptulk *ta*, natuptu *ti*; ~ here (on the back) petaw'let *ai*; ~ here (on the shoulder) petuptu *ti*; ~ or carry toward (on the back) elaw'let *ai*; ~ or carry (on the back) petaw'lalk *ta*, petaw'latm *ti*; start to ~ poqtaw'lalk *ta*, poqtaw'latm *ti*; poqtaw'let *ai* [CB]

lukewarm kisupaqsijik (pl) *an*, kisupa:q *ii* (of a liquid); nunmi-p'sit *ai*, nunmi-p'tek *ii*; ~ water eppetek *ii*

lumber cut ~ kmu:je:ket *ai*; piece of ~ kmu:j *in* (sg only); ~ **-ing** kmu:je:kaqan

lump kluk (klukk) *an*

lunch eat ~ ketaqama:sit *ai* [BC]

lung my ~ npn *an*

M

machine mulin; sewing ~ mulinji:j

mackeral am'lmekw *an* [BR]; am'lmaw (am'lmaq) *an*

mad ~ at weka'iyuktaq *ta*, weka'iyuktm *ti*

Madelein Matle:n *an* (Fr *Madeleine*)

maggot kullpatkij *an*; wijaw (wijaq) *an* [BC]

magic do ~ tricks keskmap'lkikwa:teket *ai*; perform ~ keskma:teket *ai*; posses ~ keskmsit *ai*; put ~ on keskmap'lkikwa:lek *ta*, keskmap'lkikwa:tu *ti*

magician keskmsit *ai*; a ~ nuji-milamukwa:teket *ai (an)*; nuji-sa:se:wamukwa:teket *ai (an)*

maid nuktoqtejkwej *an*

mail pitkimk *ta*, pitkitm *ti*

mainland Nova Scotian ~ enmiktaqamu:k

mak-e eli:k *ta*; elitu *ti*; elltu *ti*; etlitu *ti*, etli:k *ta*; ~ as such telitu *ti*, teli:k *ta*; ~ from wejitu *ti*, weji:k *ta*; ~ or build a fire (in a stove or furnance) mawksa:teket *ai*; ~ out of wejitu *ti*, weji:k *ta*; ~ something for elitaq *ta* [BR]; ~ the bottom part (of a basket) elikjepilawet *ai* [SH]; finish ~ -ing kisitu *ti*, kisi:k *ta*

make out ~ with wejimk *ta*

make up put on ~ ilapewnusit *ai*

male ~ animal lapew; nape:w *an*

malingerer a ~ pawe:k *ai*

Maliseet a ~ Indian mali:sit *ai*

mammal female ~ lkwetuk *an*; lukwetuk *an*; skweyoq *an*

mammary my ~ nm'lakejm *an* [SH]

man ji:nm (ji:nmuk) *an*; act like a ~ ji:nmuqamiksit *ai*; become a ~ ji:nmuwit *ai*; black ~ kanntakwey *an* [PEI]; ~ chaser ji:nmuwe:sm (ji:nmuwe:smuk) *an*; my ~ nji:n'mum *an*; solid ~ melki-ji:n'm *an*; strong ~ melki-ji:n'm *an*; strong ~ or woman m'lkiknewinu *an*; white ~ aklasiyew *an* [BR]; young Canadian ~ kanatiye:si:s *an*; young ~ ji:n'mji:j *an*; lpa:tu *an* [SH] (16–18 years of age); lpa:tu:s *an*

manage neta:sumk *ta*, neta:sutm *ti*

manager a ~ nutsuteket *ai (an)*

manhood enter into ~ (post puberty) ji:nmji:ju:wet *ai*; enter into ~ (i.e. become ready for marriage) ji:nmuwit *ai*

manner cooked in such a ~ teloqsit *ai*, teloqtek *ii*

manure epkenikn; pkenikn

many pikwelk *ai, ii* [BR]; pukwelk *ai, ii*; have ~ buildings pukwelikanik *ii*

map pekita:wey

maple hard rock ~ snawey; ~ grove jiyoqjimusi-a:qamikt [SH]; ~ syrup jiyoqsimusi apu [SH]; soft ~ malsnawey

marble waqalo:pskw'saw [BR]; wa:qalopsk'saw [SH]

March si:kewiku:s; sikowiku:s; siwkewiku:s [CB]

mare te:sipowi:skw (te:sipowi:skwaq) *an*

Maria (Québec) keskapekiyaq *ii*

Marie Mali *an* (Fr *Marie*) [BC]

marie copain neyasiskowey (a medicinal salve)

mark jilapa:l'k *ta*, jilapa:tu *ti*; jilapa:teket *ai*; keknukwalk *ta*, keknukwatm *ti*; knukwatikn *an*; have a single ~ newtuwi:kas'k *ii*, newtuwi:kasit *ai (an)*; ~ down ewi:k'k *ta*, ewi:km *ti*; ~ or scar (with a knife) jilsawet *ai*; ~ or scar with an axe jilte:k *ta*, jilte:m *ti*; ~ with a line or string jilapaqte:k *ta*, jilapaqte:m *ti*; elapaqtesmk *ta*; ~ with a saw jila:kipulk *ta*, jila:kittu *ti*; ~ -ed jilpit *ai*, jiltek *ii*; jilta:sik *ii*, jilta:sit *ai*; ~ -er knukwaqan; leave a direction or ~ keknukwatiket *ai*

market qo:tlo:mek [SH]; ~ place netukuluwo:mi [SH]

marriage maliye:wuti; toqo-pukuwa:lltimk; ~ agreement keluluwemk [BC]; arrange ~ -s peji-kluluwet *ai*

marrow wi:n; ~ bone kuwikn; wi:newey waqanntew

marr-y maliye:wit *ai*; toqo-pukuwa:l'kik (pl) *ta*; ~ out tew-maliye:wit *ai*; ~ -ied tepqatk (tepqatm) *ai*; ~ out (off the reserve) tewitpaqatk (tewipaqatm) *ai*

marten apistanewj (apistanewjik) *an*

Mary Mali *an*; Mali:j(i:j) (dim) *an*

Mary Rose Mali lo:s *an* (Fr *Marie-Rose*)

mass alame:s (Fr *à la messe*); funeral ~ nepm'kewey alame:s [BC]; nepuwitewey alames; Indian ~ nnu a:sutmamk; midnight ~ nipi-alasutmamk [SH]; nipi-a:sutmamk

massage ilisqa:l'k *ta*, ilisqa:tu *ti*
mast mto:kn [CB]
mastigate soqte:ket *ai*
mat naqsun *an* [SH]
match sq'sikwetestaqan [SH]
matchmaker a ~ kluluwet *ai (an)*; nuji-keluwet
  ai (an) [SH]; nuji-k'luluwet *ai (an)* [BC];
  postewit *ai (an)*
material piece of ~ seyekn-ji:j
maternal on the ~ side nkijewiktuk (loc)
Matthew Matiyu *an* (Fr *Mathieu*)
mattress naqsun *an* [SH]; pismuti
matur-e ke'itine:k *ai*; kisikwek *ii*, kisikwet *ai*;
  nestu:wet *ai*; tepipuna:t *ai*; ~ -ity
  tepipunamk; tepipana:mk; grow into ~
  nestu:wet *ai*
May a:siku:s [CB]; msikuwiku:s; sqoljuwiku:s
maybe jiptuk; ~ so etuk jel
me ni:n *an*
meal mijisultimk [SH]; main course of the ~
  (fish, pork, etc.) pistamun [RB][CB]
mealtime mijjiwaqan
mean winqamiksit *ai*
meanwhile jijuwaqa [SH]
measles alusol (pl) (Fr *la rougeole*); have the
  ~ alusolewit *ai*
measur-e nekaqan *an*; tape ~ n'kaqan *an*; ~
  out enkalk *ta*, enkatm *ti*; ~ up kiskajiyet *ai*;
  ~ -ment n'nkaqan; enkaqan; ~ -ing
  instrument enkemkewey
meat wiyus; ~ handler (cutter) wiyuse:j *an*;
  my ~ (of a nut or seed) nijinj (nijinjik) *an*;
  piece of ~ wiyu:ji:j; rabbit ~ wapusuwey;
  round of ~ apuwaqaj [SH]; slice or slab of ~
  piwsaw (piwsaq) *an* [BC]
medal holy picture or ~ peskmewey *an* [SH]
meddlesome ne:le:k *ai*
mediate ~ a marriage agreement keluluwet *ai*
medicine npisun; ~ bag puwowinuti
medium-sized meski:kji:jit *ii*
meet a:s'kaq *ta*, a:s'km *ti*; ~ or come together
  (by boat) a:sukwesukwijik (pl) *ai*; ~ up with
  welte:k *ta*, welte:m *ti*; ~ up with (on foot)
  welteskaq *ta*, welteskm *ti*
meeting formal ~ or gathering mawiyo:mi;
  hold a ~ mawita:jik (pl) *ai*

melt nujkima:q *ii* [SH]; nujkma:q *ii*, nujkma:t
  ai; nujkmoqs'k *ta*, nujkmoqsm *ti*; ~ or thaw
  (of the snow) saqaniyaq *ii*; ~ (through
  heating) nujkmoqsit *ai*, nujkmoqtek *ii*
memory have a short ~ wejuwowita:sit
mend mesna:l'k *ta*, mesna:tu *ti*; mesni:s'k *ta*,
  mesni:sm *ti*
menstruate wasuweka:tat *ai*
mentally lazy ~ malikwat *ai*
mention ewi:t'k *ta*, ewi:tm *ti*
merchandize malsanewey
merchant malsan *an* (Fr *marchand*)
mesmerize telap'lkikwa:l'k *ta*
mess ~ up jinewalk *ta*, jinewatm *ti*; ~ -ed up
  jinewit *ai*
messy winn'mat *ai*; have ~ hair se:saltukwat
  ai [PEI]; se:saltukwepit *ai*
meteorite puktewit *an*
methodical sipke:k *ai (an)*
Michael Mise:l *an* (Fr *Michele*)
Micmac mi:kmaw (mi:kmaq) *an*; call, say in ~
  (in Indian) nnuwi:tm *ti*; land of the ~ people
  mi:kma:ki; Maliseet word for ~ mi:km *an*;
  Restigouche term for a ~ from Big Cove
  qones *an* (pejorative); say in ~ (in Indian)
  lnuwi:tm *ti* [BR]; speak ~ mi:kmawi:sit *ai*;
  talk ~ nnuwi:sit *ai*
midday miyaw-na:kwek *ii*; miyaw-la:kwek
  [BR]
middle in the ~ mekwa'ik; miyawe:k (loc);
  the ~ of the night miyawitpa:q *ii*; the ~ of the
  day miyaw-na:kwek *ii*
midget wiklatmu:j *an* [SH]
midnight aqtatpa:q *ii*
mikmuwessu possessed by a ~
  mikmuwessuwe:ket *ai*
mild ~ (in weather) wetqane:k *ii*; ~ day
  wetqani-kisk'k [BR]
milk m'lakej *an* [SH]; m'lakejk (pl) *an*; add ~
  (to one's tea or coffee) m'lakejuwa:tat *ai*; ~
  a cow jimpeknawet *ai*; ~ pitcher or pail
  m'lakejuwo:q *an*
mill mulin (Fr *moulin*)
mind call to ~ mikwite:l'mk *ta*; mikwite:tm *ti*;
  lose one's ~ ikekkwet *ai*
mine ni:newey *an, in*

mink mujpej *an* [BR]; jiyakewj (jiyakewjik) *an*
minnow so:qomu:j *an*
minor a ~ nutqwe:k *ai*
mirage see a ~ telap'lkikwa:sit *ai*;
keskmap'lkikwa:t *ai*
mirror ankamsuti(yey); plu:jaqamati; look in
a ~ plu:jaqamat *ai*
mischievous mila:teket *ai*
miss musuwet *ai*; pesoqteskaq *ta*,
pesoqteskm *ti*; putmat *ai*; ~ an appointment
or rendez-vous with messa:l'k *ta*, messa:tu
ti; ~ connecting with pela:l'k *ta*, pela:tu *ti*; ~
in shooting at pesoqtelaq *ta*, pesoqtel'm *ti*; ~
in swinging at or striking at pesoqopsk'te:k
ta, pesoqopsk'te:m *ti*; ~ making connection
with messa:l'k *ta*, messa:tu *ti*
mission down the ~ kutank (loc); go down
the ~ kutana:sit *ai*; go up the ~ wanna:sit *ai*;
up ~ utank; up the ~ walne:k (loc) [SH][BR];
wanne:k (loc)
missionary aniyapsuwinu *an*
mistreat emeko:tm *ti*, emekweyaq *ta*;
poqwajite:l'mk *ta*, poqwajite:tm *ti*
misty kikpesanawe:k *ii* [BR]
mitt pijjaqan *an*; piljaqan *an* [BC]
mitten peljaqan *an* [SH]; pijjaqan *an*
mix ~ together wiyaqqatmu:tijik (pl) *ai*; ~ -ed
wiyaqiyaqal (pl) *ii*, wiyaqiyejik (pl) *ai*
mixed up ~ (crazy) ew'nasiyaq *ii*, ew'nasiyet
ai
moan epetoqsit *ai*
moccasin ma:kn *an*; snowshoe ~ qones *an*
[SH]
mock malikimk *ta* [BC]; malikite:l'mk *ta*,
malikite:tm *ti*; malikmk *ta*
moderately drink ~ welinqana:mat *ai*
moist ~ underneath newukulasink *ai*
molasses kastiyo:mi; add ~ (to pancakes)
m'lasisuwa:tat *ai*; put ~ on m'lasisuwa:tu *ti*
(Fr *mélasse*)
Mollygowatch malikewe:j [CB]
Monday amkwes elukutimk
money suliyewey
monger a rumour ~ puski-alaknutk (puski-
alaknutm) *ai (an)*

monkey anntaknikwej *an* [SH];
anntanqanawejit (anntanqanawejijik) *an* [SH];
kanntakknuwejit *an* [PEI]; make a ~ of
anntanqanawejuwa:l'k *ta* [SH]
Montagnais a ~ saqpi:sit *ai*
month tepknuset (tepknusejik) *an* [BR];
tepkunset (tepkunsejik) *an*; egg-laying ~
pnatmuwiku:s *an*; great (Christmas) ~
kjiku:s *an* [CB][BC]
moon tepknuset (tepknusejik) *an*; tepkunset
(tepkunsejik) *an*
moonshine tepkunsetewik *ii*
moose tiya:m (tiya:muk) *an*; calf ~ tiya:mu:j
an; female ~ tiya:mi:skw *an* [BR]; go ~
hunting natapuluwit *ai* [ESK]; hunt ~
tiya:mukwet *ai*; tiya:muwe:ket *ai* [BR]; set
out to hunt ~ naji-tiya:muwe:ket *ai*; speak ~
tiya:muwi:sit *ai*; ~ caller tiya:muwi:suti [BR]
moose bird mijjako:kwej *an* [RB];
mikjako:kwej *an*
moosefat ~ or tallow tiya:muwimi [BR]
moosehide tiya:muwekn
moosemeat tiya:muwey; dried or smoked ~
kaqaqw
more do ~ than expected me:ka:teket *ai*;
have much ~ of aji-pikweln'k *ta*, aji-
pikweln'm *ti* [BR]; aji-pukwenn'k *ta*, aji-
pukwenn'm *ti*; ~ than me: aq; piyamiw;
one ~ time mejitnewt; some ~ ! mejka:;
me: ap [SH]; me: ijka; me:jka; think ~ of
piyamite:l'mk *ta*, piyamite:tm *ti*
morning eksitpu:kw *ii*; early ~ train, boat, etc.
eksitpu:kwewulkw; early this ~ sepay [SH];
sepey; item or event pertaining to the ~
eksitpu:kowey; nice ~ weli-eksitpu:k; rise
early in the ~ eksitpu:kwiyet *ai*; tomorrow ~
eksitpu:nuk
mosquito kl'muwej *an* [BR]; pijik'njit
(pijik'njijik) *an* [SH]
moss musikn; pesaqanatkw; pesoqanatkw
mother! kiju: (voc) *an*; mam (voc.) [SH]
mother my ~ nkij *an*; nkiju:wem *an* (term of
endearment)
mother-in-law my ~ njikwi:ji:j *an* [SH];
nukumij *an* [SH]; n'niskamiji:skw *an* [SH];
n'nikamij'skw *an* [SH]; njikwi:jij *an* [SH];
njukwi:ji:j *an*

Mother's Day me:kite:l'manej kkijnaq
moult peskwiyet *ai*
mount ~ (stairs) toqjuwa:q *ii*, toqjuwa:t *ai*
mountain k'mtn *an* [SH]; m'ntn *an*; p'mtn [BR]
mourn wenmajita:sit *ai* [RB]; welma'ita:sit *ai*
    [BC]; ~ **-ing** w'lmajita:suwaqan [BC];
mouse apikji:j *an*; apukji:j *an* [BR]
moustache wear or have a ~ eli:tuwat *ai*
mouth have a big ~ maqtunat *ai*; have a
    numb ~ pissaqqutnat *ai*; have a small ~
    apsalqo:tnat *ai* [SH]; apsalqutnat *ai*;
    apsaqqutnat *ai*; have one's ~ open
    pantunepit *ai*; foam at the ~ pisewtuna:t *ai*;
    my ~ ntun; open one's ~ pantuna:sit *ai*;
    open one's ~ wide ta'utna:sit *ai*; open
    someone's ~ wide ta'utna:l'k *ta*, ta'utna:tu *ti*
move maja:sit *ai*; go or ~ along pemiyaq *ii*,
    pemiyet *ai*; go or ~ well wel-pmiyaq *ii*; wel-
    pmiyet *ai*; ~ across the river ejikliwsit *ai*; ~
    away ejikliwsit *ai*; ~ well weliyaq *ii*, weliyet
    ai; one who ~ **-s** about nuji-alapit *ai (an)*; ~
    down (to the flat) metoqwiwsit *ai*; ~ in (to
    settle down) pejiwsit *ai*; ~ out tewiwsit *ai*; ~
    up (in the world) wenaqto:sit *ai*
movement how much ~ ? ta:s ajiyet *ai*
much pikwelk *ai, ii* [BR]; pukwelk *ai, ii*; do ~
    meka:teket *ai*; me:ka:teket *ai*; eat ~
    pisoqotalk *ai*; drink too ~ of wesamqwat *ai*;
    have how ~ (many) of? ta:sunk *ta*; have ~ of
    meken'k *ta*, meken'm *ti*; how ~ ? ta:s'k *ii*,
    ta:sit *ai*; tatuji(w); how ~ (in price)? tal awtik
    ii, tal awtit *ai*; like very ~ ma:muniksalk *ta*;
    not as ~ je mu; too ~ wesamelk *ai, ii*
mucus my nasal ~ nuja:lam *an*
mud sisku; ~ **-dy** siskuwik *ii*; ~ **-dy** (dirty)
    water siskuwapu; slightly ~ **-dy** in color
    ami-siskuwapuwaq *ii*
mud hen qoqwejimuj *an* [SH]
mud turtle amaliknoqji:j *an* [SH]
muffler qotaqanikjipilaqan
mumps have the ~ w'lukwe:ket *ai*
murderer a ~ ne:pateket *ai (an)*
murky mesamu:k *ii* (of liquids) [SH]
muscle pull a ~ pestaqa:l'k *ta*, pestaqa:tu *ti*
muscular melkiyaqasit *ai*
mush sapan

mushroom lketu *an* [SH]; sqoljuwi:kan; gather
    ~ **-s** lketuweket *ai* [SH]
music make ~ ketu:muwet *ai*; make ~ for
    ketu:maq *ta*; make ~ on a horn or wind
    instrument pipukwet *ai*
musician a ~ nuji-pipukwet *ai (an)*
Muskadabit m'skuto:kuk [SH]
muskrat ki:kwesu *an*; ~ root ki:kasuwaskw;
    ki:kwesuwaskw (good for colds; mix with gin
    after boiling in water; chew on it)
mussel (freshwater) ~ sipuwe:s *an*
mustard lamutta:lt (Fr *le moutarde*)
mythical a ~ being luks *an*

N

nag ~ about sespumk *ta*, sesputm *ti*

nail pleku (Fr *les clous?*); small ~ pleku:ji:j

naive nutqwe:k *ai*

naked emisqapit *ai*; emisqe:k *ai, ii*; half ~ metaqapit *ai*, metaqatek *ii*

name wisun; ewi:t'k *ta*, ewi:tm *ti*; wisunkalk *ta*, wisunkatm *ti*; wisunkewk *ta*; have many ~ -s miliwisik *ii*, miliwisit *ai*; have many ~ -s for mili-wi:t'k *ta*, mili-wi:tm *ti*; ~ backwards kiwaskiwi:tm *ti*; say or ~ wrong o:pl-wi:t'k *ta*, o:pl-wi:tm *ti*; ~ -d or called teluwisik *ii*, teluwisit *ai*

nap take a ~ nepa:ji:jit *ai*

nape ~ of the neck walkwe:taqan [BR]; walkwi:taqanat *ai (an)*

narrow cut into ~ strips aps'sm *ti*, aps:sk *ta*; have a ~ nose apsisqonat *ai*; insufficiently ~ notqwi-jijikwe:jk *ii*, notqwi-jijikwe:jit *ai*; ~ enough wel-jijikwe:jk *ii*, wel-jijikwe:jit *ai* [BR]; too ~ wesami-jijikwe:jk *ii*

narrows tuwitn [SH]

nasal speak with a ~ twang kepitni:sit *ai* [BC]

navel my ~ nili

near kikjiw; tepaw; wejuwaqateskaq *ta*, wejuwaqateskm *ti*; lie ~ kikjiw-eloqpit *ai* [SH]

nearsighted kikjapit *ai*; kekapit *ai* [SH]; pasapit *ai*

neat pekaje:k *ai, ii*; waqamn'mat *ai*; do ~ -ly pekaja:l'k *ta*, pekaja:tu *ti*

necessarily ~ so amuj (an interjection)

necessity of ~ amujpa (an interjection)

neck an animal with a long ~ pitoqoluwajit (pitoqoluwajijik) *ai (an)*; break off at the ~ temkwa:l'k *ta*; chop off at the ~ temkwete:k *ta*, temkwete:m *ti*; cut or slice off at the ~ temkwesk *ta*, temkwesm *ti*; have a strong ~ melki:taqanat *ai*; my ~ nji:taqan; put one's arms around the ~ of ke:kuluskwa:l'k *ta*; snap off at the ~ temiskipeket *ai*

necklace p'skukun

necktie qotaqanikjipilo:qon [SH]

need ketuwapemk *ta*, ketuwapetm *ti*; menuweketu *ti*, menuweke:k *ta*; pawalk *ta*, pawatm *ti*; pewalk *ta*, pewatm *ti*; puwalk *ta*, puwatm *ti* [SH]; have ~ of wetmite:l'mk *ta*, wetmite:tm *ti*; use occasionally as ~ -ed

wetmeyaq *ta*, wetmo:tm *ti*; ~ -ed menuweket *ai*

needle sa:qati *an*; fir, pine or spruce ~ kniskwastu *an*; knitting ~ qasawo:qu:j

needly ~ or prickly (of a limb) sa:qatiju:waq *ii*

negative future ~ ma; ma:

negotiate aknutmajik (pl) *ai*

neighbour my ~ nikmaj *an*

nephew my ~ nuluks, nuluks'ji:j *an* [BR]; my ~ or niece nkoji:j *an*

nervous nepe:k *ai*

nest wisse:j; wissey; animal ~ wisnuti [BR]; bird ~ wt'si [RB]; ~ (as a bird) etnesink *ai* [SH]

net dip ~ nqani:kn *an*; ko:pikn *an*; fish with a ~ a:piyet *ai*; grilse ~ taqawan api *an*; have a ~ a:pimit *ai*; a:piya:q (a:piya:m) *ai* [SH]; my ~ nta:pim *an*; nuta:pi *an* [ESK]; pull a ~ from the water natqa:piyet *ai*; remove (fish) from a ~ mena:piyet *ai*

nettle stinging ~ kinikwejij *an*

never menaq

new piley; ~ camp pilikan; ~ cloth pilekn; ~ potato piliman *an*; very ~ maw-piley; ~ -est one pajiji-piley *an, in*; ~ -ly blazed pili-jilta:sik *ii* [BR]

New Brunswick sikniktewa:kik

New Carlisle anntakuwejuwe:kati

news aknutmaqan; surprising ~ pa:qala'iwaqan

newspaper wi:katikn

New Year give the ~ -s greeting puna:newit *ai* [BC] (Fr *Bonne Année*); ~ -'s Day puna:newumk

next stand ~ in line to (of succession) e:taqaq *ta*

nibble qaskwatalk *ai*

nice kelu:lk *ii*, kelu:sit *ai*; kelu:sit *ai*; welpit *ai*, weltek *ii*; a ~ breeze welekisk *ii*; have a ~ countenance welikwetutk (welikwetutm) *ai*; have a ~ odor welimasit *ai*, welimatek *ii*; have ~ shaped antlers or horns kesi:wesmat *ai* [BR]; kesiw'lismat *ai* [BR]; ~ and fat welkamit *ai* [RB]

nice-looking wikwasapewit

niece my ~ nsm, nsmji:j *an*; my nephew or ~ nkoji:j *an*

night tepkik (period between midnight and
  dawn); wela:kw; every ~ te:sitpa:q *ii*; how
  many ~ -s? ta:sitpa:q *ii*; in the middle of the
  ~ miyawitpa:q *ii*; last ~ wela:kwe:k; one ~
  nekwtitpa:q *ii* [BR]; six ~ -s as'kom-te:sitpa:q
  ii; stay or pass the ~ etliktuknit *ai*; stay up
  all ~ wapnapit *ai*; the ~ before last ktiki-
  w'la:kwe:k; kt'k-w'la:kw [BR]; three ~ -s
  nesitpa:q *ii*; two ~ -s tapuwitpa:q *ii*
nightfall approach or come ~ wejkwitpa:q *ii*
nine ~ (in counting) peskunatek
ninety ~ (in counting) peskunatek-te:sinska:q
  [BR]
nipple nunu:n *an*
nit kna:ji:j *an*
no moqwa
nobody moqwa: wen (wenik) *an*; moqwe wen
  (wenik) [BR]
nod ew'naskwetesink *ai* [BR]; move along ~
  ding one's head pematkwetesink *ai*
nois-e go by making a ~ pemta:q *ii*; make a
  loud ~ kesikawta:q *ii*; make a loud ~ or
  report kesikawtesiket *ai*; make a loud ~
  (with the voice) kesikawtoqsit *ai*; make
  continuous ~ sespeta:q *ii*, sespetoqsit *ai*;
  ~ -y kinta:q *ii* [EG]; sespe:k *ai, ii*; sespena:q
  ii, sespenoqsit *ai*
none moqwa: koqwey; moqwe koqowey [BR]
nonsense talk ~ papewo:kwet *ai*
noon miyawla:kwek *ii*; miyawna:kwek *ii*
no one moqwa: wen (wenik) *an*; moqwe wen
  (wenik) [BR]
normal nestuwe:k *ai*
north oqwatn; go ~ so:qiyet *ai*, so:qiyaq *ii*;
  take to the ~ so:qwa:l'k *ta*, so:qwa:tu *ti*
northeast wind wejipek *ii* [CB]
northern lights mekwatesk [SH]
northwind oqwatk *ii*
nose have a large ~ maqisqonat *ai*; have a
  cold ~ kewjisqonat *ai* [ESK]; have a narrow ~
  apsisqonat *ai*; my ~ nsisqon
nosebleed have a ~ pa:kitnet *ai* [PEI];
  pe'i:kitnet *ai*
nosey ne:tapit *ai*
nostril bleed from the ~ pe'i:kitnet *ai*;
  pejikitnet *ai*; my ~ nitn; have wide ~ -s
  maqitnat *ai*

not mo (a negative particle); mo (a negative
  particle); mu (a negative particle); can ~
  me:si (used with non negative verb); ~ as
  much je mu; ~ even je mu; jel mu (takes
  negative verb form) [BR]; ~ yet menaq
  (takes negative verb)
nothing moqwe koqowey [BR]; moqwa:
  koqwey
notice make self ~ -d ke:tane:k *ai* [PEI]
notify keknuwa:taq *ta (do)*
Nova Scotia mainland ~ elmiwktaqamu:k
  [BR]; enmiktaqamu:k
November kep't'kewiku:s
novice pile:sm (pile:smuk) *an*
now nike:; n'ke:; n'ku:; for ~ pe:l
nude emisqapit *ai*; strip self ~ emisqa:sit *ai*
numb pilse:k *ai*; pisse:k *ai*; sa:qatiju:waq *ii*
  (of a limb); become ~ pissiyet *ai*; have a ~
  mouth pissaqqutnat *ai*
nun aniyapsuwinuwi:skw
  (aniyapsuwinuwi:skwaq) *an*; patliya:si:skw
  (patliya:si:skwaq) *an*
nurser a ~ nuseskwet *ai (an)*
nut pqan [BR]
Nyanza, N.B. waqam'tkuk

oak ~ tree mimkwaqanimusi [BR]

oar ji:maqan; my ~ ntaqan [SH]; ntu:taqan; sculling ~ sno:pi [NB]

oath eluwi:tmasuti; luwi:tmasuti [BR]; take an ~ eluwi:tmasit *ai*

oats te:sipowmann (pl)

obey telisqataq *ta*

object tool or ~ requiring use of both hands tapuwapjimkewey *an, in*; useful ~ or tool wetmo:taqan

observe nutamk *ta*, nutaptm *ti* [BC]; an ~ -r nutapteket *ai (an)* [BC]

obtain ~ meat ne:patu *ti*

occasional ekel; use ~ -ly as needed wetmeyaq *ta*, wetmo:tm *ti*

ocean kta:n

ochre red ~ wewkujan *an*

o'clock ajiyet *ai*

October wikewiku:s; wikuwowiku:s [CB]

odd do ~ jobs matu:-lukwet *ai (an)*; speak in an ~ or unusual way kesmi:sit *ai*

odor have a nice ~ welimasit *ai*, welimatek *ii*; have a strong unpleasant ~ kesima:q *ii*, kesima:t *ai*

of course! tal ma:

off bite ~ temp'k *ta*; temtm *ti*; chop ~ temte:k *ta*, temte:m *ti* [CB]; get ~ kepta:s'k *ii*, kepta:sit *ai*; have a foot or leg cut ~ temikatat *ai*; knock ~ mente:k *ta*, mente:m *ti*; rip ~ menipka:l'k *ta*, menipka:tu *ti*; kick ~ menkaq *ta*, menkm *ti*; take ~ mena:l'k *ta*, mena:tu *ti*; take ~ (using the foot) menkaq *ta*, menkm *ti*; throw ~ keptaqalk *ta*, keptaqtu *ti*

offer ~ one's hand eliska:sit *ai* [BC]

often kaqi:sk

oil mimey; coal ~ ko:layl; covered with grease and ~ (as a mechanic) mimsit *ai*; hair ~ mimkwaqan [BR]; have on perfume, lotion or ~ mimkwat *ai*

OK! na to:q

old get ~ kisiku:waq *ii*, kisiku:wet *ai*; kisikuwiyet *ai* [BR]; how ~ ? ta:sipuna:t *ai*; tatuje:k *ai*; ta'uje:k *ai*; ~ animal kisiku:sm (kisiku:smuk) *an*; ~ beaver kisiku:mskw *an*; ~ camp sa:qawikan [BR]; ~ canoe or boat kisiku:lkw [BR]; ~ or worn out article sa:qawejjuwey; something ~ kisikuwey *an, in*; something that is ~ sa:qawey *an, in*; ~ -er me: kisikuwit *ai*

older sister have an ~ w'misit *ai*; my ~ numis *an* [PEI]; n'mis *an*

oldest the ~ one (person) amkwesewa:j *an*

old man kisiku *an*; kisikuwo:p *an* (pejorative) [SH]; my dear ~ nkisikum *an* (term of affection, wife to husband)

old person act like an ~ kisiku:qamiksit *ai*; ~ kisikuwa:sit *ai* [BR]; walk like an ~ kisiku:l'ka:t *ai*

old woman kisiku:skw (kesiku:skwaq) *an*; kisikuwi:skw (kisikuwi:skwaq) *an*; my dear ~ nkisikuwi:skum *an* (term of affection for a wife); my ~ nmi: (voc) (a term of affection and respect)

omipotent mawiknat *ai*

on get in or ~ (a vehicle) tepu:sit *ai* [SH]; get ~ tepa:sit *ai*; get ~ or in a vehicle teppit *ai*, teptek *ii*

once ~ long ago nekwt sa:q; ~ upon a time ki:s sa:q; nekwt sa:q [SH]

one nekwte:jk *ii*, nekwte:jit *ai* [BR]; newte: (with inanimate nouns); newte:jit *ai*, newte:jk *ii*; have ~ leg or foot newtikatat *ai*; have ~ newtunk *ta*; have only ~ of wipskunk *ta*, wipskun'm *ti*; ~ kind newtunemiksijik (pl) *an*, newtunemi:kl (pl) *in*; ~ (of something round and solid) newtapsk'sit *ai*; newtapskek *ii*; ~ day nekwti-kisk'k [BR]; ~ dollar nekwta:'ik *ii* [BR]; newkta'ik *ii*; ~ (in counting) nekwt [BR]; ne:kwt [BR]; newkt; newt; ~ (of something long and narrow, cylindrical) newtoqsit *ai*; ~ (of something round and solid) nekwtapsk'sit *ai*, nekwtapskek *ii* [BR]; ~ (of something thin and flat) newtanqasit *ai*, newtanqek *ii*; stand or slide on ~ leg newtikata:lukwet *ai*

one-eyed newtalqikwat *ai*

one-legged temikatat *ai* [PEI]

one time at ~ amkwes

on fire feel as if ~ wi:sik'sit *ai*, wi:sik'tek *ii*

onion pse:s's *an* [SH]

only pasik [CB]; pas'k; just ~ jil pas'k

onset the ~ of war poqjinntimk

on time catch or get ~ keskute:k *ta*, keskute:m *ti*; ~ for keskuteskmat *ai*

ooze ~ out tewalqiyaq *ii*, tewalqiyet *ai* [SH]

open ni:laje:k *ai* [BC]; pana:l'k *ta*, pana:tu *ti*; pantepit *ai*, pantetek *ii*; cut ~ pans'k *ta*, pansm *ti*; have one's mouth ~ pantunepit *ai*; ~ (someone's mouth) wide ta'utna:l'k *ta*, ta'utna:tu *ti*; ~ up pana:s'k *ii*, pana:sit *ai*; panta:l'k *ta*, panta:tu *ti*; ~ (the mouth) wide ta'utna:sit *ai*; run out in the ~ (from the thicket) muski:pit *ai*

operate pemeyaq *ta*, pemo:tm *ti*

operate on pans'k *ta*, pansm *ti*

opinion tel-te:qan [PEI]; have a high ~ of oneself me:kitelsit *ai*; have an ~ about tel-te:tm *ti* [PEI]; my ~ npi:nem [SH]

or kisna

orchard eletqek *ii*

order natkimk *ta*, natkitm *ti*; natkiteket *ai*

orders give ~ ilsuteket *ai*

organ ~ (taken from a pig to predict the weather) psikweta:w *an*

organize iltaqane:walk *ta*, iltaqane:watm *ti*; an ~ -er mawiyaqa:teket *ai (an)* [BC]

originate ~ from tle:yawit *ai*; wetapaqamit *ai* [SH]

orphan ns'tnaqan *an*; ~ -ed (spring-born) animal sikuniyej *an* [BR]

other ktik *an, in*; an ~ kt'k *an* [SH]; on the ~ side a:se:k (loc)

otter kiw'nik *an*

ought to lawtis [SH]

ours kinuwewey *an, in* (inclusive); ninenewey *an, in* (exclusive)

out beat ~ (a fire) naqasuwete:k *ta*, naqasuwete:m *ti*; get ~ of kepta:s'k *ii*, kepta:sit *ai*; get ~ of the water natqa:sit *ai*; pry ~ ketalqikwalk *ta*, ketalqikwatm *ti*; push ~ tewiksma:l'k *ta*, tewiksma:tu *ti*; stamp ~ (a fire) naqasuweteskaq *ta*, naqasuweteskm *ti*; stick ~ tewaqpit *ai*, tewaqtek *ii*; tewoqpit *ai*, tewoqtek *ii*; muskask'pit *ai*, muskask'tek *ii*; take or put ~ tewa:l'k *ta*, tewa:tu *ti*; take ~ from (underneath) wejiktalqa:l'k *ta*, wejiktalqa:tu *ti*; take ~ of ketalqa:l'k *ta*, ketalqa:tu *ti*

outargue ejoqjemk *ta*; we:kwa:maq *ta*

outdoors kujmuk

outhouse mi:jano:kuti [SH]; mi:jano:kuwom

outside kijimuk [BR]; kujmuk; kujm; eat ~ tewatalk *ai*; follow ~ tewukkwalk *ta*, tewukkwatm *ti*; go ~ tewiyet *ai*

outspread fall back with legs ~ panjaskiyet *ai*

outtalk apjimk *ta*; maqanimk *ta*

outwit maqana:l'k *ta*; ~ -ted maqanat *ai*

over blown ~ keskiss'k *ii*

over piyamiw; a:sispit *ai*, a:sistek *ii*; climb ~ a:sisapekit *ai*; fall ~ kewiyaq *ii*, kewiyet *ai*; fly ~ keskijaqsink *ai*; flow ~ weskitpeka:s'k *ii*, weskitpeka:sit *ai*; flown ~ keskiss'k *ii*, keskissink *ai*; go or pass ~ keskija:sit *ai*; go ~ a:sisa:sit *ai*; go ~ to quickly elateja:sit *ai*; go ~ the head of someone in authority pemkaq *ta*, pemkm *ti*; ~ the hill elqamkuk; promote ~ pemkaq *ta*, pemkm *ti*; put ~ keskija:l'k *ta*, keskija:tu *ti*; run ~ mikuteskaq *ta*, mikuteskm *ti*; mukuteskaq *ta*, mukuteskm *ti*; rush ~ toward elateja:sit *ai*; tipped ~ aputansk'pit *ai*, aputansk'tek *ii* [PEI]; turn ~ kawaska:sit *ai*; kawaskeka:l'k *ta*, kawaskeka:tu *ti*; turn ~ (while prone) kinawskismtesink *ai* [BR]; kawask'smtesink *ai*; turn self ~ kawaskisma:sit *ai*; turn (something) ~ kawaskeket *ai*; way ~ o:piyamiw

overcharge wesama:maq *ta*

overcoat weskitmaskut (weskitmaskujik *an*

overcome wissuwiknemk *ta*, wissuwiknetm *ti*

overcook wesamoqs'k *ta*, wesamoqsm *ti*; ~ -ed wesamoqsit *ai*, wesamoqtek *ii*; wasamoqsit *ai* [PEI]

overdo me:ka:teket *ai*; pajjaqamat *ai*; wesama:sit *ai* [BC]

overeat wesamatalk *ai*

overflow pa'itepeka:s'k *ii*, pa'itepeka:sit *ai*; pajitpeka:s'k *ii*, pajitpeka:sit *ai* [SH]

overhead k'p'tay

overhear ams'tk *ta*, ams'tm *ti* [SH]; keskustaq *ta*, keskustm *ti*; mikustaq *ta*, mikustm *ti*

overheard ~ talking metewo:kwet *ai*; ~ talking in anger metewiluwa:t *ai*

overload ~ (someone's) plate wesam'la:maq
   ta (do); ~ **-ed** tmaqanikju:waq *ii*,
   tmaqanikju:wet *ai*
overlook ~ an offense apiksiktaq *ta*
overpower wissuwiknemk *ta*, wissuwiknetm *ti*;
   wisuwiknemk *ta*
overturn kawaska:l'k *ta*, kawaska:tu *ti*;
   kinawska:l'k *ta* [BR]
over with kaqi net [BC]
owe tettaq *ta*; ~ a bill tettuwet *ai*; ask for
   money ~ **-d** netutmat *ai*
owl ku:ku:kwes *an* [RB]; ku:ku:wes *an*; great
   horned ~ ti:tikli *an* [SH]
own alsumk *ta*, alsutm *ti* [SH]; assumk *ta*,
   assutm *ti*; ~ all of kaqi-alsumk *ta*, kaqi-
   alsutm *ti* [BC]; something ~ **-ed** alsutaqan
   [SH]
ownership assutaqan
ox ketapet (ketapejik) *an* [SH]; kwetapet
   (kwetapejik) *an* [CB]
oyster m'ntmu *an*; t'mtmu *an*

P

Pabineau ke:kapskwesk [RB]

pacify apknuwalk *ta* [BR]; petkimk *ta*

pack ilajit *ai*; carry or ~ on the shoulder
eln'ket *ai*; ~ a pipe papnsit *ai* [BR]; stuff or ~
a pipe pi:tmat *ai*; start to ~ naji-ilajit *ai*

package (gift) ~ iloqomoqwa:taqan

pack basket anapik [SH]

pack down ~ (to make more room) sina:l'k *ta*,
sina:tu *ti*

pad writing ~ ewi:kikemkewey

paddle lu:ta:qan; uta:qan [BR]; u:ta:qan;
stern ~ sno:pi ji:matm *ti*; ji:met *ai*; Indian ~
lnuwipi [SH]; nnu wipi [CB]; my ~ nta:qan;
ntaqan; ntu:taqan; nu:ta:qan [BC]; ~ about
(while eeling) al-komit *ai* [PEI]; ~ along
pemisukwit *ai*; ~ along the shore pemi-
jajikisukwit *ai*; ~ off poqtisukwit *ai*; ~ or pole
alone or singlehanded jikalukk (jikalukum) *ai*;
~ or row along pem-ji:malk *ta*, pem-ji:matm
ti; pem-ji:met *ai*; ~ toward elisukwit *ai*; ~
toward shore wejkwi-na:taqamisukwit *ai*;
come ~ -ing toward wejkwisikwit *ai* [CB]

pail la:taqsun *an*; samqwano:q *an*; the
equivalence of a ~ in volume la:taqsuna:laq
ii, la:taqsuna:lat *ai*; milk pitcher or ~
m'lakejuwo:q *an*

paint pent (pentik) *an*; penta:l'k *ta*, penta:tu *ti*;
weskijiyama:l'k *ta*, weskijiyama:tu *ti*; ~ for
penta:tekewk *ta*

painter a ~ nuji-milamukwa:teket *ai (an)*

pair have a ~ of horns wesemuwit *ai*; a ~ (of
deuces) ta:puwaq *an*; go in ~ -s
toqwanqapultijik (pl) *ai*; have two ~ -s (of a
kind) tapu-nemi:k *ta*; work in ~ -s toqo-
lukwejik (pl); ~ -ed up (in stud poker)
toqanqajat *ai*

palate my ~ njoqj'te:kn; njoqolqote:kn'm

pale wap'staqe:q *ai*; look ~ wap'staqapewit
ai; ~ green wap'stoqon-amuksit *ai*,
wapistoqon-amu:k *ii*

pallbearer a ~ pema:teket *ai*

palm ~ of the hand lamipjan; lamiptn

pan w'laqan *an* [BR]; ash ~ t'pkwaniptaqan *an*
[SH]; frying ~ lapuwe:l *an* (Fr *la poêle*);
sisla:kwa:temkewey; iron ~ qasawo:qey
lapuwe:'lji:j; ~ bullmoose w'laqane:s *an* [BR]

pancake sisla:kwa:taqan

paper wi:katikn; piece of ~ wi:katikne:ji:j

parboil kulapuwalk *ta*, kutapuwatm *ti*

pardon apiksiktaq *ta*

parent my ~ n'nki:kw (n'nki:kuk) *an*; my ~ -s
(father dominant) nujjewijik (pl) *an*; my ~ -s
(mother dominant) nkijewijik (pl) *an*

parrot pelakwet *an* (Fr *perroquet*)

part pukwey; in ~ anapiw; reluctant to ~ with
keskel'mk *ta*, keskeltm *ti*; ~ -ly anapiw;
~ -ly strained amins'tuwe:k *ai*

partition temsaqas'k; a ~ pemsaqiyaq *ii (in)*
[SH]; ~ off ilsaqam *ti*; the other side of a ~
or obstacle a:sey

partner my ~ nmakkupe:l'm *an* [SH];
n'naqapem *an* (the godparent of one's child);
~ -s in a boat (used in guiding) wituwa:tijik
(pl) *ai*

partridge plawej *an*; young ~ plawe:si:s *an*

part-time a ~ worker matuwe:k *ai*

pass pemkaq *ta*, pemkm *ti*; ~ by crying pemi-
siyawtemit *ai* [BR]; ~ through saputa:s'k *ii*,
saputa:sit *ai*; ~ by (in the air) pemsink *ai*,
pems'k *ii*

pass out ~ (from fatigue) mesqaniyet *ai*; ~
(from drinking) pemto:kwet *ai*

past go ~ pemkaq *ta*, pemkm *ti*; go or kick ~
(in time) pemk'k *ta*, pemkm *ti* [SH]

paste sapan

pastry make all kinds of ~ miloqsawet *ai*

pasture milatuwat *ai*

patch mesni:s'k *ta*, mesni:sm *ti*; pekwi:s'k *ta*,
pekwi:sm *ti*

pate ke:kwatpan; my ~ (top of the head)
nke:kwatpan

pâté tepa:te (Fr *des pâtés*)

paternal on my ~ side nujjewiktuk (loc)

path awti:j; lead off (as of a ~) pesk'tek *ii*;
go towards the road or ~ matama:sit; reach
the end of the ~ matawa:sit *ai* [BC]

paw have small hands or ~ -s apsiptnat *ai*

pay ~ check apank'tuwowey [PEI]; ~ day
apankitatimk; apank'talinik [PEI]; ~ for
apankimk *ta*, apankitm *ti*; ~ for something
apankitaq *ta*; ~ back asita:teket *ai*

payment apankituwowey

pea alawey

peaked cap kinijkej *an* [SH]; kiniskwejewey [BC]

pear amjoqtelikn [SH]

peavey hook pi:pi *an*

peddle ~ about alankuwalk *ta*, alankuwetu *ti*; alankuwat *ai*; ~ along pemankuwat *ai*

peddler petley (petleyaq) *an*; a ~ alanku:sit *ai (an)*; elanku:sit *ai (an)* [BC]; nujintuwisket *ai (an)*

peek kimapit *ai*; ~ at kimamk *ta*, kimaptm *ti*; ~ in piskwapa:sit *ai*; ~ into pu:tapit *ai*; ~ through pu:tapa:sit *ai*

peel pekwa:q *ta*, pekwa:m *ti*; pelkoqsewet *ai* [BR]; pelkoqsawet *ai*; pelqa:l'k *ta*, pelqa:tu *ti*; ~ (as from a sunburn) pesqayet *ai*; ~ by hand pelkoqa:l'k *ta*, pelkoqa:tu *ti*; ~ with a knife pelkoqs'k *ta*, pelkoqsm *ti*; ~ -ing pelkoqsikn; ~ -ing (from a fruit or vegetable) piwtikn

peer ~ into a hollow pu:tapa:sit *ai*

pellet small lead ~ sqolu:skuji:j

pen wi:kikn *an*

penance make do ~ aniyapsu:tlk *ta*

pencil ewi:kikemkewey; wi:kikn *an*

penetrate muskask'pit *ai*, muskask'tek *ii*; pitansk'pit *ai*, pitansk'tek *ii* [SH][PEI]; pitask'pit *ai*, pitask'tek *ii*; sa:p'k *ta*, sa:pm *ti*; sepp'saqa:s'k *ii*, sepp'saqa:sit *ai*; sepp'saqa:l'k *ta*, sepp'saqa:tu *ti*; ~ beneath pitoqtek *ii*; ~ through saputaskiyaq *ii*, saputaskiyet *ai*; ~ -d into sepp'saqapit *ai*, sepp'saqatek *ii*

penis have a small ~ apso:qonmat *ai*; his ~ wilqi; my ~ nilqi [SH]; ni:p

penitent aniyapsuwinu *an*

penny maqtawa:qewey [NB]

people little ~ who live in caves tmikalmji:jk (pl) *an* [SH]; my ~ ni:kmatut (voc) *an*; (Annapolis) valley ~ kespukwitkewaq

pepper te:pisewey; te:pisawey [PEI] (Fr *des épices*); add ~ te:pisawa:tat *ai*

perch wisnaw (wisnaq) *an*; salt water ~ jakj'ke:j *an* [RB]; yellow ~ ejaqaluwej *an* [RB]

perfume masu:mi; mimkwaqan; have on ~ , lotion or oil mimkwat *ai*

perhaps etuk; jiptuk; jiptuke:l [CB]

perish ketemenejik (pl) *ai*

periwinkle jik'ji:j(i:j) *an* [RB]

permission go ask ~ (of fiancee's parents) to get married naj-kluluwet *ai*; request ~ (of parents) to marry daughter keluluwet *ai*

permit asite:l'mk *ta*; ikn'maq *ta (do)*

person nnu *an* [BR]; lnu *an*; mimajiwinu *an*; wskijin *an*; gifted ~ wskijin *an* (a Maliseet word); poor ~ ew'le:jiwanu *an* [SH]; ew'le:jiwinu *an*; tenth ~ mtl'newa:j *an*; (Annapolis) valley ~ kespukwitnewa:j *an* [SH]

personable ni:laje:k *ai*

persuade mussayaq *ta*, musso:tm *ti*

pest a ~ siwa:teket *ai (an)*

pester wetmeyaq *ta*, wetmo:tm *ti* [ESK]

pet etlipulk *ta*, etliputu *ti*; my ~ ntuwe:m *an*

photograph napuwi:kikn *an*; a ~ -er napuwi:kiket *ai (an)*

pick ~ berries ewisit *ai* [CB]; ~ up meknk *ta*, mekn'm *ti*; ~ wenaqa:l'k *ta*, wenaqa:tu *ti*; ~ hurriedly ew'nasimknasit *ai* [BR]

picker potato ~ or harvester ke:tipnewinu *an*

picture napuwi:kikn *an*; holy ~ or medal pess'mkewey *an*; take a ~ of napuwi:k'k *ta*, napuwi:km *ti*; take ~ -s napuwi:kiket *ai (an)*

pie petaqan; piece of ~ petaqanji:j (petaqanji:tl)

piece mussew (mussal) (Fr *morceau*); pukwey; a little ~ or bit musse:j; of one ~ mese:k *ai (an)* [BC]; ~ of paper wi:katikne:ji:j; small ~ mussewji:j; cut into ~ -s nuks'k *ta*, nuksm *ti*

pierce sapalqate:k *ta*, sapalqate:m *ti*; sa:p'k *ta*, sa:pm *ti*; penetrate or ~ through (with bullet or arrow) saputetelaq *ta*, saputetel'm *ti*; ~ through sapalqek *ii*; saputete:k *ta*, saputete:m *ti*; ~ -d (as in the hand or foot) mesqolit *ai*; ~ -d (by heat) paskoqsit *ai*, paskoqtek *ii*

pig kulkwi:s *an*

pigeon ples *an*

pile elamko:l'k *ta*, elamko:tu *ti*; ~ -d elamko:tas'k *ii*, elamko:tasit *ai*; ~ -d deep paspit *ai*, pastek *ii*; ~ -d together maw-amk'pijik (pl) *an*, maw- amk'tekl (pl) *ii*; ~ -d up along elm'joqtek *ii*

pillow kwa:taqan [SH]; tu:kwesmun
pimple pukliye:wey
pin safety ~ sipistaqano:suti *an*
pincers n'mtm'tqa:luwe:l (pl)
pinch mittoqopqa:l'k *ta*, mittoqopqa:tu *ti* [BC];
   m'ntoqopsqa:l'k *ta*, m'ntoqopsqa:tu *ti*;
   n'm'mtoqopqa:l'k *ta*; n'mtawa:tu *ti*;
   n'mtm'tqa:luwet *ai*
pin down hold or ~ by covering
   malkupaqteskaq *ta*, malkupaqteskm *ti*
pine kuwow (kuwaq) *an*
pinfish amjilakwej *an* [CB]
pint suppin *an*
pipe[1] tmaqan *an* (for smoking); my ~
   nutmaqan *an*; wetmamkewey; light up a ~
   pask'semk *ta*; the devil's ~ ! m'ntu
   wutmaqan (an interjection)
pipe[2] coupled ~ a:papi *an* [CB]
pipestone tmaqanapskw
pit[1] nijinj (nijinjik) *an*; wipkoman
pit[2] wowj *an*
pitch pku *an*
pitcher laklus [SH] (Fr *la cruche*); milk ~ or
   pail m'lakejuwo:q *an*; water ~ samqwano:q
   an
place ika:l'k *ta*, ika:tu *ti*; bead ~
   wayo:pskwe:kati [BR]; my ~ nt'pun; ~ -d
   epit *ai*, etek *ii*; ~ -d (in bulk) elo:l'k *ta*, elo:tu
   ti
plan ilsuteket *ai*
plane mikuteket *ai* (as in carpentry)
plank ti:ls (ti:lsik) *an* (Eng. deal)
plant ika:taqalk *ta*, ika:taqatm *ti*; ika:taquk *ai*;
   ika:taqulk *ta*, ika:taqutm *ti*; sow or ~ for
   ika:taqewk *ta*
plate lasiyet *an* (Fr *l'assiette*); nasiyet *ai* (Fr
   l'assiette; *une assiette?*); w'laqan *an* [BR];
   wooden ~ used in dice game waltes *an* [SH]
platter birchbark dish or ~ wijkwe:tlaqan *an*
play etl-te:k *ta*, etl-te:m *ti*; mila:sit *ai*; ~ a
   musical instrument ketu:muwet *ai*; ~ around
   with mila:suwalk *ta*, mila:suwatm *ti*; ~ ball
   ajje:mat *ai*; ~ for ketu:maq *ta*; ~ for (in
   cards and board games) elaqalsewk *ta*; ~
   for self elaqalsewsit *ai*; ~ house wi:k ji:jat
   ai; ~ with malikeyaq *ta*, maliko:tm *ti*

playboy act the ~ sespo:teket *ai (an)*
player a poor ~ awan-mila:sit *ai*
please ke: [BC]; tetapuwa:l'k *ta*, tetapuwa:tu
   ti; wela:l'k *ta*, wela:tu *ti*; easily ~ naqsi-
   tetapuwa:l'k *ta*; naqsi-tetapuwa:tu *ti*; hard to
   ~ miliksnqwat *ai*; ~ by one's presence
   welteskaq *ta*
pleasing ki:waje:k *ai*
pleasureable happy, joyful or ~ (place)
   weskewina:q *ii* [SH]
pledge luwi:tmasuti; make a ~ eluwi:tmasit *ai*
plenty pukweliyaq *ii*, pukweliyet *ai*; eat ~ of
   mekepk *ta*, meketm *ti*; have ~ of pikweln'k
   ta, pikweln'm *ti* [BR]; pukwenn'k *ta*,
   pukwenn'm *ti*; pick ~ of mekete:k *ta*,
   mekete:m *ti*; win ~ of mekete:k *ta*,
   mekete:m *ti*
plow elkesawet *ai*; lkeso:qon; ~ slowly
   sankewsawet *ai*; ~ the land elkesm *ti*
pluck mena:l'k *ta*, mena:tu *ti*; ~ a chicken
   pesqo:l'k *ta*; ~ a string mattaqte:k *ta*,
   mattaqte:m *ti*
plug kepijoqwa:l'k *ta*, kepijoqwa:tu *ti*;
   kepjoqikn; pkijoqikn; ~ up kepjoqte:k *ta*,
   kepjoqte:m *ti*; ~ -ged kepjoqpit *ai*,
   kepjoqtek *ii* [SH]
pocket mapos (Fr *ma poche*); mappos; my
   ~ nmaposm; ntaposm; numapposm [PEI]
point elaska:l'k *ta*, elaska:tu *ti*; bring to a ~
   sepusa:l'k *ta*, sepusa:tu *ti*; bring to a ~ (as in
   knitting a sock or a mitt) sipn'ma:q *ta*,
   sipn'ma:m *ti*; have a sharp ~ kiniskwe:k *ai*,
   ii; join together (to make a ~) sipn'mi:ket
   ai; ~ of land wesawey; ~ toward
   eli:sqaqanek *ii* [BR]; elu:kwalk *ta*, ellu:kwatm
   ti; elu:kwalk *ta*, elu:kwatm *ti*; elu:kwek *ii*,
   elu:kwet *ai*; the ~ of a tree kini:skwakum
   [SH]; the ~ of a wikwam kini:swikuwom [SH]
pointed kiniskwe:k *ai*, *ii*; sharply ~ kiniskwik
   ii, kiniskwikit *ai*; ~ in all directions telask'tek
pointer lu:kwejk [SH]
poison ivy kjimskiku [BR]
poke ~ at pu:tasknk *ta*, pu:taskn'm *ti*; ~
   around pu:tasqi:ket *ai*; ~ into pu:taska:tu *ti*
poker furnace or fireplace ~ lu:se:kn; nuse:kn
Pole pepkijatpat *ai*; po:laks (po:laksik) *an*

pole[1] sumokati [SH]; s'mkwati [CB]; canoe ~ ki:kamko:n *an* [BC]; ~ (for hanging dried meat inside the wikwam) qoti [SH]; ~ or weighty object used to secure or hold down wikwam covering malqwi:kn [SH]; wigwam ~ p'si *an* [SH]; wigwam ~ (to hold down covering) poqonaqaluskw [SH]; entranceway ~ **-s** (for a wikwam) ka:qanipsi

pole[2] ~ along pemamkwe:ket *ai*; ~ (a boat) as far as the waterway permits we:kwamkwe:ket *ai*; start off poling (in a boat) poqtamkwe:ket *ai*

policeman kast'pl *an*; a ~ (the one who takes hold of you) nujiwsuwa:teket *ai (an)*

polish wasoqote:k *ta*, wasoqote:m *ti*

pollywog sqolj (sqoljik) *an* [SH]

poor ew'le:jk *ii*, ew'le:jit *ai*; a ~ worker awanlukwet *ai*; have ~ judgement awanitplu:teket *ai*; make a ~ selection winnat *ai*; ~ condition ew'le:jk *ii*, ew'le:jit *ai*; ~ person ew'le:jiwanu *an* [SH]; ew'le:jiwinu *an*

poorly eat ~ ettamit *ai*; matuwatalk *ai*; operate or handle ~ awaneyaq *ta*, awano:tm *ti*; ~ shod winsitat *ai* [RB]; ~ shoed winkutat *ai*; see ~ winapit *ai (an)*; malapit; speak ~ mali:sit *ai*; walk ~ malikatat *ai*

poplar miti *an*

porch tusati

porcupine matuwes *an*; ~ meat matuwesewey; provision with ~ netukuluwe:set *ai* [BR]

pork kulkwi:suwey

porpoise mujpe:j *an* [BR]; sea ~ a:k'tiyepis *an*

portage the name of a ~ trail located at present-day Micmac reserve wskma:taqanejk [SH]; ~ trail unikan [SH]

Port Hood, N.S. kwe:kwiyamkek

portion a ~ ta:s'ji:jit *ai*; ta:s'ji:jk *ii*

position change ~ (while lying prone) ilisma:sit *ai*; place or put in a proper ~ iloqwa:l'k *ta*, iloqwa:tu *ti*; stand into ~ il-pukuwa:sit *ai*

possess kekkun'm *ti*, kekkunk *ta*; kelkunk *ta* [BR]; kenkunk *ta*, kenkun'm *ti*; kewkunk *ta*; wesko:tm *ti*, weskweyaq *ta* [SH]

possession my ~ ntalikem [SH]; ntalikam; ntalsutaqan

post menjipukuwejk; fence ~ llutaqanatkw

pot wow *an*; my ~ ntuwowm *an*; copper ~ wisawo:q [SH]; flower ~ wasuweko:q; large cooking ~ saska:kwit; sasqa:kwit (sasqa:kwijik) *an*; small ~ (for cooking) sasqa:kwiji:jit *an*

potato maqtewiman *an* (alternate form) [SH]; tapatat *an* [SH]; tap'tan *an* (Fr *des patates*); tepatat *an* [BR] (Fr *des patates*); Indian ~ s'kepn *an* [SH]; new ~ piliman *an*; ~ basket tap'taney; ~ bug tap'tane:j *an*; wild ~ s'kepn *an*; wild ~ place s'kepne:kati

pouch poj *an* (Fr *poche*); wijipo:ti *an* (carried around the waist) [RB]; arrow ~ pitaqan [SH]; my ~ n'musti

pound[1] n'nkatikn (measurement of weight)

pound[2] ~ ash (to make basket splints) elikpete:ket *ai*; ~ on kelapaqte:k *ta*, kelapaqte:m *ti*; ~ or hack to bits sekwiste:k *ta*, sekwiste:m *ti*; heard ~ **-ing** metete:ket *ai*

pour kuta:l'k *ta*, kuta:tu *ti*; kuta:tat *ai*; ma:munlaq *ii*; ~ in pi:t'pet *ai*; ~ into el-kuta:l'k *ta*, el-kuta:tu *ti*; ~ oneself a drink el-kuta:tat *ai*; ~ thickly pelsit *ai*, peltek *ii*

powder gun ~ psew

power m'lkiknoti

praise kin-lu:kwalk *ta* [BC]; wel-lu:walk *ta*, wel-lu:watm *ti* (Fr *louer*); highly ~ **-d** me:kite:tasit *ai*, me:kite:tas'k *ii*; mekite:tasit *ai* [BC]

prankster a ~ wetmo:teket *ai (an)*; a joker, ~ or jester nuji-mila:teket *ai (an)*

prattle ~ or gab along pemtoqsit *ai*

pray alasutmat *ai* [BR]; a:sutmat *ai*; ~ for a:sutmessewatm *ti*, a:sutmessewk *ta* (Fr *messe*)

prayer alasutmaqan [BR]; a:sutmaqan

preach pestunk (pestun'm) *ai*; stop lecturing or ~ **-ing** punewistoq (punewistu) *ai*; a ~ **-er** nuji-pestunk *ai (an)*;

precious something or someone ~ ksite:taqan

precipice pemse:k (loc)

precocious kejitme:k *ai*

predict ikanite:tm *ti* [SH]

prefer piyamiksalk *ta*, piyamiksatm *ti*

pregnancy experience (as a male) ~ symptoms (as a result of having caused a woman to become pregnant) mikulltiyat *ai*

pregnant eskmaqtmat *ai*; tele:k *ai, ii*; become ~ out of wedlock) o:ple:k *ai*

prepare iltaqane:walk *ta*, iltaqane:watm *ti*; kiskaja:l'k *ta*, kiskaja:tu *ti*; ~ for ilaji:kewk *ta*; ilajit *ai*; ilajuktaq *ta*, ilajuktm *ti*; ~ lodging for ilaji:kewk *ta*; get ~ **-d** ilaji:kewsit *ai*; ~ **-d** kisa:tasit *ai*, kisa:tas'k *ii*; kiskatpit *ai*, kiskattek *ii*

preserve anko:tm *ti*, ankweyaq *ta*; apatu *ti*; fruit ~ papkoqsikn

press jink'ja:l'k *ta*, jink'ja:tu *ti*; ~ down (basket splints) esinoqjo:tu *ti* [BC]

pretend ~ to do ewsa:tu *ti*; ~ to sleep ewsinpat *ai* [BR]

pretty weli-ankamkusit *ai* [BC]; look ~ wikwasamuksit *ai*, wikwasamu:k *ii*

prewash kesispapal'k *ta*, kesispapatu *ti*

price ask a high ~ me:kusit *ai*

priest patliya:s *an* (Fr *patriarche*)

prime in one's ~ mesk'k (meskm) *ai*

Prince Edward Island epekwitk *ii*

prize kesite:l'm'k *ta*, kesite:tm *ti*

probably etuk jel; so ~ lo:q etuk [SH]

professional make ~ **-ly** nujitu *ti*, nuji:kik (pl) *ta*

profusely bleed ~ pukweliku:niyet *ai*

progressive ~ aspect etl(i) (grammar)

projection wesawey

promise teplumk *ta*, teplutm *ti* (Fr *des promesses?*)

promote ~ over pemkaq *ta*, pemkm *ti*

prone fall ~ ketkujetesk *ii*, ketkujetesink *ai*; get into a ~ position oqolumkwa:sit *ai*; lie ~ (on the belly) ketkukjesink *ai*

propeller fan or ~ wju:sney

proper buy the ~ or right one keknu:telaq *ta*, keknu:tel'm *ti*; do what is ~ or correct keknuwa:teket *ai*; place or put in a ~ position iloqwa:l'k *ta*, iloqwa:tu *ti*; take the right or ~ way tetapuwiwsuwa:tu *ti*; wear ~ clothes (for the season) welqwanet *ai*; do correctly or ~ **-ly** keknuwa:l'k *ta*, keknuwa:tu *ti*; dress ~ **-ly** ilpilk *ta*, ilpil'm *ti*; get ~ **-ly** dressed

ilpilsit *ai*; heat up ~ **-ly** wel-p'sk *ta*, wel-p'sm *ti*

property my ~ nutumo:taqan'm; personal ~ alsutaqan

prophet nikanikjitekewinu *an* [BC]

propose keluluwet *ai* [PEI]

protect ikalk *ta*, ikatm *ti*; keliket *ai*

protrude muskansk'pit *ai* [SH]; muskask'pit *ai*, muskask'tek *ii*

protuberance chip off a ~ manapsk'te:m *ti*

proud ~ of kesite:l'm'k *ta*, kesite:tm *ti*

prove keknuwa:l'k *ta*, keknuwa:tu *ti*

provide netukulit *ai* [SH]; ~ **-r** ntuksuwinu *an* [SH]

provision kiwiksit *ai*; ~ with fowl netukuluwe:set *ai* [SH]; ~ with porcupine netukuluwe:set *ai* [BR]; my ~ **-s** ninu; set out for ~ **-s** najintukulit *ai* [BR]; stock a pantry with ~ **-s** kiwikatm *ti* [BR]; get ~ **-s** netukulit *ai*; kill for ~ **-s** netuk-siktmat *ai* [BR]; ~ **-ing** netukulimk [BR]

pry ~ loose aputaskikwalk *ta*, aputaskikwatm *ti*; mena:qikwalk *ta*, mena:qikwatm *ti*; pekwikwalk *ta*, pekwikwatm *ti*; wena:q'k *ta*, wena:qm *ti*; ~ out ketalqikwalk *ta*, ketalqikwatm *ti*; ~ toward elikwalk *ta*, elikwatm *ti*; ~ out or remove (with hands or tool) menikwalk *ta*, menikwatm *ti*

pubic hair witu:ji:tl (pl)

puddle a ~ walqopaqtek *ii* [ESK]

Puerto Rican puwi:kn-ji:j *an*; ~ woman puwi:kn-ji:je:skw *an*

puff ~ or smoke along pemikp'ta:q *ii*, pemikp'ta:t *ai*

pug-nosed kikjisqonat *ai*; sasqitnat *ai*

pull nujatejo:l'k *ta*, nujatejo:tu *ti*; wesutqa:l'k *ta*, wesutqa:tu *ti*; wetn'k *ta*, wetn'm *ti*; ~ a net from the water natqa:piyet *ai*; ~ down niseka:l'k *ta*, niseka:tu *ti*; ~ in by rope wesuwepil'm *ti*, wesuwepilk *ta*; ~ in to dance wesutqa:l'k *ta*, wesutqa:tu *ti*; ~ on (to make a sound, as a bell) mattaqa:tu *ti*; ~ out of the water (by a rope or fish line) natqapilawet *ai*; ~ up (vegetables or weeds) mena:qikwet *ai*; ~ strings (to get a job or to get in an organization) mekwasitalk *ta*

pullet koqoli:kwej *an*

pumpkin ejkw'jk [SH]

punch taqamk *ta*, taqtm *ti*

puncheon ponjin [PEI]

pung kalipu *an* [BC]

punish aniyapsu:tlk *ta*

pup have ~ -s nmu:ji:jmit *ai*; peneskwit *ai* [BC]

puppy my ~ nte:j *an* [BR]

purchase pekwateliket *ai*; pekwatelaq *ta*,
pekwatel'm *ti*; buy or ~ from there wet-telaq
ta, wet-tel'm *ti*

purgatory spa:suwe:kati

purr ~ (as a cat) eltnuwet *ai* [SH]

purse poj *an*; my ~ nijapo:ti [SH]; nujipo:ti
[BC]

pursue ela:l'k *ta*, ela:tu *ti*

pus waqayew; full of ~ waqayewiyaq *ii*

push kesma:l'k *ta*, kesma:tu *ti*; ~ across
asoqomiksma:l'k *ta*, asoqomiksma:tu *ti*; ~
against epatkwiksma:l'k *ta*, epatkwiksma:tu
ti; ~ around kitto:qiksma:l'k *ta*,
kittoqiksma:tu *ti*; ~ away ejikliksma:l'k *ta*,
ejikliksma:tu *ti*; ~ back esetiksma:l'k *ta*,
esetiksma:tu *ti* [SH]; ~ down nisiksma:l'k *ta*,
nisiksma:tu *ti*; ~ in a circle kiwto:qiksma:l'k
ta, kiwto:qiksma:tu *ti* [SH]; ~ on, in or by a
vehicle kesmoqja:l'k *ta*, kesmoqja:tu *ti*; ~
toward eliksma:l'k *ta*, eliksma:tu *ti*; ~
underneath mesatkwiksma:l'k *ta*,
mesatkwiksma:tu *ti* [BR]; try to ~
munsiksma:l'k *ta*, munsiksma:tu *ti* [SH]

put ika:l'k *ta*, ika:tu *ti*; place or ~ in a proper
position iloqwa:l'k *ta*, iloqwa:tu *ti*; ~ away
masqwa:l'k *ta*, masqwa:tu *ti*; nasko:l'k *ta*,
nasko:tu *ti* [SH]; ~ away maskwa:l'k *ta*,
maskwa:tu *ti* [PEI]; ~ away (in bulk)
masko:l'k *ta*, masko:tu *ti*; ~ away (in a
mental institution) masqwa:tasit *ai*; ~ away
quickly maskute:k *ta*, maskute:m *ti*;
masqute:k *ta*, masqute:m; ~ back in place
(as a joint) ilisqa:l'k *ta*, ilisqa:tu *ti*; ~ or set on
top ke:kwa:l'k *ta*, ke:kwa:tu *ti*; ~ where
easily found naqamasi:katu *ti* [PEI]; ~ down
maqanimk *ta*; penoqwite:l'mk *ta*,
penoqwite:tk *ti*; ~ in a garden ika:taquk *ai*;

~ off schedule malkaq *ta*; ~ on na:qoqum
ti; nasa:l'k *ta*, nasa:tu *ti*; ~ on make up
ilapewnusit *ai*; ~ on shoes and socks
pept'skna:sit *ai* [SH]; ~ out naqasuwa:l'k *ta*,
naqasuwa:tu *ti*

puwowin act like a ~ puwowina:teket *ai*

Q

quack pentoqsit *ai* [SH]; heard ~ **-ing** metetoqsit *ai* [SH]

quarrel wejeyatijik (pl) *ai*

quarter kalkiyey; kaltiyey [SH] (coin); one ~ (of time, etc.) ka:l (Fr *quart*)

queen eleke:wi:skw *an*; ~ card eleke:wi:skw *an*; wennjujkwej *an*

queer wi:kuwe:k *ai, ii*

quick jaqal'k *ai, ii*; do ~ **-ly** jaqala:l'k *ta*, jaqala:tu *ti*; finish off ~ **-ly** (as in boxing or cards) jaqal-te:k *ta*, jaqal-te:m *ti*; go away ~ **-ly** ejikl-ajija:sit *ai*; go by ~ **-ly** kaqawa:s'k *ii*, kaqawa:sit *ai*; heal ~ **-ly** naqsi-nijkik *ii*, naqsi-nijkit *ai*; make a ~ killing jaqal-te:k *ta*, jaqal-te:m *ti*; make money ~ **-ly** jaqal-te:k *ta*, jaqal-te:m *ti*

quick-dry ~ clothing jaqali-piyas'k *ta*, jaqali-piyasm *ti*

quicksand wowj *an*

quick-tempered eluwe:wit *ai*; wisqiluwe:wit *ai*

quiet jenpit *ai*, jentek *ii*; jiktek *ii*; wantaqe:k *ai*; wetayaq *ta* [SH]; ~ (of animals) wansit *ai* [RB]; stay ~ wantaqpit *ai*, wantaqtek *ii*; sit ~ **-ly** wantaqpit *ai*, wantaqtek *ii*

quill ~ work kawey; kawiyey; do ~ work kawiye:ket *ai*; porcupine ~ kawi *ai*; ~ box awiyo:qopilaqan [SH]; kawiyo:qolaqan [SH]

quilt my ~ ntoqwan [BC]

quintuplet nanupe:j *an*

quit puna:l'k *ta*, puna:tu *ti*

quiver pitlan; my ~ npijo:qati(m)

R

rabbit apli:kmuj *an* [SH]; wapus *an*; ~ meat wapusuwey; ~ skin wapusuwekn

raccoon amaljikwej *an* [SH]

race ikatne:wet *ai*

racer ikatne:we:sm (ikatne:we:smuk); horse ~ ikatne:siwinu *an*;

radiate epsawek *ii*, epsawet *ai*; wasoqonawek *ii*, wasoqonawet *ai*

raffle contribution ~ (following a wake) salitewa:taqatimk [ESK]; ~ off eleketoq (eleketu) *ai*

raft sawtaqa:taqan; s'nkatikna:teket *ai*; s'nkatikn; ~ (of logs) s'nkatikna:taqan; work on a ~ s'nkatikna:teket *ai*

rafter ~ (of a house) mtuwi:kan; a ~ s'nkatikna:tekewinu *an*

rag miseknuj

raggedy get ~ misissiyaq *ii*, misissiyet *ai*

rain kikpesaq *ii*; kikpesan; look like ~ kikpesana-mukwiyaq *ii*; ~ heavily ma:munlaq *ii*; wenaqala:maq *ii* [PEI]; ~ inside piskw'laq *ii*; ~ slightly kikpesa:ji:jk *ii*; turn to ~ kikpesanewiyaq *ii* [SH]

rainbow m'nqwan [SH]; walqwan *an*; ~ (in the bay) u:npekw

raise anko:tm *ti*, ankweyaq *ta*; kisikwen'm *ti*, kisikwenk *ta*; nikwen'm *ti*, nikwenk *ta*; ~ a child es'pkw'tl'k *ta* [SH]; ~ or lift up neps'tkwa:l'k *ta*, neps'tkwa:tu *ti*; have a ~ -d tail nepsluwat *ai*

raisin jijjawiknej *an*; sqato:min *an*

rake jikk'putaqan; jikk'puteket *ai*; ~ toward elipulk *ta*, eliputu *ti*

ramrod pitqasawaqan; load (a gun) with gunpowder and ~ pitqasawet *ai*

rape ki:kaja:l'k *ta*, ki:kaja:tu *ti*

rapid flow ~ -ly me:ka:sik *ii* [SH]

rapids qapskwamkitk *ii* [BR]

rapport make a loud ~ (as a cannon or gun) kesikawtewesikek *ii*, kesikawtewesiket *ai*

rare awije:jk *ii*, awije:jit *ai*

rascal kji-apluwew *an*

rasp la:kittaqan

raspberry red ~ klitaw (klitaq) *an* [SH][BC][RB]; kmu:jemin *an*

rat kji-apluwew *an* [SH]

raven kji-kaqaquj *an*

raw eske:k *ai, ii* [BC]; eat ~ esk'pk *ta*, esk'tm *ti*; eat ~ food esk'tamit *ai*

reach kisapskn'm *ti*, kisapsknk; tepn'k *ta*, tepn'm *ti*; have a long ~ pijiptnat *ai*; ~ or stretch toward (as a cable or rope) eltaqayaq *ii*, eltaqayet *ai*; try to ~ (with the hand) weji-tepn'k *ta*, weji-tepn'm *ti*

read ejiljet *ai*; ekijjet *ai*; ekimk *ta*, ekitm *ti*; ~ entrails ikanite:tm *ti* [SH]; ~ poorly awan-kijjet *ai*; ~ properly or correctly keknu:kijjet *ai*; ~ properly or well wel-kijjet *ai*

ready kiskatpit *ai*, kiskattek *ii*; get ~ (for) ilajit *ai*; ilajuktaq *ta*, ilajuktm *ti*; get ~ ilaji:kewsit *ai*; kiskaja:l'k *ta*, kiskaja:tu *ti*; go get prepared or ~ naji-ilajit *ai*; ~ or available immediately kiskaje:k *ai*; stand at the ~ kiskat-pukuwit *ai* (said of the sun when it is on the verge of rising) [BR]

real ~ one kjitmey *an, in*

re-align ilaska:l'k *ta*, ilaska:tu *ti*

really! lpa (an emphatic particle)

rear[1] kisikwen'm *ti*, kisikwenk *ta*

rear[2] break off at the tail or ~ end temaluwa:l'k *ta*, temaluwa:tu *ti*; in the ~ paqaqamk [SH]; in the ~ of wpaqamk

reasonable good or ~ (in price) wel-awtik *ii*, wel-awtit *ai*

recall mikwite:l'mk *ta*, mikwite:tm *ti* [PEI]

recede ~ (of the tide) elm'kiyaq *ii* [BR]; el'm'kiyaq *ii* [SH]; enmikiyaq *ii*

receive mesn(')k *ta*, mesn'm *ti*

recently kejikow; kejikaw [SH]; wejuwow

recite ekimk *ta*, ekitm *ti*

recluse a ~ jipaluwet *ai (an)*; jipaluwejit *ai (an)*; nkutuko:pj *an*

recognize nenaq *ta*, nen'm *ti*

recollect nestuwita:sit *ai*

re-cook minuwoqs'k *ta*, minuwoqsm *ti*

record eptaqan *an*

recover ila:sit *ai*; ~ from an illness iltaqayet *ai*; saputawsit *ai*; start to ~ from bad times pem-pukuwa:sit *ai*; ~ -ed (from being ill) wela:s'k *ii*, wela:sit *ai*

recuperate ni:taqa:t *ai*

red mekwe:k *ai, ii*; flash ~ mekwatesink *ai*, mekwatesk *ii*; make ~ mekwa:l'k *ta*, mekwa:tu *ti*; round and ~ mekwapsk'sit *ai*, mekwapskek *ii*; turn ~ mekwe:saqa:sit *ai*; turn ~ (as of the sky) mekloqiyaq *ii* [SH]; ~ -dish mekwamuksit *ai*, mekwamu:k *ii*;

Red Bank met'pna:kiyaq [RB]

redeem westawitu *ti*, westawi:k *ta*; ~ -ed sape:wik *ii*, sape:wit *ai*; ~ -er westawu:lkw (westawu:lkwaq) *an*

red-faced mekwe:saqsit *ai*

refuse esa:q *ta*, esa:m *ti*; ese:k *ta*

regain ~ conciousness apajiyaq *ii*

regrettable wenqaje:k *ii* [PEI]

regular embark ~ -ly i:pusit *ai*

reheat minu:p'sk *ta*, minu:p'sm *ti*

rein wtunapi

reject aluwa:l'k *ta*, aluwa:tu *ti*; ~ because of the appearance aluwamk *ta*, aluwaptm *ti*

relate ~ what happens aknimk *ta*, aknutm *ti*

related wettaqiyet *ai*; ~ (as kin) wo:kumatijik (pl) *ai*; ~ (as brothers or sisters) wijik'tijik (pl) *ai*; ~ as such telakutijik (pl) *ai*; ~ through descent wetakutk (wetakutm) *ai*; ~ to as such telakumk *ta*

relative have as a ~ wijikumk *ta*; my ~ nikmaq *an*; no:kumaw (no:kumaq) *an* [SH]; close ~ -s or relations kikjakutijik (pl) *ai*; distant ~ -s or relations knek wetakutijik (pl) *ai*

release elaqtu *ti*; ika:l'k *ta*, ika:tu *ti*; tewalqa:l'k *ta*, tewalqa:tu *ti*; tewaqqa:l'k *ta*, tewaqqa:tu *ti*

relief ~ blanket tpi:tnewqwan

religion my ~ ntalasutmaqan'm [PEI]; nta:sutmaqan'm

reluctant ~ to part with keskel'mk *ta*, keskeltm *ti*

remainder eskwiyaq *ii*, eskwiyet *ai*; piwiyaq *ii*

remember mikwite:l'mk *ta*, mikwite:tm *ti*; nestuwita:sit *ai*

reminded ~ of pe:kwamk *ta* [PEI]

remove kepta:l'k *ta*, kepta:tu *ti*; mena:l'k *ta*, mena:tu *ti*; ~ bark (from a tree) menipqwa:wet *ai* [SH]; ~ by striking mente:k *ta*, mente:m *ti*; ~ from tewalqa:l'k *ta*, tewalqa:tu *ti* [SH]; ~ (fish) from a net mena:piyet *ai*; ~ from the water natqa:l'k *ta*,

natqa:tu *ti*; take off or ~ bark menipqwa:l'k *ta*, menipqwa:tu *ti* [SH]

repair elukwalk *ta*, elukwatm *ti*; kisa:l'k *ta*, kisa:tu *ti*; mesna:l'k *ta*, mesna:tu *ti* [SH]; include in the ~ -s maw-lukwalk *ta*, maw-lukwatm *ti*

repeat ~ after nasplutaq *ta*; ~ what is said minuwi:tm *ti*; cry ~ -edly puskimt'k *ai*; laugh ~ -edly pusk-elmit *ai*

reply ~ or talk back to asite-klulk *ta* [SH]; ~ to keta:maq *ta*; ~ to in kind asitemk *ta*

report aknutmaqan; ~ on aknimk *ta*, aknutm *ti*

repossessor a ~ nuji-koqqwa:luwet *ai (an)*

reproduction minuwitaqan

reptile mteskm (mteskmuk) *an*

request kelumk *ta*, kelutm *ti*; ~ from etamk *ta*; ~ permission (of parents) to marry daughter keluluwet *ai*

required menuweket *ai*

rescue ketuwapsmu:tlk *ta* [PEI]; ~ (by grabbing) weji-koqqwa:l'k *ta*

resemblance bear a family ~ elat *ai*

resemble elaq *ta*

reserved enmikjepit *ai*, enmikjetek *ii*

reside eyk (ey'm) *ai*, *ii* [BC]; eyt *ai* [BR]; ~ or dwell there wikit *ai*

respect kepmite:l'mk *ta*, kepmite:tm *ti*; me:kite:l'mk *ta*, mekite:tm *ti* [PEI]; nenuwite:l'mk *ta*, nenuwite:tm *ti* [BR]

respectfully act ~ keknuwe:k *ai*, *ii*

responsible ~ for nujeyaq *ta*, nujo:tm *ti*

rest atlasmit *ai*; atlasmu:l'k *ta*; give a ~ to atlasmu:l'k *ta*; ~ one's head on etu:kwesmit *ai*; stretch out for a ~ ilapsk'smu:kwet *ai*; take a short ~ atlasmu:teket *ai*

restaurant eat in a ~ tewatalk *ai*

Restigouche speak or imitate the ~ dialect listukujewa:tuwat *ai*

Restigouche Reserve land area surrounding ~ qoptm'n

restless jikajiyet *ai*; sespa:sit *ai*

restrain kelkaq *ta*, kelkm *ti* [PEI]; naqan'm *ti*, naqank *ta*; ~ by leash or rope keltaqan'm *ti*, keltaqank *ta*

resurrected minu:nsit *ai*; wenakiyet *ai*

resussitate sapa:l'k *ta*, sapa:tu *ti*

retainer put a claim, deposit, ~ or down payment on kelte:k *ta*, kelte:m *ti*

retaliate asita:teket *ai* [PEI]

retarded amatpa:t *ai*

return apaja:sit *ai*; apajiyaq *ii*; never ~ apja:'it *ai*; apja:sit *ai*

reunite apajitqwa:majik (pl) *ai*

revenge get ~ asita:teket *ai*; get ~ on kiskaja:l'k *ta*, kiskaja:tu *ti*

revers-e do (something) in ~ order (e.g. skip rope backwards, paddle in reverse) apatto:sit *ai*; ~ **-ing** tide apatpa:q *ii* [SH]

revive kinuwa:l'k *ta*, kinuwa:tu *ti* [SH]; minuwa:l'k *ta*, minuwa:tu *ti*

rhubarb lupapl [BC]; sewlukowey (sewlukowe:k) *an*

rib pikaqan; my ~ npikaqan; ~ (of a splint basket) pikaqan *an* [MARIA]

ribbon hair ~ saqalo:pi *an*

ribs part of animal between ~ and belly wa:naw (wa:naq) *an*

rice tulijewe:l (pl) (Fr *du riz*); grain of ~ apjelmultimkewey [BR]; aptelmultimkewey

rich milesit *ai*

rid-e wejkwatejimkwet *ai* (come riding on or in); ~ a horse ali:puluwet *ai*; ~ along on horseback pemi:puluwet *ai*; come ~ **-ing** on or in wejkwatejimkwet *ai*

right koqwattek *ii* [SH]; cut ~ or correctly tetapu:s'k *ta*, tetapu:sm *ti*; do ~ by tetapuwa:l'k *ta*, tetapuwa:tu *ti*; do the ~ way tetapuwa:teket *ai*; on the ~ inaqanek; put ~ side up illjo:qwa:l'k *ta*, illjo:qwa:tu *ti*; ~ side inaqan; set ~ keknuwa:l'k *ta*, keknuwa:tu *ti*; the ~ size tepaqapit *ai*, tepaqatek *ii*; toward the ~ inaqaneke:l

right away nankmiw; simtuk; smtuk

right-handed inaqanmit *ai*

right on! ansmajiw [ESK]; a:toq [ESK]; kijka:tata:n (an interjection)

rigid melkikiyaq *ii*, melkikiyet *ai* [BC]; flat and ~ elsaqapit *ai*, elsaqas'k *ii*

rigor mortis undergo ~ mejkiyet *ai*

rilely esiyamkek *ii* [BR]

rind psaqa:kw

ring nasoqwa:taqan; diamond ~ wasoqwa:toqan [BC]

ringworm misuwes *an*

rinse ~ out jinqamisteket *ai*; ~ water sikuwapatikn

rip ~ off menepqa:l'k *ta*, menepqa:tu *ti*; menipka:l'k *ta*, menipka:tu *ti*; ~ or tear off or out menina:l'k *ta*, menina:tu *ti*; ~ or tear up sekwiskina:l'k *ta*, sekwiskina:tu *ti* [BR]; ~ **-ped** off temine:k *ai*, *ii*

ripe essit *ai*, ettek *ii*; kislassit *ai*, kislastek *ii*

rise pempa:q *ii* (of the tide); sekewa:t *ai* (of the sun or moon); wenaqa:s'k *ti*, wenaqa:sit *ai*; get up or ~ menja:sit *ai*; start to ~ (of the tide) pempeka:s'k *ii*; ~ (from a prone position) nemja:sit *ai* [BR]; nenja:sit *ai* [SH]; incoming or ~ ing tide wejkwapa:q *ii*; ~ **-n** (as dough) apita:q *ii*, apita:t *ai*; where the sun ~ **-s** wesekewa:nek (loc) (a religious expression)

river sipu

river drive psi:kikwaqan [BC]; psi:kukwaqan; pesi:kukwet *ai*

road awti; make or clear a ~ or path awtiket *ai*; go towards the ~ or path matama:sit

roast etoqtasit *ai* [BR]

robin jipjawej *an* [SH]; kapjakwej *an*; swamp ~ kloqiyej *an*

rock[1] nanamiyaq *ii*, nanamiyet *ai*; nanma:l'k *ta*, nanma:tu *ti*; ~ a baby nanama:l'k *ta*; ~ to and fro nanamo:qiyaq *ii*, nanamo:qiyet *ai*

rock[2] kunntew (kunntal); a kind of ~ wapskw [BR]; Indian ~ lnapskw [SH]; ~ **-y** kunntewapskek *ii*

rocking chair kjitloqomuwaqan; nanamiyaqawey; nanamiyemkewey [SH]

rock maple ~ tree jiyoqsimusi [SH]; joqsimusi

rod connecting ~ (automobile) pulljikn

roe nijinj (nijinjik) *an*; winjinj (winjinjik) *an* [BR]; my fish ~ nijinj (nijinjik) *an*

roll elipqama:l'k *ta*, elipqama:tu *ti* [NB]; elipqamu:l'k *ta*, elipqamu:tu *ti*; te:tipja:l'k *ta*, te:tipja:tu *ti*; ~ a cigarette eloqo(n)maqa:tu *ti* [BR]; ~ over tet'piyet *ai* [SH]; te:t'pjiyet *ai*; ~ (something long and round) over te:tipjo:l'k *ta*, te:tipjo:tu *ti*

rookie pile:sm (pile:smuk) *an*; sqapantiyej [AN]
room a:sey [SH]
roomy ewe:ke:k *ai, ii*
rooster jikijo:n (jikijo:naq) *an* [SH]; kikli:kwej *an* [BR]; lape:w *an* [SH]; nape:w *an* [BR]
root[1] wjip'sk; a fine ~ used in basketry wt'pi *an* [SH]; a type of ~ s'kepn *an*; lily ~ sapoqwani-pako:sit [SH]; muskrat ~ ki:kasuwaskw; ki:kwesuwaskw (good for cold; mix with gin after boiling in water; chew on it); my ~ nt'pi (a fine ~ used for stitching quill basket covers); water ~ paqo:si (eaten by moose); harvest ~ -s or tubers (e.g. potatoes, carrots, turnips) ke:tipnet *ai*
root[2] ~ (as a pig) jikni:ket *ai*
rope a:papi *an*; carry along in the hand (by means of ~, strap, handle, etc.) pemapilk *ta*, pemapil'm *ti*; carry by means of a ~ or handle pemapilawet *ai*; haul or ~ aboard teppil'm *ti*, teppilk *ta*; reel or ~ in (from the water) natqapil'm *ti*, natqapilk *ta*; send across by ~ or cable elpil'm *ti*, elpilk *ta*
rosary sulmin *an* [SH]; sunmun *an*
rotten sukul'kaq *ii*, sukul'kat *ai*; taste or smell ~ sukul'kma:q *ii*, sukul'kma:t *ai*
rouge mekwa:taqan; mkwa:taqan [SH]; put on ~ mekwa:tat *ai*
roughly wake up ~ tukwipnn'k *ta*
rough up ewsa:l'k *ta*
round mimtoqopsk'sit *ai*, mimtoqopskek *ii* [BR]; become large and ~ pemimqapsk'sit *ai*, pemimqapskek *ii* [SH]; big and ~ meptoqopsk'set *ai* [PEI]; big and ~ or oval shaped telapsk'sit *ai*, telapskek *ii*; four solid, ~ (globular) objects newapsk'sijik (pl) *ai*, newapskekl (pl) *ii*; good and ~ in size weloqsit *ai*; half ~ menjapsk'sit *ai*, menjapskek *ii*; have a big and ~ belly maqapsk'tiyat *ai*; large and ~ kesi-maqapsk'sit *ai*, kesi-maqapskek *ii*; maqapsk'sit *ai*, maqapskek *ii*; one (of something ~ and solid) newtapsk'sit *ai*; newtapskek *ii*; ~ and hollow elltuknapskek *ii*, elltuknapsk'sit *ai*; ~ and red mekwapsk'sit

ai, mekwapskek *ii*; ~, cylindrical, or tubular piptoqopsit *ai*, piptoqwa:q *ii*; kittoqoqsit *ai* [CB]; ~ or circular kittukwakik *ii*, kittukwakit *ai* [CB]; piptukwakik *ii*, piptukwakit *ai*; ~ or globular piptoqopsk'sit *ai*, piptoqopskek *ii*; kiptoqapsk'sit *ai* [CB]; short and ~ elapsk'pit *ai*, elapsk'tek *ii*; toqopsk'sit *ai*, toqopskek *ii*; apjoqji:jk *ii*, apjoqji:jit *ai*; smooth and ~ musikapsk'sit *ai*, musikapskek *ii*; three ~ (globular) objects nesapsk'sijik (pl) *ai*, nesapskekl (pl) *ii*; three ~ (cylindrical) objects nesa:ql (pl) *ii*
row[1] ji:matm *ti*; ji:met *ai*; paddle or ~ along pemi-ji:met *ai*; ~ about alu:l'k *ta*; ~ to the end we:kwi-ji:met *ai*; come ~ -ing or padding toward wejkwisukwit *ai*
row[2] five in a ~ nanoqoskl (pl) *ii*; five lying in a ~ nanoqosmiya:tijik (pl) *ai*
rowboat welipot [SH]
rub amaqan'm *ti*; a:mekn'k *ta*, a:meken'm *ti*; etlipulk *ta*, etliputu *ti*; ~ in amipulk *ta*, amiputu *ti*; ~ off menkaq *ta*, menkm *ti*; ~ on amipulk *ta*, amiputu *ti*; ~ (something) on oneself a:meknusit *ai*; ~ self against amipusit *ai*
rubber boot tepot *an* [ESK] (Fr *des bottes*)
rude pepsitelket *ai*; pepsite:l'mk *ta*
ruler nekaqan *an*; n'kaqan *an*
rumble ~ inside the stomach tetuwipskuna:t *ai* [SH]
rumour lutmaqan; a ~ monger puski-alaknutk (puski-alaknutm) *ai (an)*; go around spreading ~ -s puski-alaknutk (puski-alaknutm) *ai (an)*; spread ~ -s lutmaqaniket *ai*
rump mijimij *an*; my ~ ninoqwey; ns'kun; nsukun [SH]
run ketkwi:k (ketkwi:m) *ai*; come on the ~ wejkwitukwi:k (wejkwitukwi:m) *ai* [BR]; wejkutukwi:k (wejkutukwi:m) *ai*; ~ across as'komi:pit *ai* [BR]; ~ along pemi:pit *ai*; pem-tukwi:k (pem-tukwi:m) *ai*; ~ along slowly pemi-kekwi:pit *ai* [SH]; ~ atop ke:kwi:pit *ai*; ~ away wesumukwat *ai*; ~ fast kesikawi:pit *ai*; ~ fast with head bobbing kesikawatpi:pit *ai* [BR]; ~ for office

elaqalsewsit *ai*; ~ off with wesmi:pulk *ta*,
wesmi:putu *ti*; ~ out in the open (from the
thicket) muski:pit *ai*; ~ over mikuteskaq *ta*,
mikuteskm *ti*; mukuteskaq *ta*, mukuteskm *ti*;
~ slowly kekwi:pit *ai*; ~ through
saputeteskaq *ta*, saputeteskm *ti*; ~ toward
el-tukwi:k (el-tukwi:m) *ai*

run around give the ~ to amsalimk *ta*

runner a fast ~ kji-kawa:suwinu *an*; a ~
(professional) nuji:pit *ai (an)*

runt tkulmi:s *an*

rush ketaqa:sit *ai*; ~ over toward elateja:sit
ai; ~ toward eli:pit *ai*

rusty jijiwa:qiyaq *ii*, jijiwa:qiyet *ai*

rythmically beat or move ~ etl-tesk *ii*,
etl-tesink *ai*

S

sack m'nuti [BR]; munnti; pqasqaqan [SH]; little ~ munnte:j; my ~ n'munntek

sacrifice one who ~ -s aniyapsuwinu *an*

sad welma'ita:sit *ai*; ~ -den (by one's departure) kiwatteskaq *ta*; taqawaja:l'k *ta*; ~ -ness w'lma'itasuwaqan

safe ~ and sound westawit *ai*

safekeeping hold in ~ keleyaq *ta*, kelo:tm *ti*; kept for ~ kekkunas'k *ii*, kekkunasit *ai*; leave for ~ eptoqalk *ta*, eptoqatm *ti*; ettoqalk *ta*, ettoqatm [BR]

said it is ~ (that) na to:q

sail seki:kn *an*; ~ along pemaqteket *ai*; ~ along by pemsiyawaqteket *ai*; ~ around (about) alaqteket *ai*; ~ home elmaqteket *ai* [CB]; ~ toward elaqteket *ai*; come sailing wejkwaqteket *ai*

sailboat sallpo:l [CB]; sallpo:k [CB]; small ~ sallpo:lku:j [CB]

sailor matlot (matlotaq) *an* (Fr *matelot*) [SH]

saint aniyapsuwinu *an* [SH]; patron ~ kji-sape:wit *ai (an)*

Sainte-Anne Se:ta:n *an*; ~ -s Day Se:ta:newimk; Se:tanewumk

Saint Patrick's Day patliks'te:wumk

salamander taqtatoq *an* [SH]

salary on ~ awtit *ai*

salesman a ~ netuwisket *ai (an)*; nujintuwisket *ai (an)*

saliva luskwatikn; pne:sukwati

salmon plamu *an*; a kind of ~ punamu *an* [BR]; black ~ pqalmawj (pqalmawjik) *an*; fish for ~ plamukwet *ai*; hook-nose male ~ napiklej *an* [RB]; large, hook-nosed male ~ wapiklej *an*

salt salawey (Fr *sel*); add ~ salawa:tat *ai*; ~ -y salawe:k *ai, ii*

salve a kind of ~ niya:sikowey

same wijey; all the ~ lpa wijey; ~ as nkutey; pana; st'ke:; at the ~ time nespiw [CB]; ~ here lpa wijey (an emphatic paricle); just the ~ as ankutey

Samuel Samuwel *an*

sand atuwomk; wiskipk; fine ~ amalamkw *an* [SH]; where there are many varieties of ~ amalamkuk [SH]

sand piper jijikwatej *an*

sane partly ~ amins'tuwe:k *ai*

sap balsam ~ pu:kowij *an*; puku:kewij [PEI]

sardine so:qomu:j *an*

Satan kji-m'ntu *an*

satisfactory find ~ mikuwa:l'k *ta*, mikuwa:tu *ti*

satisfy tetapuwa:l'k *ta*, tetapuwa:tu *ti*

Saturday kesp'tek

saucer lasiyetji:j *an* [SH]; sa:slji:j *an*

saunter ~ along sankewa:s'k *ii*, sankewa:sit *ai*

save apatu *ti*; masqwa:l'k *ta*, masqwa:tu *ti*; mawte:k *ta*, mawte:m *ti*; westawitu *ti*, westawi:k *ta*; ~ from mishap sapa:l'k *ta*, sapa:tu *ti*; ~ -d sape:k *ai*; ~ -d up masqo:tasit *ai*

Savior westawu:lkw (westawu:lkwaq) *an*

savory lasupe:ji:j

saw ela:kipulk *ta*, ela:kittu *ti*; tela:kipulk *ta*, tela:kittu *ti*; tma:kittaqan; ~ down tema:kipulk *ta*, tema:kittu *ti*

sawwhet kopkej *an* [SH]; koqkwej *an* [RB]

sawyer a ~ nuja:kitteket *ai (an)*

say teluwet *ai*; call or ~ in Micmac (in Indian) nnuwi:tm *ti*; ~ backwards kawaskuwi:tm *ti*

scab wjiki; my ~ nujkim [SH]

scabb-y wejkiyet *ai*; ~ -iness wejkiyemkewey

scale[1] tetpaqikn; ~ or measure enket *ai*; enkalk *ta*, enkatm *ti*

scale[2] (fish) ~ pipukwes *an*; piwikes *an*

scaler a ~ (in lumbering) nujinket (nujinkejik) *ai (an)*

scallop sasqale:s *an* [BC]

scapular etu:kutewe:k (pl) *an*

scar mark or ~ (with a knife) jilsawet *ai*; ~ -red jilta:sik *ii*, jilta:sit *ai*; wesikwat *ai*; wise:k *ai, ii*; wisikat *ai*

scarce awije:jk *ii*, awije:jit *ai*

scare we:kwata:l'k *ta*

scared jipasit *ai*; we:kwata:sit *ai*

scarf a:pij [ESK]; qotaqanikjipilaqan [SH]

scar-faced wesikwat *ai*; wisikat *ai*

school nuji-kina:muwo:kuwom [NB]; sku:l

schoolmaster sku:lma:stl *an*

scissors pair of ~ tm'tqe:kn; tm'tqe:kne:l (pl) [SH]

scold majiyaqa:l'k *ta*; wetapulk *ta*

scoop nqani:kn *an*; ~ out naqani:ket *ai*

scoot ~ home elmoqwe:set *ai* [CB]; trot or ~ along home enm'kate:pit *ai*

scout postewit *ai (an)* (Fr *poste*); ~ around nutapit *ai*

scowl wetajikwet *ai*; winikwa:sit *ai*

scrap food ~ piwtikn; ~ of cloth or paper piwsikn; eat the ~ -s matu:p'k *ta*, matu:tm *ti*

scrape jilapa:l'k *ta*, jilapa:tu *ti*; kesipoqwat *ai* [SH]; nassi:k'k *ta*, nassi:km *ti*; ~ a frying pan nassi:kwalk *ta*, nassi:kwatm *ti*; ~ (as one's knee or foot) pesqatesm'k *ta*, pesqatestu *ti*; ~ off mena:qikwalk *ta*, mena:qikwatm *ti*; ~ off a protuberance jilapsk'te:m *ti*; ~ the ground pelqoqte:kniket *ai* [SH]; ~ with an instrument pesqate:k *ta*, pesqate:m *ti*

scraps eat the ~ matu:p'k *ta*, matu:tm *ti*

scratch jilapa:l'k *ta*, jilapa:tu *ti*; kesipa:l'k *ta*, kesipa:tu *ti*; ~ hard kesipte:k *ta*, kesipte:m *ti*; ~ oneself (as an animal) kesipto:sit *ai*; ~ oneself etlapensit *ai*; ~ with an instrument kesipte:k *ta*, kesipte:m *ti*; ~ with fingernails kejkapa:l'k *ta*, kejkapa:tu *ti*; start to ~ poqtapa:teket *ai*; ~ -y kesipkuwek *ii*, kesipkuwet *ai*; ~ -ing place ksipo:qwan [SH]

scream ~ at seskwalk *ta*; se:skwalk *ta* [SH]

scream seskwet *ai*

screech owl ku:ku:kwes *an*

screw ~ on kelapaqam *ti*, kelapaqq *ta*; na:sapa:qam *ti* [SH]

scrotum my ~ n'munnti

scrub ~ on one's hands and knees nutkul-papatiket *ai*

scruff carry by the ~ of the neck (as a cat) pemapilawet *ai*

sculpin klakw (klakwaq) *an* [SH]

scum salt water ~ oqopekiyaq

scurry ~ about alatija:sit *ai*

scythe pskweso:qon

sea heavy ~ -s maqatkwik *ii*

seagull kloq'ntiyej *an*

seal[1] waspu *an*

seal[2] sepusa:l'k *ta*, sepusa:tu *ti*; sipma:m *ti*

seam kepjoqi:s'k *ta*, kepjoqi:sm *ti*; sepusi:s'k *ta*, sepusi:sm *ti*

sea porpoise aqatiyepis *an* [SH]

search panawijqanawet *ai*; ~ about kwiluwasit *ai*; ~ for fir boughs stoqone:ket *ai*; ~ for kwilaq *ta*, kwil'm *ti*

seat epa:l'k *ta*; my ~ nt'pun; ntupun [PEI]; ~ -ed epit *ai*, etek *ii*

seaweed kata:skw'l (pl) [PEI]; paqo:si (sometimes used as a cold remedy medicine by boiling it)

second the ~ one ta:puwowa:j *an*; ta:puwowey

secret laugh ~ -ly kim-elmit *ai* [BR]; kim-enmit *ai* [SH]; talk ~ -ly kim-ewo:kwet *ai*

section upper (rear) ~ of wikwam kataqam [SH]

secure kejipil'm *ti*, kejipilk *ta*

seduce sespeyaq *ta*, sespo:tm *ti*

see nemiteket *ai*; nemitu *ti*, nemi:k *ta*; make someone ~ things that are not there keskmap'lkikwa:lek *ta*, keskmap'lkikwa:tu *ti*; ~ a mirage keskmap'lkikwa:t *ai*; ~ again after a long separation or absence pe:kwamk *ta*, pe:kwaptm *ti*; ~ all around pe'ikwapit *ai*, pe'ikwatek *ii*; ~ poorly malapit; ~ the break of dawn wapnapit *ai*; try to ~ kweji-n'mitu *ti*, kewji-n'mi:k *ta*

seed nijinj (nijinjik) *an*; skilmin; skinmin; skniman [BR]; winjinj (winjinjik) *an* [SH]

seek hunt or ~ for a woman e:pitewe:ket *ai*; ~ assistance from elulk *ta*

seep ~ in putlaq *ii* [SH]

seer nikanita:suwinu *an*

segments cut into ~ or chunks temapsk'sk *ta*, temapsk'sm *ti*

seldom awisiw; ~ see pe:kwi-n'mitu *ti*, pekwi-n'mi:k *ta*

selection make a poor ~ winnat *ai*

sell netuwisketu *ti*; ~ (as a pimp) netuwiskalk *ta*; ~ for someone (as a sales representative) netuwiskewkw *ta*; go ~ -ing or peddling natanku:sit *ai*; a ~ -er or salesman netuwisket *ai (an)*

semen eskmoqon; mi:poq *an*

send el'm'kitm *ti* [SH]; enm'kitm *ti*; pitkimk *ta*, pitkitm *ti*; ~ across by rope or cable elpil'm *ti*, elpilk *ta*; ~ for natkimk *ta*, natkitm *ti*; natkiteket *ai*; wikimk *ta* [SH]; wikumk *ta*; ~

forth elkimk *ta*, elkitm *ti*; ~ home enmikimk
ta, enmikitm *ti*; ~ home elmikimk *ta* [BR]; ~
off poqtikimk *ta*; ~ up toqju:kimk *ta*,
toqju:kitm *ti*

sense talk ~ to nestuwimk *ta*

senseless knock ~ or silly ewayatpete:k *ta*
[SH]

senses back to one's ~ (after drinking)
sinu:wet *ai*; come back to one's ~
nestu:tesink *ai*; regain one's ~ sinutesink *ai*
[BR]

sensible nestuwe:k *ai*

sensitive menata:t *ai*; ~ to the cold menawjit
ai

sentence ilsumk *ta*, ilsutm *ti*

separat-e niktuwa:tijik (pl) *ai*; niktuwa:l'k *ta*,
niktuwa:tu *ti*; tepkisa:l'k *ta*, tepkisa:tu *ti*; go ~
ways niktuwa:tijik (pl) *ai*; ~ -d niktuwe:k *ai*,
ii; punalltijik (pl) *ai*; ~ -d (in marriage)
maskelket *ai*; ~ -ion niktuwa:taqan

September maja:sitewiku:sk [SH];
wikumkewiku:s

serendipitous ~ happening welitpa:s'k *ii*,
welitpa:sit *ai*

serene wantaqe:k *ai*

seriously! meluwijoqo na; mewlijoqo na [SH]

serpent jujij *an*; horned ~ jupijka:m *an*

servant naqap (naqapaq) *an*; nuktoqtejkwej
an; my ~ n'naqapem *an*; nunaqapem *an*

serve ela:q *ta*, ela:m *ti*; e:l'k *ta*, e:l'm *ti* [BC]; ~
food e:liku *ti* [BC]; ~ self ela:mat *ai* [ESK]

set¹ ila:l'k *ta*, ila:tu *ti*; ~ up iltaqane:walk *ta*,
iltaqane:watm *ti*; build or ~ a fire (in a stove
or furnace) moqsa:l'k *ta*, moqsa:tu *ti*; ~ a
net eltaqa:teket *ai* [RB]; ~ a table elm'joqtek
ii; ~ a trap ilsaqa:tu *ti*

set² ~ (as the sun) elmi-walqwasiyet *ai* [CB]

settle illjo:qwa:l'k *ta*, illjo:qwa:tu *ti*

settlement old camp site or ~ ujikana:qamikt
[BR]

seven ~ (in counting) lluwikn'k

seventy ~ (in counting) lluwikn'k-te:sinska:q

sever ~ with a knife tems'k *ta*, temsm *ti*

several pikwelk *ai*, *ii* [SH]; pukwelk *ai*, *ii*

sew eli:sawet *ai*; eli:sewet *ai* [SH]; eli:s'k *ta*,
eli:sm *ti*; kisi:s'k *ta*, kisi:sm *ti*; mesni:s'k *ta*,

mesni:sm *ti* [SH]; ~ by hand wpitni:sawet *ai*
[SH]; wpitni:sewet *ai*; ~ closed the gap of a
pointed article (such as a sock or mitt)
sepusi:s'k *ta*, sepusi:sm *ti*; ~ for eli:sawewk
ta; ~ right or correctly tetapuwi:s'k *ta*,
tetapuwi:sm *ti*

shad msamu *an*

shade window ~ lekepilaqan

shadow have a ~ wjijaqamiju:wet *ai*; my ~
njijaqamiju:wiyey [SH]; njijaqamiju:wey;
njijaqamij *an*

shady aqjikatek *ii*

shake etl-tesk *ii*, etl-tesink *ai*; ewsa:l'k *ta*;
mattesk *ii*, mattesink *ai*; pepuwetesink *ai*,
pepuwetesk *ii*; ~ hands with pusu:lewiktaq
ta; ~ off pepuwetestu *ti*; pewaqtesm'k *ta*,
pewaqtestu *ti*; ~ out tewalqatesm'k *ta*,
tewalqatestu *ti* [SH]; tewaqqatesm'k *ta*,
tewaqqatestu *ti*; ~ (something) pepuweket
ai; ~ without cease putuktesink *ai*

shallow ~ water pakwejk *ii*

shaman npuwowin *an* [CB]; puwowin
(puwowinaq) *an*

shame netako:qona:l'k *ta*; ntaqo:qon

shameful netaqasit *ai* [SH]

shank ~ of meat qones *an* [BR]

shape have a nice ~ welikk *ii*, welikit *ai*; ~ -d
like telikk *ii*, telikit *ai*; ~ -d to fit ji:kate:k *ta*,
ji:kate:m *ti*

share mawa:tajik (pl) *ai*; naskwa:tatijik (pl) *ai*;
~ the load toqonasit *ai*; ~ the same belief
mawiktlams'tasultijik (pl) *ai* [BC]

shark siklati *an* [SH]; wipitmekw (wipitmaq) *an*
[SH]

sharp ki:k *ai*, *ii*

sharpen esipulk *ta*, esiputu *ti*; kiniskayipulk *ta*,
kiniskayiputu *ti*; ~ -er siputaqan

sharp-sighted ne:tapit *ai*

shave peske:mat *ai* [SH]; peskutuwe:k *ta*,
peskutuwe:m *ti*; peskutuwe:mat *ai* [BC];
peskutuwe:maq *ta (do)* [BC]; ~ oneself
peskutuwo:sit *ai*; a ~ -r nujipskutuwe:muwet
ai (an) [BC]

shaving wood ~ pu:tlaqan

shawl anqono:sun [SH]; sa:l (Fr *châle*)

she nekm

shed¹ tusati

shed² peskwiyet *ai*; pi:kwatiknmit *ai*; ~ hair pi:kwatikn; pesqayet *ai* [BC]

sheen ~ (used for weaving baskets) lisknuwaqan [SH]; cut ~ **-s** (for basket making) eltaqsawet *ai*;

sheep jijkluwewj (jijkluwewjik) *an*

sheet anqoni:kn [SH]

shell bird tmaqani *an* [SH]

shelter epqwalk *ta*, epqwatm *ti*; nqani:kuwom; temporary ~ epqwas'k

shield ~ or conceal (with a cloth) elaqpil'm *ti*, elaqpilk *ta*

shimmer ~ (of the sun) etlanqatesk *ii*

shine wasoqote:k *ta*, wasoqote:m *ti*; ~ through ne:ya:ta:q *ai* [SH]; ~ through (as the sun) ne:yaseniket *ai*

shiny welasek *ii*, welaset *ai*

ship pnasu:lkw [SH]; sallpo:k [CB]; sallpo:l; three-master sailing ~ lapukwan (Fr *la boucane*)

shirt atla:y *an* (Basque pidgin *atouray*; Basque *atorra*)

shiver nenk'tesink *ai*, nenk'tesk *ii*

shod poorly ~ winsitat *ai* [RB]; winkutat *ai*

shoe mk'sn *an*; wennjuksnan *an* [SH]; wennjusknan *an*; have nice ~ **-s** or boots welipteskna:q (welipteskna:m) *ai*; my ~ n'muksn *an*; ~ a horse mkuniye:jo:tlk *ta*

shoed poorly ~ winkutat *ai*

shoelace laqpa:taqan [SH]; mk'snapi *an*; my ~ n'muksnapi

shoeless sesaki:k (sesaki:m) *ai*

shoes and socks put on ~ pept'skna:'it *ai* [SH]; pept'skna:sit *ai* [SH]

shoestring mk'snapi *an*

shoot pe:skikek *ii*, pe:skiket *ai*; ~ at mattelaq *ta*, mattelm *ti*; pe:sk'k *ta*, pe:skm *ti* (with a gun); ~ dead siktelaq *ta*; wesaqalk *ta* [BR]; ~ down nistelaq *ta*, nistel'm *ti*; ~ toward eltaqa:m *ti*

shop go ~ **-ping** makasana:sit *ai*

shore sitm; a little way off ~ apaqtu:jk; along the ~ jajiktuk (loc) [SH]; move or walk along the ~ pemi-jajika:sit *ai*; off ~ apaqtuk; on the ~ tajiktuk; paddle along the ~ pemi-

jajikisukwit *ai*; paddle toward ~ wejkwina:taqamisukwit *ai*

shore up ettoqalk *ta*

short tekwaqti:jk *ii* [BR]; tewaqji:k *ii*, tewaqji:jit *ai* [BR]; toqopaqji:jk *ii*, toqopaqji:jit *ai* (in length); toqwaqji:jk *ii*, toqwaqji:jit *ai* (in height); ~ and round toqopsk'ji:jit *ai*; elapsk'pit *ai*, elapsk'tek *ii*; take or bring by the ~ **-est** route keskma:l'k *ta*, keskma:tu *ti*; too ~ wesamitwaqji:jit *ai*; very ~ kesitwaqji:jit *ai*

shortcut a ~ kesk'mtek *ii*; take a ~ keskma:sit *ai*

short-legged toqopskikatat *ai*

short-tempered eluwe:wit *ai*

shot take down with a ~ mesqanatelaq *ta* [CB]; mesqani:telaq *ta*

should lawtis

should? etuk

shoulder carry on the ~ pemn'kalk *ta*, pemn'katm *ti*; carry or pack on the ~ eln'ket *ai*; carry or pack on the ~ eln'kalk *ta*, eln'katm *ti*; carry toward on one's back or ~ eluktulk *ta*, eluktu *ti*; my ~ ntlmaqan; my ~ blade ntlaw (ntlaq) *an*; ntlmaqanatkw; ~ pack pemn'ket *ai*; have big ~ **-s** kekitlmaqanat *ai* [PEI]

shout seskwet *ai*

shove kesmaqalk *ta*, kesmaqtu *ti*; kesmeket *ai*; ~ backwards esetekjeket *ai*; ~ down nisaqalk *ta*, nisaqtu *ti*; ~ toward elipulk *ta*, eliputu *ti*; ~ (with foot) kesmteskaq *ta*, kesmteskm *ti*

shovel mulqwekn; qaliputi; qalaputi [SH]; qalipit *ai*; qalipilk *ta*, qalipitm *ti*

shower a (rain) ~ kikpesa:ji:jk *ii*; take a ~ kesispapalsit *ai* [BR]

show how ~ to do keknu:tmaq *ta*

show off ewsitutk (ewsitutm) *ai*; me:ka:teket *ai*

show up ne:ya:s'k *ii*, ne:ya:sit *ai*

shred sekwiskiyaq *ii*, sekwiskiyet *ai*

shrink we'ita:q *ii*, we'ita:t *ai*; ~ from ketkite:l'mk *ta*, ketkite:tm *ti* [BC]

shrivel apitapuwek *ii*, apitapuwet *ai*; ~ **-ed** up alm'stapuwek *ii*, alm'stapuwet *ai*

Shubenacadie s'kepne:kati

shut ilta:l'k *ta*, ilta:tu *ti*; kepjoqpit *ai*, kepjoqtek *ii*; kepsaqa:l'k *ta*, kepsaqa:tu *ti*; kepsoqpit *ai*, kepsoqtek *ii*; ~ firmly ilteket *ai*; slam ~ iltijiyeket *ai*

shy netake:k *ai*; a ~ person ntaqo:pj *an* (pejorative)

sibling have as a ~ (brother or sister) wijikumk *ta*; wijikimk *ta* [BR]; ~ -s wijik'tijik (pl) *ai*; wijikitijik (pl) *ai* [BR]

sick kesinukwat *ai* [BR]; kesnukwat *ai*; fall ~ ikekkwet *ai*; look ~ kesnukw-amuksit *ai*; kesnukwi-ankamkusit *ai*; very ~ kesiksinukwat *ai*; very weak (from being ~) kesis'wikna:t *ai*; ~ -ness ksnukowaqaan

sickle peskwete:kemkewey

sickly nenestawe:k *ai*, *ii*

side hip or ~ of one's body wpmepikaj [BR]; lie down on one's ~ wpmesma:sit *ai* [BR]; lie on one's ~ wpmesink *ai* [BR]; on one's ~ wpmetuk (loc) [BR]; on the opposite ~ qame:k (loc); on the other ~ a:se:k (loc); ~ elqamkuk [SH]; on the ~ kmetuk; pmetuk; upmetuk; push from the ~ taqamoqiksma:l'k *ta*, taqamoqiksma:tu *ti*; take the ~ of ikalk *ta*, ikatm *ti*; sit to one ~ anapiw pemkopit *ai*

sight ilamk *ta*, ilaptm *ti*; follow (with one's eyes) until out of ~ we:kwamk *ta*, we:kwaptm *ti*

silently cry ~ kimtemit *ai*

silk lapli:sikn

silly amassit *ai*; ewayatpat *ai*

silver suliyewey

simpl-e matuwe:k *ai*; live ~ y matu:-mimajit *ai*

sin pata:taqan; pata:teket *ai*; winjik *ii*, winjit *ai*; a ~ winjik *ii*; winjit *ai*; ~ -ner pata:tekewinu *an*

sinew tnuwan *an*

sing etlintoq (etlintu) *ai*; ketapekiyatm *ti* [CB]; ketapekiyet *ai*; ~ along pemintoq (pemintu) *ai*; know how to ~ natawintoq (natawintu) *ai*; ~ until dawn wapnintoq (wapnintu) *ai*; start to ~ poqjiktapekiyet *ai* [BR]; start to holler or ~ ketu:k (ketu:m) *ai*; ketuk *ai* [BR]; start to ~ poqjintoq (poqjintu) *ai*; heard ~ -ing

metewintoq (metewintu) *ai*; wetewintoq (wetewintu) *ai* [BR][SH]; finish ~ -ing kisintoq (kisintu) *ai*; a ~ -er nujintoq (nujintu) *ai (an)*; a good ~ -er natawintoq (natawintu) *ai*

single newtukwa:lukwet *ai*; have a ~ mark newtuwi:kas'k *ii*, newtuwi:kasit *ai (an)*

single file go ~ naploqqatultijik (pl) *ai*

singlehanded paddle or pole alone or ~ jikalukk (jikalukum) *ai*

sink[1] ketapa:q *ii*, ketapa:t *ai*; kutapuwalk *ta*, kutapuwatm *ti* [BC]; kwetapa:q *ii* [BR]; kwetapa:l'k *ta*, kwetapa:tu *ti* [BC]; ~ in wesawa:q *ii*, wesawa:t *ai* [BR]; wesuwa:q *ii*, wesuwa:t *ai* [BR]; wesuwaskiyaq *ii*, wesuwaskiyet *ai*

sink[2] mjikapu:lkw; dirty ~ mejiku:lkw [BR]

sinker k'lpisun; kullpisun; ~ -s sqolu:skw

sinner pata:tekewinu *an*

siphon maple syrup ~ tlaqan *an*

sirloin tnuwanoq *an*

sister my older ~ n'mis *an*; numis *an* [PEI]; my younger ~ nkwe:ji:j *an*

sister-in-law my ~ (female speaker) n'magtam *an* [BC]; nsukwis *an* [PEI]; my ~ (male speaker) nilmus *an* [PEI][BC]

sit ~ down epa:sit *ai*; ~ down atop ewt'pa:sit *ai*; ~ next to epa:suwalk *ta*, epa:suwatm *ti*; ~ in the way a:jelpit *ai*, a:jeltek *ii*; ~ on epa:suwalk *ta*, epa:suwatm *ti*; epitm *ti*; ewt'paskaq *ta*, ewt'paskm *ti*; paskaq *ta*, paskm *ti*; start to ~ down pempa:sit *ai*; ~ all about allkopijik (pl) *ai*; ~ (or set) facing toward wejkwajepit *ai*, wejkwajetek *ii*; ~ (or set) up high esp'pit *ai*, esp'tek *ii*; ~ quietly wantaqpit *ai*, wantaqtek *ii*; ~ to one side anapiw pemkopit *ai*; ~ with witpitaq *ta*, witpitm *ti*

six as'kom-te:s'kl (pl) *ii*, as'kom-te:sijik (pl) *ai*; have ~ of as'kom-te:sunkik (pl) *ta*; ~ (in counting) as'kom; ~ (of something cylindrical in shape) as'kom-te:soqsijik (pl) *ai*

sixty ~ (in counting) as'kom-te:siska:q; as'kom-te:sinska:q [BR]

skate na:qum *an*; ~ about alipqamit *ai* [ESK]; coast or ~ along pemipqamik *ii*, pemipqamit *ai*; ice ~ elipqamit *ai*; na:qoqumaq *ai*

skeleton waqanntewatpat (waqanntewatpajik) *an*

skin m′kekn; rabbit ~ wapusuwekn; kesipsa:l′k *ta*; musika:l′k *ta*, musika:tu *ti*; ~ a fish kesipsaqalk *ta* [BR]; pesa:l′k *ta*; ~ an animal pesqa:l′k *ta*; ~ inside out esetekjipsa:l′k, esetekjipsa:tu *ti* [SH]

skinny alu:saq *ii*, alu:sat *ai*

skip wenaqja:t *ai*; ~ around iwtoqoto:sit *ai* [SH]; ~ correctly koqqaji-w′naqto:sit *ai* [BR]; ~ rope kikto:qoto:sit *ai*; kiwto:qoto:sit *ai* [SH]; wenaqto:sit *ai* [SH]; ~ the cross (in jump rope) klujjewtaqto:sit *ai* [SH]; ~ wrong o:pli-w′naqto:sit *ai* [SH]

skull waqanntewatpat (waqanntewatpajik) *an*; animal ~ mi:saqatp [SH]; my ~ nsaqatp [BR]; nusaqatp [SH]

skunk apikjilu *an*; apukjilu *an* [PEI][BR]; hit with a ~ (in cribbage) apikjilute:k *ta*

sky musikiskw

sky blue musswan-amuksit *ai* [BR]

slab ~ of wood slaps (slapsik) *an*; ~ of meat piwsiw (piwsaq) *an* [BC]

slam ~ or throw down paqiyatkwe′itesm′k *ta*, paqiyatkwe′itestu *ti*; ~ shut iltijiyeket *ai*

slander pisuwimk *ta*

slap jaqpije′ite:m *ti* [SH]; ~ along the side of head epme:tkwete:k *ta* [SH]; ~ in the face pesikwe′ite:k *ta*; pesikwete:k *ta* [PEI]; ~ on the back of the head peji:taqanete:k *ta* [PEI]; ~ on the back of the head or neck peji:taqane:′ite:k *ta*

slapstick ji:kmaqan (a piece of rolled up birch bark used in drumming)

slate mtasoq; ~ colored wataptek *ii*

slaughterer a ~ ne:patat *ai (an)*

slave kisteju *an*; naqap (naqapaq) *an*

sled tapaqan [BR]; tepaqan; coasting ~ kulkwis *an*; short ~ (with wide runners) kulkwisuwatp [SH]

sleep nepaq *ii*, nepat *ai*; drift off to ~ kepskiyet *ai*; feign ~ ewsinpat *ai*; go to ~ najinpat *ai*; lie down to ~ nepasma:sit *ai*; pretend to ~ ewsinpat *ai* [BR]; put to ~ kepska:l′k *ta*; nepa:l′k *ta*; ~ easily or without trouble naqsinpat *ai*; ~ over ketkunit *ai*; ~

there ketkunit *ai*; ~ together toqosinkik (pl) *ai*; ~ until dawn wapnuksit *ai* [SH]; wapunkusit *ai*; ~ with eyes open wapinpat *ai*

sleepy ketuksit *ai*; get ~ ketuksiyet *ai*

sleet msi:kw (msi:kuk) *an*

sleeve my ~ np′ssan; nt′p′ssan [PEI]

sleigh kalipu *an*; kaliyulk (Fr *carriole*); tapaqan; tepaqan; my ~ nutepaqan

sleight of hand keskma:taqan

slice tems′k *ta*, temsm *ti*; cut or ~ off at the neck temkwesk *ta*, temkwesm *ti*; ~ in half naskwoqs′k *ta*, naskwoqsm *ti*; ~ or cut accidentally pess′k *ta*, pess′m *ti*; ~ a slab of meat piwsaw (piwsaq) *an* [BC]

slide elipqamulk *ta*, elipqamutu *ti*; pemipqamik *ii*, pemipqamit *ai*; ~ down nisateja:lukwet *ai*

slightly rain ~ kikpesa:ji:jk *ii*; ~ muddy in color ami-siskuwapuwaq *ii*; ~ warm ami-p′sit *ai*; ~ deaf amistaqanat

slim a ~ person nikoqji:j *an* [BC]

slime eskmoqon

slimy sisqallpo:qiyaq *ii*, sisqallpo:qiyet *ai*

sling tlansu (Fr *trente-sous*) (slang word for a quarter)

slip[1] saqatuwetesink *ai*; sesupa:lukwet *ai*; let ~ from the hand pesaqopska:sit *ai*

slip[2] lame:kewey (an undergarment)

slipper lamikuwome:j *an* [ESK]

slippery kesikaq *ii*, kesikat *ai*; sesupe:k *ai*, *ii*; wesase:k *ii* [BC]

slither ~ along pemtaqayet *ai*

slope nunmaqek *ii*, nunmaqet *ai*

sloppy winn′mat *ai*

slouched ~ over sawepit *ai*, sawetek *ii*

slow kekwe:k *ai*, *ii*; malja:t *ai*; ~ down jena:s′k *ii*, jena:sit *ai*; get out of the water ~ -ly paw-natqa:sit *ai*; grow ~ -ly malikwek *ii*, malikwet *ai*; move ~ -ly kekwa:s′k *ii*, kekwa:sit *ai*; pawa:s′k *ii*, pawa:sit *ai*; plow ~ -ly sankewsawet *ai*; run ~ -ly kekwi:pit *ai*; run along ~ -ly pemi-kekwi:pit *ai* [SH]; talk ~ -ly sankewewo:kwet *ai*; sankewi:sit *ai*; think ~ -ly sankewi-ankita:sit *ai*

slowpoke a ~ mala:sit *ai (an)*; pawe:k *ai*; sipke:k *ai (an)*

slush ~ (on the river) makun

slushy mekunik *ii*
small apje:jk *ii*, apje:jit *ai*; have a ~ head
　　apsatpat *ai*; have a ~ mouth apsalqo:tnat *ai*
　　[SH]; apsalqutnat *ai*; apsaqqutnat *ai*; have ~
　　eyes apsalqikwat *ai*; have ~ hands or paws
　　apsiptnat *ai*; ~ and round apjoqji:jk *ii*,
　　apjoqji:jit *ai*; take or withdraw in ~ amounts
　　qasko:tm *ti*, qaskweyaq *ta*; too ~ ewsami-
　　apje:jk *ii* [CB]; wemsami-apje:jk *ii* [BR];
　　make ~ **-er** apsa:l'k *ta*, apsa:tu *ti*;
smallpox lapikot *an*; have ~ lapikotewit *ai*
smart seskwe:k *ai*; sma:tewit *ai*
smarten up sma:tewa:sit *ai*
smartly act or do ~ sma:tewa:sit *ai*
smash sekwistesmk *ta*, sekwistestu *ti* [BR]; ~
　　to bits nukte:k *ta*, nukte:m *ti*; ~ **-ed**
　　sekwisto:kwek *ii*, sekwisto:kwet *ai*
smear eljaqam *ti*, eljaqq *ta*; ~ over
　　weskijiyama:l'k *ta*, weskijiyama:tu *ti*
smell pese:k *ta*, pesetu *ti*; pesemk *ta*, pesetm
　　ti; have a certain (nice) ~ welitpima:q *ii*,
　　welitpima:t *ai*; have such a ~ telima:q *ii*,
　　telima:t *ai*; ~ bad jijjema:q *ii*, jijjema:t *ai*;
　　metuwima:q *ii*, metuwima:t *ai*; ~ good
　　welima:q *ii*, welima:t *ai*; ~ of smoke
　　wikplatewma:t *ai*, wikplatewma:q *ii*; taste or
　　~ rotten sukul'kma:q *ii*, sukul'kma:t *ai*; a
　　faeces ~ **-er** mi:janimat *ai (an)*
smelt kaqpesaw (kaqpesaq) *an*; wisnanaw
　　(wisnanaq) *an* [SH]
smile weskowikwa:sit *ai*; ~ to oneself
　　kim-elmit *ai*; wear a ~ welikwetutk
　　(welikwetutm) *ai*
smoke mklu:tew; mtlu:tew [BR]; nklu:tew;
　　ntlu:tew [BR]; ~ or steam etlikp'ta:q *ii*,
　　etlikp'ta:t *ai*; metlu:sit *ai*, metlu:tek *ii*;
　　kwetamat *ai* [BR]; a (cigarette) ~
　　wetmamkewey; kwetmat *ai* [BR]; light up or
　　smoke pask'setmat *ai*; wetmat *ai* [RB]; give
　　a ~ (cigarette) to wetmaq *ta (do)*; smell of ~
　　wikplatewma:t *ai*, wikplatewma:q *ii*; ~ a fish,
　　etc. pukkwana:l'k *ta*, pukkwana:tu *ti* (Fr
　　boucane); ~ food pukkwana:teket *ai*; a ~ **-d**
　　fish pukkwanata:sit n'me:j *an*; ~ **-d** fish (e.g.
　　herring) or ham pukkwanaw (pukkwanaq)
　　an; ~ **-ed** (such as meat) wikplasit *ai*,
　　wikplatek *ii*; a heavy ~ **er** wikmat *ai*; place,

apparatus or utensil for ~ **ing** meat
　　pukkwana:taqan; ~ **-y** metlu:sit *ai*, metlu:tek
　　ii; netlu:sit *ai*, netlu:tek *ii* [BC]; smell ~ **y**
　　wikplatewma:t *ai*, wikplatewma:q *ii*
smooth sasqe:k *ai*, *ii*; welnuksik *ii*, welnuksit
　　ai; ~ and round musikapsk'sit *ai*,
　　musikapskek *ii*; ~ out jiktaqam *ti* [SH];
　　jitnaqa:m *ti*; musikwatm *ti* [PEI];
　　siw'noqikwatm *ti*; ~ sheens (for basketry)
　　jiktaqawet *ai*; do nicely or ~ **-ly** weljaqk *ta*,
　　weljaqam *ti*
smother aptlama:l'k *ta*, aptlama:tu *ti*
snack qaskwatalk *ai*; have a good ~ (on
　　bread) wel-pistamit *ai*; have a ~
　　matuwatalk *ai*
snail sea ~ jik'ji:j(i:j) *an* [RB]
snake mteskm (mteskmuk) *an*
snap ~ in two temeket *ai*; ~ off at the tail
　　temaluweket *ai* [BR]; ~ off at the neck
　　temiskipeket *ai*
snare na:puktaqan [BR]; puktaqan [BR];
　　la:puktaqan; la:puktaqannikalk *ta*; set
　　(rabbit) ~ **-s** la:puktaqaniket *ai*
sneak ~ around kimiyet *ai*; ~ up eli-
　　kimskuwet *ai* [BR]; ~ up on eli-kimskuwatm
　　ti, eli-kimskuwalk *ta* [BR]; kimteskaq *ta*,
　　kimteskm *ti*; ~ up to el-kimskuwet *ai*; ~ **-y**
　　kime:k *ai* [SH]
sneeze ejkwit *ai*; eskwit *ai*; ewskwit *ai*
sniff kwejipsemk *ta*, kwejipsetu *ti*; pitna:tat *ai*;
　　wejisetmit *ai*; wejipsemk *ta*, wejipsetm *ti*;
　　give a ~ to pitna:taq *ta*; pitnewey
snipe jijikwatej *an* [RB]; jikatej *an* [RB]
snob me:ko:pj (me:ko:pjik)
snobbish emteskit *ai*
snor-e kin-tewoqsink *ai*; heard ~ **-ing**
　　wetewoqsink *ai* [SH]
snort kesikawitnet *ai*
snot wja:law (wja:laq) *an*
snow pesaq *ii*; at the end of the ~ period
　　paniyanuk (loc); fallen ~ wastew; light ~
　　pesa:ji:jk *ii*; ~ heavily ma:munipsaq *ii*; ~
　　mist pesanakik *ii* [BR]; start to ~ poqjipsaq;
　　wade around in the ~ alasumteket *ai*; wet ~
　　saqpipsaq *ii*
snowball wali:j *an*; wastew tu:waqan [RB]
snow-blinded wisqap'lkikwa:t *ai*

snow-covered oqonaliyaq *ii*, oqonaliyet *ai*
snowdrift wali:kik (pl) *an*
snowfall psan; heavy ~ e:pluwipsaq *ii* [ESK]; pastesk *ii*; light ~ psanji:j
snowshoe aqam *an* [SH]; my ~ ntaqam *an*; aqami:k (aqami:m) *ai* [SH]; laskuwaw (laskuwaq) *an*; ~ about alaqami:k (alaqami:m) *ai*; make tracks with ~ -s jilaqami:k (jilaqami:m) *ai*
so ki:wajiyaq *ii*, ki:wajiyet *ai*; klamen; kulaman [BC]; lo:q; toqo; is that ~ ? toqo na; it shall be ~ na to:q; make ~ telitu *ti*, teli:k *ta*; ~ bashful tetujintake:k *ai*; ~ many years old tetuje:k *ai*; te'uje:k *ai*; ~ probably lo:q etuk [SH]; ~ that lo:q; ~ then toqo t'lisip [CB]; sound ~ telta:q *ii*, teltoqsit *ai*; treat ~ teleyaq *ta*, telo:tm *ti*
soak wetqapalsit *ai*; wetqapalk *ta*, wetqapatu *ti*
soap ksispa:taqan [SH]; suspanikn
sob ejkwe:mat *ai*
so be it na tliyaq *ii*
sober pa:ke:k *ai*
sock sikn; ankle length ~ siksuti
soda apita:taqan
sofa soppey
soft nukwe:k *ai*, *ii*; ~ -en nukwa:l'k *ta*, nukwa:tu *ti*; nujkmoqs'k *ta*, nujkmoqsm *ti*
softly talk ~ kim-ewo:kwet *ai*
soggy alm'sta:q *ii*, alm'sta:t *ai*
soldier sma:knis *an*; become a ~ sma:knisuwit *ai*
solicit salite:wit *ai* (Fr *charité*)
solid melke:k *ai*, *ii*; ~ man melki-ji:n'm *an*; ~ -ly built melkikit *ai*
solidify melka:s'k *ii*, melka:sit *ai*
solitary ~ person nkuto:pj: *an*; nkuta:pewj *an* [BC]
so many ~ kinds te:sunemiksit *ai*, te:sunemi:k *ii*; ~ years old te:sipuna:t *ai*
some alt
somebody ta:n wen
someone nat wen; ~ else me: wen (me: wenik) *an*
something nat koqwey; ta:n koqwey
sometimes jijuwaqa

somewhat ~ big meski:kji:jit *ii*; ~ cold (of the weather) amitke:k *ii*
somewhere na: tami; se:k; ~ or someplace else me: na: tami [SH]
sommersalt jammpo:qiyet *ai*
so much te:s'k *ii*, te:sit *ai* (many); have ~ or so many te:sun'm *ti*, te:sunk *ta*
son! kwi:s (voc)
son my little ~ nkwitji:j (dim) *an*; my ~ nkwis *an*; have a ~ wkwisit *ai*
song ktapekiyaqan
son-in-law my ~ ntlu:suk *an*; act like a ~ lu:sukwewa:sit *ai*
sonny! kwitji:j (voc)
soon apukjik; ekipjik [BR]; keket; wikipjik; wipukjik [BR]; as ~ as ta:n tlinqase:k
soot muspusi *an* [BR]; puksetew; ~ -y puksetewik *ii*
sop bread spread or ~ (e.g., fat, molasses) pistamun; ~ up (e.g., gravy, molasses) with bread pistamit *ai*; epistamit *ai*
sore my ~ nujkim; wjiki [BR]; cause (a body part) to get ~ (from sleeping on it) elkaq *ta*, elkm *ti*; ~ (of a body part) kitaqet *ai*, kitaqek *ii*; ~ (of a person) kitaqasit *ai*
sorrow meskata:suwaqan; w'lma'itasuwaqan
sorry meske:k *ai*
sort of kimu:tuk; ~ good ami-klu:lk *ii*, ami-klu:sit *ai*;
so-so ami-klu:lk *ii*, ami-klu:sit *ai*
soul my ~ njijaqamij *an*
sound[1] of ~ mind nestuwe:k *ai*
sound[2] have a good ~ (of music) welta:q *ii*, weltoqsit *ai*; like the ~ of wels'taq *ta*, wels'tm *ti*; ~ sickly kesnukwitoqsit *ai*; ~ hoarse kepitnetoqsit *ai*; ~ (the voice) in such a manner tel-kisutnat *ai*; ~ like telta:q *ii*, teltoqsit *ai*; make ~ -s pentoqsit *ai*
soup lasup (Fr *la soupe*); pea ~ wennju-a:p'tew
sour sewl'k *ai*, *ii*
south kp'te:sn; tp'te:sn; go ~ metoqiyaq *ii*, metoqiyet *ai*; take ~ metoqwa:l'k *ta*, metoqwa:tu *ti*
southerner tp'te:snukowa:j
southpaw patatujo:q *an*

southwest senusaqtn [SH]; ~ wind senusaqt'k *ii* [SH]

southwind pekte:s'k *ii*

sow eleket *ai*; ika:taqalk *ta*, ika:taqatm *ti*; ika:taquk *ai*; ika:taqulk *ta*, ika:taqutm *ti*

spade a ~ (in cards) maqtewipqaji:jit (maqtewipqaji:jijik) *an* [SH]; pi:k (pi:kaq) *an* (Fr *pique*)

spank matte:k *ta*, matte:m *ti*

sparkle wasoqotesk *ii*, wasoqotesink *ai*

sparrow msikuwe:j *an*

spawn sika:law (sika:laq) *an* [SH]; sika:lat *ai*; sika:tat *ai* [SH]

speak kelusit *ai*; begin to ~ poqtewo:kwet *ai* [BR]; ~ carefully menaqajewo:kwet *ai*; ~ English aklasiyewi:sit *ai* [BR]; ~ falsely of pilsimk *ta*; ~ hoarsely kepitnetoqsit *ai*; ~ in an odd or unusual way kesmi:sit *ai*; ~ loudly kesikawewo:kwet *ai*; ~ many languages milatuwat *ai*; ~ Micmac mi:kmawi:sit *ai*; ~ poorly mali:sit *ai*; ~ succinctly menaqajewo:kwet *ai*; ~ the truth (as a preacher) nestuwapukuwet *ai*; ~ to kelulk *ta*; ~ truthfully to keknuwimk *ta*; ~ wet saqpi:sit *ai*; ~ with a deep or husky voice maqi:sit *ai*; ~ with a nasal twang kepitni:sit *ai* [BC]

speak for nesssutmasewk *ta*

spear sumokati; eel ~ nikoq [BR]; nikoqol; small two-pronged ~ nikoqji:j; tlawo:qte:k *ta*, tlawo:qte:m *ti*;

special keknuwe:k *ai*, *ii*

specifically nkutey

specs my ~ npu:kwe:l (pl)

speech know how to make a ~ natawatuwet *ai*; make a ~ pestunk (pestun'm) *ai*

spell cast a ~ puntat *ai*; cast a ~ on puntalk *ta*, puntatm *ti*

spider awo:wejit (awowejijik) *an* [BR]; ko:qwejij *an*; ~ web awo:wejituwo:pi [BR]; ko:qwejijiwa:pi

spike-horn ~ bull (two points) niktuwoqonej *an* [SH]

spill kutatestat *ai*; kutatesmk *ta*, kutatestu *ti*; kuteket *ai*

spin elisknuwet *ai* [BR]; kitto:qiyaq *ii*, kitto:qiyet *ai*; ~ around kiwto:qoto:sit *ai* [BC]; ~ thread eltaqanewet *ai*

spinal cord my ~ no:kwin

spinster kisiku:skwe:j *an*; nkutilj *an*

spirit Great ~ kji-niskam *an*; my ~ njijaqamij *an*

spit eluskwatamit *ai*; luskwatikn

spite ketank *ta*, ketantu *ti*; act for ~ ki:kaje:k *ai* [PEI]; do for ~ ki:kajeyaq *ta*, ki:kajo:tm *ti*; go for ~ ki:kaja:sit *ai*; in ~ of ki:kaj; toqqatu

spiteful ketanuwet *ai*; ketanteket *ai*

splash elpaq'nte:m *ti* [BR]; ~ along pempaqto:sit *ai*; ~ oneself elapaqto:sit *ai*; ~ water on elapaqte:k *ta*, elapaqte:m *ti*

splint finger ~ pitlan

split naskwina:l'k *ta*, naskwina:tu *ti*; naskwine:k *ai*, *ii*; paskinete:k *ta* [SH]; ~ lengthwise (with a heavy blow) naskoqte:k *ta*, naskoqte:m *ti*; ~ open nawswoqwa:t *ai* [SH]; ~ up as kindling elask'te:m *ti* [SH]; ~ with the hand naskoqwa:l'k *ta*, naskoqwa:tu *ti*; ~ wood naskoqte:ket *ai*; pesikte:ket *ai*

spooked em'lsiktmat *ai*

spool papn-ji:j *an*; amqwanji:j *an*; ~ of thread a:papi:j *an*

spoon emqwanji:j *an* [BR]; mqwan(ji:j) *an* [SH]

spotted jilpit *ai*, jiltek *ii*

spouse get a ~ from there weja:teket *ai*; my ~ nikma:j *an*

spout putuwatamit *ai*

sprain o:plisqatestu *ti*; ~ -ed kelkwisketesk *ii*; kelkwiske:k *ii*; o:plisqatesk *ii*, o:plisqatesink *ai*

spread eljaqam *ti*, eljaqq *ta*; ileko:tm *ti* [PEI]; bread ~ or sop (fat, molasses, etc.) pistamun; ~ (in mixed colors) amjaqamuksit *ai*, amjaqamu:k *ii*; ~ around (as a sickness) ala:s'k *ii*, ala:sit *ai*; ~ around se:sikwalk *ta*, se:sikwatm *ti*; ~ on amjaqam *ti*, amjaqq *ta*; amjaqamat *ai*; ~ out elaqpit *ai* [SH]; eleko:l'k *ta*, eleko:tu *ti*; se:sa:l'k *ta*, se:sa:tu *ti*; se:sa:s'k *ii*, se:sa:sit *ai*; sipela:l'k *ta* [BR]; sipeleka:l'k *ta*, sipeleka:tu *ti* [BR]; sipeleka:l'k *ta*, sipleka:tu *ti*; ~ out the blanket elaqsensit *ai*

spring[1] siwkw [BR][CB]; sikkw [BR]; about or toward ~ sikkwe:l [BR]; last ~ sikun; next ~ sikunuk; turn ~ sikuniyaq *ii* [SH]; have ~ fever sikowiyet *ai*; ~ -born animal sikune:ji:j *an*

spring[2] ~ water lenpok; l'npok [SH]; tk'poq; bubbling ~ tkupoq

spring[3] wenaqteskasit *ai*; ~ back apattesk *ii*, apattesink *ai*

spring from wetapaqamit *ai*

sprinkle dab or ~ self (with powder or perfume) amjaqto:sit *ai*

sprinkler holy water ~ lapatikn

sprint wisqi:pit *ai*; ~ along pemi-wisqi:pit *ai* [BR]

sprout nikik *ii*, nikit *ai*; saqaliyaq *ii*, saqaliyet *ai*

spruce kawatkw (kawatkuk) *an*; ~ bough enaqan *an* (used as floor covering in wikwam) [SH]; ~ , fir or balsam tree stoqonaqsi *an* [SH]; spread ~ boughs enaqet *ai* [SH]; break off a ~ bough menastatm *ti*; break off ~ boughs menastet *ai*; collect ~ gum menipku:sit *ai* [BC]

spy awisku:k (awisku:kaq) *an* [SH]; ~ on kimamk *ta*, kimaptm *ti*

spy glass laputi

square tetpitsaq

squash[1] ejkw'jk

squash[2] nukjaqa:l'k *ta*, nukjaqa:tu *ti*

squat nisnusit *ai*

squeeze jink'ja:l'k *ta*, jink'ja:tu *ti*; paskija:l'k *ta*, paskija:tu *ti*; ~ or press in piji-jink'ja:l'k *ta*; piji-jink'ja:tu *ti*; ~ together ash strands in basketry esinapito:tu *ti* [ESK]; ~ unintentionally peji-jink'ja:l'k *ta*, peji-jink'ja:tu *ti*

squid seta:su *an* [SH]; sete:su *an*

squint winikwetuwet *ai*; ~ at winikwetaq *ta*

squirm sespa:sit *ai*; ~ around milipusit *ai*

squirrel atu:tuwej *an*; flying ~ sasqatu *an*; imitate a ~ atu:tuwejuwi:sit *ai*

stab sapaqqate:k *ta*; tlawo:qte:k *ta*, t'lawo:qte:m *ti*

stable nqani:kuwom

stack ~ -ed elamko:tas'k *ii*, elamko:tasit *ai*; ~ -ed upright el-pukuwo:tasit *ai*, el-pukuwo:tas'k *ii*

stagger al-ja:t *ai*; ~ along enmoqtesink *ai*; pemi:pukwet *ai*; ~ along by pemi-siyawi:pukwet *ai* [BR]; ~ home enmoqtesink *ai*; ~ toward eli:pukwet *ai*

stalk ketanqikalk *ta* [CB]

stamp ~ out (a fire) naqasuweteskaq *ta*, naqasuweteskm *ti*

stand kaqamik *ii*, kaqamit *ai*; ~ at the ready kiskat-pukuwit *ai* (said of the sun when it is on the verge of rising) [BR]; ~ atop ke:kwi-pukuwit *ai* [SH]; facing toward wejkupukuwit *ai*; ~ in the way a:jel-pukuwik *ii*, a:jel-pukuwit *ai*; ~ like a ginap kin-pukuwit *ai*; ~ outside the door tew-pukuwit *ai*; ~ or slide on one leg newtikata:lukwet *ai*; ~ straight up tetpaqqamit *ai*, tetpaqqamik *ii*; ~ tall kin-pukuwit *ai*; ~ together toqo-pukuwa:l'kik (pl) *ta*; ~ up kaqama:s'k *ii*, kaqama:sit *ai*; ~ up high esp'pukuwik *ii*, esp'pukuwit *ai*

star kloqowej *an*

stare ~ at kesi-ankamk *ta*, kesi-ankaptm *ti*

starling puk'tli:kej *an* ("black robin") [ESK]

start ~ after poqt'teskaq *ta*, poqt'teskm *ti*; ~ off poqtamka:sit *ai*; ~ off to church najitko:tk (najitko:tm) *ai*; ~ out poqtamkiyaq *ii*, poqtamkiyet *ai*; ~ out to fish najiwsket *ai*; ~ out to hunt and kill najiktanteket *ai* [CB]; ~ to bald poqji-m'mkatpa:t *ai* [BR]; ~ to get cool poqji-newek *ii*; ~ to pack naji-ilajit *ai*; ~ to sing poqjiktapekiyet *ai* [BR]; ~ to snow poqjipsaq

starvation pestmo:qon

starve aptaqanet *ai*; pestmat *ai*

statue (human) ~ nnuwoqta:w *an*

stay ~ for a long time pekitqatk (pekitqatm) *ai*; ~ here and there pe'ikwaqatk (pe'ikwaqatm) *ai*; ~ , live or situated at weskowa:s'k *ii*, weskowa:sit *ai*; ~ or live together toqwa:majik (pl) *ai*; ~ permanently aptaqatk (aptaqatm) *ai*; ~ quiet wantaqpit *ai*, wantaqtek *ii*; ~ such a length of time telipkitqatm *ai*; ~ up all night wapnapit *ai*

steady illjo:qon'm *ti*, illjo:qonk *ta*; my ~ (girl or boyfriend) np'lkoqom *an*

steal kemutnek *ii*, kemutnet *ai*; kmutnet *ai*; kemutnalk *ta*, kemutnatm *ti*; kimutnalk *ta*; kimutna:l'k *ta* [SH]; kmutnalk *ta*, kmutnatm *ti*; ~ from kemutmk *ta*

stealthfully kimu:tuk

steam etlikp'ta:q *ii*, etlikp'ta:t *ai*; piksapekiyaq *ii* [EG]; ~ and boil etlikmiyet *ai*; steamy piksa:q *ii*, piksa:t *ai*

steamboat puktewulkw

steel sqana:kw

steep kesaqek *ii*, kesaqet *ai*

steeple jejuwejkwatp; jijuwejkwatp

steer ilkwi:t'k *ta*, ilkwi:tm *ti*; ~ along pemkwi:tm *ti*

step ~ outside tew-pukuwa:sit *ai*

stepchild my ~ nijjus *an*

stepdaughter my ~ nkoji:j *an*

stepfather my ~ niskamij *an* [BC]

Stephen Ekiyan *an* [BC]

stepmother my ~ niskamiji:skw *an* [BC]

stern in the rear or ~ (of a boat) setamk (loc) [BR]; satamk [BC]

stick¹ kmu:j *in*; candle ~ wasoqonmaqanatk; forked ~ na:po:qon; small ~ kmu:ji:j [BR]; bundle of ~ -s (used for fuel) oqon; beat with a ~ kmutte:k *ta*, kmutte:m *ti*

stick² oqoskijikuwek *ii*, oqoskijikuwet *ai*; ~ on mekwasa:l'k *ta*, mekwasa:tu *ti*; ~ out muskask'pit *ai*, muskask'tek *ii*; tewoqpit *ai*, tewoqtek *ii*

stick³ ~ in enn'ma:l'k *ta*, enn'ma:tu *ti*; pitask'pit *ai*, pitask'tek *ii*

sticky pekuwik *ii*, pekuwit *ai*; pesqojikuwek *ii*, pesqojikuwet *ai* [SH]; pesqojukuwek *ii*, pesqojukuwet *ai*; have ~ fingers pesqojukuwiptnat *ai* [BC]; ~ -fingered pekuwiptnat *ai*; pkuwiptnat *ai (an)*

stiff metkwe:k *ai, ii*; petkwe:k *ai* [BC]; ~ all over kaqi-petkwe:k *ai* [BC]; get ~ mejkiyet *ai*; ~ with fright (from a nightmare) melkwiskat *ai*

still ki:kaj; me:; even ~ me:j; mi:soqo me:j [BC]; ~ water wantaqpekitk *ii*

stimulate massaqte:ket *ai*; sexually aroused or ~ -d massaqiyet *ai*

sting sapte:k *ta*, sapte:m *ti*

stingy amase:ke:k *ai* [SH]; keskeltmat *ai* [BC]; nepaqt'k (nepaqtm) *ai*; ~ with one's drinks metu:pet *ai*

stink jijjema:q *ii*, jijjema:t *ai*; keslet *ai*, keslek *ii* [SH]

stir mesiyapoq'k *ta*, mesiyapoqm *ti*; ~ up trouble asiketk (asiketm) *ai*; ~ with an instrument mesiyapoqte:k *ta*, mesiyapoqte:m *ti*; heard ~ -ring or bustling about metewe:k *ai*

stitch ~ on kelapaqte:k *ta*, kelapaqte:m *ti*

stock ~ a pantry with provisions kiwikatm *ti* [BR]

stocking sikn; my ~ ntisikn; nt'sikn [PEI]

stomach my ~ ntlamilu

stomach ache have a ~ sewtiya:t *ai* [SH]

stomp ~ to bits nukjaqteskaq *ta*, nukjaqteskm *ti*; break by kicking or ~ -ing temteskaq *ta*, temteskm *ti* [BR]

stone kunnte:j; kunntew (kunntal)

stool have a hard ~ melk'jat *ai*; have a large ~ maqijjikwat *ai*

stoop ejaqjepit *ai*; nisnusit *ai*; ~ down nisa:kwa:sit *ai*; ~ facing backwards enmikjo:kwet *ai*; ~ to drink (human or animal) kukwa:sit *ai*

stop enqa:l'k *ta*, enqa:tu *ti*; enqa:s'k *ai*, enqa:sit *ai*; naqa:l'k *ta*, naqa:tu *ti*; naqa:sit *ai*; nqa:s'k *ii*, nqa:sit *ai*; ~ (by nudging) naqte:k *ta*, naqte:m *ti*; ~ crying puntemit *ai*; ~ doing punajeyaq *ta*, punajo:tm *ti*; ~ laughing pun-el'mit *ai* [SH]; ~ lecturing or berating punajimk *ta*; ~ lecturing or preaching punewistoq (punewistu) *ai*; ~ working for pun-lukwewk *ta*; ~ -ped enqapit *ai*, enqatek *ii*

store¹ makasan (Fr *magasin*); general ~ malsano:kuwom [SH]

store² masko:l'k *ta*, masko:tu *ti*; masqwa:l'k *ta*, masqwa:tu *ti*; nasko:l'k *ta*, nasko:tu *ti*;

stories je:k [BC]

storm mtukunoqt; act like a ~ is approaching mtukunoqtnukwet *ai* (said of a horse); ~ -y metukuna:q *ii*; metu:na:q *ii*

story a:tukwaqan; tell a ~ a:tukwet *ai*; tell a ~ to a:tukwewk *ta*; the end of the ~ (the sound) kespiyatoqsit *ai*

storyteller a:tukwewinu *an*; a ~ nuji-nutmaqaneket *ai (an)*

stout toqopsk'ji:jit *ai*

stove epsaqtejk *an*; kepsaqtejk *an* [SH]; wood ~ puksukey epsaqtejk

stove pipe wsitney

straddle nasuwoqkaq *ta*, nasuwoqkm *ti*; sit a ~ sawkwatepit *ai* [BR]

straight koqwattek *ii*; tekpaqikk *ii*, tekpaqikit *ai*; tetpaqpit *ai*, tetpaqtek *ii*; tetpaqsit *ai*, tetpaqtek *ii*; tetpaqik *ii*, tetpaqikit *ai*; cut ~ tetpaqs'k *ta*, tetpaqsm *ti*; follow one another in a ~ line naploqqatultijik (pl) *ai*; long and ~ peka:q *ii*, pekoqsit *ai*; place ~ tetpaqqama:l'k *ta*, tetpaqqama:tu *ti*; put ~ illjo:qwa:l'k *ta*, illjo:qwa:tu *ti*; sit ~ tetpaqopit *ai*; sit up ~ sinuwoqpa:sit *ai* [BC]; stand ~ up tetpaqqamit *ai*, tetpaqqamik *ii*

straighten tetpaqa:l'k *ta*, tetpaqa:tu *ti* [PEI]; ~ out iloqwa:l'k *ta*, iloqwa:tu *ti*; iltaqa:l'k *ta*, iltaqa:tu *ti*; ~ out as pipe or a net iltaqo:l'k *ta*, iltaqo:tu *ti*

strain enqalk *ta*, enqan'm *ti*; pestaqa:l'k *ta*, pestaqa:tu *ti*; ~ to look munsapit *ai*

strand braid or ~ lisknuwapi [MARIA]

strange istuwe:k *ai, ii*; wi:kuwe:k *ai, ii*; look ~ or different to piltuwamk *ta*, piltuwaptm *ti*; look ~ or weird kesmapewit *ai*; see something ~ in piltuwamk, piltuwaptm *ti*

stratified lipqamu:k

straw sikuwaqs'te:kn

strawberry atuwomkemin *an* [BR][RB]; klitaw (klitaq) *an*

streaked pemapaqtesink *ai*, pemapaqtesk *ii*

streamlined kesmikit *ai*

strength m'lkiknoti

stretch siptaqa:s'k *ii*, siptaqa:sit *ai*; siptaqa:l'k *ta*, siptaqa:tu *ti*; ~ and yawn sipit *ai*; ~ out sipleka:l'k *ta*, sipleka:tu *ti*; sisqa:taq *ta*; ~ out for a rest ilapsk'smu:kwet *ai*; ~ -ed out siptaqesink *ai*

stretcher alapilawemkewey

stricken grief ~ welmaje:k *ai*

strik-e me:te:k *ta*, me:te:m *ti*; ~ or hit accidentally pette:k *ta*, pette:m *ti*; ~ with a knife tlawo:qs'k *ta*; finish ~ -ing kaqte:k *ta*

string fiddle ~ tapiya:jijk api *an* [SH]; ~ a line eltaqa:teket *ai* [RB]; ~ beads na:pawet *ai* [BC]; ~ toward eltaqa:l'k *ta*, eltaqa:tu *ti*; ~ up (as a clothesline) eltaqa:l'k *ta*, eltaqa:tu *ti* [BC]

stringy strong and ~ melk'tqasit *ai*, melk'tqek *ii* [BC]

strip musika:l'k *ta*, musika:tu *ti*; musiko:l'k *ta*, musiko:tu *ti*; ash ~ (for weaving baskets) likpete:knapi; ash ~ (for making baskets) wikpe:tlaqan; beat (ash) into ~ -s elanqate:m *ti*; ~ ash elikpetamit *ai* [SH]; ~ a person emisqo:t'lk *ta*; ~ bare musik'nja:tm *ti*; ~ off menepqa:l'k *ta*, menepqa:tu *ti*; ~ off (birchbark) meni:kwet *ai*; papqwa:tu *ti* [SH]; ~ off (with an axe) pelkoqte:k *ta*, pelkoqte:m *ti*; ~ or split well welikpa:q *ii*, welikpa:t *ai*; ~ while dancing emisqatesink *ai*; ~ -ped of clothing emisqatesk *ii*, emisqatesink *ai*; remove by ~ -ping menipka:l'k *ta*, menipka:tu *ti*

strive ketanteket *ai*; ~ to obtain ketank *ta*, ketantu *ti*; ~ to save munsi-sapa:l'k *ta*, munsi-sapa:tu *ti*

stroke etlipulk *ta*, etliputu *ti*; ~ toward elipulk *ta*, eliputu *ti*

stroll ~ toward elenqwe:set *ai*

strong melkiknaq *ii*, melkiknat *ai*; have a ~ grip melkapjit *ai*; have a ~ neck melki:taqanat *ai*; have a ~ , unpleasant odor kesima:q *ii*, kesima:t *ai*; ~ and stringy melk'tqasit *ai*, melk'tqek *ii* [BC]; ~ brew m'lsuwapu; ~ enough tepiknaq *ii*, tepiknat *ai*; ~ man melki-ji:n'm *an*; ~ man or woman m'lkiknewinu *an*; very ~ kesi-m'lkiknat *ai*

structure long enclosed ~ pittaqapekisk *ii*

struggle ketuwapsit *ai*; matnakket *ai*; ~ to get through munsi-sapa:l'k *ta*, munsi-sapa:tu *ti*; ~ to survive munsi-sapa:l'k *ta*, munsi-sapa:tu *ti*

strum etl-te:k *ta*, etl-te:m *ti*

strung ~ up na:pasit *ai*, na:pas'k *ii*

strut ~ around kinateja:sit *ai*

stub ~ one's toe ejaqannjeteskmat *ai*
stuck amjimoqpit *ai*, amjimoqtek *ii*;
    amjimoqtesk *ii*, amjimoqtesink *ai*; get ~
    inside amjimoqwa:l'k *ta*, amjimoqwa:tu *ti*; ~
    inside apt'tesk *ii*, apt'tesink *ai*; ~ into
    eln'mik *ii*, eln'mit
stuck up me:ke:k *ai*; ~ person me:ko:pj
    (me:ko:pjik)
stud ~ horse latto:law *an* (Fr *le taureau*)
stuff pitkmalk *ta*, pitkmatm *ti*
stumble pesoqteskmat *ai*; ~ about al-ja:t *ai*;
    ~ and fall paqiyatkwe'itesink *ai*
stump tree ~ wji:k'j
sturgeon komkotamu *an* [RB]
submerge ketapa:sit *ai*; kwetapa:sit *ai* [BR]
substitute temporarily ~ or fill in for nespit *ai*
succinctly speak ~ menaqajewo:kwet *ai*
such behave or act in ~ a manner tela:sit *ai*;
    have ~ a smell telima:q *ii*, telima:t *ai*; have ~
    a taste telima:q *ii*, telima:t *ai* [SH]; seems as
    ~ teleyaq *ii*; ~ time tele:k *ai*, *ii*; treat as ~
    teleyaq *ta*, telo:tm *ti*
suck nujitat *ai*; nunat *ai*; nunalk *ta*, nunatm *ti*
sucker komkwej *an* (a fish)
suckle nunat *ai*; ~ an infant nusalk *ta*; ~ from
    the breast etlitat *ai*
suddenly fall ~ ill jaqalipnet *ai*; go or move ~
    jaqala:sit *ai*
suds pisew
suet m'ni:maqanu:min [PEI]
suffer welmaje:k *ai*; ~ in spirit welma'ita:sit
    ai; ~ from a long term illness pekijipnet *ai*
sufficient tepiyaq *ii*, tepiyet *ai*
suffocate aptlamik *ii*, aptlamit *ai*
sugar sismoqwan [BR]; sismo:qon; ~ ant
    sismo:qone:j *an*; ~ bowl sismo:qono:q
summer nipk *ii*; last ~ ktiki-nipn; last ~ nipn;
    next ~ nipnuk; paniyanuk (loc) [PEI]
summit k'petaq *ii*; the ~ k'p'tay
sun na:ku:set *an*
sun-blinded wisqatenmat *ai* [PEI]; kesatenmat
    ai
Sunday ak'ntiyewimk [BC]; aq'ntiye:wumk;
    ek'ntiye:wimk [CB]; kek'ntiye:wimk [SH];
    observe ~ aq'ntiye:wit *ai*

sun dog menoqwam (small rainbow seen next
    to sun at sunrise and sundown) [BR]
sunny na:ku:setewik *ii*
sunset kalqwasiyet *ai*
superior act ~ to emteskite:l'mk *ta*,
    emteskite:tm *ti*
supernatural person who has ~ powers
    mikmuwessu *an*
supper wela:kwewey; eat ~ w'loqotalk *ai*
supple sipikpa:t *ai*, sipikpa:q *ii*
supplement ankuwa:taqan; ankuwa:l'k *ta*,
    ankuwa:tu *ti*
support ettoqalk *ta* [BR]; give ~ to
    wpaqama:l'k *ta*; ~ from falling kelte:k *ta* [PEI]
surface weskijinuwit *ai*
surplus piwiyaq *ii*; piyamiyaq *ii*, piyamiyet *ai*
surprise pa:qala'iwaqan; catch by ~
    keskuteskaq *ta*, keskuteskm *ti*; wiskuteskaq
    ta [PEI]; take by ~ wisqateskaq *ta*; ~ -d
    pa:qala'ik *ai*
surroundings have nice ~ welqatmit *ai*
survive sapawsit *ai*; sape:k *ai* [SH];
    saputawsit *ai*; struggle to ~ munsi-sapa:l'k
    ta, munsi-sapa:tu *ti*
suspended ~ (on a rope or string) elo:pitek *ii*,
    elo:pisit *ai*
swaddling ~ clothes qopisunikn [BC]
swallow[1] pukwales *an*
swallow[2] mesa:tamit *ai*; mesa:l'k *ta*, mesa:tu
    ti; meseket *ai*; meso:tamit *ai* [BC]; chew
    and ~ mawkutamit *ai*
swamper head ~ ikanawtiket (ikanawtikejik)
    ai (an)
swan wapi *an*
swap sa:se:wit *ai*
swarm ~ (as bees) mawiya:tijik (pl) *ai*
sway mato:qiyaq *ii*, mato:qiyet *ai*;
    nanmo:qiyet *ai*, nanmo:qiyaq *ii*
swear ~ off eluwi:tmasit *ai*
sweat tekniyaq *ii*, tekniyet *ai*; tknu; bead of ~
    tkniyewati
sweep pewa:m *ti*; pewi:ket *ai*
sweet sekkw *ai*, *ii*; sismoqonima:q *ii* [BR]
sweeten sewa:tat *ai*
sweetener sekkwewey
sweet flag i:wesuwaskw (a medicinal plant or
    herb) [RB]; ki:wesuwaskw [RB]

sweetgrass kjimskiku [BC]; weljema:qewe:l
(pl) [RB]; weljemajkewe:l (pl); collect ~
msikuwe:ket *ai*; ~ ceremony pekitne:min
[CB]

swell pemimkwik *ii*, pemimkwit *ai* [BR]; ~ up
put'pekiyaq *ii*, put'pekiyet *ai*

swelling kluk (klukk) *an*; my ~ n'luk *an*

swift a ~ current kesikawitk *ii*

swim tekismit *ai*; ~ about ala:q (ala:m) *ai*; ~
across as'komi:kwe:k (as'komi:kwe:m) *ai*
[BR]; asoqoma:q (asoqoma:m) *ai*; ~ along
pema:q (pema:m) *ai*; pemi:kwe:k
(pemi:kwe:m) *ai* [SH]; ~ away ejikli:kwe:k
(ejikli:kwe:m) *ai* [SH]; ~ forth e:l'k (e:l'm) *ai*
[BC]; know how to ~ natawa:q (natawa:m)
ai; ~ on the back atuwa:sikwe:k *ai* *ai* [BR];
atuwa:skwa:q (atuwa:skwa:m) *ai*; ~ toward
ela:q (ela:m) *ai*; eli:kwe:k (eli:kwe:m *ai* [BR];
elkwi:tm *ti* [BR]; a ~ -**mer** nuja:q (nuja:m) *ai*
(an)

swing nanamiyaqan [NB]; nanamiyaqawey;
etlo:piyet *ai*; nanamiyaq *ii*, nanamiyet *ai*; ~
around in a circle kitto:qopeka:l'k *ta*,
kitto:qopeka:tu; ~ down niso:piyet *ai*; ~ or
spin around kiwto:qa:l'k *ta*, kiwto:qa:tu *ti* [SH];
turn or ~ around kitto:qa:l'k *ta*, kitto:qa:tu *ti*

switch nipisoqon [BC]; n'mispaqan; ~ (from a
tree) npisoqon [SH]; beat with a ~
n'mispaqannte:k *ta*; n'mispaqannte:m *ta*

swollen mekwik *ii*, mekwit *ai*; mowpek *ii*,
mowpet *ai*

swordfish kniskunej *an*

syrup maple ~ jiyoqsimusi-apu [SH]

T

table pataluti [BR]; pata'uti
tack pleku:j
tackle wesuwejo:qa:l'k *ta*, wesuwejo:qa:tu *ti*
tadpole sqolj (sqoljik) *an* [SH]
tag kukwejultimk (a game); ~ along wije:wet *ai*; ~ along with majukkwalk *ta*, majukkwatm *ti* [PEI]
tail break off at the ~ end (by slamming) temaluwetesm'k *ta* [BR]; break off at the ~ or rear end temaluwa:l'k *ta*, temaluwa:tu *ti*; have a raised ~ nepsluwat *ai*; my ~ nsukuni; snap off at the ~ temaluweket *ai* [BR]
tailbone my tailbone nsukun
take ~ along nespn'm *ti*, nespnk *ta*; ~ good care of weleyaq *ta*, welo:tm *ti*; ~ hold of wesuwa:l'k *ta*, wesuwa:tu *ti*; ~ out tewaqqa:l'k *ta*, tewaqqa:tu *ti*; ~ out of tewalqa:l'k *ta*, tewalqa:tu *ti*; ~ the side of ikalk *ta*, ikatm *ti*; ~ place tele:k *ai, ii*; put or ~ off kepta:l'k *ta*, kepta:tu *ti*; ~ well weliwsuwa:tu *ti*
tale a:tukwaqan; tell tall ~ **-s** kluskapewit *ai*
talk etlewistu *ai*; kelusit *ai*; ~ a long time pekitewo:kwet *ai*; ~ about wesku:mk *ta*, wesku:tm *ti*; ~ about this and that miltoqsit *ai*; ~ loud jakkwet *ai* [PEI]; ~ loudly kesikawwek *ii*, kesikawwet *ai*; ~ on and on sespewo:kwet *ai*; ~ over aknutmajik (pl) *ai*; ~ secretively kim-ewo:kwet *ai*; ~ softly sankewewo:kwet *ai*; ~ together maw-aknutmajik (pl) *ai*; walk or ~ in one's sleep we:kwanqe:ket *ai*; heard ~ **-ing** metewenk (metewen'm) *ai*; meto:kwet *ai* [PEI]; stop ~ **-ing** punewenk (punewen'm) *ai*; a good ~ **er** netawet *ai*
tall pita:q *ii*, pitoqsit *ai*; very ~ kesi-pitoqsit *ai*
tallow m'ni:maqanu:min [EG]; moosefat or ~ tiya:muwimi [BR]; tiya:mu:mi
tame wansit *ai*
tamp pack or ~ down esinnteskaq *ta*, esinnteskm *ti*
tandem work in ~ toqo-lukwejik (pl)
tank fish ~ or bowl n'me:juwo:q *an*
tanned maqtawoqsit *ai*, maqtawoqtek *ii*
tap samte:k *ta*, samte:m *ti*

taper wasoqwa:taqan
tart tepa:te [SH] (Fr *des pâtés*)
tast-e kwetp'k *ta*, kwettm *ti* [BR]; mesp'k *ta*, mestm *ti*; wetp'k *ta*, wettm *ti*; have such a ~ telima:q *ii*, telima:t *ai* [SH]; like the ~ of wikp'k *ta*, wiktm *ti*; ~ bad metuwima:q *ii*, metuwima:t *ai*; ~ good wikapuksit *ai*, wikapu:k *ii* [SH]; try the ~ of kwetp'k *ta*, kwettm *ti* [BR]; ~ **-y** wikk *ii*
tattletale a ~ nuji-nutmaqaneket *ai (an)*
tea p'tewey; have a ~ break p'teweye:mat *ai*; take ~ p'teweye:mat *ai*
teaberry kakaju:man [BR]; kaqaju:man [SH]; ka:qakuju:man
teach kekina:maq *ta*; kekina:muwet *ai*; kina:muwet *ai*; ~ to keknu:tmaq *ta*; ~ well wel-knu:tmaq *ta*; ~ what is proper wel-knu:tmaq *ta*; a ~ **-er** nuji-kina:muwet *ai (an)*
teakettle ji:kitlo:q *an*; ti:kitlo:q *an*
team my ~ (of horses) nutapaqan [SH]; nutepaqan
teamster a ~ nuji-asiketk (nuji-asiketm) *ai (an)*
teapot p'teweyo:q *an*
tear[1] naskwina:l'k *ta*, naskwina:tu *ti*; ~ or rip paskina:l'k *ta*; ~ or rip off or up temina:l'k *ta*, temina:tu *ti*
tear[2] shed ~ **-s** saqpiku:niyet *ai*; burst into ~ **-s** paqsikpetemit *ai* [PEI]
teardrop saqpiku:n
tease ki:kaje:k *ai* [BC]; ki:kajeyaq *ta*, ki:kajo:tm *ti*; ki:kassit *ai*; malikimk *ta* [BC]; malikmk *ta*; oqotqomk *ta* (about a member of the opposite sex); ~ **-r** ki:kassuwinu *an*
teeth crush with the ~ pasp'k *ta*, pastm *ti*; have ~ wipitmit *ai*; take out ~ nuji-m'napita:teket *ai (an)*
telegram send a wire or ~ mattaqte:ket *ai* [SH]
telephone kelusimkewey [SH]; mattaqa:tu *ti* [BR]; mattaqa:tmkewey [SH]; mattaqa:taq *ta (do)* [BC]
tell ekinuwa:l'k *ta* [SH]; elaq *ta* [SH]; telimk *ta*; know how to ~ stories netawi-a:tukwet *ai*; ~ on aknimk *ta*, aknutm *ti*; mesimk *ta*; ~ the fortune of wesikalk *ta*; ~ (something) to aknutmaq *ta*
temperamental nepe:k *ai*

temple epme:tkwaj *an*; memkwan (of the head) [SH]

temporary ~ thing maqatewey

ten mtnn [EG]; ~ dollars metla:sa:'ikl (pl); ~ in counting mtl'n [SH]; nekwtinska:q [BR]

ten-card newtiska:qawa:j *an*

tend ~ bar pitupet *ai* [SH]

tenderize nukwa:kipulk *ta*, nukwa:kittu *ti*

tenderloin tnuwanoq *an* [SH]

tendon tnuwan *an*; my ~ ntnuwan *an* [SH]

tense make ~ jipkaq *ta*

tenth the ~ one mtl'newey *an, in*; ~ person newtiska:qawa:j *an*

terminate kaqa:l'k *ta*, kaqa:tu *ti*

test kweja:l'k *ta*, kweja:tu *ti* [BR]; wejeyaq *ta*, wejo:tm *ti*

test-drive we'i-teja:l'k *ta*, we'i-teja:tu *ti*

testicle k'lsu *an*; have large ~ **-s** maqapskusuwat *ai*; my ~ nsaqtaqan *an*; n'lsu *an*

tethered pittaqpisit *ai*

thankful ~ for mi:walk *ta*, mi:watm *ti*

Thanksgiving ~ Day mi:wat(i)mkewey na:kwek

thank you! wela:lin; ke:n [SH]

that ala; ala: [BR]; a:t; nekla (obv.); over ~ way ala: te:l [SH]; who's ~ ? wen net

thaw ~ out apuwa:'l'k *ta*, apuwa:tu *ti*

theirs nekmowowey *an, in*

them nekmow

then aqq; toqo [CB]; and ~ toqojiyu; so ~ toqo t'lisip [CB]; until ~ we:kaw

there be ~ eyk (ey'm) *ai, ii*; eyt *ai*; bring down from ~ weji-nisa:l'k *ta*; come from ~ wejiyaq *ii*, wejiyet *ai*; fall from ~ weji-nisiyaq *ii*, weji-nisiyet *ai*; from ~ on weja:tekemk; get ~ pekisk *ii*, pekisink *ai*; over ~ ala tet; na te:l [CB]; way over ~ ala: tet [SH]

therefore klamen; kulaman [BC]

these weket; wekla

they nekmow

thick pase:k *ai, ii*; paspit *ai*, pastek *ii*; peltek *ii* (as of liquids, porridge); have ~ body or facial hair pasi:tukwat *ai* [SH]; have ~ hair pasaltukwat *ai*; have ~ whiskers pasi:tuwat

ai; nice and ~ wel-paspit *ai*, wel-pastek *ii* [RB]; pour ~ **-ly** pelsit *ai*, peltek *ii*

thicket pukwatqek; clear the brush or ~ musikte:ket *ai*; go through the ~ pematqayet *ai*; hard going (through a ~) metuwatqek *ii* [CB]; try to get out of a ~ kweji-pawnatqa:t *ai*

thick-headed ekkatpat *ai*; pasatpa:t *ai*

thief kmutnes *an*; a ~ pekuwiptnat *ai (an)*

thigh my ~ nulukun

thimble poqwas'tiyey; poqwasutiyej *an* [SH]

thin pepke:jk *ii*, pepke:jit *ai*; cut someone's hair ~ pepk'te:maq *ta (do)*; cut ~ pepka:'ipulk *ta*, pepka:kittu *ti*; ~ down splints ess'ntaqo:tu *ti* [SH]; ~ out a liquid pepka:l'k *ta*, pepka:tu *ti*

thin-headed pepkatpat *ai*

think etlite:l'mk *ta*, etlite:tm *ti*; ~ about tel-te:l'm'k *ta*, tel-te:tm *ti*; ~ about all kinds of things milita:sit *ai*; ~ ahead about nikanite:tm *ti*; ~ highly of me:kite:l'mk *ta*, mekite:tm *ti*; ~ slowly sankewi-ankita:sit *ai*; ~ so tel-ta:sit *ai*; tel-te:l'm'k *ta*, tel-te:tm *ti* [CB]

thinker a quick ~ ne:tata:sit *ai*

thin-skinned nepe:k *ai*

third the ~ person si:stewa:juwit *ai*; the ~ one si:stewa:j *an*; si:stewey

thirty-three ~ (in counting) nesinska:q jel si:st [BR]; nesiska:q je si:st

this ula [SH]; u:t; weket (obv.); wekla (obv.); who's ~ ? wen net; who's this? wen tana

thistle kawiksaw (kawiksaq) *an*; kelikwet *an*; kinikwejij *an* [BC]

thong moose ~ tiya:muwapi

thorn kawiksaw (kawiksaq) *an*

thornberry kokomin *an* [BR]

thornbush ko:kuminaqsi *an*; ~ berry ko:kemin *an* [SH]

thorn wood ~ genus kawikso:musi [SH]

those neket; nekla

thousand a ~ (in counting) pituwiptnnaqan; pituwimtlnaqan [BR]; ten ~ (in counting) mtl'n te:s pituwimtlnaqan

thrash matte:k *ta*, matte:m *ti*; ~ (as of wheat) pewaqs'te:ket *ai*

thrasher pewaqs'te:kney (used in farming)

thread a:papi:j *an*

three ~ days nesi-kisk'k *ii* [BR]; ~ dollars nesa'ikl; ~ flat (sheetlike) objects nesaqpijik (pl) *ai*, nesaqtekl (pl) *ii*; ~ (in counting) si:st; ~ of them ne:siskl *ii*, ne:sisijik *ai*; take or have ~ of a kind nesu-nemi:k *ta*; ~ round (cylindrical) objects nesa:ql (pl) *ii*, nesoqsijik (pl) *ai*; ~ round (globular) objects nesapsk'sijik (pl) *ai*, nesapskekl (pl) *ii*

throat have a hoarse voice or ~ kepa:tat *ai*; my ~ nqotaqan

throttle kestuna:l'k *ta*

through cut or knock ~ (with a tool) saputete:k *ta*, saputete:m *ti*; dig ~ saputalqatm *ti*; go ~ saputa:s'k *ii*, saputa:sit *ai*; pass ~ (as a tunnel) sapalqek *ii*; penetrate or pierce ~ (with a bullet or arrow) saputetelaq *ta*, saputetel'm *ti*

throw eleket *ai*; ~ at elaqtaq *ta (do)* [ESK]; ~ away ejikleket *ai*; ~ down nisaqalk *ta*, nisaqtu *ti* [BR]; ~ in pijeket *ai*; ~ lengthwise eloqeket *ai* [BR]; ~ off keptaqalk *ta*, keptaqtu *ti*; ~ out tewajjiyeket *ai*; teweket *ai*; ~ over a:siseket *ai*; ~ quickly wisqeket *ai*; ~ toward elaqalk *ta*, elaqtu *ti*; ~ under pijeket *ai*; ~ up in the air wenaqeket *ai*

throw in ~ (for office) eleket *ai*

thumb my ~ ntijin

thunder kaqtukwawik *ii*; kaqtukwaw (kaqtukwaq) *an*; ~ stick kaqtukwewe:sn *an*

Thunderer the ~ kaqtukwewe:sn *an* (a mythical spirit)

Thursday ne:wowey

thus klamen; kulaman [BC]; act ~ telqamiksit *ai*; cooked ~ teloqsit *ai*, teloqtek *ii*

tickl-e kiklikjnk *ta*; ~ **-ish** kikliksit *ai*, kikliksik *ii*

tide jikwapa:n [BR]; kjikapa:n; dog ~ nmu:ju:pa:q *ii*; dry ~ niwetek *ii*; high (full) ~ waju:pa:q *ii*; high ~ maju:pa:q *ii* [RB]; incoming ~ jikwapan [SH]; kjikapan; wjikapan; wejkapa:q *ii* [RB]; neap ~ lmu:ju:paq *ii* [SH]; nmu:ju:pa:q *ii*; reversing ~ apatpa:q *ii* [SH]; very low ~ paqtlusk'tek *ii*; weak ~ mikpa:q *ii*

Tide head qaskusi-a:qamikt

tidy waqamn'mat *ai*

tie keltaqpil'm *ti*, keltaqpilk *ta*; ~ self up ilpilsit *ai*; ~ tight sekkipil'm *ti*, sekkipilk *ta*; ~ up kelpilk *ta*, kelpil'm *ti*; ~ up properly ilpilk *ta*, ilpil'm *ti*; ~ up with a rope kejipil'm *ti*, kejipilk *ta* [SH]; ~ **-d** up kelpisit *ai* [PEI]

tight hang on ~ melkunasit *ai* [BC]; hold ~ sekki-kln'k *ta* [PEI]; tie ~ sekkipil'm *ti*, sekkipilk *ta*

tightly close ~ sekki-ap'sqa:tu *ti* [PEI]; gather ~ wesuwisepilasit *ai*; wesuwisepilas'k *ii*; hold on ~ (with hands) sekkapjit *ai* [PEI]

time at that ~ na tujiyu; tujiyu; each ~ ta:n te:s; from that ~ on weja:tekemkek; have a good ~ ise:k *ai*; keep in ~ with majukkwalk *ta*, majukkwatm *ti*; majulkwalk *ta*, majulkwatm *ti*; put in ~ piskwa:l'k *ta*, piskwa:tu *ti* [CB]; some other ~ pe: ap ta:n tujiyu; ten ~ **-s** metla:siska:q; what ~ ? tal e:k *ii*; ta:s ajiyet *ai*

timid nenestawe:k *ai*, *ii*; nesawet *ai* [SH]

tin lapawji:jitewey

tiny apje:ji:jk *ii*, apje:jijit *ai*; have ~ eyes apsalkikwat *ai* [PEI]; apsalqikwa:ji:jit *ai*

tipped ~ over ukumejepit *ai*, ukumejetek *ii*; aputansk'pit *ai*, aputansk'tek *ii* [PEI]

tipsy menakwisk *ii*, menakwisink *ai*

tiptoe kimskwet *ai*; walk on ~ **-s** kimteskawit *ai* [PEI]

tire car ~ kiwiyo:qiyaq *ii* (*in*) [SH]

tired kispnek *ii*, kispnet *ai*; feel ~ kispniyet *ai*; look ~ kispnapewit *ai*; make ~ kispnulk *ta*; sound ~ kispnetoqsit *ai*; ~ of hearing about siws'taq *ta*; ~ of moving along siw-pmiyet *ai*; ~ of seeing siwwam'k *ta*; ~ of waiting siwiskmat *ai*

tire out ~ with talk siktewa:l'k *ta*

tithe la:ti [BC]; lati:m (Fr *la dîme*)

toad amqoqjaji:j *an* [SH]; samqwani:j *an*; tqolj *an* [SH]

toadstool mi:mije:maqan

tobacco tmawey; chewing ~ ja:wey; my ~ nutmawey

tobaggan kulkwis *an* [BR]

today kiskuk

toe my big ~ nmaqaqjikewe:m; ntijinikat [BR];
my ~ n'maqjikewe:m; ntluwiknikat [BR];
nto:jm

together toqwe:kik (pl) *ai*; call ~ (pl) maw-
kimk *ta*; maw-kitm *ti*; chip in ~ mawa:tajik
(pl) *ai*; gathered ~ mawe:kik (pl) *ai*; live ~
mawe:kik (pl) *ai*; piled ~ maw-amk'pijik (pl)
an, maw- amk'tekl (pl) *ii*; sit ~ toqpijik (pl) *ai*
[BC]; sleep ~ toqosinkik (pl) *ai*; stay or live ~
toqwa:majik (pl) *ai*; stand ~ toqo-
pukuwa:l'kik (pl) *ta*; talk ~ maw-aknutmajik
(pl) *ai*

toilet go to the ~ najijjikwat *ai*

tomato tmato:s *an*

tomcod punamu *an*

tomorrow sapo:nuk; the day after ~ ktiki-
sapo:nuk; iktiki-sapo:nuk

tongue have a large ~ maqi-wilnuwit *ai*; my ~
nilnu [BR]; ninnu

tonight w'lo:nuk

tonsil my ~ nulukw *an* [SH]

tonsilitus have ~ w'lukwiyet *ai* [SH]

too elk; elp; elt; nkutey; push ~ hard
pajijiksma:l'k *ta*, pajijiksma:tu *ti*; ~ good
wesam-klu:lk *ii*; ~ much wesamelk *ai*, *ii*; ~
small ewsami-apje:jk *ii* [CB]; wemsami-
apje:jk *ii* [BR]; ~ wide wesamikske:k *ii*

tool digging ~ mulqwekn; ~ or object
requiring use of both hands
tapuwapjimkewey *an*, *in*; useful ~ or object
wtmo:taqan [SH]

too much! nnim (an exclamation); llim

too much not ~ mu nnim

tooth my ~ nipit

top[1] put or set on ~ ke:kwa:l'k *ta*, ke:kwa:tu *ti*;
sit on ~ of ewt'pa:suwalk *ta*, ewt'pa:suwatm
ti; sit or set on ~ weskitpit *ai*, weskittek *ii*;
sit down on ~ ewt'pa:sit *ai*

top[2] (toy) ~ llipqama:taqan [NB]

topple kewa:salk *ta*, kewa:satm *ti* [BR];
kewe:salk *ta*, kewe:satm *ti* [SH]; kewiyaq *ii*,
kewiyet *ai*; kews'k *ta*, kews'm *ti*

torch come with a light or ~ petasenmat *ai*; ~
fish (or hunt) saqsikwet *ai* [PEI]

torchlight saqsikwemkewey

torn ripped or ~ paskine:k *ai*, *ii*

tornado ekulamsn *an*; ew'lamsn *an*

torture amaskipnn'k *ta*

totem have a ~ or benefactor wtuttemit *ai*;
my ~ ntuttem *an*

touch sama:l'k *ta*, sama:tu *ti*; in close ~ with
teko:tm *ti*, tekweyaq *ta*; ~ slightly samte:k *ta*,
samte:m *ti*

touchy nepe:k *ai*

tough melkiyaqasit *ai*; ~ and stringy
melkapekisk *ii*; ~ to eat melkapek *ii* [SH]

tow sawtaqa:l'k *ta*, sawtaqa:tu *ti*; ~ along
pempil'm *ti*, pempilk *ta*; ~ by boat nuta:lutm
ti

toward bent ~ wejku:jink *ai*; wejkuwijink *ai*
[BR]; stand facing ~ wejkupukuwit *ai*; take
or bring ~ ela:l'k *ta*, ela:tu *ti*

town kjikanji:j; utan; go to ~ kutana:sit *ai*

toy papitaqan; ~ top llipqama:taqan [NB]; ~
with mila:suwalk *ta*, mila:suwatm *ti*

trace napuwi:k'k *ta*, napuwi:km *ti*; draw or ~
pictures napuwi:kiket *ai (an)*

track na:piptme:k *ta*; railroad ~ pullja'in awti
[SH]; make ~ -s toward elaptoq (elaptu) *ai*;
make ~ -s with snowshoes jilaqami:k
(jilaqami:m) *ai*

trade ~ or do one's business there wejo:tasit
ai

trail awaqan [SH]; awti; awti:j; a ~ blazer
ikanawtiket (ikanawtikejik) *ai (an)*; lead or
take off the ~ or road peska:l'k *ta*, peska:tu
ti; leave or go off the ~ or road peska:sit *ai*

trailer sawtaqa:taqan

train ka:s; pullja'in [SH]

translate kiwaskiwi:tm *ti* [CB]; kinawskwiwi:tm
ti [BR]; kuwaskuwi:tm *ti* [BC]

translation nesutmalsewuti

transport awjo:l'k *ta*, awjo:tu *ti* [BC]; ewjo:l'k
ta, ewjo:tu *ti*

transportation my means of ~ (boat, car, etc.)
ntul

trap loqte:knikalk *ta*; loqte:kn; loqte:kniket *ai*;
go check ~ -s nassikwet *ai*; set a ~
elsaqa:tu *ti* [BR]; set ~ -s loqte:kniket *ai*; set
a ~ for loqte:knikalk *ta*; ~ lobsters
jakejuwe:ket *ai*;

tray ash ~ sipiska:sutiyo:q

treasure kesite:taqan [PEI]; my ~ nk'sitaqan;
nt'ksite:taqan

treat ~ as such teleyaq *ta*, telo:tm *ti*; ~
(people) badly emeko:teket *ai (an)*; ~ right
tetapuwa:l'k *ta*, tetapuwa:tu *ti*; ~ so teleyaq
ta, telo:tm *ti*

tree kmu:j (kmu:jik) *an* [BR]; miti:s *an*; stoqon
an [BC]; a kind of ~ (related to the ash;
grows near the water) pa:mikli *an*; a dead
sagging ~ kuwasun [BR]; apple ~ wennju:-
su:naqsi; beech ~ munkwaqanemusi [PEI];
cherry ~ maskwe:simanaqsi *an*; lumber ~
kmu:j (kmu:jik) *an*; type of ~ jikmuwatk
(used in medicine) [PEI]

tremble nenk'tesink *ai*, nenk'tesk *ii*;
pepuwetesink *ai*, pepuwetesk *ii*

trey ~ (playing card) si:stewa:j *an*; pair of ~ -s
(in cards) si:staq (pl) *an*

trial ilsutaqan

trick eluwe:wa:l'k *ta*

Trickster mikmuwessu *an*

trifling kesnqo:we:k *ai*

trim ji:kate:k *ta*, ji:kate:m *ti*; ~ a Christmas
tree kekno:tlk *ta*; ~ (someone's) hair
matu:te:maq *ta*; ~ slowly sankewsawet *ai*;
~ to fit eloqomqwalk *ta*, eloqomqwatm *ti*;
eloqwalk *ta*, eloqwatm *ti* [BR]; ~ tree
branches pesikte:ket *ai*; ~ wood ji:kate:ket
ai

trip ejaqannjeteskmat *ai*; nesikateskmaq *ta*;
pesoqteskmat *ai*; ~ over peji:taqamat *ai*

tripe elanqayejit (elanqayejijik) *an*; winisqi [SH]

triplet nesupe:j *an*

triviality ksno:qonewey (pejorative) [RB]

troll pukulatmu:j

trot ~ along pemikate:pit *ai*

trouble lkowaqana:l'k *ta*, lkowaqana:tu *ti*;
lukwaqana:l'k *ta*, lukwaqana:tu *ti*; make or
cause ~ lukwewaqana:teket *ai*

troublesome lukowaqanit *ai*

trough mjikapu:lkw [SH]

trousers pitaqawe:mkl (pl) [CB]; pita:qawe:l
(pl)

trout atoqwa:su *an*; fish for ~
atoqwa:suwe:ket *ai*

true ki:wajiyaq *ii*, ki:wajiyet *ai*; teliyaq *ii*; ~ (as
in carpentry) tekpaqikk *ii*, tekpaqikit *ai* [CB];
tetpaqik *ii*, tetpaqikit *ai* [CB]

trunk l'sqi:kn [BC]; clothes ~ lesqe:kn

Truro, N.S. we:kopekitk

trust sankewite:l'mk *ta*, sankewite:tm *ti*

truth speak the ~ (as a preacher)
nestuwapukuwet *ai*

truthful speak ~ to keknuwimk *ta*

try kule:k *ai* [BR]; kweja:l'sit *ai* [BR]; ~ on
kwet-nasa:l'k *ta*, kwet-nasa:tu *ti*; ~ on there
wet-nasa:l'k *ta*, wet-nasa:tu *ti*; ~ out
kweja:l'k *ta*, kweja:tu *ti* [BR]; wejeyaq *ta*,
wejo:tm *ti*; ~ out (sexually) wejimk *ta*; ~ the
taste of kwetp'k *ta*, kwettm *ti* [BR]; ~ to
catch kwejiks'kuteskaq *ta*; wejiks'kuteskm
ti; ~ to catch up with wet-tepne:k *ta*, wet-
tepne:m *ti*; ~ to get out of a thicket kweji-
pawnatqa:t *ai*; ~ to grasp kwejimsn'm *ti*,
kwejimsnk *ta*; ~ to push munsiksma:l'k *ta*,
munsiksma:tu *ti* [SH]; ~ to see kweji-n'mitu
ti, kewji-n'mi:k *ta*

tub ku:la:ji:j [SH]; lapa:y *an* (Fr *la baille*)

tuberculosis have dry ~ epskuninet *ai*;
wepskuninet *ai* [SH]; have gastric ~
nujumuwit *ai*; person who has gastric ~
nujumu *an*

tubers harvest roots or ~ (e.g. potatoes,
carrots, turnips) ke:tipnet *ai*

tuck ~ in the flaps (in basket making)
temaqjo:tu *ti* [SH]

Tuesday ta:puwowey

tugboat nuta:lutewey

tumble te:tipjiyet *ai*

tumbler glass ~ tm'letji:j

tune catch a ~ nasapaqteskm *ti* [BR]

tunnel elalqek *ii*

turkey apatapekiyejit (apatapekiyejijik) *an*

turn at (on) the ~ aquwoqomqek (loc); ~
about kikto:qo-pukuwa:sit *ai* [NB]; ~ around
(while seated) kawak'pa:sit *ai*;
kinawsk'pa:sit *ai* [BR]; ~ around (while
standing up) kinawski-pukuwa:sit *ai* [BR]; ~
back kiwanska:sit *ai* [SH]; make a ~
aquwoqomwa:s'k *ii*, aquwoqomwa:sit *ai*;
make someone's head ~ ew'naskwatpa:l'k

ta; ~ one's head about kinawsklapa:sit *ai*
[BR]; ~ over kiwaska:sit *ai* [BC]; ~ over
(while prone) kinawskismtesink *ai* [BR]; ~
over (with a tool) aputaskikwalk *ta*,
aputaskikwatm *ti*; ~ upside down
aputaska:l'k *ta*, aputaska:tu *ti*

turn down esa:q *ta*, esa:m *ti*; ese:k *ta*

turnip tanaps (tanaps'k) *an* [SH]; wennju:-
sukapun *an*; wennju:s'pekn *an* [BC]; wennju:-
s'kepn *an* [BC]

turtle mikjikj (mikjikjik) *an*

twang kesikawlusit *ai* [CB]

twentieth the ~ one tapuwinska:qewa:j *an* [BR]

twenty ~ (in counting) tapuwiska:q;
tapuwinska:q [BR]; ~ persons or objects
tapuwiska:qal (pl) *ii*, tapuwiskeksijik (pl) *ai*

twenty-five cents tlansu (Fr *trente-sous*)

twig green ~ eskikloqon [SH]

twilight become ~ pem-piskiyaq *ii*; piskiyaq
ii

twin tqope:j *an*

twist mim'ntawa:l'k *ta*, mim'ntawa:tu *ti* [SH];
m'ntawa:l'k *ta*, m'n'tawa:tu *ti*; n'm'ntawa:l'k
ta, n'm'ntawa:tu *ti*; ~ with a quick motion
m'ntawaqalk *ta*, m'ntawaqtu *ti*; a ~ **-ed** foot
wkatistuwik *ii*

twitch ewskwapet *ai*, ewskwapek *ii*; ~ or pull
logs nujatejo:l'k *ta*, nujatejo:tu *ti*;
nujatejo:teket *ai*; a ~ **-er** nutatijo:tasit *ai (an)*
[PEI]; nujatejo:ta:sit (nujatejo:ta:sijik) *ai (an)*;

two have ~ (of) tapunkik (pl) *ta*, tapunmann
(pl) *ti*; ~ (in counting) ta:pu; ~ (of something
cylindrical in shape) tapuwoqskekl (pl) *ii*,
tapuwoqsijik (pl) *ai*; ~ (of something flat)
tapu-saqpit *ai*, tapu-saqtek *ii*; ~ (of
something globular or round in shape)
tapuwapskekl (pl) *ii*, tapuwapsk'sijik (pl) *ai*; ~
of them tapusijik (pl) *ai*, tapu:kl (pl) *ii*

two by two go ~ toqwanqapultijik (pl) *ai*

two-dollar ~ bill tapu a'ikewey [SH]

tyrant emeko:teket *ai (an)*

U

ugly winapewit *ai*; winikk *ii*, winikit *ai*

uh! a'ej [SH]; a'ij (hesitation form; noun and verb substitute) [PEI]

ulcer my ~ ntalsuwikn [BC]

umbilical cord wili api

umbrella poqwatikn

unable me:si

unannounced arrive ~ (or unexpectedly or by surprise) pejila:'it *ai*; pejila:sit *ai*

unappetizing eat ~ food o:platalk *ai*

unaware awana:qiyet *ai*

unbalanced menakwisk *ii*, menakwisink *ai*; act ~ amatpesmat *ai*

uncertain awana:qiyet *ai*

uncle my ~ nklamuksis *an* (also, a term of respect for an older man) [SH]

uncomfortable si:kasit *ai*; make ~ si:kaq *ta*; make the body ~ (by the presence of a foreign or intrusive object) muskulkukumat *ai*

uncrowded ewe:ke:k *ai*, *ii*

uncured eskik *ii*, eskit *ai*

underground lipqamu:k; lamkmu:k; lamqamu:k (loc)

underneath lame:k *ai*, *ii*; burn ~ pitoqtek *ii*; crawl ~ pitapekit *ai*; go ~ pija:sit *ai*; lie ~ nekoqpit *ai*, nekoqtek *ii* [SH]; moist ~ newukulasink *ai*; put ~ nekwasa:l'k *ta*, nekwa:satu *ti* [BR]; sit (set) ~ pitoqpit *ai*, pitoqtek *ii*

undershirt lamqwan *an* [SH]

understand nestasit *ai* [BC]; nestaq *ta*; nest'k (nestm) *ai*

underweight naqji:sit *ai*

undeveloped nutqwe:k *ai*

undo apkwa:l'k *ta*, apkwa:tu *ti*

undress menikna:sit *ai* [BC]; musika:sit *ai*; musiko:tlk *ta*

uneven an'stawe:k *ai*, *ii*; istuwik *ii*, istuwikit *ai*; milqamikek *ii*

unevenly cut ~ or crookedly istu:s'k *ta*, istu:sm *ti*

unexpectedly arrive unannounced, or ~ , or by surprise pejila:'it: *ai*; pejila:sit *ai*; happen ~ and pleasantly welitpa:s'k *ii*, welitpa:sit *ai*; turn out ~ piltuwa:s'k *ii*, piltuwa:sit *ai*

unfortunate ansuwe:k *ii*

unintentionally burn ~ pejoqs'k *ta*, pejoqsm *ti*; chop down ~ peji-ku:te:m *ti*; squeeze ~ peji-jink'ja:lek *ta*, peji-jink'ja:tu *ti*

unless jiptuk

unload kepta:l'k *ta*, kepta:tu *ti*

unlock pansaqam *ti*, pansaqq *ta*

unpleasant an ~ (ugly) color kajj-amuksit *ai*, kajj-amu:k *ii*

unsafe an'stawpit *ai*, an'stawtek *ii*

unsalted pilse:k *ai*, *ii*

unsavory find ~ poqwajite:l'mk *ta*, poqwajite:tm *ti*

unscrew menapaqam *ti*, menapaqq *ta*

unsophisticated matuwe:k *ai*

unsteady anastawto:kwek *ii*, anastawto:kwet *ai* [CB]

unsure ~ of or about an'stawite:l'mk *ta*, an'stawite:tm *ti*

untie apkwa:l'k *ta*, apkwa:tu *ti*

untied apkwa:'ik *ii*, apkwa:'it *ai* [PEI]; become ~ apkwa:s'k *ii*, apkwa:sit *ai*

until mi:soqo; we:kow

untouched left ~ (by fire) eskoqsit *ai*, eskoqtek *ii*

untrim musiko:tlk *ta*

up k'p'tay; crawl ~ toqjuwapekit *ai*; go ~ so:qwa:t *ai*; go ~ (in altitude) so:qiyet *ai*, so:qiyaq *ii*; go ~ (stairs) toqjuwa:q *ii*, toqjuwa:t *ai*; pick ~ wenaqa:l'k *ta*, wenaqa:tu *ti*; send ~ toqju:kimk *ta*, toqju:kitm *ti*; take ~ (in altitude) so:qwa:l'k *ta*, so:qwa:tu *ti*; throw ~ (in the air) wenaqeket *ai*; ~ above toqjuwe:k (loc)

uphill run ~ pemisqoqi-tukwi:k (pemisqoqi-tukwi:m) *ai*

upright el-pukuwik *ii*, elp-ukuwit *ai*; stacked ~ el-pukuwo:tasit *ai*, el-pukuwo:tas'k *ii*

upside down turn ~ aputaska:l'k *ta*, aputaska:tu *ti*

upstairs ke:kwey; chase ~ toqju:teskaq *ta*; run ~ pemitqoju:tukwi:k (pemitqoju:tukwi:m) *ai*; toqjuwitukwi:k (toqjuwitukwi:m) *ai* [SH]

upstream pi:taw

up to mi:soqo

urin-e skuti; my ~ ns'kuti; nsukuti; ~ **-ate**
sekit *ai*; ~ **ate** into pu:taskilk *ta*, pu:taskitm *ti*;
~ **ate** on oneself sekilsit *ai* [BC]

us kinu (inclusive); ninen (exclusive)

U.S.A. pastunkewa:ki; pastun ("Boston")

use e:w'k *ta*, e:w'm *ti*; able to ~ menuweketu
ti, menuweke:k *ta*; have ~ for wetmite:l'mk
ta, wetmite:tm *ti*; make ~ of eweketu *ti*,
eweke:k *ta*; e:w'k *ta*, e:w'm *ti*; make ~ of
(for the first time) sik'ntaq *ta*, sik'ntm *ti*; ~ up
kaqo:tm *ti*; want to ~ ketu-apemk *ta*, ketu-
apetm *ti*; ~ to like puskiksatmap *ti*; ~ **-d** so
teluwekek *ii*, teluweket *ai*; ~ **-d** (scrubbing)
water mjikapu [SH]; what ~ **-d** for?
taluwekaq *ii*, taluweket *ai*

useful weliyaq *ii*, weliyet *ai*; wetapsunik *ii*,
wetapsunit *ai*; wtapsunik *ii*, wtapsunit *ai*; ~
object or person wtapsun; ~ object or tool
wetmo:taqan; wtmo:taqan [SH]

useless ~ object ksnqoweyey

utensil (food) ~ mikwije:maqan

uterus masqutek *ii* (*in*)

V

vacate tewiwsit *ai*; start to move or ~ (a house, camp) poqjiwsit *ai*

vaccination smallpox ~ lapikot *an* (Fr *la picote*)

vague hear ~ **-ly** about ams'tmat *ai*

vain emteskit *ai*; ki:nujink *ai*; ~ person me:ko:pj (me:ko:pjik)

valley (Annapolis) ~ people kespukwitkewaq; (Annapolis) ~ person kespukwitnewa:j *an* [SH]

valuable my ~ nk'sitaqan [SH]; nk'site:taqan [BR]; nt'ksite:taqan

value kesite:l'm'k *ta*, kesite:tm *ti*; something or someone cherished or ~ **-d** ksite:taqan

vanish keskatesk *ii*, keskatesink *ai*; make or cause to ~ or disappear keskamukwa:l'k *ta*, keskamukwa:tu *ti*; ~ **-ed** keskamukwa:s'k *ii*, keskamukwa:sit *ai*

vanquish matte:k *ta*, matte:m *ti*

variety ~ (of something) milamuksit *ai*, milamu:k *ii*

vase wasuweko:q

veer ~ off aquwoqomwa:s'k *ii*, aquwoqomwa:sit *ai*

vehicle tepaqan; have a ~ wtulit *ai*

vein mija:kaj *an*; wija:qajim [PEI]; my ~ ntnuwan *an*; nuja:kaj [BR]

venereal have a ~ disease winpnet *ai*

Veronica Pelonik *an* (Fr *Véronique*)

vertical el-pukuwik *ii*, el-pukuwit *ai*

very ~ fat mawkamik *ii*, mawkamit *ai*; ~ happy or pleased mawi-w'lta:sit *ai*; ~ new maw-piley; ~ sick kesiksinukwat *ai*; ~ strong kesi-m'lkiknat *ai*; ~ tall kesi-pitoqsit *ai*

vessel pnasu:lkw; sallpo:k [CB]

vest weskit (weskijik) *an*

Veteran's Day sma:knisuwey na:kwek

vibrate nenk'tesink *ai*, nenk'tesk *ii*; pepuwetesink *ai*, pepuwetesk *ii*

view ankamk *ta*, ankaptm *ti*; catch full ~ of wilokamk *ta*, wilokaptm *ti*

village kjikanji:j; Indian ~ (reserve) lnuwe:kati [BR]; nnuwe:kati

vindictive ketanteket *ai*

vinegar penikl(ewey); te:pineklewey (Fr *des vinaigres*)

violinist tapiya:jijke:j *an* [SH]

virgin a ~ mespit *ai (an)*

Virgin Mary Ma:li

visit emittukwalk *ta*, emittukwatm *ti*; emittukwet *ai*; mittukwalk *ta*, mittukwatm *ti*; mittukwet *ai*; go ~ naji-ne:yamk *ta*

vocal cords my ~ nsitunapi:l (pl)

voice have a hoarse ~ or throat kepa:tat *ai*; have a husky ~ kepi:sit *ai*; have a ~ like a bird jipji:ju:kisutnat *ai*; my ~ nsitun

voice box my ~ nsitun

vomit so:qotemit *ai*; so:qotmun

voyeur a ~ winapit *ai (an)*

W

wade ~ across as'komasikwet *ai* [BR];
asoqomasukwet *ai*; ~ around in the snow
alasumteket *ai*; ~ around in the water
alasukwet *ai*; ~ toward in the water
elasukwet *ai*; ~ forth through the snow
elasumteket *ai*

wag ~ the tail mataluwat *ai*

wagon low-bottomed ~ slapn

wail kesimt'k (kesimtm) *ai*; weto:temit *ai*

waist put one's arm around the ~ of
te:tipoqja:l'k *ta*, te:tipoqja:tu *ti*

wait eskmat *ai*; ~ for eskmalk *ta*, eskmatm *ti*;
~ a long time for pekiji-eskmalk *ta*, pekiji-
eskmatm *ti*; tired of ~ **-ing** siwiskmat *ai*

wake ~ (by making a loud noise) tukwteskaq
ta; ~ up (by shaking) tukweyaq *ta*; ~ up
tukwa:l'k *ta*; tukwiyet *ai*; ~ up roughly
tukwipnn'k *ta*

walk take (a dog) for a ~ on a leash al-
k'ltaqan'k *ta*; ~ along peml'ka:t *ai* [BR]; ~
around with a light alasenmat *ai*; ~ back and
forth to asu:teskaq *ta*, asu:teskm *ti*; ~ like an
old person kisiku:l'ka:t *ai*; ~ or stride back
apatl'ka:t *ai*; ~ or talk in one's sleep
we:kwanqe:ket *ai*; ~ poorly malikatat *ai*

wall pemsaqas'k *ii*; temsaqas'k

wallet poj *an*

waltes play ~ waltestat *ai*

wander ~ off unintentionally matuwa:sit *ai*

want pawalk *ta*, pawatm *ti*; pewalk *ta*, pewatm
ti; puwalk *ta*, puwatm *ti*; ~ an alcoholic drink
ketuktnukqwanet *ai*; ~ or intend to go home
ketu:lmiyet *ai*; ~ there el-puwalk *ta*,
el-puwatm *ti*; ~ to use ketu-apemk *ta*,
ketu-apetm *ti*

war mat'ntimk; the onset of ~ poqjinntimk

warm light and ~ (of a breeze) epoqek *ii*;
nice and ~ wel-p'sit *ai*, wel-p'tek *ii*; slightly ~
ami-p'sit *ai*; ~ house kisuwe:k *ii* [ESK]; ~
liquid eppaqsijik (pl) *ai*; eppa:q *ii*; ~ up
eps'k *ta*, epsm *ti*; ~ up (by body heat)
apu:jenk *ta*, apu:jen'm *ti*; ~ up (by the fire)
apu:s'k *ta*, apu:sm *ti*; ~ weather ami-p'tek *ii*
[BR]; am-p'tek *ii*; dress ~ **-ly** kisu:piso:tlk *ta*;
~ **-ly** dressed kisu:k'k (kisu:km) *ai*

warrior matnakkewinu

warship manasu:lkw [SH]

wart my ~ nijkikm; nnijkikm; nujkikm [BR]

wash kesispa:l'k *ta*, kesispa:tu *ti*; ~ clothes
kesistaqanewet *ai*; ~ floors, etc.
kesispa:teket *ai*; ~ off kasapuwek *ii*,
kasapuwet *ai*; object pertaining to the ~ **-ing**
of clothes ksispa:tekemkewey

washing machine kesispa:tekemkewey

wasp amuwow (amuwaq) *an*

watch na:ku:setewey; wpukikwa:l'k *ta* [SH];
wpukukwa:l'k *ta*, wpukukwa:tu *ti*; keep ~
over keleyaq *ta*, kelo:tm *ti*

watchman a ~ nuji-alapit *ai (an)*

water samqwan; (sweet) ~ sapoqwan [SH];
dirty ~ mjikapu; muddy (dirty) ~ siskuwapu;
salt ~ salawapu; sugar ~ (for babies)
sismo:qonapu; crystal-clear ~ wasapa:q *ii*
[BR]; calm ~ wantaqpa:q *ii*; still ~
wantaqpekitk *ii*; frozen ~ kep't'k *ii*; enter
the ~ paqasa:sit *ai*; enter the ~ (by
watercraft) m'nawa:sit *ai*; fall in the ~
paqasiyet *ai*; get out of the ~ natqa:sit *ai*;
get out of the ~ slowly paw-natqa:sit *ai*; go
ahead down in the ~ elmi-nikanipqa:sit *ai*
[BR]; pull a net from the ~ natqa:piyet *ai*;
put in the ~ ekwija:l'k *ta*, ekwija:tu *ti*; put in
the ~ (river) paqasa:l'k *ta*, paqasa:tu *ti*; pull
out of the ~ (by a rope or fish line)
natqapilawet *ai*; remove from the ~ natqa:l'k
ta, natqa:tu *ti*; sit (set) in the ~ ekwijink *ai*,
ekwitk *ii*; throw in the ~ paqasaqalk *ta*,
paqasaqtu *ti*; wade around in the ~
alasukwet *ai*; ~ (a horse) samoqo:tlk *ta*;
sapoqo:tlk *ta* [SH]; esapoqo:tlk *ta*;
esamuqo:tlk *ta*

watercraft enter the water by ~ m'nawa:sit *ai*

waterfall qapskw; little ~ qapsku:j; tiny ~
qapskuji:j

waterfowl sisip *an*; hunt ~ pi:mat *ai*

waterlily pako:si (a particular type) [PEI];
paqo:si

waterway pole (a boat) as far as the ~ permits
we:kwamkwe:ket *ai*; where the ~ ends
we:kwamkuk

watery samqwank *ii*; samqwanapuwa:q *ii*;
samqwanik *ii*

wave¹ tku *an*; big ~ **-s** maqatkwik *ii*

wave² ~ around kiwto:qa:l'k *ta*, kiwto:qa:tu *ti* [SH]

wavy ~ (of the sea) tkuwik *ii*

way get in the ~ a:jela:s'k *ii*, a:jela:sit *ai*; hurry that ~ enmateja:sit *ai*; hurry this ~ wejkwateja:s'k *ii*, wejkwateja:sit *ai*; in the ~ kejimoqpit *ai*, kejimoqtek *ii*; tetkuwek *ii*, tetkuwet *ai*; wetmkuwet *ai*; lie in the ~ a:jelisink *ai*; sit in the ~ a:jelpit *ai*, a:jeltek *ii*; stand in the ~ a:jel-pukuwik *ii*, a:jel-pukuwit *ai*

we kinu (inclusive); ninen (exclusive)

weak menaqanaq *ii*, menaqanat *ai*; have a ~ back malukunat *ai* [BR]; physically ~ maljat *ai*; so ~ tel-m'naqanaq *ii*, tel-m'naqanat *ai*; very ~ (from being sick) kesis'wikna:t *ai*

wean naqanu:salk *ta*

weapon pkumaqan [BC]; poqomati [CB]; pukumaqan; my ~ npoqomatim [CB]; npukumaqan [BC]

wear naskaq *ta*, naskm *ti*; ~ hair to the shoulders (of a man) sa'ukwat *ai*

wear out kaqqmat *ai*; ~ (one's footwear) kaqteskmat *ai*; ~ (one's shoe on one side) ejaqannjeteskmat *ai*; ~ (an article of clothing) kaqqaq *ta*, kaqqm *ti*

weasel sku:s *an* [RB]; wskus *an*

weav-e elisknuwet *ai*; eltaqte:ket *ai*; ~ a handle on elisqanpeka:tu *ti* [SH]; fine- ~ apsisknuwet *ai*; ~ the bottom (of a basket) elikjipil'm *ti* [SH]; ~ -ing lisknuwaqan

web spider ~ awo:wejituwo:pi [BR]; ko:qwejijiwa:pi

Wednesday si:stewey

weed musikunnkete:ket *ai*

week aq'ntiye:wuti

weep atkitemit *ai*; atk'temit *ai* [CB]; ~ -ing atkitemuwaqan [BC]

weigh enkalk *ta*, enkatm *ti*; tetpaqam *ti*, tetpaqq *ta*; ~ such an amount teliksukulk *ai*, teliksukk *ii*

weight feel the ~ of we:tunk *ta*, we:tun'm *ti*

weir nisaqan [SH]

weird wi:kuwe:k *ai*, *ii*

welcome! pjila:si

welcome wela:luwet *ai*; wel-ta:suwalk *ta*, wel-ta:suwatm *ti*

welfare tpi:tnewey; ~ day tepi:timk

well¹ lo:q

well² wele:k *ai*; do ~ by wela:l'k *ta*, wela:tu *ti*; eat ~ weltamit *ai*; fit ~ wela:q *ii*, weloqsit *ai*; welkaq *ta*, welkm *ti*; get ~ ila:sit *ai*; move ~ weliyaq *ii*, weliyet *ai*; read properly or ~ wel-kijjet *ai*; turn out ~ wela:s'k *ii*, wela:sit *ai*

well³ ~ (of water) nqano:pati

well-built kesmikit *ai*

well-cooked weloqsit *ai*, weloqtek *ii* [RB]

well-dressed welpisit *ai*; kesmpisit *ai*; wel-knesit *ai*; wel-kutat *ai* [SH]; weli-a:su:na:q (weli-a:su:na:m) *ai*

well-dried weli-piyasit *ai*, weli-piyatek *ii*

well-furnished welseksit *ai*

well-grooved welina:q *ii*, welina:t *ai*

well-heated have a ~ house wel-p'smat *ai*

well-placed welpit *ai*, weltek *ii*

well-populated pukwelikanik *ii*

well-proportioned kesmikit *ai*

well-shoed wel-k'snet *ai*

well-supplied welseksit *ai*

west pi:taw; tkesn; tk'sn; go ~ pi:tawa:sit *ai*, pi:tawa:s'k *ii*; in the ~ pi:tawe:k (loc); take to the ~ pi:tawa:l'k *ta*, pi:tawa:tu *ti*

westerner pi:tawkowa:j *an*; tk'snukowa:j *an*

wet saqpe:k *ai*, *ii*; speak ~ saqpi:sit *ai*; ~ snow saqpipsaq *ii*

wet-bottomed saqpikjat *ai*

whale put'p *an*; grampus ~ sapate:mekw [SH]; small ~ put'pe:j *an*

what ~ for? koqwey ta; koqwey wjit; ~ is that? koqwey net; ~ is this? koqwey net; ~ is this (that)? koqowey n't [BR]

what? koqwey; ta:n koqwey

whatever ta:n koqwey

wheat klumk

wheel kiwiyo:qiyaq *ii* (in)

when ta:n tujiw

when? ta:n

whenever ta:n tujiw

where etl(i)

where? tami

wherever ta:n tett

whetstone siputaqan; sipiki:taqan; supiki:taqan [SH]

which? teken

while ke:s; ke:skw [SH]; after a ~ tel-kne:kek; in a little ~ pe:(l) apukjik [BC]; once in a ~ ekel

whiney mikutiyat *ai* [PEI]

whip kumaqan; a horse ~ te:sipow kumaqan

whipperwill kloqiyej *an*

whisker my ~ nitu; have thick ~ **-s** pasi:tuwat *ai*; ~ **-ed** pukwi:tuwat *ai* [BC]; wituwit *ai*; pukwatqasik *ii*, pukwatqasit *ai*

whiskey puktewijk

whisper kim-ewistoq (kim-ewistu) *ai*

whistle pipukwaqanji:j; wikwasmukwet *ai*; ~ along pemi-wikwa:smukwet *ai* [BR]; a ~ **-r** nuji-pipukwet *ai (an)*

white wape:k *ai, ii*; grey or ~ hair wapkwan; look ~ wapamuksit *ai*, wapamu:k *ii*; ~ birch bark maskwi *an*; turn ~ wapa:s'k *ii*, wapa:sit *ai*; ~ hair wasapun [SH]; ~ man aqalasiyew; ~ woman wenuji:skw *an* [SH]

white ash aqamoq *an* [RB]

whitish wape:jik *ii*, wape:jit (wape:jijik) (pl) *ai*

whittle amaliksawet *ai* [SH]; amaloqsawet *ai* [PEI]; amalsawet *ai*; mils'k *ta*, milsm *ti*

who ~ is he? wen tana; the one ~ ta:n (ta:nik) *an* [BC]; ~ **-'s** that? wen net; wen n't [SH]; ~ **-'s** this? wen n't

who? n't (a question particle)

who? wen (wenik) *an*

whole mese:k *ai (an)*

whopper tell a ~ to eksupukuwa:l'k *ta*

whover ta:n wen

why ~ not? koqwey wjit; the reason ~ tela:tekek *ii*, tela:teket *ai*

Whycogamagh, N.S. we:koqoma:q

wide keske:k *ai, ii*; maqiske:k *ai, ii*; have ~ nostrils maqitnat *ai*; too ~ wesamikske:k *ii*; ~ and deep (e.g., a canoe, chair) keskulq'k *ii*; ~ and round (cylindrical) maqa:q *ii*, maqoqsit *ai*

widen keska:l'k *ta*, keska:tu *ti*; ~ (as a river) keskapekiyaq *ii*

widow "grass" ~ piley jijjawiknej *an*; young ~ siku:skwe:j *an*

widow siku:skw (siku:skwaq) *an*

widower sikuwap (sikuwapaq) *an*; young ~ sikuwapji:j *an*

wife my ~ nte:pitem *an*; my ex- ~ nte:pitemt'p *an*

wiggle milikjetesink *ai*, milikjetesk *ii*

wikwam ujikan; wikuwom [BR]; the point of a ~ kini:swikuwom [SH]; upper (rear) section of the ~ kataqam [SH]

wild cat tqoqwej *an*

wild man wintiku *an*

wildman a legendary, greedy ~ kukwes *an*

wild rice grain of ~ m'no:man

William Suliyan *an*

win kaniye:wit *ai*; ~ a race ikatne:wet *ai*; ~ back apatte:k *ta*, apatte:m *ti*; apatte:mat *ai*; ~ plenty of mekete:k *ta*, mekete:m *ti*

wind[1] ~ up atapaqalk *ta* [PEI]; atapaqam *ti*, atapaqq *ta*

wind[2] wju:sn; a mild ~ (the southwest wind that precedes a thunderstorm) putuwesk *ii*; break ~ putuwet *ai*; east or northwest ~ wejipek *ii*; gale force ~ me:kiwju:s'k *ii* [SH]; in the ~ wju:sniktuk (loc); west ~ teks'k *ii*; ~ **-y** weju:s'k *ii*

window tuwop'ti

windpipe my ~ nsitun

wine moqopa:q

wing his ~ unisqi [BR]; my ~ nilisqi *an*

wink japikwetuwet *ai*; ~ at japikwetaq *ta*

winner the ~ kespu:tuwet *ai (an)*

winter kesik *ii*; a nice ~ welipuk *ii*; all ~ newtipuk *ii*; become ~ poqjipu:k [ESK]; experience ~ pejipunmit *ai*; every ~ te:sipuk [BR]; forthcoming ~ ksinuk; have a nice ~ welipunsit *ai*; last ~ ktipun; one ~ newtipuk *ii*; past ~ ksin; settle in for the ~ pejipunsit *ai*; something associated with ~ kesikewey *an, in*; spend or pass the ~ apipunsit *ai*; ~ arrives pejipuk *ii*

wipe ka:s'k *ta*, ka:sm *ti*; ~ dry niwika:s'k *ta*, niwika:sm *ti*; ~ or rub off kasa:l'k *ta*, kasa:tu *ti*; ~ out ketmete:k *ta*, ketmete:m *ti*; ~ **-d** out ketmete:mat *ai*

wire send a ~ or telegram mattaqte:ket *ai* [SH]

wisdom ne:tata:suwaqan

wise ne:tata:sit *ai*; wordly ~ natawe:k *ai*

witch puwowinujkwej *an*; male ~ qones *an* [BR]

with sit ~ witpitaq *ta*, witpitm *ti*

withdraw take or ~ in small amounts qasko:tm *ti*, qaskweyaq *ta*

withstand ~ the cold melkajit *ai* [BC]

witness a ~ (at a wedding) nujo:teket *ai (an)*

wobble majo:qiyaq *ii*, majo:qiyet *ai*

wobbly menakwisk *ii*, menakwisink *ai*

wolf paqtasm (paqtasmk) *an*; paqt'sm (paqt'smuk) *an* [BR]

wolverine ki:kwaju *an*

woman e:pit (e:pijik) *an*; act like a ~ e:pitewqamiksit *ai*; a young ~ e:pite:s *an*; an unmarried ~ e:pite:s *an*; become a ~ e:pitewit *ai*; Canadian ~ kanatiyesuwi:skw *an*; hunt or seek for a ~ e:pitewe:ket *ai*; white ~ wenuji:skw *an* [SH]; ~ of high rank saqama:skw (saqama:skwaq) *an*; young Canadian ~ kanatiyesuwi:skwe:j *an*

woman-chaser e:pitewe:sm *an* [PEI]; e:pitewsm (e:pitewsmuk) *an*

womanhood enter into ~ (post menstruation) e:pite:siwwet *ai*; enter into ~ (ready for marriage) e:pitji:jiwwet *ai*

wonders do ~ me:ta:teket *ai* [BR]

wondrous do ~ things me:ki-w'la:teket *ai* [SH]

wood dressed ~ ji:ka:taw (ji:ka:taq) *an*; ~ stove puksukey epsaqtejk; ~ shaving piwsikn

woodchuck m'lumkewej *an* [RB]; munumkwej *an* [ESK]

wood-pecker Russian (red-headed) ~ antawe:s *an* [SH]

woodpecker apo:qajej *an* [BC]; apoqnej *an* [RB]; apo:qatej *an* [SH]; yellow hammer ~ w'lukuni *an* [SH]

woods nipukt; come out of the ~ panatqa:sit *ai*

woodsman nipuktukewe:sn *an*

wool jijkluwewjiwapi; wayekn [CB]

woolen ~ material jijkluwewjiwapiyey

work elukwek *ii*, elukwet *ai*; elukwe:k *ta*; lukowaqan; do different kinds of ~ mil-lukwet *ai*; do such and such ~ tel-lukwet *ai*, tel-lukwek *ii*; make ~ elukwe:k *ta*; ~ for elukwewk *ta*; ~ out tew-lukwet *ai*; ~ to one's limit attikna:s'k *ii*, attikna:sit *ai*; use for ~ elukwetu *ti*; the first ~ day amkwes elukutimk; ~ **-er** lukowinu *an* [SH]; lukwewinu *an* [BR]; a part-time ~ **-er** matuwe:k *ai*; good ~ nata:-lukwet *ai*

world ws'tqamu; bring into the ~ ws'tqamuwa:l'k *ta*; come into the ~ ws'tqamuwit *ai*; the end of the ~ kespaqami:k *ii*

worm weti *an*

worry ~ about sespete:l'mk *ta*, sespete:tm *ti*

worse aji-winjik *ii*, aji-winjit *ai*; get ~ me:ka:sit *ai*, me:ka:s'k *ii*

worship emtoqwalk *ta*, emtoqwatm *ti*

worst the ~ pajiji-winjik *ii*, pajiji-winjit *ai* [SH]

worth ~ so much tel awtik *ii*, tel awtit *ai*; ~ the price tepawtik *ii*, tepawtit *ai*

worthless ~ object ksnqoweyey

worthy wel-te:l'sit *ai* [BC]

wound deep ~ or gash la:qan

wrap elpiso:tulk *ta*; oqonisqopil'm *ti*, oqonisqopilk *ta*; ~ a gift iloqomoqwa:l'k *ta*, iloqomoqwa:tu *ti*; ~ around kitto:qopilk *ta*, kitto:qopil'm *ti*; ~ up lengthwise eloqo(n)maqa:tu *ti* [BR]; ~ **-ped** up oqopisit *ai*; ~ **-ping** paper iloqomoqwa:taqan; ~ **per** loqomoqa:taqan; oqono-qopisaqan; oqopisaqan

wrestler a ~ nuji-koqqwa:luwet *ai (an)* [NS]

wring ~ out jimpeknawet *ai*; jimpekn'k *ta*, jimpekn'm *ti*; ~ out quickly m'ntawaqalk *ta*, m'ntawaqtu *ti*

wrinkle atkikwati; ~ **-d** (of the head and neck) atkikwa:t *ai*

writ-e ewi:kikek *ii*, ewi:kiket *ai*; ewi:k'k *ta*, ewi:km *ti*; ~ with Micmac characters komkwejuwi:kiket *ai*; ~ to ewi:kmaq *ta*; ~ **-ing** pad ewi:kikemkewey

wrong chop ~ o:p'lte:k *ta*, o:p'lte:m *ti*; do ~ o:pla:l'k *ta*, o:pla:tu *ti*; o:pla:teket *ai*; o:ple:k *ai*; eat ~ o:platalk *ai*; go ~ amsala:s'k *ii*, amsala:sit *ai*; opla:sik *ii*, opla:sit *ai*

Y

yard lape:lis (a measurement, Fr. la verge)

yarn jijkluwewjiwapi

yawn ikte:k (ikte:m) *ai* [SH]; iktewsit *ai* [PEI];
ikto:sit *ai*

year five ~ -s nanipunq'k *ii*; one hundred ~ -s
old kaskimtlnaqanipuna:t [BR];
kask'ptnnaqanipuna:t *ai*; one ~ newtipunqek
ii; one ~ old nekwtipuna:t *ai* [BR]; so many
~ -s old te:sipuna:t *ai*; kaqi:siskekipuna:q *ii*,
kaqi:siskekipuna:t *ai*; ten ~ -s
metla:sipunq'k; ten ~ -s old metla:sipuna:t
ai; three ~ -s nesipunqek *ii*; two ~ -s
tapuwipunqek; two ~ -s old tapuwipuna:t *ai*

yearn long or ~ for kiwajeyaq *ta*, kiwajo:tm *ti*

yeast so:kwistaqan

yellow wataptek *ii* [BR]; wisawe:k *ii*

yellowish wisaw-amuksit *ai*, wisaw-amu:k *ii*

yes amuj (in contradicting a negative
statement); e:; e:'e

yesterday w'laku; the day before ~ jktiki-
w'la:ku; peku:laks [BR]

yet ki:kaj [BR]; me:

you ki:l (sg); kilow (pl)

you are created! kisu:l (expression of
surprise) [BR]

you bet! jki:n je:k (an exclamation)

young maljewe:juwit *ai*; ~ -er me:
maljewe:juwit *ai*

youngster luks'ji:j *an*; maljewe:j *an*

yours kilewewey (pl) *an, in*; ki:lewey (sg) *an,
in*; kilowewey (pl) *an, in*